Big Data and Data Science Initiative in India - Upcoming Job Opportunities (Vol.-2)

By Ajit Kumar Roy

Copyright: akroy@2017

Dedication:

Dedicated to my granddaughter
'ANGANA'

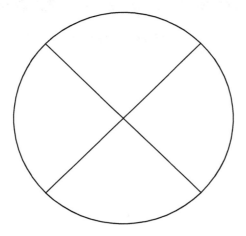

PREFACE

The first volume of the book entitled *'Big Data and Data Science Initiative in India-Upcoming Job Opportunities'* was published in July 2016.Since then a lot of events have taken place India like Demonetization, Cashless economy, GST bill etc. besides smart city project, make in India, digital healthcare and New India Vision. Some argue that the hidden purpose of demonetization was to push digital economy. Whatever may be the argument it is a fact that post demonetization scenario is quite different in many ways particularly in terms of transparency in economy, digital push and black money control and tax collection. Prime Minister Narendra Modi has launched an ambitious initiative to digitize India by making Internet access available to over two lakh villages by 2019, promoting e-governance, e-banking, e. education and e-health, and transforming India into a knowledge economy.

When Prime Minister Narendra Modi made the demonetization announcement on the night of 8 November, it started an administrative chain reaction focused on squeezing money launderers, promoting less-cash economy and of course remonetizing the banking system. Indian financial system has several players' foreign banks, public sector banks, private banks, cooperative banks, rural banks, credit cooperatives, and the specialized non-banking financial corporations. The FIU and the RBI will be saddled with heaps of complex transaction data from the post-demonetization months.

The CAG's Centre for Data Management and Analytics (CDMA) is going to play a catalytic role to synthesize and integrate relevant data into auditing process. CDMA aims to build up capacity in the Indian Audit and Accounts Department in Big Data Analytics to exploit the data rich environment in the Union and State Governments.

One of the biggest projects under USOF is Bharat Net wherein the government plans to connect 250,000 *gram panchayats* via the Internet. The project cost for Bharat Net has gone up to Rs. 75,000 crores wherein the government plans to connect 250,000 *gram panchayets* via the Internet. Global consulting firm McKinsey has said digital finance is a $700 billion opportunity for India, offering 11.8 per cent boost to GDP by 2025, benefitting millions of people. Digitization is creating tremendous opportunities for economies across the globe. India realized this opportunity, and used a three-pronged approach: (i) JAM Jan Dhan Yojana (government payments transferred into one account digitally) (ii) Aadhaar (national biometric identification system to simplify account opening) (iii) mobile (use of a mobile number to allow clients to link accounts for easy recollection).

Agriculture plays a vital role in India's economy. Along with fisheries and forestry, agriculture is one of the largest contributors to the Gross Domestic Product (GDP). Prime Minister Modi and his cabinet have already given the green light to development of an Online National Agriculture Market to oversee online trading and ensure smooth processing of transactions, which would possibly also include storage and transportation of farm produce following their online sale. From precision agriculture to real-time price updates, advanced data analytics can help farmers usher in a new era in farming

There were 342.65 million Internet connections by the end of March 2016, of which 20.44 million were wired connections. In total, 149.75 million were on broadband (3G + 4G + wire line broadband) and 192.9 million on "Narrowband". Narrowband Internet subscriber base was 192.90 million (2G and wire line broadband). Click here for state wise broadband and narrowband data.

The Indian government has launched a *Big Data Initiative. It aims at ensuring the government services are made available to citizens electronically by reducing paperwork.* The Open Government Data

Platform, data.gov.in, created by NIC for Indian government departments and ministries for easy and open access by citizens. Besides pet project of building, 'one hundred smart cities' calling for a robust cloud computing backend coupled with real-time surveillance and big data analytics technologies. It is believed that 30-50 million people would be actively contributing to Mygov.in, given its current pace of growth. The UID-Aadhaar project will be the largest such citizen database on the planet. One of the major issues of the government is timely tracking of projects for public good, monitoring and tracking the direct benefit transfer for poor people. There is a silent revolution happening in this side in the government's approach to deal with these burning issues. Using Big Data one can analyze the satellite picture to find the truth about the progress of projects.

The government has huge complex transaction data from the post-demonetization months. Now it is time to leverage data analytics capabilities to track down those who may have tried to game the banking system. With this flood of data, the need to unlock actionable value becomes more acute, thereby rapidly increasing demand for Big Data skills and qualified data scientists. Big Data bring new opportunities to modern society and challenges to data scientists. Big Data is supposed to be a $25 billion industry and India has the great opportunity to take a large share from it. *According to an industry report by NASSCOM in partnership with Blue Ocean Market Intelligence, the analytics market in India could more than double from the current $1 billion to $2.3 billion by the end of 2017-18 and* Big Data Analytics Sector in India to Reach $16 Billion by 2025. *Keeping in view the major initiative by various departments of Govt. of India and private sectors in applying Big data and data science indifferent aspects of business, banking, healthcare, economy the book entitled* **'Big Data and Data Science Initiative in India-Upcoming Job Opportunities (Vol.-2)** is compiled with up-to-date information. The book highlights the latest development in big data usage in India particularly post demonetization Scenario in the following chapters.

Ch-1: Understanding Big data and Data Science

Ch-2: Trends in Big Data Analytics

Ch-3: Big data and Data Science Application by Govt. of India

Ch-4: Data Science Application by Private Sectors

Ch-5: Big data Applied in Agriculture

Ch-6: Digital Transformation Initiative in India

The compiled book will help you understand and learn about basics of data science and big data analytics. Indian initiative in digital India program & initiative of big data analytics in science & technology are creating lakh of jobs. The book will be useful for researchers of social, political, economic, legal, and business and marketing fields, besides engineering or other sciences engaged in Data-intensive applications, challenges, techniques and technologies. Thanks to the original contributors of the articles presented in the book for bringing awareness among the interested readers.

AJIT KUMAR ROY

ABOUT THE BOOK

The first volume of the book entitled *'Big Data and Data Science Initiative in India-Upcoming Job Opportunities'* was published in July 2016.Since then a lot of events have taken place India like Demonetization, Cashless economy, GST bill etc. besides smart city project, make in India, digital healthcare and New India Vision. When Prime Minister Narendra Modi made the demonetization announcement on the night of 8 November, it started an administrative chain reaction focused on squeezing money launderers, promoting less-cash economy and of course remonetizing the banking system.

The CAG's Centre for Data Management and Analytics (CDMA) is going to play a catalytic role to synthesize and integrate relevant data into auditing process. FIU and the RBI will be saddled with heaps of complex transaction data from the post-demonetization months. Indian financial system is also generating huge data with several players' foreign banks, public sector banks, private banks, cooperative banks, rural banks, credit cooperatives, and the specialized non-banking financial corporations. Presently the Income Tax department of GOI will reportedly use big data analytics to comb through personal bank deposits money holders. As per reports, the analytics tool was used in the past for corporate tax reporting. Now, for the first time it will be used on a massive scale to rule out any in discrepancies found in personal taxes and records.

India aims to create a cleaner, more transparent economy via digitalization that will lead to an improved climate for foreign investment, boost economic growth, and ultimately propel the country to the next chapter of its emerging markets story. India by making Internet access available to over two lakh villages by 2019, promoting e-governance, e-banking, e. education and e-health, and transforming India into a knowledge economy. **Digital India** is a visionary initiative of the GOI to ensure that government services are made available to citizens electronically. Universal Banking

Initiative in India in focusing on simplifying the customer experience, India used a three-pronged approach: (i) JAM Jan Dhan Yojana (government payments transferred into one account digitally) (ii) Aadhaar (national biometric identification system to simplify account opening) (iii) mobile (use of a mobile number to allow clients to link accounts for easy recollection).

Government will invest Rs4.5 lakh crores in the Digital India program which will generate 18 lakh jobs. "Reliance Industries (RIL) Chairman Mukesh Ambani said that he will invest Rs2.5 lakh crores which will create employment for over five lakh people. Cyrus Mistry said that Tata Group will hire 60,000 IT professionals, this year. K.M. Birla said that the Aditya Birla Group would invest Rs. 44,500 crores in next five years in the infra and digital space.

Prime Minister Modi and his cabinet have already given the green light to development of an Online National Agriculture Market to oversee online trading and ensure smooth processing of transactions, which would possibly also include storage and transportation of farm produce following their online sale.

The government has huge complex transaction data from the post-demonetization months. Now it is time to leverage data analytics capabilities to track down those who may have tried to game the banking system. *Demonetization, the necessary evil, is touted to flush out black money from our economy. But to accomplish this, the government is leverage on Big Data analytics to build an intelligent data capturing mechanism by integrating various data sources. In a country where we are creating the best analytics talent for the world there is enough room for individuals to be used in crunching data that matters for the country.* Tools such as Big Data can be effective in collecting information about financial misappropriation. The data provided by banks can be analyzed to find unusual activity in currency flow, whether at an individual or a regional level," Further, the use of Big Data can however complement reforms in India's traditional statistical machinery to help generate better data and frame more informed policies.

India just crossed 1 Billion Mobile Subscribers Milestone and the Excitement's Just Beginning India internet user is expected to almost double to 600 million users by 2020 from approximately 343 million users currently. There were 342.65 million Internet connections by the end of March 2016, of which 20.44 million were wired connections. In total, 149.75 million were on broadband (3G + 4G + wire line broadband) and 192.9 million on "Narrowband". Narrowband Internet subscriber base was 192.90 million (2G and wire line broadband).

Global consulting firm McKinsey has said digital finance is a $700 billion opportunity for India, offering 11.8 per cent boost to GDP by 2025, benefitting millions of people. Digital financial services delivered via mobile phones, the Internet or cards linked to a digital payment system could be a boon to individuals, businesses, and governments across the country boosting GDP and making the aspiration of financial inclusion a reality.

Keeping in view the major initiative by various departments of Govt. of India and private sectors in applying Big data and data science indifferent aspects of business, banking, healthcare, economy the book entitled **'Big Data and Data Science Initiative in India-Upcoming Job Opportunities (Vol.-2)** is compiled. The book highlights the latest development in the initiative of GOI & private sectors and tools that Data Scientists use through the following chapters

Ch-1: Understanding Big data and Data Science
Ch-2: Trends in Big Data Analytics
Ch-3: Big data and Data Science Application by Govt. of India-
Ch-4: Data Science Application by Private Sectors
Ch-5: Big data Applied in Agriculture
Ch-6: Digital Transformation Initiative in India

The compiled book will be useful for researchers of social, political, economic, legal, and business and marketing fields, besides engineering or other sciences engaged in Data-intensive applications, challenges, techniques and technologies.

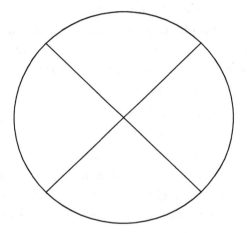

Contents

Chapter 1: Understanding Big Data and Data Science 1

1.1   What is data science? Here's How to Understand the Subject 2

1.2   Data Science Summarized in One Picture 4

1.3   What is Big Data? 5

1.4   All You Need to Know about Big Data 8

1.5   From Patterns to Profits: How Big Data is Unleashing Value for Startups and Industry Leaders 10

1.6   Big Data, Analytics and the Path from Insights to Value 15

1.7   How to Monetize Your Data 34

1.8   How Data Science is the Driving Force behind Successful Digital Transformation 35

1.9   Top 10 Hot Big Data Technologies 40

1.10   How Big Data Is Impacting the E-Commerce Industry 43

1.11   Big Data Analytics Solutions – The Pulse of the New Age Data 48

1.12   Looking into the Future with Big Data and Analytics 53

1.13   The Flood of Data from IoT Is Powering New Opportunities — for Some 58

1.14   IoT and Developing Analytics-Based Data Products 62

1.15   Cloud Computing Has Cut the Cost of Analytics, Say Experts 63

1.16   Applied Statistics Comes to the Rescue of Big Data 65

xiii

1.17   The Tools of Big Data Science: The Technologies & Languages of Statistical Analysis 67

1.18   Big Data - Big Security 78

Chapter 2: Trends in Big Data Analytics 81

2.1   Steps of Data Digitization Process 81

2.2   Data Science, the Future of Digitization 84

2.3   25 Big Data Terms You Must Know To Impress Your Date (Or whoever you want to) 86

2.4   Beginner's Guide to the History of Data Science 93

2.5   Data Science vs. Big Data vs. Data Analytics 97

2.6   Data Science and Big Data: Two very Different Beasts 104

2.7   Data Science and its relationship to Big Data and Data-Driven Decision Making 108

2.8   Evolution of the Data Scientist through the Decade: What's changed 110

2.9   A Tale of Two India's – a Digital Paradox 116

2.10   Data and innovation in the Economic Survey 120

2.11   Big Data Initiative 122

2.12   Big data analytics and the India equation 124

2.13   EMC-Hive India Think Tank - The power equation Big Data + Social in Governance 129

2.14   The impact of Big Data Analytics on Management Consulting and Human Resources in India 132

2.15   Broad contours of DST initiated BDI programme 135

2.16   Taking the step forward: Government Initiatives in Analytics 136

2.17   RKMVU's launches India's first Masters Level Degree Course: M.Sc. in Big Data Analytics 139

2.18   Top 10 Analytics Trends in India to watch out for in 2017 141

2.19   Ten Emerging Analytics Startups in India to watch for in 2016 149

2.20   Ten startups that are changing the face of Virtual Reality in India 156

2.21   Top 10 Analytics Training Institutes in India – Ranking 2016 165

2.22   10 Startups in India that are leading the race of Artificial Intelligence 181

2.23   Top 10 Analytics Courses in India – Ranking 2016 190

2.24   Ten Super exciting Data Science / Machine Learning / Artificial Intelligence based startups in India 207

2.25   Big Data and the Internet of Things don't make business smarter, Analytics and Data Science do 214

2.26   AI, Data Science, Machine Learning: Main Developments in 2016, Key Trends in 2017 218

2.27   Data Science, Predictive Analytics Main Developments in 2016 and Key Trends for 2017 231

2.28   Machine Learning & Artificial Intelligence: Main Developments in 2016 and Key Trends in 2017 235

2.29   How to Build a Data Science Team 244

2.30   Top 10 Big Data Trends 2017 247

2.31   The Demand for Big Data Scientists in India will grow in 2017: Report 254

2.32   Big Data, Data Analytics to Play Vital Role in Financial, Banking Services 257

2.33   2017: Digitization of Medical Sector Is Good For Our Health 259

2.34   Data Science Comes of Age................................... 262

2.35   Data Science Trends to Look Out For In 2017 264

2.36   Big Data Analytics- Big Security........................... 268

2.37   Preparing for a 'Cloud'y Year- Top Cloud Telephony Trends for 2017... 271

2.38   Guide for Library Links on Digitization, Preservation, Curation and Data Management: Big Data / Data Science 274

Chapter 3: Big Data and Data Science Application by Government of India....................283

3.1   How Big Data is improving Lives for the Better in India 283

3.2   Data Sciences Can Save India and here is why............... 286

3.3   Why Data Science matters and how to approach it for your Digital Transformation 292

3.4   How Data Analytics Can Help Modi Government Catch the Demons of Demo 296

3.5   Data and Innovation in the Economic Survey 301

3.6   Use of Big Data in Government's Overarching Policies and Reforms 305

3.7   CAG Readies to Meet Big Data Challenges Sri Shashi Kant Sharma Inaugurates Centre for Data Analytics... 312

3.8   How Big Data Analytics Can Help in Making the Most of Data from Demonetization 313

3.9   Demonetization: Five Ways in Which Big Data Analytics Can Trace Black Money in India 318

3.10   Data Analytics Post Demonetization in India 320

3.11   Demonetisation: Data Analytics Could Have Traced Black Money in India............................... 322

3.12   Big Data Can Drive India from 'Cashful' To 'Cashless' 324

3.13   Demonetization – A Heady Cocktail Served
        With Big Data & Analytics the Hangover
        Continues.. 328

3.14   Niti Aayog Brings in Big Data Big Gun to
        Track Fraud in Jan Dhan A/Cs.................................. 332

3.15   Big Data Analytics Will Help Bridge India's
        Tax Gap. Here's how! 335

3.16   Income Tax Department to Use Big Data to
        Scrutinize Bank Accounts... 337

3.17   Tax Department Leans on Big Data Analytics
        to Mark Out Multiple PAN Holders.......................... 339

3.18   Tax Official Use Big Data and Analytics To
        Combat Black Money Menace 341

3.19   Tax Officials Are Using Big Data Analytics to
        Crack a Whip on Black Money Hoarders.................. 342

3.20   How   Big   Data   Enables   a   Successful
        Implementation of Demonetization in India 344

3.21   Data Analytics post Demonetization in India 347

3.22   Leveraging Data in Real Estate – The New
        Beginning.. 349

3.23   How Big-Data to Be A Big Part of India's
        Weather Insurance in the Year 2016......................... 352

3.24   Big Data, Data Analytics to Play Vital Role in
        Financial, Banking Services...................................... 356

3.25   Big Data for Anti-Poverty Programmes: A
        Politically Embedded View....................................... 357

3.26   68% of Indian businesses ready to thrive in a
        digital world: Microsoft study................................. 361

3.27   Cashing in This Diwali & Halloween with Big
        Data & Analytics 365

3.28   Intel & DST - Innovate for Digital India
        Challenge 2.0.. 370

3.29 Mygov, Intel & DST Announce the Top 10 Innovators from Intel & DST – Innovate for Digital India Challenge 2.0 374

3.30 Modi Government Using Big-Data & Social Media to Assess Public Mood and Trending Issues 376

3.31 Arun Jaitley to Address Auditors General of Commonwealth Nations 378

3.32 How Big Data Is Revolutionizing Indian Railways to Ease The Pain of Getting Tatkal Ticket 380

3.33 Analytics Sector Will Figure among World Top Three: Nasscom 383

3.34 Big Data Analytics Sector in India to Reach $16 Billion by 2025: Nasscom 385

3.35 Nasscom Sees India among the Top 3 Destinations for Analytics By 2025 387

3.36 Indian Analytics Sector Set to Grow 8 Times 389

3.37 Nasscom Aims to Make India A Force In Big Data, Analytics 390

Chapter 4: Data Science Application by Private Sectors 393

4.1 Aditya Birla Financial Services Group Picks Teradata EDW to Gain More Business and Customer Insights 393

4.2 Microsoft Showcases the Power of Analytics and Machine Learning to Transform Businesses and Drive Inclusive Growth 396

4.3 GE Digital: Driving the Next Industrial Revolution through Analytics 399

4.4 Driving Digital Transformation with Data Science 401

4.5   From Data Science to Data Stories: Bridging
        the Gap to Digital Transformation (Highlights)............ 408

4.6   The role Big Data plays in Digital
        Transformation.. 409

4.7   Realizing the Potential of Big Data and
        Analytics... 412

4.8   Microsoft India Projects itself as Open Source
        Champion, Says AI is the Next Step 416

4.9   Industries of the Future: The Race for
        Robotics, Genomics, Analytics, Cyber security
        and Digital Transactions................................... 418

4.10   15 Indian Big Data Companies to Watch Out
        For In 2015... 428

Chapter 5: Big Data Applied in Agriculture 433

5.1   Launch of Digital India: A programme to
        transform India into a digitally empowered
        society and knowledge economy......................... 433

5.2   Challenges in the Adoption of ICTs for Rural
        sector - Learning from Nano Ganesh ICT in
        India.. 434

5.3   Digital-Agriculture 437

5.4   How Will Digital India Impact on Agriculture
        in India? 439

5.5   Farming goes digital: the 3rd Green Revolution 441

5.6   Digital Agriculture Empowers Farmers.................. 444

5.7   Agrow Book– Empowering the Agriculture
        Industry as a Whole 449

5.8   The Rise of Digital Farming 453

5.9   Big Data for the Next Green Revolution 455

5.10   Precision Agriculture in the Digital Era.................. 458

5.11   How Big Data will revolutionize the Global
        Food Chain.. 465

5.12   Would You Like To Learn More About Our Consumer Packaged Goods Practice?...................... 467

Chapter 6: Digital Transformation Initiative in India.............471

6.1   "Make in India", "Skill India" and "Digital India" Positive signals of new Transformation................ 471

6.2   Make in India... 473

6.3   Digital India: Transforming India Into a Knowledge Economy.. 477

6.4   What we need is Digital Disruption 482

6.5   The Next-Generation Operating Model for The Digital World 487

6.6   The Case for Digital Reinvention........................ 496

6.7   The seven decisions that matter in a digital transformation: A CEO's guide to reinvention 504

6.8   Digital Transformation in India........................... 511

6.9   Union Budget (2017-18): Promoting Digital Payments (Digital Economy) Towards Less-Cash Society. 515

6.10   What Do the Numbers Reveal About India's Digital Acceptance Post-Demonetization? 517

Chapter 1: Understanding Big Data and Data Science

Several articles have been published emphasizing why data should be treated as an organizational asset. And there are many that focus on deriving value by analyzing the structured data and Big Data to gain deep business insights.

New Delhi | Published: March 9, 2017 3:44 AM

Data science enables conversion of the data assets into data products. Not surprisingly, demand is very high for this hot new profession. Companies are now taking a step further to turn their data assets into products / services which in themselves would carry commercial value.

IDC predicts a need for 181,000 such professionals in the US by 2018 and a requirement for five times that number of positions with data management and interpretation capabilities. McKinsey Global Institute estimates the shortage of data scientists in 2018 at 190,000. Glassdoor has listed the role of a data scientist as the top job of 2016 from among 25 best jobs in America. The average salary of a data scientist is likely to be 50-80% higher than that of a business analyst.

1.1   What   is   data   science?   Here's   How   to   Understand the Subject

Data science helps uncover hidden patterns from large volume of structured and unstructured data which can then be deployed commercially. What differentiates it from standard business intelligence is that one is not sure what one is looking for and instead, attempts to uncover hidden patterns of commercial value.

For instance, an attempt to classify video clips as, say, political, sports, humour, self-improvement, etc., without manually opens each file. To achieve this, the data scientist will need to study numerous subjective characteristics of the video clip, such as voice modulation, sentiment analysis, colour, speech to text, NLP, or other parameter yet unknown, to detect repeatable patterns that will enable classification of the video clips accurately.

As a discipline of study, data science combines the technology of data analysis, visualization, statistics, mathematics, and the knowledge of business prerogatives. Statistics plays a central role in fitting patterns to data sets. With descriptive statistics one can qualify, categories and describe what is shown by the available data, while inferential statistics helps in deducing possibilities beyond the available data. While statistical techniques provide quantitative insight, sound business knowledge helps translate it into business outcome.

Given that we are now generating more data than ever, the need for identifying patterns from such huge volumes of data has never been more relevant. And with technological advances, it is becoming all the more feasible. This can only mean that there is little excuse for organizations to overlook the value that can be gained through data science.

Turning data into product

Creating a data product involves defining a problem; postulating the desired outcome; determining the data required for analysis and ensuring its cleanliness, completeness and authenticity; using statistics, visualization techniques, domain knowledge to analyze the data from several perspectives to uncover patterns, or trends; upon observation of a pattern, design experiments to confirm the accuracy and repeatability in different scenarios; represent the successful pattern as an algorithm / build models which a machine can learn and use for analysis.

Some considerations for creating a data product

Quality of data: To succeed with a data product, it is essential to have quality data. This ensures that the patterns being fitted to the data are not obscured by errant or outlying data. Thus, the clean and relevant data helps shorten the pattern identification cycle and increases the success of the data product.

A viable business model: Typically, data products are bundled with other offerings that generate revenue. However, it is essential to estimate the additional value the data product will bring to such products and whether the effort spent on creating the data product is justifiable.

Benefits of data science

Data science finds critical usage in many key sectors. In the financial domain, data science is being used to unearth frauds or test risk models to evaluate credit risks. In retail, targeted offers to prospective buyers are increasing conversion rates. In fact, data science finds applications in every industry that generates data. Traditional businesses are also exploiting data science to build data products that will propel their respective businesses.

The writer, Jay Shah, is associate vice-president and ERP head, Nihilent Technologies

http://www.financialexpress.com/lifestyle/science/what-is-data-science-heres-how-to-understand-the-subject/580066/

1.2   Data Science Summarized in One Picture

Posted by <u>Vincent Granville</u> on February 26, 2017 at 1:00pm

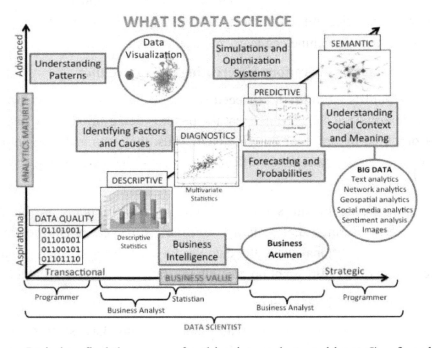

I tried to find the source for this picture, but could not. I've found it on LinkedIn, posted by <u>Mathias Golombek,</u> CTO at Exasol. This picture was also spotted <u>here.</u>

Are there any components that you would add? I would definitely add automated data science (machine-to-machine or device-to-device communications, automated transactions such as algorithms that automatically purchase keywords on ad networks.) This article also helps clarify what data science, machine learning, automation, algorithms and data architectures are about.

http://www.datasciencecentral.com/profiles/blogs/data-science-summarized-in-one-picture

1.3   What is Big Data?

Lisa Arthur ,   **CONTRIBUTOR:** *I write about how data & data-driven marketing are changing business.* Opinions expressed by Forbes Contributors are their own.

Big data is new and "ginormous" and scary –very, very scary. No, wait. Big data is just another name for the same old data marketers have always used, and it's not all *that* big, and it's something we should be embracing, not fearing. No, hold on. That's not it, either. What I meant to say is that big data is as powerful as a tsunami, but it's a deluge that can be controlled . . . in a positive way, to provide business insights and value. Yes, that's right, isn't it?

Over the past few years, I have heard big data defined in many, many different ways, and so, I'm not surprised there's so much confusion surrounding the term. Because of all the misunderstanding and misperceptions, I have to ask:

CMOs, when you talk about "big data" in the C-suite, do you know if everyone's on the same page? And even closer to home, are you certain there's consensus within your marketing organization?

You won't get far untangling your big data hairball if, for example, half of your company is forgetting to include traditional data in the calculus or if some don't think social network interactions "really" matter. So, please, take a minute to get back to basics and do a simple self-check. Ask yourself, your team, the C-suite:

How *do* we define big data?

While I fully expect your company to add its own individual tweaks here or there, here's the one-sentence definition of big data I like to use to get the conversation started:

Big data is a collection of data from traditional and digital sources inside and outside your company that represents a source for ongoing discovery and analysis.

Some people like to constrain big data to digital inputs like web behavior and social network interactions; however, the CMOs and CIOs I talk with agree that we can't exclude traditional data derived from product transaction information, financial records and interaction channels, such as the call center and point-of-sale. All that is big data, too, even though it may be dwarfed by the volume of digital data that's now growing at an exponential rate.

In defining big data, it's also important to understand the mix of unstructured and multi-structured data that comprises the volume of information.

Unstructured data comes from information that is not organized or easily interpreted by traditional databases or data models, and typically, it's text-heavy. Metadata, Twitter tweets, and other social media posts are good examples of unstructured data.

Multi-structured data refers to a variety of data formats and types and can be derived from interactions between people and machines, such as web applications or social networks. A great example is web log data, which includes a combination of text and visual images along with structured data like form or transactional information. As digital disruption transforms communication and interaction channels—and as marketers enhance the customer experience across devices, web properties, face-to-face interactions and social platforms—multi-structured data will continue to evolve.

Industry leaders like the global analyst firm Gartner use phrases like "volume" (the amount of data), "velocity" (the speed of information generated and flowing into the enterprise) and "variety" (the kind of data available) to begin to frame the big data discussion. Others have focused on additional V's, such as big data's "veracity" and "value."

One thing is clear: Every enterprise needs to fully understand big data – what it is to them, what is does for them, what it means to them – and the potential of data-driven marketing, starting *today*. Don't wait. Waiting will only delay the inevitable and make it even more difficult to unravel the confusion.

Once you start tackling big data, you'll learn what you don't know, and you'll be inspired to take steps to resolve any problems. Best of all, you can use the insights you gather at each step along the way to start improving your customer engagement strategies; that way, you'll put big data marketing to work and immediately add more value to both your offline and online interactions.

https://www.forbes.com/sites/lisaarthur/2013/08/15/what-is-big-data/#7e696fc15c85

1.4   All You Need to Know about Big Data
GAUTAMI RAO, 20 MAY 2016

Big Data – the term that organizations worldwide have been obsessed with for some time now – refers to data sets that are so huge or complex that traditional software tools are inadequate to capture, curate, manage, and process them. With the world's technological per capita capacity to store information multiplying every other year, big data and its challenges has gained much hype in the recent past.

In 2001, Gartner Inc., an American research and advisory firm, had evolved a "3Vs" model to define data growth challenges and opportunities. They defined big data as "high volume, high velocity, and/or high variety information assets that require new forms of processing to enable enhanced decision making, insight discovery and process optimization."

Intensive research activities on sampling of big data and deriving its optimum benefits soon took the IT sector by storm. Since then, various processing models have continued to evolve to manage this vast cluster of ever-growing information. In 2000, a C++ based distributed file-sharing framework for data storage and query was developed by Seisint Inc., which was followed by more advances and better approaches like MapReduce and Hadoop in later years.

Volume 1 of the Big Data and Advanced Analytics Survey, 2015, by Evans Data Corporation presented the following insights:

- 6 per cent of all big data apps developed for manufacturing were being created by enterprises.
- 2 per cent of all big data and advanced analytics apps in use were in customer-facing departments.
- 2 per cent of all big data and advanced analytics developers were concentrating on the software and computing industry.
- Enterprises competing in the software and computing industry, manufacturing and financial industry were investing the heaviest in big data and analytics app development.
- Marketing departments have quickly become the most common users of big data and advanced analytics apps, followed by IT and R&D departments.

Evidently, we are seeing a rapid evolution in how organizations are dealing with big data today. Employees interpreting big data must bring a broad skillset to the table--statistical and technical expertise coupled with an analytical mindset and an acute business sense. Statistical and technical expertise is needed as data is the fuel that feeds the machine. Employees must have an intimate knowledge of data analysis, data security, data visualization and data quality. They must be comfortable with massive volumes of unstructured data and be able to organize it in a consumable way. Employees must be open to using advanced technology and tools in machine learning.

Today, data segmentation has crossed the barriers of demography and has begun to run through the veins of organizations as a whole. With advances in machine learning, analytics and computing power, there has been a huge improvement in the ability of organizations to target customers at the individual level and create personalized offers for each customer.

Enterprises today have enormous opportunities to harness big data to improve their competitiveness. In this new age of the Internet-of-Things (IoT), around 80 per cent information and data comes from a multitude of different sources worldwide.

We're entering an era where companies are no longer just keeping up with technology, but are instead exploring ways to reshape their business processes to take advantage of big data. Every industry today is realizing that this Internet-connected world is providing them with the information they need to change and grow – to introduce new products or offer better service based on that information. By 2018, we're going to see virtually every enterprise taking advantage of big data.

(Disclaimer: The views and opinions expressed in this article are those of the author and do not necessarily reflect the views of Your Story.)

https://yourstory.com/2016/05/big-data-introduction/

1.5   From Patterns to Profits: How Big Data is Unleashing Value for Startups and Industry Leaders
MADANMOHAN RAO: 24 JUNE 2015

Driven by startups and some savvy industry leaders, Big Data and analytics are becoming more widely accepted, and the activity of numerous practitioners and investors is showing the way to successful models.

The power of being able to gather, identify, understand and execute upon patterns of data is critical for long-term success of companies as well as for advancement of humanity, according to authors Rob Thomas and Patrick McSharry in their new book, 'Big Data Revolution: what farmers, doctors and insurance agents teach us about discovering Big Data patterns.'

Rob Thomas is Vice President of Product Development for Big Data and Information Management at IBM. Patrick McSharry is a Senior Research Fellow at the Smith School of Enterprise and the Environment, Oxford University.

The 272-page book covers Big Data at work in vertical sectors like farming, health, insurance, retail, energy, manufacturing and government services. Each chapter covers broad historical trends, and the book ends with ethical and strategy recommendations for business leaders (some of these topics are better explained in other books).

For better insights on how to gather and use data, see my reviews of the books 'The Code Halos' and 'Connected by Design,' as well as 'Big Data Marketing' (for internal culture change) and 'BigData @ Work' (for corporate and startup strategies).

Here are my key takeaways from the case stories in the book; for more details and a range of podcasts, see the online companion of the book.

Farming has evolved through phases like subsistence farming (1700s), large for-profit farms (barns: 1800s), animal-powered farming (horses: early 1900s) and machine farming (late 1900s). We are now entering the era of data-powered farming, via large scale open data sets on weather and yields, IoT, drones and smart tractors. In future, digital tools will be as important as traditional farming tools in the agricultural sector.

For example, Ground Cover uses farm imagery to map and predict potato yields; its Canopy Check app adds geo-location information for farmers using smartphones. Monsanto's Integrated Farming System (IFS) uses science-based analytics tools like Field Script for planting advice, precision seeding and genetic gain; it bought the Climate Corporation in 2013 for $930 million. Grow Safe Systems uses sensors and analytics to track the movement and health of cattle and help farmers deal with disease detection and prevention.

The **medical field** is still strongly dominated by opinion in diagnosis – which is why it is common for patients to get a 'second opinion' before going in for surgery. The first medical schools were established in the 1200s in Italy; the scientific method was applied in medical research from the 1900s onwards. Investors like Vinod Khosla are now promoting Big Data approaches in the medical field, and several analysts are urging inclusion of more statistical and Big Data skills in medical education.

Cell Scope has developed a smartphone-enabled otoscope for patients to examine ears on their own and share the data with doctors. True Colours lets users enter and track their health data and monitor their progress online, and also aggregates data across cohorts. Quantus tracks real-time cardio-vascular data to get better insights into fighting heart disease. Health Tap harnesses the power of the crowd by letting them ask experts questions, and track patterns in consumer health trends.

Insurance practices began with the Babylonians in 1700 BC (marine insurance), followed by the rise of insurance businesses (1600s), life and crop insurance (1700s), and car insurance (1900s). Today, insurance is increasingly powered by better data, quicker workflow and more informed decision making. Online channels and IoT sensors are helping companies like All State and Progressive Insurance map, predict and manage risk for automobile policies in real-time. Governments and industry are getting together to share large data sets on natural catastrophes, such as the Global Earthquake Model and Oasis Loss Modeling Framework.

Retail has evolved through phases like local corner stores (1900s), department stores (1920s-1940s), malls (1940-1970), superstores (Walmart: 1970-1990) and e-commerce (1990s onwards). Shoppers feel that the sense of intimacy of smaller stores is being lost with scaling – but Big Data can bring back some of that personalization and customization. Stitch Fix, Keaton Row and Zara are using nimble business processes and scalable curation informed by real-time data to better serve their customers.

Energy firms like GE are riding the three waves of innovation: industrial revolution, Internet revolution and Industrial Internet. Machine data will be critical in the renewable energy sector, e.g., for monitoring massive wind turbine installations which are often in remote areas. Aeron Labs uses drones to inspect and manage energy sites like turbines and rigs. Tesla doesn't just make electric cars: its Vehicle Management System gathers insightful data which can be used to mine patterns across all Tesla cars and fleets on the road in real-time.

The largest power outage in history occurred during the summer of 2012 in northern India – but the application of data and pattern analysis could have foreseen the risk and prevented the blackout. Data networks are as important as data sources, and will re-shape entire industries. Global utility company expenditure on Big Data analytics could reach $3.8 billion in 2020, according to GTM Research. Smart meters and smart grids could also help 'nudge' consumers towards better energy utilization.

Governments can now use Big Data to come up with better evidence-based policy making, and emerging economies can leapfrog straight into mobile-driven data gathering networks for market and sentiment analysis. The open data movement, open access to content and hackathons are useful ways for governments to engage with society and industry – but concerns over security and privacy will have to be managed as well.

Examples include the Willis Research Network (risk modeling), and catastrophe insurance networks formed in the aftermath of earthquakes in Turkey and Florida. New financial tools like social impact bonds and development impact bonds are showing the way for the Children's' Investment Fund Foundation in India. Other firms profiled in the book are Zen Desk (providing customer service across interactive media channels) and Sky Catch (commercializing use of drones in sectors like construction).

The book also stresses the importance for companies to systematically sense data, apply feature extraction and post-processing, and ensure quality and security of data. Data does not just improve existing products, but creates new competitive advantage and even leads to the rise of data itself as a product. The chapter on data factors illustrates the wide range of **data pattern** advantages: building new applications, reducing subjective distortions, defining new channels, democratizing data access and usage, and enabling real-time response options.

For example, Intuit has turned data gathered from its products (TurboTax, QuickBooks, Quicken) into a valuable competitive advantage that even the mighty Microsoft could not beat. Dun & Bradstreet is a good example of a company which leverages **data as product**; it has spun off other successful companies like Nielsen, Cognizant, Moody's and IMS Health.

Major **culture change** will be needed, however, for organizations to accept the power of data-driven decisions, improve internal skillsets, speed up innovation, harness the power of algorithms and machine learning, design new processes and architectures, and especially create new business models.

"Data is much more than an opportunity; it is an imperative," the authors conclude.

https://m.yourstory.com/2015/06/big-data-unleashing-value-for-startups/

1.6   Big Data, Analytics and the Path from Insights to Value

Steve LaValle, Eric Lesser, Rebecca Shockley, Michael S. Hopkins and Nina Kruschwitz - Magazine: Winter 2011 Research Feature December 21, 2010

Data & Analytics, Analytics & Performance

How the smartest organizations are embedding analytics to transform information into insight and then action. Findings and recommendations from the first annual New Intelligent Enterprise Global Executive study:

In every industry, in every part of the world, senior leaders wonder whether they are getting full value from the massive amounts of information they already have within their organizations. New technologies are collecting more data than ever before, yet many organizations are still looking for better ways to obtain value from their data and compete in the marketplace. Their questions about how best to achieve value persist.

Are competitors obtaining sharper, timelier insights? Are they able to regain market advantage, neglected while focusing on expenses during the past two years? Are they correctly interpreting new signals from the global economy — and adequately assessing the impact on their customers and partners? Knowing what happened and why it happened are no longer adequate. Organizations need to know what is happening now, what is likely to happen next and what actions should be taken to get the optimal results.

FULL REPORT

This article presents the highlights of our Special Report Analytics: The New Path to Value. The full report includes complete survey questions and answers.

To help organizations understand the opportunity of information and advanced analytics, *MIT Sloan Management Review* partnered with the IBM Institute for Business Value to conduct a survey of nearly 3,000 executives, managers and analysts working across more than 30 industries and 100 countries. (See "About the Research.")

Among our key findings: Top-performing organizations use analytics five times more than lower performers. (See "Analytics Trumps Intuition.") Overall, our survey found a widespread belief that analytics offers value. Half of our respondents said that *improvement of information and analytics was a top priority in their organizations.* And more than one in five said they were under intense or significant pressure to *adopt advanced information and analytics approaches.*

About the Research: To understand the challenges and opportunities associated with the use of business analytics, *MIT Sloan Management Review*, in collaboration with the IBM Institute for Business Value, conducted a survey of more than 3,000 business executives, managers and analysts from organizations located around the world. The survey captured insights from individuals in 108 countries and more than 30 industries and involved organizations from a variety of sizes. The sample was drawn from a number of different sources, including MIT alumni and *MIT Sloan Management Review* subscribers, IBM clients and other interested parties.

ANALYTICS TRUMPS INTUITION

The source of the pressure is not hard to ascertain. Six out of 10 respondents cited *innovating to achieve competitive differentiation* as a top business challenge. The same percentage also agreed that their *organization has more data than it can use effectively*. Organizational leaders want analytics to exploit their growing data and computational power to get smart, and get innovative, in ways they never could before. Senior executives now want businesses run on data-driven decisions. They want scenarios and simulations that provide immediate guidance on the best actions to take when disruptions occur — disruptions ranging from unexpected competitors or an earthquake in a supply zone to a customer signaling a desire to switch providers. Executives want to understand optimal solutions based on complex business parameters or new information, and they want to act quickly.

These expectations can be met — but with a caveat. For analytics-driven insights to be *consumed* — that is, to trigger new actions across the organization — they must be closely linked to business strategy, easy for end-users to understand and embedded into organizational processes so that action can be taken at the right time. That is no small task. It requires painstaking focus on the way insights are infused into everything from manufacturing and new product development to credit approvals and call center interactions.

Top Performers say Analytics is a Differentiator

Our study clearly connects performance and the competitive value of analytics. We asked respondents to assess their organization's competitive position. Those who selected "substantially outperform industry peers" were identified as top performers, while those who selected "somewhat or substantially underperform industry peers" were grouped as lower performers. We found that organizations that strongly agreed that *the use of business information and analytics differentiates them within their industry* were twice as likely to be top performers as lower performers.

Top performers approach business operations differently than their peers do. Specifically, they put analytics to use in the widest possible range of decisions, large and small. They were twice as likely to use analytics to guide *future strategies*, and twice as likely to use *insights* to guide *day-to-day operations*. (See "The Analytics Habits of Top Performers.") They *make decisions based on rigorous analysis* at more than double the rate of lower performers. The correlation between performance and analytics-driven management has important implications to organizations, whether they are seeking growth, efficiency or competitive differentiation.

Three Levels of Capabilities Emerged, Each with Distinct Opportunities

Organizations that know where they are in terms of analytics adoption are better prepared to turn challenges into opportunities. We segmented respondents based on how they rated their organization's analytics prowess, specifically how thoroughly their organizations had been transformed by better uses of analytics and information. Three levels of analytics capability emerged — Aspirational, Experienced and Transformed — each with clear distinctions. (See "The Three Stages of Analytics Adoption.")

THE ANALYTICS HABITS OF TOP PERFORMERS

Aspiration: These organizations are the furthest from achieving their desired analytical goals. Often, they are focusing on efficiency or automation of existing processes and searching for ways to cut costs. Aspirational organizations currently have few of the necessary building blocks — people, processes or tools — to collect, understand, incorporate or act on analytic insights.

Experienced: Having gained some analytic experience — often through successes with efficiencies at the Aspirational phase — these organizations are looking to go beyond cost management. Experienced organizations are developing better ways to collect incorporate and act on analytics effectively so they can begin to optimize their organizations.

THE THREE STAGES OF ANALYTICS ADOPTION

Transformed: These organizations have substantial experience using analytics across a broad range of functions. They use analytics as a competitive differentiator and are already adept at organizing people, processes and tools to optimize and differentiate. Transformed organizations are less focused on cutting costs than Aspirational and Experienced organizations, possibly having already automated their operations through effective use of insights. They are most focused on driving customer profitability and making targeted investments in niche analytics as they keep pushing the organizational envelope.

Transformed organizations were three times more likely than Aspirational organizations to indicate that they *substantially outperform their industry peers.* This performance advantage illustrates the potential rewards of higher levels of analytics adoption.

Data is not the Biggest Obstacle

Despite popular opinion, getting the data right is not a top challenge that organizations face when adopting analytics. Only about one out of five respondents cited *concern with data quality or ineffective data governance* as a primary obstacle.

The adoption barriers that organizations face most are managerial and cultural rather than related to data and technology. The leading obstacle to widespread analytics adoption is *lack of understanding of how to use analytics to improve the business*, according to almost four of 10 respondents. More than one in three cite *lack of management bandwidth due to competing priorities.* (See "The Impediments to Becoming More Data Driven.")

Information Must Become Easier to Understand and Act Upon

Executives want better ways to communicate complex insights so they can quickly absorb the meaning of the data and take action. Over the next two years, executives say they will focus on supplementing standard historical reporting with emerging approaches that make information come alive. These include data visualization and process simulation as well as text and voice analytics, social media analysis and other predictive and prescriptive techniques.

THE IMPEDIMENTS TO BECOMING MORE DATA DRIVEN

New tools like these can make insights easier to understand and to act on at every point in an organization, and at every skill level. They transform numbers into information and insights that can be readily put to use, versus having to rely on further interpretation or leaving them to languish due to uncertainty about how to act.

What Leaders Can Do to Make Analytics Pay off — A New Methodology

It takes big plans followed by discrete actions to gain the benefits of analytics. But it also takes some very specific management approaches. Based on data from our survey, our engagement experience, case studies and interviews with experts, we have been able to identify a new, five-point methodology for successfully implementing analytics-driven management and for rapidly creating value. The recommendations that follow are designed to help organizations understand this "new path to value" and how to travel it. While each recommendation presents different pieces of the information-and-analytics value puzzle, each one meets all of these three critical management needs:

Reduced time to value: Value creation can be achieved early in an organization's progress to analytics sophistication. Contrary to common assumptions, it doesn't require the presence of perfect data or a full-scale organizational transformation.

Increased likelihood of transformation that's both significant and enduring: The emerging methodology we've identified enables and inspires lasting change (strategic and cultural) by tactically overcoming the most significant organizational impediments.

Greater focus on achievable steps: The approach used by the smartest companies is powerful in part because each step enables leaders to focus their efforts and resources narrowly rather than implementing universal changes — making every step easier to accomplish with an attractive ROI.

Whether pursuing the best channel strategy, the best customer experience, the best portfolio or the best process innovation, organizations embracing this approach will be first in line to gain business advantage from analytics.

First, Think Biggest

Focus on the biggest and highest-value opportunities - Does attacking the biggest challenge carry the biggest risk of failure? Paradoxically, no — because big problems command attention and incite action. And as survey participants told us, management bandwidth is a top challenge. When a project's stakes are big, top management gets invested and the best talent seeks to get involved.

It's extraordinarily hard for people to change from making decisions based on personal experience to making them from data — especially when that data counters the prevailing common wisdom. But upsetting the status quo is much easier when everyone can see how it could contribute to a major goal. With a potential big reward in sight, a significant effort is easier to justify, and people across functions and levels are better able to support it.

Conversely, don't start doing analytics without strategic business direction, as those efforts are likely to stall. Not only does that waste resources, it risks creating widespread skepticism about the real value of analytics.

In our discussions with business executives, we have repeatedly heard that analytics aligned to a significant organizational challenge makes it easier to overcome a wide range of obstacles. Respondents cited many challenges, and none can be discounted or minimized: Executive sponsorship of analytics projects, data quality and access, governance, skills and culture all matter and need to be addressed in time. But when overtaken by the momentum of a single big idea and potentially game-changing insight, obstacles like these get swept into the wake of change rather than drowning the effort.

[RECOMMENDATION 2]

Start in the Middle

Within each opportunity, start with questions, not data

Organizations traditionally are tempted to start by gathering all available data before beginning their analysis. Too often, this leads to an all-encompassing focus on data management — collecting, cleansing and converting data — that leaves little time, energy or resources to understand its potential uses. Actions taken, if any, might not be the most valuable ones. Instead, organizations should start in what might seem like the middle of the process, implementing analytics by first defining the insights and questions needed to meet the big business objective and then identifying those pieces of data needed for answers.

By defining the desired insights first, organizations can target specific subject areas and use readily available data in the initial analytic models. The insights delivered through these initial models will illuminate gaps in the data infrastructure and business processes. Time that would have been spent cleaning up all data can be redirected toward targeted data needs and specific process improvements that the insights identify, enabling iterations of value.

Companies that make data their overriding priority often lose momentum long before the first insight is delivered, frequently because a data-first approach can be perceived as taking too long before generating a financial return. By narrowing the scope of these tasks to the specific subject areas needed to answer key questions, value can be realized more quickly, while the insights are still relevant.

Also, organizations that start with the data or process change often end up with unintended consequences — such as data that is not extensible or processes that are ultimately eliminated — that require rework and additional resources to solve.

Speeding Insights into Business Operations: Compared with other respondents, transformed organizations are good at data capture. (See "What Data-Transformed Companies Do.") Additionally, transformed organizations are much more adept at data management. In these areas, they outpaced Aspirational organizations up to tenfold in their ability to execute.

WHAT DATA-TRANSFORMED COMPANIES DO

Enterprise processes have many points where analytic insights can boost business value. The operational challenge is to understand where to apply those insights in a particular industry and organization. When a bank customer stops automatic payroll deposits or remittance transfers, for example, who in the organization should be alerted and tasked with finding out whether the customer is changing jobs or planning to switch banks? Where customer satisfaction is low, what insights are needed, and how should they be delivered to prevent defections?

To keep the three gears moving together — data, insights and timely actions — the overriding business purpose must always be in view. That way, as models, processes and data are tested, priorities for the next investigation become clear. Data and models get accepted, rejected or improved based on business need. New analytic insights — descriptive, predictive and prescriptive — are embedded into increasing numbers of applications and processes, and a virtuous cycle of feedback and improvement takes hold.

[RECOMMENDATION 3]

Make Analytics Come Alive

Embed insights to drive actions and deliver value

New methods and tools to embed information into business processes — use cases, analytics solutions, optimization, work flows and simulations — are making insights more understandable and actionable. Respondents identified trend analysis, forecasting and standardized reporting as the most important tools they use today. However, they also identified tools that will have greater value in 24 months. The downswings in "as-is" methods accompanied by corresponding upswings in "to-be" methods were dramatic. (See "Where Are Data-Driven Managers Headed?")

Today's staples are expected to be surpassed in the next 24 months by:

(i)   Data visualization, such as dashboards and scorecards

(ii)   Simulations and scenario development

(iii)   Analytics applied within business processes

(iv)   Advanced statistical techniques, such as regression analysis, discrete choice modeling and mathematical optimization

Organizations expect the value from these emerging techniques to soar, making it possible for data-driven insights to be used at all levels of the organization. For example, GPS-enabled navigation devices can superimpose real-time traffic patterns and alerts onto navigation maps and suggest the best routes to drivers.

WHERE ARE DATA-DRIVEN MANAGERS HEADED?

Similarly, in oil exploration, three-dimensional renderings combine data from sensors in the field with collaborative and analytical resources accessible across the enterprise. Production engineers can incorporate geological, production and pipeline information into their drilling decisions.

Beyond 3-D, animated maps and charts can simulate critical changes in distribution flow or projected changes in consumption and resource availability. In the emerging area of analytics for unstructured data, patterns can be visualized through verbal maps that pictorially represent word frequency, allowing marketers to see how their brands are perceived. Innovative uses of this type of information layering will continue to grow as a means to help individuals across the organization consume and act upon insights derived through complex analytics that would otherwise be hard to piece together.

New Techniques and Approaches Transform Insights into Actions - New techniques to embed insights will gain in value by generating results that can be readily understood and acted upon:

Dashboards that now reflect actual last-quarter sales will also show what sales *could* be next quarter under a variety of different conditions — a new media mix, a price change, a larger sales team, even a major weather or sporting event.

Simulations evaluating alternative scenarios will automatically recommend optimal approaches — such as the best media mix to introduce a specific product to a specific segment, or the ideal number of sales professionals to assign to a new territory.

Use cases will illustrate how to embed insights into business applications and processes.

New methods will also make it possible for decision makers more fully to *see* their customers' purchases, payments and interactions. Businesses will be able to *listen* to customers' unique wants and needs about channel and product preferences. In fact, making customers, as well as information, come to life within complex organizational systems may well become the biggest benefit of making data-driven insights real to those who need to use them.

[RECOMMENDATION 4]

Add, Don't Detract

Keep existing capabilities while adding new ones

When executives first realize their need for analytics, they tend to turn to those closest to them for answers. Over time, these point-of-need resources come together in local line of business units to enable sharing of insights. Ultimately, centralized units emerge to bring a shared enterprise perspective — governance, tools, methods — and specialized expertise. As executives use analytics more frequently to *inform day-to-day decisions and actions*, this increasing demand for insights keeps resources at each level engaged, expanding analytic capabilities even as activities are shifted for efficiencies. (See "How Analytics Capabilities Grow with Adoption.")

HOW ANALYTICS CAPABILITIES GROW WITH ADOPTION

Sophisticated modeling and visualization tools, as noted, will soon provide greater business value than ever before. But that does not mean that spreadsheets and charts should go away. On the contrary: New tools should supplement earlier ones or continue to be used side by side as needed. That lesson applies to nearly every way that analytics capabilities should be nurtured as an organization becomes more ambitious about becoming data driven: The process needs to be additive. As analytics capabilities are added upstream at increasingly central levels of management, existing capabilities at point of need shouldn't be subtracted. Nor should they be transplanted to central locations. As new capabilities come on board, existing ones should continue to be supported.

There are other ways that capabilities grow and deepen within an organization. Disciplines like finance and supply chain are inherently data intensive and are often where analytics first take root. Encouraged by early successes, organizations begin expanding analytic decision making to more disciplines. (See "How Analytics Propagates Across Functions.") In Transformed organizations, reusability creates a snowball effect, as models from one function are repurposed into another with minimal modifications.

Over time, data-driven decision making branches out across the organization. As experience and usage grow, the value of analytics increases, which enables business benefits to accrue more quickly.

HOW ANALYTICS PROPAGATES ACROSS FUNCTIONS

Add Value with an Enterprise Analytics Unit Organizations that first experience the value of analytics in discrete business units or functions are likely soon to seek a wider range of capabilities — and more advanced use of existing ones. A centralized analytics unit, often called either a center of excellence or center of competency, makes it possible to share analytic resources efficiently and effectively. It does not, however, replace distributed and localized capabilities; rather, the central unit is additive, built upon existing capabilities that may have already developed in functions, departments and lines of business.

We found that 63% more Transformed organizations than Aspirational organizations use a *centralized enterprise unit as the primary source of analytics*. A centralized analytics unit can provide a home for more advanced skills to come together within the organization, providing both advanced models and enterprise governance through establishing priorities and standards by these practices:

(i)   Advance standard methods for identifying business problems to be solved with analytics.

(ii)   Facilitate identification of analytic business needs while driving rigor into methods for embedding insights into end-to-end processes.

(iii)   Promote enterprise-level governance on prioritization, master data sources and reuse to capture enterprise efficiencies.

(iv) Standardize tools and analytic platforms to enable resource sharing, streamline maintenance and reduce licensing expenses.

In three distinct areas — application of analytic tools, functional use of analytics and location of skills — we found that adding capabilities without detracting from existing ones offers a fast path to full benefits from analytics-driven management.

[RECOMMENDATION 5]

Build the Parts, Plan the Whole

Use an information agenda to plan for the future

Big data is getting bigger. Information is coming from instrumented, interconnected supply chains transmitting real-time data about fluctuations in everything from market demand to the weather. Additionally, strategic information has started arriving through unstructured digital channels: social media, smart phone applications and an ever-increasing stream of emerging Internet-based gadgets. It's no wonder six out of 10 respondents said their organization *has more data than it knows how to use effectively*.

All this data must be molded into an information foundation that is *integrated*, *consistent* and *trustworthy*, which were the leading data priorities cited by our respondents. (See "What Managers Want Most in Their Data.") Therefore, even though smart organizations will start down the analytics path by selectively attacking the biggest problems (and selectively building out the parts of the data foundation most relevant to gaining insight about them), they'll need to understand how each piece of this data foundation aligns to overall information agenda. The information agenda accelerates the organization's ability to share and deliver trusted information across all applications and processes. It sets up information to serve as a strategic asset for the organization.

WHAT MANAGERS WANT MOST IN THEIR DATA

The information agenda identifies foundational information practices and tools while aligning IT and business goals through enterprise information plans and financially justified deployment road maps. This agenda helps establish necessary links between those who drive the priorities of the organization by line of business and set the strategy, and those who manage data and information.

A comprehensive agenda also enables analytics to keep pace with changing business goals. An executive at one company, for example, told us they "had it down to a science" when it came to understanding the impact of price changes on single products and single channels. But they were blindsided when the company shifted to a customer-centric strategy, restructuring around bundled products and dynamic pricing across channels. Because their data marts had been developed de facto over time, they found themselves struggling to understand which tools and information were needed to go forward.

Last, building the analytics foundation under the guidance of a forward-looking information agenda enables organizations to keep pace with advances in mathematical sciences and technology. Without an enterprise wide information agenda, units are likely to explore these new developments independently and adopt them inconsistently, a difficult path for gaining full business benefits from analytics.

Outline for an Information Agenda The information agenda provides a vision and high-level road map for information that aligns business needs to growth in analytics sophistication, with the underlying technology and processes spanning the following:

(i) Information governance policies and tool kits: from little oversight to fully implemented policies and practices

(ii)   Data architecture: from ad hoc to optimal physical and logical views of structured and unstructured information and databases

(iii) Data currency: from only historical data to a real-time view of all information

(iv)   Data management, integration and middleware: from subject-area data and content in silos to enterprise information that is fully embedded into business processes with master content and master data management

(v)   Analytical tool kits based upon user needs: from basic search, query and reporting to advanced analytics and visualization

The information agenda is a key enabler of analytics initiatives by providing the right information and tools at the right times based upon business-driven priorities.

Set Yourself Up for Success

Aware that analytics-driven opportunities are central to growth and success, organizations seek to capture value. They want to find the best place to begin, but for many, that entry point is elusive.

If you are Aspirational: Assemble the best people and resources to make the case for investments in analytics. To get sponsorship for initial projects, identify the big business challenges that can be addressed by analytics and find the data you have that fits the challenge.

If you are Experienced: Make the move to enterprise analytics, and manage it by keeping focus on the big issues that everyone recognizes. Collaborate to drive enterprise opportunities without compromising departmental needs while preventing governance from becoming an objective unto itself.

If you are Transformed: Discover and champion improvements in how you are using analytics. You've accomplished a lot already with analytics but are feeling increased pressure to do more. Focus your analytics and management bandwidth to go deeper rather than broader, but recognize it will be critical to continue to demonstrate new ways of how analytics can move the business toward its goals.

Techniques to Get Started - Hurdles on the path to effective analytics use are highest right at the start of adoption. Here is a way to begin.

Pick your spots - Search for your organization's biggest and highest priority challenge, and create a diagram to describe it. Show available data sources, models to be built and processes and applications where analytics will have an impact. (For a full example of what such a diagram can look like, see "Figure 5" in the complete special report "Analytics: The New Path to Value.") Create multiple diagrams if you're selecting from a strong list of possible initiatives. Keep in mind that your biggest problems, such as customer retention, anti-fraud efforts or advertising mix, are also your biggest opportunities. Change is hard for most, so select an initiative worthy of sustained focus that can make the biggest difference in meeting your most important business goals. Remember that focus is critical during these initial efforts. Do not get distracted once the targeted area is identified.

Prove the value - Use reason and benchmarks for initial executive sponsorship, but use a proof-of-value pilot to keep sponsors engaged. Estimate how much revenue can be gained, how much money can be saved and how much margins can be improved. Employ techniques to embed analytics to illustrate and prioritize the types of organizational changes that are needed to achieve the value. Pull it all together using an implementation road map with a clear starting point and a range of options for future opportunities.

Roll it out for the long haul - The challenge should be big, the model insightful and the business vision complete. However, the first implementation steps can be small, as long as they fit your agenda. Reduce your rework by using business analytics and process management tools that you have selected for the long haul — information governance, business analytics and business rules. As you make progress, don't forget to analyze feedback and business outcomes to determine where your analytics model and business vision can be improved.

Make Analytics Pay off - It takes big plans followed by discrete actions to gain the benefits of analytics. But it also takes some very specific management approaches. Each of our recommendations meets three critical management needs:

(i)   Reduced time to value

(ii)   Increased likelihood of transformation that's both significant and enduring

(iii) Greater focus on achievable steps

To start on the fastest path to value, keep everyone focused on the big business issues and select the challenges that you know analytics can solve today — within an agenda for the future. Build on the capabilities you know you already have. And always keep pressing to embed the insights you've gained into business operations.

ABOUT THE AUTHORS

Steve La Valle is the global strategy leader for IBM's Business Analytics and Optimization service line. Eric Lesser is the research director and North American leader of the IBM Institute for Business Value. Rebecca Shockley is the business analytics and optimization global lead for the IBM Institute for Business Value. Michael S. Hopkins is editor-in-chief of MIT Sloan Management Review. Nina Kruschwitz is an editor and the special projects manager at MIT Sloan Management Review.

ACKNOWLEDGMENTS

Essential contributions to the research and this article were made by Fred Balboni, GBS global leader: Business Analytics and Optimization, IBM; Michael Haydock, GBS global leader: Customer Analytics, IBM; Deborah Kasdan, writer: Corporate Communications, IBM; Christine Kinser, global leader: Strategic Communications, IBM; and Katharyn White, vice president of marketing, IBM Global Services.

1.7   How to Monetize Your Data

Barbara H. Wixom and Jeanne W. Ross - Magazine: Spring 2017 IssueResearch Highlight January 09, 2017

These days, most companies are awash in data. But figuring out how to derive a profit from the data deluge can help distinguish your company in the marketplace.

The possession of rich amounts of data is hardly unique in today's world. Indeed, data itself is increasingly a commodity. But the ability to monetize data effectively — and not simply hoard it — can be a source of competitive advantage in the digital economy.

Companies can take three approaches to monetizing their data: (1) improving internal business processes and decisions, (2) wrapping information around core products and services, and (3) selling information offerings to new and existing markets. These approaches differ significantly in the types of capabilities and commitments they require, but each represents an important opportunity for a company to distinguish itself in the marketplace.

Theoretically, companies can pursue more than one approach to data monetization at the same time. In practice, adopting each approach requires management commitment to specific organizational changes and targeted technology and data management upgrades. Thus, it's best to identify your most promising opportunity and start there. In doing so, you will enhance your data in ways that will accelerate subsequent efforts related to the other approaches. More importantly, you'll build your company's capacity for monetizing its data.

Improving Internal Processes

Using data to improve operational processes and boost decision-making quality may not be the most glamorous path to monetizing data, but it is the most immediate. Executives often underestimate the financial returns that can be generated by using data to create operational efficiencies. Companies see positive results when they put data and analytics in the hands of employees who are positioned to make decisions, such as those who interact with customers, oversee product development, or run production processes. With data-based insights and clear decision rules, people can deliver more meaningful services, better assess and address customer demands, and optimize production.

When Satya Nadella became CEO of Microsoft Corp. in February 2014, he urged employees to find ways to improve the company's processes with data. Within sales, executives believed that, with the right tools and systems, they could improve the productivity of their salespeople by 30%. To do so, Microsoft's sales leaders sought to deploy tools that would help salespeople spend more of their time engaging with customers — and in more effective ways — by arming them with key computed insights, such as how likely a sale is to close and when.

http://sloanreview.mit.edu/article/how-to-monetize-your-data/

1.8   How Data Science is the Driving Force behind Successful Digital Transformation

Ben Rossi: **7 OCTOBER 2016**

Data science needs to be a fundamental component of any digital transformation effort.

In a recent report from Forrester Research, nearly 40% of global data and analytics decision-makers said they are already implementing and expanding big data technology, with an additional 30% planning to do so over the next year.

Big data is bringing with it the ability to transform industries and the potential to turn traditional, long-standing business models on their head. For businesses, the issue to be addressed is how to make the most of all this data, turning it into actionable insights.

Help is at hand in the form of data science. The analysis of patterns in the data allows organizations to build models that create forecasts of what can happen under different scenarios.

By doing so, companies can state objectives in a mathematical language, optimize over possible actions, and recommend be best action to the user. This form the basis for transformative software, creating solutions that reliably turn data into actionable insights.

Cloud elasticity

Data science has seen a rapid increase in adoption levels, evolving from being a question of if it should be used to a question of what frequency.

It has become a necessity as technologies have exploded the volume of data available for analysis and as cloud computing has made storing and analyzing the data more affordable and feasible.

Central to cloud computing's contribution to data science is the elasticity of its computing power. We now have the ability to add CPU horsepower as needed to execute analysis, however complex, on data, however large. There was a time when any science design was only as good as its ability to run within a timeframe determined by the available CPU power. With cloud computing and the ability to add processing power on demand, those limitations are no longer in place. This gives rise to things like computationally expensive machine learning where the software can learn and evolve.

Ultimately, the real question for a business that wants to leverage data science is how to use it to make better decisions and improve operations. If it's to be of use, it needs to be consumable – meaning the algorithms employed by the software shouldn't be a black box where the user has little sense (or trust) in what is happening in the background.

On the other hand, software should not over-power the user with so much information that they are left confused. There is a middle ground where the science is accessible by the user. Here, users are given a basic knowledge of the logic employed, the majority of recommendations can be accepted automatically, and in the few instances where the user requires more information, it is made available to them.

Real-world applications

Data science is enabling the next generation of enterprise software, resulting in solutions that tell users what is going to happen and what they should do about it today.

How much inventory should we carry today to meet future demand? How should we price our items to guarantee future profitability? Which port should we have a shipment depart from and come into in order to de-risk the estimated time of arrival? What products should we recommend to customers to increase the probability of a cross-sell?

Across industries, it's valuable to have a CRM application with the ability to predict which customers are most likely to make the next purchase, which products will be part of that purchase, and which customers are at risk for attrition.

An intelligent CRM engine should be able to identify the individual products a customer is most likely to purchase and the probability that the purchase will occur within a specified time. Sales associates can make use of this information to prioritize which customers they contact or to filter customers based on specific products they want to push.

For counter sales locations, the CRM software can alert checkout staff to remind customers about complementary purchases they might have forgotten. And, in retail environments, customers can receive coupons or recommendations on arrival in a shop, instead of at the checkout when the sale is already completed.

In a business environment where supply chains are increasingly complex and interdependent, the smooth operation of the global supply chain is essential if businesses are to avoid costly delays and inventory shortages.

Data scientists are making full use of increased computing power and global supply chain data to automatically model supply chain timelines and anticipate where disruptions are likely to occur. This enables businesses to take the necessary steps to mitigate against them.

The combination of machine learning and big data provides a better overall understanding of which delays are normal and which are true system-wide disruptions (e.g. strikes and natural disasters).

There are systems available to continuously monitor the data feed in real time, which will the send out a notification if there is a problem, before going on to suggest a whole range of solutions.

When there is a disruption, businesses can dive into affected shipments, for example, with a view to understanding the impact of the disruption for each individual shipment. And, by integrating this data across an entire business, it helps to deepen the understanding of where the business's priorities lie.

So, how will it affect the business downstream? Which shipments are more important? What's the optimal trade-off – faster shipping times or additional costs? In short, as well as helping to identify disruptions, data science has a significant role to play in a charting a successful course around any supply chain bottlenecks.

By better connecting global companies to their many and varied partners throughout the world, the solutions enabled by data science afford businesses real-time visibility of order and shipment statuses, helping decision makers to optimize their supply chains for greater agility, increased flexibility and lower costs.

New data sources

By utilizing RFID and in-store sensors, retailers, distributors and manufacturers can search every piece of inventory in stores and warehouses – seeing not only what inventory is available but also detecting its movement in the store or warehouse.

The wealth of data this is providing from traditional brick-and-mortar locations will allow data scientists to conduct analysis that was never possible before.

Across retail, this data can also be used to understand cannibalization effects, as one item is picked up and another is put down. Additionally, customer foot patterns in the store will allow for the creating of better store layouts.

In the retail fashion, businesses will be able to use the data gathered by sensors to assess the fit of items based on the frequency of items that don't make it out of the fitting room. And away from the shop floor, warehouse and inventory managers can use similar solutions to obtain accurate inventory levels, without the need for a time-consuming and error-prone manual count.

Data science is the only sure-fire way of creating and validating solutions to improve decision-making across the board. For modern, forward-thinking businesses that find themselves with more data than they know what to do with, the appliance of data science will be the difference between sink or swim.

Sourced from Ziad Nejmeldeen, chief scientist, <u>Infor</u>

<u>http://www.information-age.com/data-science-driving-force-behind-successful-digital-transformation-123462527/</u>

1.9   Top 10 Hot Big Data Technologies

As the big data analytics market rapidly expands to include mainstream customers, which technologies are most in demand and promise the most growth potential? The answers can be found in *Tech Radar: Big Data, Q1 2016*, a new Forrester Research report evaluating the maturity and trajectory of 22 technologies across the entire data life cycle. The winners all contribute to real-time, predictive, and integrated insights, what big data customers want now.

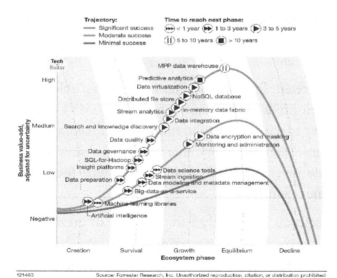

Here is my take on the 10 hottest big data technologies based on Forrester's analysis:

Predictive analytics: software and/or hardware solutions that allow firms to discover, evaluate, optimize, and deploy predictive models by analyzing big data sources to improve business performance or mitigate risk.

NoSQL databases: key-value, document, and graph databases.

Search and knowledge discovery: tools and technologies to support self-service extraction of information and new insights from large repositories of unstructured and structured data that resides in multiple sources such as file systems, databases, streams, APIs, and other platforms and applications.

Stream analytics: software that can filter, aggregate, enrich, and analyze a high throughput of data from multiple disparate live data sources and in any data format.

In-memory data fabric: provides low-latency access and processing of large quantities of data by distributing data across the dynamic random access memory (DRAM), Flash, or SSD of a distributed computer system.

Distributed file stores: a computer network where data is stored on more than one node, often in a replicated fashion, for redundancy and performance.

Data virtualization: a technology that delivers information from various data sources, including big data sources such as Hadoop and distributed data stores in real-time and near-real time.

Data integration: tools for data orchestration across solutions such as Amazon Elastic MapReduce (EMR), Apache Hive, Apache Pig, Apache Spark, MapReduce, Couchbase, Hadoop, and MongoDB.

Data preparation: software that eases the burden of sourcing, shaping, cleansing, and sharing diverse and messy data sets to accelerate data's usefulness for analytics.

Data quality: products that conduct data cleansing and enrichment on large, high-velocity data sets, using parallel operations on distributed data stores and databases.

Forrester's Tech Radar methodology evaluates the potential success of each technology and all 10 above are projected to have "significant success." In addition, each technology is placed in a specific maturity phase—from creation to decline—based on the level of development of its technology ecosystem. The first 8 technologies above are considered to be in the Growth stage and the last 2 in the Survival stage.

Forrester also estimates the time it will take the technology to get to the next stage and predictive analytics is the only one with a ">10 years" designation, expected to "deliver high business value in late Growth through Equilibrium phase for a long time." Technologies #2 to #8 above are all expected to reach the next phase in 3 to 5 years and the last 2 technologies are expected to move from the Survival to the Growth phase in 1-3 years.

Finally, Forrester provides for each technology an assessment of its business value-add, adjusted for uncertainty. This is based not only on potential impact but also on feedback and evidence from implementations and market reputation. Says Forrester: "If the technology and its ecosystem are at an early stage of development, we have to assume that its potential for damage and disruption is higher than that of a better-known technology." The first 2 technologies in the list above are rated as "high" business value-add, the next 2 as "medium," and all the rest "low," no doubt because of their emerging status and lack of maturity.

Why did I add to the list of hottest technologies two that are still in the Survival phase—data preparation and data quality? In the same report, Forrester also provides the following data from its Q4 2015 survey of 63 big data vendors:

http://www.forbes.com/sites/gilpress/2016/03/14/top-10-hot-big-data-technologies/#1806f5547f26

1.10 How Big Data Is Impacting the E-Commerce Industry
DURJOY PATRANABISH, 18 NOVEMBER 2016

In recent years, India has become one of the fastest developing markets in the e-commerce industry. With an online user base of around 100 million in 2016, the e-retail business in India is expected to touch the $100 billion revenue mark by 2020. As per an Assocham survey, consumer demand is witnessing a market growth of as much as 40 percent in the ongoing festival season, as compared to 2015. This exponential growth can largely be attributed to the massive chunks of data available with companies. Availability of data has created the opportunity to utilize past trends and performances for growth, allowing companies to improve customer satisfaction via better products and services.

As retailers prepare for the big season sale, the use of Big Data has become a critical force in growing revenues. Big Data Analytics is helping retailers stay in front of a new breed of consumer, the omni-channel shopper. Consumers are today shopping across multiple channels, from brick-and-mortar stores and catalogues to online websites and mobile devices. This transformation is in large part driven by advances in portable devices, digital media and geo-based technology.

The omni-channel shopping revolution has put the customer in control, compelling the retailers to look for a single, seamless approach that lets them interact with their customers anytime and anywhere, across any and all channels. The ability to foster a sales experience that melds the world of physical stores with online shopping has led both the consumers and the retailers to embrace omni-channeling retailing. E-commerce companies have now turned to Big Data Analytics for focused customer group targeting, evaluating campaign strategies and maintaining a competitive advantage, especially during the festive shopping season.

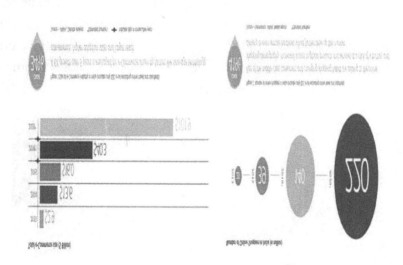

Source: Deloitte

Here are some of the many ways in which companies use Big Data to provide a personalized customer shopping experience.

Customer Journey and Behaviour

Big Data plays an important role in tracking the entire journey of a customer, from entry to exit. An average online shopper may not realize that every click is being monitored and that all purchases being made are captured from beginning to end. Dividing customers into different segments based on a combination of purchase patterns and demographic details makes it easier to target them better. Such categorizations are even more critical during campaigns and festive sales, when companies invest heavily to attract new customers and retain existing base.

Search and purchase information of buyers three or four months prior to the sale yields a deep understanding of current trends and actual demand. This is extremely useful as sellers can then stock their inventory accordingly and optimize shelf space. For example, based on historical data, Electronics, Automobiles and Apparel & Clothing are some of the categories that see the highest purchase volumes during festivals; hence, demand forecasting and inventory stocking of merchandise before the sale period can be utilized to give optimum discounts, thus maximizing revenue.

Demographics also play an important role in demand. It has been observed that Kolkata and other major cities witness a spike on Durga Puja, while North India is expected to pick up pace in the coming days. Big Data helps in predictive analysis and inventory management by analyzing customer behaviour.

Personalized Offers and Recommendations

E-retailers make huge investments to attract new customers to their websites and maximize their return on investment. This is where campaigns, referral programmes and coupons act as triggers to attract new traffic to websites. Amongst competitors, it is a matter of how the data being captured is analyzed, extrapolated and converted into business decisions and strategies that decides the market leader.

As a next step to customer behavioural analysis, e-retailers use recommender systems to generate recommendations autonomously for individual users based on past purchases and searches, as well as on the behaviour of other, similar users. This not only provides an interactive and richer experience to customers, but also improves the retailer's ability to increase sales through cross-sell and up-sell. For example, recommending mobile accessories to a person searching for or buying a phone will increase the odds of a cross-sell. Retailers can also extract useful insights from a buyer's search history and his actions on social media (likes and clicks), thereby being able to provide personalized advertisements that can enrich the customer's overall shopping experience.

Customer feedback

Customer feedback is undoubtedly the most important tool for companies looking at improving their business. It can be safely assumed that the growth of a company is directly proportional to the satisfaction of its customers - the happier the customers, the more they tend to indulge in the services offered. Analyzing customer feedback provides actionable insights not only to create better customer experience, but also to improve existing products or services.

One of the most important utilizations of feedback data is sentiment analysis of reviews and ratings. Sentiment analysis is a method of identifying customers' reviews and opinions about products and services. Big Data helps in processing a large amount of reviews that are not in similar formats, and stores the combination of data, which is more efficient. With the use of text analytics and machine learning, positive and negative reviews are categorized into different buckets and analyzed to gather useful insights about customer satisfaction and the overall business. This processed data can be a useful asset for organizations looking for direct customer touch-points.

Moving computation is always cheaper than moving data, and Big Data follows the same approach. Online companies generate click stream data in huge volumes. With the help of analytics, e-retailers analyze customer feedback from both their and the competitors' previous campaigns to improve their strategies by determining issues and resolving them in the next sale.

Big Data has helped the e-commerce industry in many ways, but there are still an infinite number of possibilities to explore. Many companies have already started using Big Data for real-time analysis. Real-Time Big Data Analytics (RTBDA) can result in improved sales and higher profits by detecting and resolving issues at the time of purchase rather than post purchase. RTBDA can help satisfy customers by resolving issues on the spot and detecting fraud at the same time. In the future, machines using RTBDA will be able to respond like humans in a critical situation.

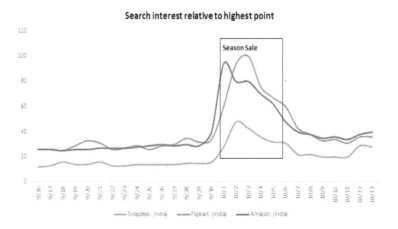

Source: Google trends

Big Data when combined with the Internet of Things can certainly open endless opportunities for decision making. IoT connects multiple devices via the internet, generating vast amounts of data. This data, if utilized properly, can be very useful, allowing the e-commerce industry to predict precisely what, where and when a buyer is willing to pay.

While Big Data is being used for providing insights from transactional and behavioural data, what if it is used for voice-based search as well? A few companies have already started working in this direction by storing and analyzing voice data. Once more organizations start seeing value in creating new use cases instead of replicating what is already done; it will soon generate a new methodology for e-commerce companies to grow their businesses.

(Disclaimer: The views and opinions expressed in this article are those of the author and do not necessarily reflect the views of Your Story.)

https://yourstory.com/2016/11/big-data-impacting-e-commerce-industry/

1.11 Big Data Analytics Solutions – The Pulse of the New Age Data

Posted on May 10, 2016

Big Data comes as a great indispensable addition to the enterprises in the wake of the extremely high volumes of data expected to be handled, coming in from versatile sources. The Returns on investments realized because of the integration of Big Data Analytics into the enterprise workflow is tremendous as critical data is being effectively captured and analyzed like no other could have. Enterprises are considering the future with Big Data emerging as the pulse of the new age data.

What Makes Big Data really BIG – the Growing Importance of Big Data Analytics

Big Data is a term coined after fathoming the volume, velocity and versatility of data. Different people have different views on why data today is considered big or intricate. And there are interesting reasons, why it is called so and how it becomes important to enterprises today.

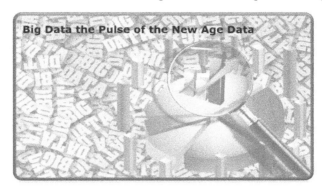

Most of the people feel that the traditional large data files comprise the most important of the data assets of enterprises and need to be stored efficiently. But, the new age data needs to be handled differently as well. Big Data with its capacity of handling structured and unstructured data, becomes an all important part of the process of collecting and curating data generated by social media. Contemporary techniques putting to use the concept of location based services; powered by the simple sensor based techniques to the very sophisticated satellite communications, rely heavily on Big Data Analytics Solutions for data capture, organization and presentation. Devices like beacons, smartphones, tablets, and wearables; almost anything under the sun wired by IoT or other niche concepts bank on Big Data.

Advanced analytics is an all-important technique depending on a robust Big Data set up and is instrumental in giving a logical direction to enterprises. Big data is the driving force behind precise analytics and becomes critical to the success of an organization. Data Visualization techniques too depend on the appropriateness of data to measure up and become a relevant concept.

Big Data Analytics -The Concerns

Every innovation comes with its own risks and challenges which need to be attended to. While implementing big data into their organization, companies face some common challenges.

Securing enterprise systems from unauthorized access and other vulnerabilities is the foremost concern a company can have. Keeping this data safe is a major task for all. Another huge challenge is to get an infrastructure and the other nitty gritties in place for implementing Big Data, summing up to higher budgets.

Enterprises wishing to integrate Big Data Analytics Solutions into the existing systems need have a better planning and a judicious vision to ensure the correctness of the setup.

At times enterprises get into this data handling methodology without really needing it. Without the relevant applications, they end up having no fruitful advantages for these.

Engaging the correct resources for Big Data is a huge challenge for many and can give nightmares to enterprises.

With Cloud based services becoming more practical today, this too can be obtained as a flexible, scalable and a feasible service in the Cloud at least as a step to ease out many of these problems.

Big Data Consulting Revolutionizing the Businesses

It is more than clear today that Big Data revolutionizes the ways of work in a very similar way that the internet did, decades ago. Enterprises are adopting this technology, blending it in into other contemporary techniques with the help of efficient Big Data Consulting practices. Companies who have already implemented this see remarkable competitive advantages in big data and are rapidly progressing to make their own data practices.

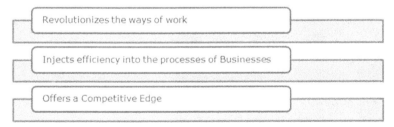

Data specialists predict data driven business outcomes from big data and its compatible technologies. The outcome requires ability to mobilize information across the enterprise. As more and more data becomes available, it requires quick categorization as well.

Big Data Driving Businesses to Success Big Data – The Big Transformation

Big Data Analytics is all set to radically change the enterprises want in the experiences they set out to provide to their users with. The users of the system right from the employees, field force staff, dealers, and partners and of course the most important of them all, the customer.

- Precision in Manufacturing
- Prudency in Planning
- Designing appropriate strategies
- Optimized Processes
- Better Team Organizations

Making use of modern day devices and the novel technologies, Big Data extends its benefits to much more transforming every process it touches within the organization.

- Focused Data Collection
- Improved Management of Versatile Data
- Precise Reporting
- Conducive Use for Keypersons
- Supports Self-Service Concepts
- Insightful Data Presentation Enabler

In a Nutshell

Big Data Complements Businesses like no other and the forecasts by both GE and Accenture tell a promising story.

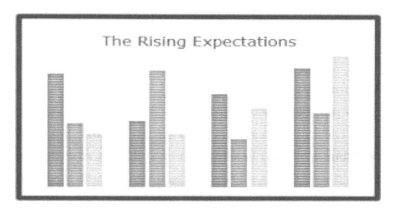

According to a study conducted by GE and Accenture

☐ 87% of enterprises think that Big Data Analytics Solutions are all set to completely change the competitive landscape in the next three years

☐ 73% of the businesses invest more than 20% of their total technology budget on Big Data analytics

☐ 76% of industry experts believe that Big Data is likely to grow more in the coming years

https://blog.spec-india.com/big-data-analytics-solutions-pulse-new-age-data/

1.12 Looking into the Future with Big Data and Analytics

Posted on February 9, 2016

Big Data comes of age today. From its humble beginnings as a shift from traditional databases to a grand, comprehensive repository of data, organized to suit the requirements of the data itself; today Big Data and Analytics promises a logical connect to predictions, suggestions, finances and hence assured returns on investments.

Predictive Analytics emerges as a powerful tool to be used in conjunction with Big Data to combine real time data with statistical data to foresee and expect the future trends. Intelligent predictions assist the enterprises to encash opportunities as also prevent catastrophic mistakes.

Modern day tools like Big Data Analytics and Business Intelligence scrap the old-school methods of relying on descriptive data and reports. The businesses today rely on tools which not only help in decision making; they also generate new insights into the strategies, with an aim to finalize the future course of actions. Proactive participation is promoted by these modern methods by introducing self-service facilities, empowering key decision makers to use their own acumen to foresee and face the future.

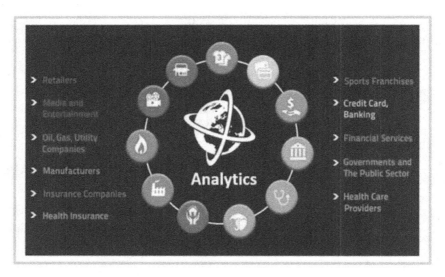

Applications of Big Data and Analytics

This technology along with Predictive Analytics is mainly used to find out the trends, knowing the customers and their behaviour; it helps the business with decision making and business performance improvement.

Fraud Detection and Security

With predictive Big Data Solutions, enterprises control the losses due to any deceitful activities before the occurrence. They achieve high performance, greater accuracy and make better predictions by various methods, such as

- Business Rules
- Anomaly Detection

Today, cyber security is a major concern and these highly reliable analytics helps controlling such vulnerabilities.

Marketing

Businesses use Analytics for identifying the potential clients, predicting their responses as well as promoting cross-sell opportunities.

Operations

With intelligent Big Data and Analytics, organizations increase operational efficiency.

- Predictive Analytics Models are used to manage inventory and factory resources in many organizations
- Organizations make use of the predictive models generated from the Big Data to decide the sales expected according to the trends and be prepared to combat the demand

Risk Analysis

Predictive Analytics with Big Data and Analytics is extensively used for credit scoring, a method to assess individual capacity to purchase an asset or worthiness for obtaining insurance. Credit score is a number that is generated by a predictive model, incorporating all the data of the person to know his creditworthiness.

Getting into Real Life

Big Data Solutions have interesting applications in real life, for various industries across domains.

Credit Card, Banking and Financial Services

- Detect and control fraud
- Manage credit risk
- Maximize cross-sell opportunity
- Intelligent customer relationship management
- Improve marketing campaigns

Governments and the Public sector

- Control improper payments of tax
- Analyze misuse of funds and taxpayer's money
- Detect criminal activities and patterns
- Relevant details for the citizens

Health Care

- Predicting health concerns in accordance with geographies and populations
- Analyzing the effectiveness of
- Medical & pathological tests
- Treatments & medications
- Predicting requirements in patient care and providing for the facilities accordingly
- Active data sharing with Research organizations and universities to determine patterns

Health insurers

- Controlling insurance claims related fraud
- Identifying patients prone to risks, especially for chronic and life threatening diseases
- Quality of life betterment with prudent foresight generated through Analytics

Insurance companies

- Regulating premium rates for insurance
- Controlling insurance claims related fraud
- Improvising claims processes
- Managing clients and Improving viability
- Enhancing marketing campaigns & increasing their effectivity

Manufacturers

- Predicting factors related to compromise in quality
- Combating machinery & production failure
- Enhancing service resources and distribution

Media and Entertainment

- Identifying influencing attributes & hence trends
- Improving the insight of the business in a quick and cost-effective manner

Oil, Gas and Utility Companies

- Predicting future resource demands
- Sharing useful parameters helping in exploration

Retailers

- Estimating the effectiveness of
- Promotional events
- Marketing campaigns
- Prudent inventory management across stores with predicted demands
- Analyzing online as well as offline consumer behavior to get a complete perspective of consumer behavior

Sports franchises

- Predictions help in strategizing sports and games

- Estimating the moves and behavior of the competitor beforehand drives games using modern technology

On a Parting Note

With diverse and interesting applications of Big Data solutions, Big Data and Analytics is a trend to look out for. Complementing each other, Big Data, Business Intelligence and Predictive Analytics need to be explored and use in innovative and interesting ways.

https://blog.spec-india.com/looking-into-the-future-with-big-data-and-analytics/

1.13 The Flood of Data from IoT Is Powering New Opportunities — for Some

Sam Ransbotham: January 31, 2017 Reading Time: 3 min

Companies that got into IoT early are reaping rewards in more timely, accurate, detailed, and reliable data.

It comes as no surprise that an important part of data analytics is the data itself. In fact, the appeal of the internet of things (IoT) largely relates to the role of connected devices in gathering this valuable resource.

With hyperbole, rampant about the new "oil," "soil," "coal," or even "gold," is we becoming inured to data's promise? And even if we aren't, how effective is IoT at delivering on the promise of these data riches?

Recently, Stephanie Jernigan, David Kiron, and I researched the effect that IoT is having on organizations. A combination of interview and survey responses from 1,480 managers resulted in a summary report of this research, "Data Sharing and Analytics Drive Success with IoT".

One aspect of our findings that we were unable to cover in the summary report was the relationship between organizational experience with IoT projects and organizational data. Our understanding of this relationship flows from responses to two questions: First, we asked organizations how much experience they had with IoT projects, ranging from none (27%) to actively using IoT for more than 2 years (13%). Second, we asked organizations to assess the data they've collected along four dimensions: its timeliness, accuracy, detail, and reliability. Figure 1 summarizes these results.

What we found was that increased experience with IoT projects is associated with improvements in the timeliness, detail, accuracy, and reliability of data. This is certainly comforting to those investing the time and resources in deploying these devices. A greater volume of data from IoT devices seems inevitable. But beyond that, organizations improve over time in their ability to get better *quality* data, not just greater quantities.

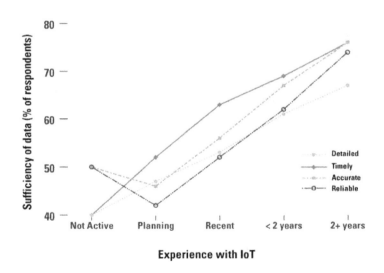

Figure 1: Data Quality and Experience with IoT

Of these data quality measures, timeliness exhibits the largest difference. About 40% of respondents whose organizations aren't active with IoT reported that their data has "mostly" or "completely" sufficient timeliness; in contrast, 76% of respondents who have 2 years or more of IoT experience said their data was sufficiently timely. As systems monitor and transmit data closer to the source, delays associated with data gathering decrease. Accuracy of data takes longer to improve but eventually reaches the same level of sufficiency as the timeliness dimension.

How Are Companies Using IoT Now?

We also asked respondents for their favorite example of how IoT has been used in their organization. Respondents certainly spoke to timeliness, accuracy, detail, and reliability. Descriptions of these projects provide qualitative support for the empirical findings but also offer insight and richness in unexpected ways, including:

- Improved customer experience by sharing more accurate and more timely data
- Early warning on poor equipment performance and failure
- Automated alerting for critical systems
- Real-time alerts for immediate action
- Real-time contextual collaboration between all stakeholders in an open and honest environment

In this way, IoT can be particularly beneficial in reducing bullwhip effects with projects that "improve supply chain performance to meet variable demand."

Opportunities Abound

While many examples focused on improved speed and efficiency through data, some also spoke of entirely new opportunities that resulted from IoT projects. One respondent noted, for example, that "analytics of the data from IoT is being bundled as a service and is one of the strategies for growth," while another commented that IoT permitted "developing new modules and linking them with existing products." Still another commenter described, "Testing key biometrics from a small group of employee volunteers to see if there are any specific client interactions [meetings, phone calls, help desk, etc.] with specific clients that create employee stress" — a far cry from industrial equipment monitoring.

Perhaps as another indication of the potential for IoT, some respondents were cagey. We got comments such as, "I can't tell you; it is proprietary!!!" and "we are in stealth mode, so ... no comment." Such comments indicate the potential for competitive advantage that IoT may contain.

And yes, there were certainly those who did not provide examples. Some were optimistic that examples will come, with such comments as "... I can only hope," while others noted that investments were still required ("It really hasn't borne fruit yet" and "We are in the early stages") or complementary changes needed ("We aren't really using it yet; our business model needs changing to make it happen"). It can take considerable effort and investment to get ready for IoT.

So, while the internet of things is associated with more data, making use of IoT isn't just about quantity — and fortunately for organizations investing in IoT devices, quality do not seem to suffer in the deluge.

ABOUT THE AUTHOR

Sam Ransbotham is an associate professor of information systems at the Carroll School of Management at Boston College and the *MIT Sloan Management Review* guest editor for the Data and Analytics Big Idea Initiative. He can be reached at sam.ransbotham@bc.edu and on Twitter at @ransbotham.

http://sloanreview.mit.edu/article/the-flood-of-data-from-iot-is-powering-new-opportunities-for-some/

1.14 IoT and Developing Analytics-Based Data Products

Thomas H. Davenport, Stephan Kudyba, and Steven Paul: January 09, 2017

There are many ways for organizations to monetize data, including selling "data products" directly to consumers. A seven-step model shows the way real-life companies are developing those products and services.

In their recent *MIT Sloan Management Review* article, "Designing and Developing Analytics-Based Data Products," authors Thomas H. Davenport and Stephan Kudyba note that a large variety of data products now enhance the consumer experience. LinkedIn's "People You May Know" feature is one example. So, too, is Zillow's Zestimate, which uses publicly accessible housing data to predict what price a homeowner might get for the sale of his or her house.

But as ubiquitous as this kind of incorporation of data and analytics into the consumer experience now feels, relatively little has been written about the process of *developing* these new generations of data products, say Davenport and Kudyba. They're changing that.

To find out what leading companies are actually doing in the field to create, refine, and generate value from data products, Davenport and Kudyba interviewed data scientists, met with representatives from large companies that are exploring data- and analytics-based products and services (including State Street Corp., GE, Monsanto, the World Bank, Thomson Reuters, and Caterpillar), and interviewed managers at more than 40 companies that had some data product development activities underway.

The result is a model by Davenport and Kudyba of seven steps that companies go through in the development of data products. Taking their lead from a 1996 article by Marc H. Meyer and Michael H. Zack that outlined specific steps in designing and developing information products, Davenport and Kudyba have augmented and updated the Meyer-Zack model. "Data product development activities today are rarely undertaken in a traditional product development sequence that involves identifying the need, developing the product, and then taking it to market," they write. "Rather, product development activities often take place in a continuous, iterative fashion, with the important activities conducted in parallel." The sequence also includes a few new steps that they have identified.

http://sloanreview.mit.edu/article/iot-and-developing-analytics-based-data-products/

1.15 Cloud Computing Has Cut the Cost of Analytics, Say Experts

1 Jan 2017

Cloud computing forms a key component of most enterprises' overall IT infrastructure, and firms are using analytics atop the cloud for greater efficiency, agility, experts say

Mumbai: Cloud computing today forms a key component of most enterprises' overall IT infrastructure and companies are increasingly using Big Data analytics atop the cloud for greater efficiency and agility. This was the consensus among panel lists who included Mukesh Kripalani, chief officer (business process transformation and IT) at Marico Ltd; Prashant Yadav, partner (management consulting) and lead (data and analytics) at KPMG; Sankarson Banerjee, chief technology officer (projects) at National Stock Exchange of India Ltd; and Vyom Upadhyay, head of analytics and business intelligence at ICICI Bank Ltd.

How are you using analytics in your organization?

Kripalani: We set an aspiration target for a decade and identified five transformation areas—innovation, goes-to-market, talent, IT and analytics, and value management. For analytics, we adopted the Gartner framework. It starts with data at one end and goes on to decision-making and thereby action at the other end. We also deployed a data visualization tool so that the data comes visually alive. Post that, we focused on predictive analytics.

Setting the right flows was important. We had a master data gateway and did some proofs of concept in the beginning. We also took feedback from our customers to correct any mistakes. Earlier, while we had central data, different departments used to collate data in a different fashion. With the new solution, the time needed to collate data got reduced and we were able to generate actionable insights.

What are the challenges in getting insights from data?

Sankarson: A key challenge is that people focus on the front-end part (interface of the portal) rather than collection or storage of the data. A key problem with Indian companies is that the data they collect just reinforces their opinions; they never collect data on what they do not agree with. That is where the cloud comes in. For instance, at NSE, we have been able to store the humongous amounts of data the stock market generates. The biggest challenge is, if you forget to collect historic data, then how do you regenerate it for deriving insights? Fortunately, thanks to the cloud, you can set up an account cheaply and conduct analytics experiments relatively easily and quickly.

How do you think has the usage of analytics evolved?

Yadav: The journey started typically with business intelligence and most organizations have now jumped on to predictive analytics. There is migration to the cloud, making a lot more resources available. The cost of doing analytics has also improved significantly in the last couple of years.

What role do you see for analytics in your industry and what challenges exist?

Upadhyay: Banking is central to the service industry and analytics plays an essential role. One needs to know what the interaction points are, exactly where service failures are happening, and constantly look at data in order to serve customer needs better. As regards ICICI Bank, we have had a fully functional data warehouse for the last 10 years. The challenge is that with the technology and business landscape changing fast, we must adapt to those changes quickly.

http://sciencejunction.in/cloud-computing-has-cut-the-cost-of-analytics-say-experts/

1.16 Applied Statistics Comes to the Rescue of Big Data
Written by **PeterBajorski May 27th, 2015**

Today's businesses, governments, and other organizations collect a large amount of data about their operations and their customers. Classic examples include data about Amazon customers, call centers, or Twitter. All that information is aggregated and analyzed to predict future customer needs, provide sensible purchase suggestions, and personalize the organization's engagement with customers.

Another example includes Google Flu Trends (GFT), an algorithm that attempts to predict flu outbreaks based on online search patterns. Although GFT is often used as a success story about the power of Big Data, the GFT's performance has been questioned in Nature [1] and more recently in Science [2]. GFT missed the non-seasonal influenza pandemic in 2009. It turns out that GFT was only partially detecting the flu, and partially just the winter season, since the two events mostly coincided. After the prediction failure in 2009, the GFT algorithm was updated, and it continues to be improved by Google. Nevertheless, Lazer et al. [2] demonstrate that GFT suffers from a frequent Big Data hubris by assuming that the availability of a large amount of data makes traditional data collection and analysis obsolete. The authors also show that a straightforward application of some traditional statistical methods would have avoided many problems with GFT.

Jeff Leek[3] describes other examples, where the lack of statistical expertise led to fundamental errors in genomics and economics. For instance, incorrect predictions of responses to chemotherapy resulted in major consequences and cancelled clinical trials. In another example, two economists published a paper claiming that GDP growth was hindered by high government debt. Ultimately, the data did not support their claim. In this instance, the impact was more difficult to assess, but we do know that the paper was widely cited by regulators in many countries worldwide after the recent financial crisis and might have contributed to the exceptionally slow rate of recovery. Errors such as these can have serious consequences and can be mostly avoided through the use of proper applied statistical techniques.

Leek [3] also points out the absence of statisticians in many Big Data initiatives, including some high-impact events and organizations. One way to improve this situation is to produce more statisticians with applied skills, who can work in the current environment of Big Data and analytics; and collaborate with experts from other fields.

Courses in Applied Statistics are designed to serve that very purpose, so that the problems described earlier can be avoided when working on Big Data and analytics projects. Students gain the knowledge and skills in all major areas of applied statistics. Various elective courses provide a wide range of specialized topics, including data mining, machine learning, and predictive analytics –all necessary skills while working with data sets of all sizes.

Students can choose between two paths: one, an Advanced Certificate which consists of only four courses; two, a Master's Degree which requires 10 courses to complete. Our Master's program offers five concentrations: Predictive Analytics, Data Mining/Machine Learning, Industrial, Biostatistics, and Theory.

https://www.rit.edu/ritonline/blog/index.php/applied-statistics-comes-to-the-rescue-of-big-data/

1.17 The Tools of Big Data Science: The Technologies & Languages of Statistical Analysis

You've read about many of the kinds of big data projects that you can use to learn more about your data in What Can a Data Scientist Do for You? Article—now, we're going to look at tools that data scientists use to mine that data: performing statistical techniques like clustering or linear modeling, and then turning them into a story through visualization and reporting.

You don't need to know how to use these yourself, but having a sense of the differences between these tools will help you gauge what tools might be best for your business and what skills to look for in a data scientist.

ANALYTICAL TOOLS

R: THE MOST POPULAR LANGUAGE FOR DATA SCIENCE

Once the data scientist has completed the often time-consuming process of "cleaning" and preparing the data for analysis, R is a popular software package for actually doing the math and visualizing the results. An open-source statistical modeling language, R has traditionally been popular in the academic community, which means that lots of data scientists will be familiar with it.

R has literally thousands of extension packages that allow statisticians to undertake specialized tasks, including text analysis, speech analysis, and tools for genomic sciences. The center of a thriving open-source ecosystem, R has become increasingly popular as programmers have created additional add-on packages for handling big datasets and parallel processing techniques that have come to dominate statistical modeling today.

- **Parallel** helps R take advantage of parallel processing for both multicore Windows machines and clusters of POSIX (OS X, Linux, UNIX) machines.

- **Snow** helps divvy up R calculations on a cluster of computers, which is useful for computationally intensive processes like simulations or AI learning processes.

- **Rhadoop** and **Rhipe** allow programmers to interface with Hadoop from R, which is particularly important for the "MapReduce" function of dividing the computing problem among separate clusters and then re-combining or "reducing" all of the varying results into a single answer.

R is used in industries like finance, health care, marketing, business, pharmaceutical development, and more. Industry leaders like Bank of America, Bing, Facebook, and Foursquare use R to analyze their data, make marketing campaigns more effective, and reporting.

JAVA & THE JAVA VIRTUAL MACHINE

Organizations that seek to write custom analytics tools from scratch increasingly use the venerable language Java, as well as other languages that run on the Java Virtual Machine (JVM). Java is a variation of the object-oriented C++ language, and because Java runs on a platform-agnostic virtual machine, programs can be compiled once and run anywhere.

The upside of using the JVM over a language written to run directly on the processor is the reduction in development time. This simpler development process has been a draw for data analytics, making JVM-based data mining tools very popular. Also, Hadoop—the popular open-source, distributed big data storage and analysis software—is written in Java.

Java has rich open-source libraries for data mining, including Mahout and Weka, and the JVM provides robust memory management and exception handling. Other programming languages that can be used with the JVM include:

- **Scala**: This programming language has the same efficiency as Java because it's run on the JVM. However, it's also become increasingly popular in data mining because it permits developers to use object-oriented programming (OOP) as well as functional programming. *Users of Scala include The Guardian, LinkedIn, Foursquare, Novell, Siemens, Twitter, and the SPARK data mining environment at the UC Berkeley AMP Lab.*

- **Clojure**: A dialect of the 1980s-era artificial intelligence language LISP, Clojure is a primarily (although not 100%) functional language that also runs on the JVM. Clojure keeps data static and was designed for running concurrent processes. These features are important because, in contrast, object-oriented code executing concurrent processes will sometimes attempt to write to the same variable simultaneously. Keeping data structures immutable avoids this problem. Clojure has access to Java libraries, and the same development efficiencies as Java. Clojure can use the LISP macro facility to integrate with Hadoop and SQL. *Users of Clojure include Netflix, Zendesk, Citibank, WalMart Labs, and Spotify.*

PYTHON: A HIGH-LEVEL PROGRAMMING LANGUAGE WITH EXCELLENT DATA LIBRARIES

Python is a high-level language, meaning that the creators automated certain housekeeping processes in order to make code easier to write. Python has robust libraries that support statistical modeling (Scipy and Numpy), data mining (Orange and Pattern), and visualization (Matplotlib). Scikit-learn, a library of machine learning techniques very useful to data scientists, has attracted developers from Spotify, OKCupid, and Evernote, but can be challenging to master.

EXCEL: POWERFUL DATA ANALYTICS ON A SMALLER SCALE

Excel can accomplish a lot of sophisticated analysis—plus, it's easy to use and widely available. While it's not best for analyzing truly massive, unstructured datasets—for example, a massive dataset of some 30 million healthcare records distributed via Hadoop across dozens of servers—it is surprisingly powerful when used for a variety of data analytics projects at a small scale. These can include clustering, optimization, and predictive modeling using supervised AI learning or forecasting techniques.

SAS (STATISTICAL ANALYSIS SYSTEM): DATA MINING SOFTWARE SUITE

Used for advanced analytics, data management, and social media analytics, SAS is a robust suite that's popular for business intelligence analysis of large data and unstructured datasets. In 2015, SAS topped the Gartner Magic Quadrant list in terms of "ability to execute" in the category of advanced analytics platforms due to the breadth and quality of its predictive modeling and data mining techniques. With a well-regarded visualization tool and integration with open-source tools like R, Hadoop and Python, SAS also puts significant effort into making tools backwards compatible, an important feature when looking at older historical datasets.

Why is backwards compatibility so important? Say, for example, a company's sales records were prepared for use by SAS in 1998. With backwards compatibility, they can still be read today. In large organizations, employee turnover over the years puts a premium on the continuity of tools. So, when a data scientist retires, you won't lose the ability to access their work if they preferred older software that no one new to the position knows how to use.

SAS can be costly, has a complicated licensing structure that some customers have found to be annoying, and has a steep learning curve. Although it's expensive and complicated, it's a very popular option, with more than 65,000 customers.

IBM: SPSS MODELER AND SPSS ANALYTICS

Forrester Research Wave ranks IBM's advanced data analytics platform as the top offering in the advanced analytics category for its breadth of tools that handle all elements of big data modeling: loading, "cleaning," preparing, and then predictive modeling, whether using statistical or machine learning techniques.

SPSS Modeler and SPSS Statistics were acquired by IBM in 2009, and have a loyal following among statisticians. These tools integrate Hadoop to facilitate file-system computing using big datasets. The Social Media Analytics product helps data scientists harvest data from Twitter, Facebook, and other platforms to perform customer sentiment analysis. Gartner reports that the IBM advanced analytics platform has lower customer satisfaction ratings than average, largely due to weak customer support, inadequate documentation, and a challenging installation process.

Other makers of highly rated commercial tools for advanced data analytics include SAP, KNIME, RapidMiner, Oracle, and Alteryx.

SQL VS NOSQL DATABASES: TACKLING THE "MESSINESS" OF BIG DATA

Another important distinction in the world of data is SQL databases vs. NoSQL databases, both of which are well suited to different types of datasets. Here's a quick look at what makes them different in the context of data analysis.

The traditional "relational" database was designed for an era in which data was far more expensive to collect and to store—and much more carefully organized. **Structured Query Language (SQL)** has been the means by which programmers transfer data to and from those neatly categorized rows and columns. (Read up on the basics of databases in our Guide to Database Technology.)

However, modern data is not so easily categorized. In 2011, Abhishek Mehta, CEO of big data company Tresata, estimated that only 5% of the world's information was structured data—and the rest consists of articles, photos, videos, social media posts, machine-to-machine communication, product inventory, and technical documents. So data scientists turned to a different standard for data storage called "NoSQL."

If the traditional relational database was a carefully curated boutique with a small collection, the NoSQL database is more like a chaotic big box warehouse, with many different kinds of data scattered all over the place. Storing data in bulk in this *ad hoc* way requires more processing power and storage capacity than if the data were better organized—but that's why Hadoop has become so popular as a way to divvy up storage and processing tasks on clusters of inexpensive commodity hardware.

Which database is right for you? Once you clearly outline the problem you seek to solve, figure out your objective, and determine the size of the dataset to be handled, you'll have a much better idea of which one could be best for your needs.

Database management systems you might consider include:

MYSQL: OPEN-SOURCE RDBMS

Purchased by Oracle in 2009, MySQL is a widely used RDBMS (relational database management system) and one part of the LAMP software stack. This free, open-source database management system is used by web applications like WordPress, Drupal, Facebook, Twitter, and YouTube.

MONGODB

The most popular NoSQL database system available on the market is the open-source MongoDB, which has been used by Metlife, The Weather Channel, Bosch, and Expedia. MongoDB has well-regarded customer service, and the tool is particularly popular with startups.

One of the fastest-growing big data projects involving MongoDB is Apache Spark, a distributed computing framework from the Apache Software Project that's designed to operationalize real-time analytics. Paired up with MongoDB, Spark allows organizations to put real-time analytics reporting to use.

Other commonly used open-source NoSQL databases include HBase, MariaDB, and Cassandra.

ORACLE

Oracle has nearly 50% of the traditional relational database market, with products such as Oracle Database and Oracle Times Ten. The database behemoth has also entered the market for unstructured data storage with Oracle NoSQL, and for open-source SQL databases that compete with its proprietary offerings. While popular and considered to be top-notch by many, they're expensive.

SQL Server DBMS: Enterprise-Level Database Management

Microsoft SQL Server DBMS is a competitive enterprise-level database management system that includes support for SQL or no SQL architectures, in-memory computing, the cloud, and analytics on transactions. Existing customers are generally impressed with its performance. Gartner reports that SQL Server has a poor image with developers, which had made the product less popular. Also, customers gave the product's pricing model the lowest score of any tested.

Other strong performers in the market include SAP, IBM, EnterpriseDB, InterSystems, and MarkLogic.

If your organization has room in the budget, then the full-service option from Oracle is the way to go in terms of reliability and customer service. But if your back-end developer can handle hacking their way through an open-source solution without a huge amount of expensive support calls, then an open-source solution like MariaDB or MongoDB will help you cut costs.

Hadoop: File System Computing

What is "file system computing"? It's a way to store and tackle the analytics for truly massive datasets. For example, 2 billion data points from sensors on an auto assembly line area that are stored on a cluster of servers, with each connected to multiple drives would be enormous. Because this kind of dataset is too large to extract from the drives to a place where it can be analyzed, software like Hadoop was created.

Hadoop is an open-source software tool specially designed to help data scientists manage the unwieldiness of big data. It eliminates the need to extract data from the storage devices altogether, bringing the analytics *to the data* so it can be processed in place. It has increasingly become the industry standard for file system computing projects involving big data, with prominent users including Facebook, Yahoo, and The New York Times.

There are many other platforms that do file system computing, such as SciDB, but Hadoop has risen to the top with user contributions that extend its functionality, like Hive, Pig, Spark, and MapReduce. Even software giants like Microsoft and IBM have created their own Hadoop tools, rather than reinventing the wheel. Learn more about Hadoop's key features in our Guide to Hadoop.

A/B TESTING

Big data analysis involves finding correlations in unexpected places in your data. The technique known as "A/B testing," in which users see different versions ("A" versus "B") of a website design in order to see which attracts more clicks, has taken over the tech world. Big data is very good at telling you "what works."

Consider this example from an Optimize customer, which proves how A/B testing can overrule older "best practices" and yield better results. A retailer was testing a homepage layout, and had previously been putting any new-related items in one corner of the homepage grid—a carry-over from print and magazine best practices. But, by testing different versions of the design against one another using the Optimize A/B platform, the company found users responded more to having news-related items front and center. Moving forward, the company always utilized that area of the homepage for items it wanted prioritized. This is how A/B testing works—it can find a correlation between a layout and how users respond to it, then allow you to adjust for the best results.

A/B testing terms to know:

- **Multivariate testing** allows you to test more than two different versions of a page against one another. For example, if you're testing out the sales conversion rate against two versions of a drop-down menu, three different textual descriptions of a product offer, and two large photos on a page, you'll have 12 different versions of the page to test, not just an "A" and a "B."

- **Multi-platform functionality** helps ensure your design or layout performs well on all kinds of devices, from PCs to smartphones.

Optimize

Optimize has a simple and intuitive user interface that the company intends for organizations of all sizes. And the easier the tool is to use, the more likely employees are to experiment and discover unknown correlations. Both Forrester Wave and TrustRadius found Optimize less effective than some competitors with more complicated forms of A/B testing. Optimize is the most commonly used A/B testing platform across the top 10,000 largest websites. *Clients include Microsoft, NBC, The Guardian, Disney, and Starbucks.*

Maxymyser

TrustRadius' top rated A/B testing tool among large "enterprise" customers (along with Monetate), Maxymyser requires web managers to insert a single line of code into a page and then begins analyzing for basic testing. More advanced tests with multiple variables require coding and may end up requiring help from Maxymyser customer support. Because the tool is powerful, web managers may need to allot themselves some training time to get things running smoothly. *Clients include Ramada, Alaska Airlines, Virgin Media, and HSBC.*

Adobe Target (formerly Test & Target)

This powerful A/B testing tool integrates well with the other components within the Adobe Analytics suite. With Target, web developers can engage in more elaborate segmentation and custom

JavaScript-based experimentation. For example, Target has a particularly nimble interface that makes the cumbersome process of multivariate testing simple and assigns different statistical weights. *Clients include Marriott, AOL, and Redbox.*

Other A/B and multivariate testing platforms include: Monetate, A/B Tasty, Qubit, Visual Website Optimizer, and Unbounce.

Ready to hire a data analysis expert? Browse data analytics pros on Up work, and dig deeper into the world of data with our Guide to Database Technology article.

Get more work done, faster with freelance help. Post a job today **and get started!**

Sources Consulted

- Clojure website, http://dev.clojure.org/display/community/ Clojure+Success+Stories, accessed April 21, 2015.

- Jared Dean, Big Data, Data Mining and Machine Learning: Value Creation for Business Leaders and Practitioners, (New York: Wiley, 2014), pp. 43-54.

- Donald Feinberg, Merv Adrian, Nick Heudecker, "Magic Quadrant for Operational Database Systems," http://www.gartner.com/ technology/reprints.do?id=1-23A415Q&ct=141020&st=sb, October 16, 2014.

- John W. Foreman, Data Smart: Using Data Science to Transform Information Into Insight (New York, Wiley, 2013), pp. 1-28.

- Gareth Herschel, Alexander Linden, Lisa Kart, "Magic Quadrant for Advanced Analytics Platforms," (Gartner: 2015), http://www.gartner.com/technology/reprints.do?id=1-2A881DN&ct=150219&st=sb.

- Jonothon Morgan, "Don't Be Scared of Functional Programming," *Smashing Magazine*, July 2, 2014.

- "Expert to Expert: Brian Beckmen and Rich Hickey — Inside Clojure," http://channel9.msdn.com/shows/Going+Deep/Expert-to-Expert-Rich-Hickey-and-Brian-Beckman-Inside-Clojure/," accessed April 21, 2015

- Abhishek Mehta, "Big Data: Powering the Next Industrial Revolution," Tableau Software white paper, 2011, http://www.tableau.com/learn/whitepapers/big-data-revolution.

- Scikit-Learn website, http://scikit-learn.org/stable/, accessed April 21, 2015.

- Viktor Mayer-Schönberger and Kenneth Cukier, Big Data: A Revolution That Will Transform How We Live, Work, and Think (New York: Eamon Dolan/Houghton Mifflin Harcourt, 2013), pp. 45-46.

- Joe Stanhope, "The Forrester Wave: Online Testing Platforms, Q1 2013," http://success.adobe.com/assets/en/downloads/forrester/30317.The_Forrester_Wave_Online_2013.pdf, February 7, 2013.

- Ashlee Vance, "Open Source as a Model for Business Is Elusive," New York Times, November 29, 2009.

BY ANDREW ROSENBLUM - WRITER

Andrew Rosenblum reports on drones, artificial intelligence, security, and the commercial space business for Popular Science, MIT Technology Review, Wired, Fortune, and other publications.

https://www.upwork.com/hiring/data/big-data-science-tools/

1.18 Big Data - Big Security

Ratan Jyoti, Chief Information Security Officer (CISO), Ujjivan Small Finance Bank Published on February 5, 2017

Big Data Analytics is and can be most effective fortifications against cyber intrusions. Accurate, speedy and effective information can help us in lessening of critical time from detection to remediation and thus proactively defend and protect your information and infrastructure. If we call the Intrusion Detection and Prevention System as First generation of the Security System, the second generation belongs to Security Information and Event Management (SIEM) which were without the data analytics. The third generation belongs to Big Data Analytics based Security Information and Event Management (SIEM) which is typically the Next generation SIEMs and are heavily relying on Big data and its analytical capabilities. A Big Data security analytics ecosystem can give firms enhanced visibility into their users, applications, network and information. Following are some of the usage of big data which if utilized suitably will make differences:

1.   Real Time Transaction and Fraud Monitoring

For last few decades the Card and delivery transaction frauds have been challenge for banks and payments systems. Fraud detection on a real time basis is one of the most visible applications of big data analytics and data mining and as s a result the real time Risk Based transaction monitoring has become feasible. Many Fraud Risk Management (FRM) solutions rely upon the big data capabilities and the best part is that they are still evolving.

2.   Improved Security Analytics and advanced Security Operation Centre

The Big Data Analytics unleashes fresh capabilities of security analytics. Security Operations Centers (SOCs) have traditionally relied on trademarked Security Information and Event Response Systems (SIEMS) for their security analytics proficiencies. New security analytics capabilities have evolved because of Big Data Security Analytics which helps in real-time alerts, real time anomaly detection, real time correlation etc. at amazing speed.

3.   <u>Big data analytics and building threat intelligence</u>

Cyber Threat intelligence is all about empowering Cyber Security decision-making and response.

Most of the organizations today ignore some or many security alerts or events as they are overwhelmed by the deluge of events and alerts. Question remains are they ignoring something that they shouldn't? Are they inviting possible breach? What is the tradeoff – possibly automated system which can suppress false positives or unconnected information and thus answer is the accurate Threat Intelligence. Although use of Big data analytics is already evident in the way of Threat Intelligence but I foresee a level of maturity in this area.

4.   **Cloud Security with Big Data analytics**

Data breaches and theft can be disastrous and if this cloud based data theft or breaches as it can cause significant loss to business and reputation because they handle enormous amount of data and information. Because of shared resources it is even more vulnerable as weakness of one shared resources can impact all other. Techniques like "attribute based encryption "and big data analytics can help in providing the security to the cloud emphatically. Anomaly and behavior change can be detected using "feature extraction".

Big data analytics and its application can help in preventing and detecting threats at an early stage, using more erudite pattern analysis and correlating multiple sources in no time.

https://www.linkedin.com/pulse/big-data-analytics-security-ratan-jyoti

Chapter 2: Trends in Big Data Analytics

2.1   Steps of Data Digitization Process

March 2, 2016 · by Eminenture in Data, Infographics

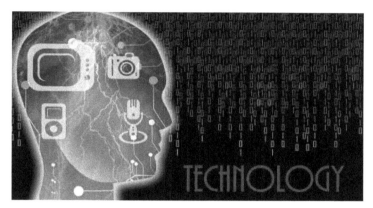

The change is in the air. Digitization aces a test of today's high end technology. We are profusely hooked up to your smartphone, laptop, iPad and many more gadgets. It seems these have become our lifeblood. Our life is orbiting around digitization. Business, sports, entertainment, education and so on are embracing it with loud cheer. And internet meshes up all verticals together. Of course, it's the miracle of big data. The appetite for more data motivates to extract data which is infinite. What! Won't you believe it? Take an example of Google.

Undoubtedly, the statistics are enough to make you dumbstruck. Data extraction services of India and many more are madly indulged in extracting vital information every day. The purposes are various. Biz, like market research, requires it to spin million dollars as revenue. Data is its cash cow. It's all possible only through data digitization. Is your curiosity piqued to know how actually digitization works? Let's catch up the data digitization process:

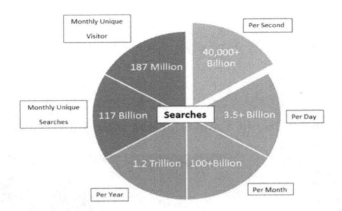

Data digitization process

Let have its intro first: Data digitization holds the centre of the stage for decades. The advent of computers, scanners and multimedia technology has sparked it in to a flame. Industries, like e-Commerce, automotive, insurance, education and market as well as business research, have started picking up visual data, art, videos, images and photographs. Online revolution is incomplete without these. And computers hold the keys. Application software stores and manipulates data into digital form.

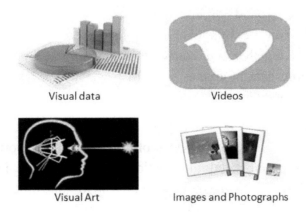

Visual data   Videos

Visual Art   Images and Photographs

Data Capturing: But it needs the help of processes. An optimal clubbing of experts and technology gives digitization a flying start.

Scanning devices, like digital camera, scanner, take care of data capturing. And computers hold the keys. Application software stores and manipulates data into digital form.

Automatic Identification and data capture (AIDC): This term identifies various methods of data identification, collection and entering the computer application. It teams up all the tools and techniques to obtain external data. What it comprises are below:

- Bar Codes
- Radio Frequency Identification
- Biometrics
- Magnetic stripes
- Optical Character Recognition (OCR)
- Smart Cards
- Voice recognition

Streamline the data: Data capturing is followed up by sorting. Manual checks and software checks are run afterwards. This responsibility is discharged to the reliable shoulders of the geek editors, proof readers and analysts.

Finally, the digitized data is all set to catch thousands of eyeballs on internet or specific community. Data digitation services of India as well as many more countries offshore are adhering to the same procedure. It's flawless, swift, effective, mind blowing and worth to million dollars when administering the corporate as well as knowledge imparting motive.

(http://www.eminenture.com/blog/steps-of-data-digitization-process/)

2.2   Data Science, the Future of Digitization

Global data science market to be worth $320 billion in 5 years, says expert

Thiruvananthapuram, May 6: Large corporations such as Amazon, Ebay, Google, Face book and LinkedIn are as much data science companies as they are leaders of specific domains.

Global data science market is projected to be worth $320 billion by year 2020, says Graham Williams, data scientist at data processor company Togaware as well as the Australia Taxation Office. According to McKinsey, there will be shortage of over 1.8 lakh data scientists in the US by 2018, given the explosive growth rate of the sector.

Data mining tool

Williams was speaking at a three-day workshop on 'Data mining and analytics with R' organized here by the International Centre for Free and Open Source Software. 'R' is the most widely-used data mining and analytics tool globally for statistics and data science.

Data mining is the process of excavating data in an attempt to uncover hitherto unknown but useful patterns, particularly in large datasets. It is intended to discover new insights and knowledge and to develop predictive models.

The 'R' tool is being used in different disciplines such as retail, financial services, health research, weather modeling, astronomy, psychology, and social sciences.

As computerization becomes common in governments, enormous volumes of data are generated.

Significance of open source

Open source tools domains such as data mining, analytics and big data, previously used mostly by the IT Industry, is increasingly becoming important for governments around the world, Williams said. Open source tools such 'R' are of immense use in this context, given their significant power, very low cost, rapid adoption of new technology, vibrant communities and license-free regimes.

Massive datasets

Governments are increasingly applying tools such as data mining, analytics and visualization on massive datasets to uncover patterns of interest including fraud and tax evasion.

The Australian government uses 'R' for data mining at the Australian Tax office, and office of Immigration and Border Control, and Health and Human Services.

As more governments join the open data movement, it is expected that the use of 'R' will increase even further.

According to Satish Babu, Director of hosts International Centre for Free and Open Source Software, better training in 'R' could help India to leverage the potential of this domain.

http://www.thehindubusinessline.com/news/national/data-science-the-future-of-digitisation/article7180728.ece

2.3   25 Big Data Terms You Must Know to Impress Your Date (Or whoever you want to)

Posted by Ramesh Dontha **on January 31, 2017**

Big Data can be intimidating! If you are new to Big Data, please read 'What is Big Data', 'Who coined Big Data', 'Big Data … So, what' to get you started. With the basic concepts under your belt, let's focus on some key terms to impress your date or boss or family. By the way, I am putting together a much more exhaustive list of Big Data terms (almost 100) and if you are interested in that, please leave a comment below with a note 'I want more of Big data' or something like that.

So, let's get going with this shorter list. Also, check out the infographic midway through this article.

Algorithm: A mathematical formula or statistical process used to perform an analysis of data. How Algorithm is related to Big Data? Even though algorithm is a generic term, Big Data analytics made the term contemporary and more popular. (Bonus: Here's a pickup line on your date, 'you show me your algorithms and I'll show you mine. …. Ok, Ok, I'll stop! No more cheesy jokes)

Analytics: Most likely, your credit card company sent you year-end statement with all your transactions for the entire year. What if you dug into it to see what % you spent on food, clothing, entertainment etc.?

You are doing 'analytics'. You are drawing insights from your raw data which can help you make decisions regarding spending for the upcoming year. What if you did the same exercise on tweets or Facebook posts made by your friends/network or your own your company. Now we are talking Big Data analytics. It is about making inferences and story-telling with large sets of data. There are 3 or 4 different types of analytics depending on who you talk to.

Descriptive Analytics: If you just told me that you spent 25% on food, 35% on clothing and 20% on entertainment and the rest on miscellaneous items last year using your credit card, that is descriptive analytics. Of course, you can go into lot more detail as well.

Predictive Analytics: If you analyzed your credit card history for the past 5 years and the split is somewhat consistent, you can safely forecast with high probability that next year will be like past years. The fine print here is that this is not about 'predicting the future' rather 'forecasting with probabilities' of what might happen. In Big data predictive analytics, data scientists may use advanced techniques like data mining, machine learning, and advanced statistical processes (we'll discuss all these terms later) to forecast weather, economy etc.

Prescriptive Analytics: Still using the credit card transactions example, you may want to find out which spending to target (i.e. food, entertainment, clothing etc.) to make a huge impact on your overall spending. Prescriptive analytics builds on predictive analytics by including 'actions' (i.e. reduce food or clothing or entertainment) and analyzing the resulting outcomes to 'prescribe' the best category to target to reduce your overall spends. You can extend this to big data and imagine how executives can make data-driven decisions by looking at the impacts of various actions in front of them.

Batch processing: Even though Batch data processing has been around since mainframe days, Batch processing gained additional significance with Big Data given the large datasets that it deals with.

Batch data processing is an efficient way of processing high volumes of data where a group of transactions is collected over a period. Hadoop, which I'll describe later, is focused on batch data processing.

Cassandra, a beautiful name, is a popular open source database management system managed by The Apache Software Foundation. Apache can be credited with many big data technologies and Cassandra was designed to handle large volumes of data across distributed servers.

Cloud computing: Well, cloud computing has become ubiquitous so it may not be needed here but I included just for completeness sake. It's essentially software and/or data hosted and running on remote servers and accessible from anywhere on the internet.

Cluster computing: It's a fancy term for computing using a 'cluster' of pooled resources of multiple servers. Getting more technical, we might be talking about nodes, cluster management layer, load balancing, and parallel processing etc.

Dark Data: This, in my opinion, is coined to scare the living daylights out of senior management. Basically, this refers to all the data that is gathered and processed by enterprises not used for any meaningful purposes and hence it is 'dark and may never be analyzed. It could be social network feeds, call center logs, meeting notes and what have you. There are many estimates that anywhere from 60-90% of all enterprise data may be 'dark data' but who really know.

Data Lake: When I first heard of this, I really thought someone was pulling an April fool's joke. But it's a real term! Data lake is a large repository of enterprise-wide data in raw format. While we are here, let's talk about Data warehouse which is similar in concept that it is also a repository for enterprise-wide data but in a structured format after cleaning and integrating with other sources. Data warehouses are typically used for conventional data (but not exclusively). Supposedly data lake makes it easy to access enterprise-wide data you really need to know what you are looking for and how to process it and make intelligent use of it.

Data mining: Data mining is about finding meaningful patterns and deriving insights in large sets of data using sophisticated pattern recognition techniques. It is closely related the term Analytics that we discussed earlier in that you mine the data to get analytics. To derive meaningful patterns, data miners use statistics (yup, good old math), machine learning algorithms, and artificial intelligence.

Data Scientist: Talk about a career that is HOT! It is someone who can make sense of big data by extracting raw data (did u say from data lake?), massage it, and come up with insights. Some of the skills required for data scientists are what a superman/woman would have: analytics, statistics, computer science, creativity, story-telling and understand business context. No wonder they are so highly paid.

Distributed File System: Distributed File System is a data storage system and is meant to store large volumes of data across multiple storage devices and it will help to decrease the cost and complexity of storing large amounts of data.

ETL: ETL stands for extract, transform, and load. It refers to the process of 'extracting' raw data, 'transforming' by cleaning/enriching the data for 'fit for use' and 'loading' into the appropriate repository for the systems use. Even though it originated with data warehouses, ETL processes are used while 'ingesting i.e. taking/absorbing data from external sources in big data systems.

Hadoop: When people think of big data, they immediately think about Hadoop. Hadoop (with its cute elephant logo) is an open source software framework that consists of what is called a Hadoop Distributed File System (HDFS) and allows for storage, retrieval, and analysis of very large data sets using distributed hardware.

MUST KNOW BIG DATA TERMS

TO IMPRESS YOUR DATE (OR WHOEVER)

Big Data can be intimidating! This infographic will help you feel at home with Big Data.

by Ramesh Dontha
LinkedIn: https://www.linkedin.com/rameshdontha
Twitter: @rkdontha1
www.DigitalTransformationPro.com

1 ALGORITHM

Algorithm is a mathematical formula or statistical process used to perform an analysis of data.

2 BIG DATA ANALYTICS

Big data analytics is the process of examining large data sets to uncover hidden patterns, unknown correlations, market trends, customer preferences and other useful business information.

3 DATA LAKE

Data lake is a large repository of enterprise-wide data in raw format.

4 DATA WAREHOUSE

Data warehouse is a repository for enterprise-wide data but in a structured format

5 DATA MINING

Data mining is about finding meaningful patterns and deriving insights in large sets of data using sophisticated pattern recognition techniques.

6 DATA SCIENTIST

Data Scientist is someone who can make sense of big data by extracting raw data, massage it, and come up with insights, analytics. Skills needed: Statistics, computer science, creativity, story-telling and understand business context.

7 HADOOP

Hadoop is an open source software framework that consists of a Hadoop Distributed File System (HDFS) and allows for storage, retrieval, and analysis of very large data sets using distributed hardware.

8 IN-MEMORY COMPUTING

In-memory computing is a technique to moving the working datasets entirely within a cluster's collective memory and avoid writing intermediate calculations to disk thus making it faster. Apache Spark is an example of this.

9 MACHINE LEARNING

Machine learning is a method of designing systems that can learn, adjust, and improve based on the data fed to them.

10 MAPREDUCE

Hadoop MapReduce is a software framework for distributed processing of large data sets on compute clusters of commodity hardware.

11 NOSQL (NOT ONLY SQL)

NoSQL, Not Only SQL, refers to database management systems that are designed to handle large volumes of data that does not have a structure or schema.

12 (APACHE) SPARK

Apache Spark is a fast, in-memory data processing engine to efficiently execute streaming, machine learning or SQL workloads that require fast iterative access to datasets.

If you really want to impress someone, talk about YARN (Yet another Resource Scheduler) which, as the name says it, is a resource scheduler. I am really impressed by the folks who come up with these names. Apache foundation, which came up with Hadoop, is also responsible for Pig, Hive, and Spark (yup, they are all names of various software pieces). Aren't you impressed with these names?

In-memory computing: In general, any computing that can be done without accessing I/O is expected to be faster. In-memory computing is a technique to moving the working datasets entirely within a cluster's collective memory and avoids writing intermediate calculations to disk. Apache Spark is being an in-memory computing system and it has huge advantage in speed over I/O bound systems like Hadoop's MapReduce.

IoT: The latest buzzword is Internet of Things or IOT. IOT is the interconnection of computing devices in embedded objects (sensors, wearable, cars, fridges etc.) via internet and they enable sending / receiving data. IOT generates huge amounts of data presenting many big data analytics opportunities.

Machine learning: Machine learning is a method of designing systems that can learn, adjust, and improve based on the data fed to them. Using predictive and statistical algorithms that are fed to these machines, they learn and continually zero in on "correct" behavior and insights and they keep improving as more data flows through the system. Fraud detection, online recommendations based.

MapReduce: MapReduce could be little bit confusing but let me give it a try. MapReduce is a programming model and the best way to understand this is to note that Map and Reduce are two separate items. In this, the programming model first breaks up the big data dataset into pieces (in technical terms into 'tuples' but let's not get too technical here) so it can be distributed across different computers in different locations (i.e. cluster computing described earlier) which is essentially the Map part. Then the model collects the results and 'reduces' them into one report. MapReduce's data processing model goes hand-in-hand with Hadoop's distributed file system.

NoSQL: It almost sounds like a protest against 'SQL (Structured Query Language) which is the bread-and-butter for traditional Relational Database Management Systems (RDBMS) but NOSQL actually stands for Not ONLY SQL :-). NoSQL refers to database management systems that are designed to handle large volumes of data that does not have a structure or what's technically called a 'schema' (like relational databases have). NoSQL databases are often well-suited for big data systems because of their flexibility and distributed-first architecture needed for large unstructured databases.

R: Can anyone think of any worse name for a programming language? Yes, 'R' is a programming language that works very well with statistical computing. You aren't a data scientist if you don't know 'R'. (Please don't send me nasty grams if you don't know 'R'). It is just that 'R' is one of the most popular languages in data science.

Spark (Apache Spark): Apache Spark is a fast, in-memory data processing engine to efficiently execute streaming, machine learning or SQL workloads that require fast iterative access to datasets. Spark is generally a lot faster than MapReduce that we discussed earlier.

Stream processing: Stream processing is designed to act on real-time and streaming data with "continuous" queries. Combined with streaming analytics i.e. the ability to continuously calculate mathematical or statistical analytics on the fly within the stream, stream processing solutions are designed to handle high volume in real time.

Structured v Unstructured Data: This is one of the 'V's of Big Data I.e. Variety. Structured data is basically anything than can be put into relational databases and organized in such a way that it relates to other data via tables. Unstructured data is everything that can't – email messages, social media posts and recorded human speech etc.

Hope this list was helpful. Also, if you are interested in the much more exhaustive list, please leave a comment below with a note 'I want more of Big Data' or something like that. Thank you for reading.

http://www.datasciencecentral.com/profiles/blogs/25-big-data-terms-you-must-know-to-impress-your-date-or-whoever

2.4 Beginner's Guide to the History of Data Science
HANNAH AUGUR · MARCH 11, 2016

"Big data" and "data science" may be some of the bigger buzzwords this decade, but they aren't necessarily new concepts. The idea of data science spans many different fields, and has been slowly making its way into the mainstream for over fifty years. In fact, many considered last year the fiftieth anniversary of its official introduction. While many proponents have taken up the stick, made new assertions and challenges, there are a few names and dates you need know.

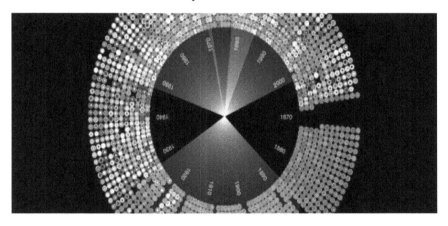

1962. **John Tukey** writes "Analysis. "Published in The Annals of Mathematical Statistics, a major venue for statistical research, he brought the relationship between statistics and analysis into question. One famous quote has since struck a chord with modern data lovers:

"For a long time, I have thought I was a statistician, interested in inferences from the particular to the general. But as I have watched mathematical statistics evolve, I have had cause to wonder and to doubt...I have come to feel that my central interest is in data analysis, which I take to include, among other things: procedures for analyzing data, techniques for interpreting the results of such procedures, ways of planning the gathering of data to make its analysis easier, more precise or more accurate, and all the machinery and results of (mathematical) statistics which apply to analyzing data."

1974. After Tukey, there is another important name that any data enthusiast should know: **Peter Naur.** He published the Concise Survey of Computer Methods, which surveyed data processing methods across a wide variety of applications. More importantly, the very term "data science" is used repeatedly. Naur offers his own definition of the term: "The science of dealing with data, once they have been established, while the relation of the data to what they represent is delegated to other fields and sciences." It would take some time for the ideas to really catch on, but the general push toward data science started to pop up more and more often after his paper.

1977. The International Association for Statistical Computing (IASC) was founded. Their mission was to "link traditional statistical methodology, modern computer technology, and the knowledge of domain experts to convert data into information and knowledge." In this year, Tukey also published a second major work: "Exploratory Data Analysis." Here, he argues that emphasis should be placed on using data to suggest hypotheses for testing, and that exploratory data analysis should work side-by-side with confirmatory data analysis. In **1989,** the first Knowledge Discovery in Databases (KDD) workshop was organized, which would become the annual ACM SIGKDD Conference on Knowledge Discovery and Data Mining (KDD).

In 1994, the early forms of modern marketing began to appear. One example comes from the Business Week cover story "Marketing. "Here, readers get the news that companies are gathering all kinds of data to start new marketing campaigns. While companies had yet to figure out what to do with all the data, the ominous line that "still, many companies believe they have no choice but to brave the database-marketing frontier" marked the beginning of an era.

In 1996, the term "data science" appeared for the first time at the International Federation of Classification Societies in Japan. The topic was "Data science, classification, and related methods" The next year, in 1997, **C.F. Jeff Wu** gave an inaugural lecture titled simply "Statistics = Data Science?"

Already in 1999, we get a glimpse of the burgeoning field of big data. Jacob Zahavi, quoted in "Mining Data for Nuggets of Knowledge" in Knowledge@Wharton had some more insight that would only prove to true over the following years:

"Conventional statistical methods work well with small data sets. Today's databases, however, can involve millions of rows and scores of columns of data... Scalability is a huge issue in data mining. Another technical challenge is developing models that can do a better job analyzing data, detecting non-linear relationships and interaction between elements... Special data mining tools may have to be developed to address web-site decisions."

And this was only in 1999! **2001** brought even more, including the first usage of "software as a service," the fundamental concept behind cloud-based applications. Data science and big data seemed to grow and work perfectly with the developing technology. One of the many more important names is **William S. Cleveland.** He co-edited Tukey's collected works, developed valuable statistical methods, and published the paper "Data Science: An Action Plan for Expanding the Technical Areas of the field of Statistics." Cleveland put forward the notion that data science was an independent discipline and named six areas in which he believed data scientists should be educated: multidisciplinary investigations, models and methods for data, computing with data, pedagogy, tool evaluation, and theory.

2008. The term "data scientist" is often attributed to Jeff Hammerbacher and DJ Patil, of Facebook and LinkedIn—because they carefully chose it. Attempting to describe their teams and work, they settled on "data scientist" and a buzzword was born. (Oh, and Patil continues to make waves as the current Chief Data Scientist at White House Office of Science and Technology Policy).

2010. The term "data science" has fully infiltrated the vernacular. Between just 2011 and 2012, "data scientist" job listings increased 15,000%. There has also been an increase in conferences and meetups devoted solely to data science and big data. The theme of data science hasn't only become popular by this point, it has become highly developed and incredibly useful.

2013 was the year data got really big. IBM shared statistics that showed 90% of the world's data had been created in the preceding two years, alone.

2016 may have only just began, but predictions are already begin made for the upcoming year. Data science is entrenched in machine learning, and many expect this to be the year of Deep Learning. With access to vast amounts of data, deep learning will be key towards moving forward into new areas. This will go hand-in-hand with opening up data and creating open source data solutions that enable non-experts to take part in the data science revolution.

In the past decade, the idea of data science exploded and slowly became what we recognize today. One vital point analysts understand is that data science and big data are not simply "scaling up" data. Instead, it means a shift in study and analysis. Despite seeming almost completely ordinary in today's world, like something that could not possibly be removed from research and study, the nature and importance of data science was not always so clear, and its exact nature will continue to develop alongside technology.

http://dataconomy.com/2016/03/beginners-guide-history-data-science/

2.5   Data Science vs. Big Data vs. Data Analytics

Avantika Monnappa: Published on April 5, 2016

Data is everywhere. In fact, the amount of digital data that exists is growing at a rapid rate, doubling every two years, and changing the way we live. According to IBM, 2.5 billion gigabytes (GB) of data was generated every day in 2012.

An article by Forbes states that Data is growing faster than ever before and by the year 2020, about 1.7 megabytes of new information will be created every second for every human being on the planet; which makes it extremely important to at least know the basics of the field. After all, here is where our future lies.

In this article, we will differentiate between the Data Science, Big Data, and Data Analytics, based on what it is, where it is used, the skills you need to become a professional in the field, and the salary prospects in each field.

Let's first start off with understanding what these concepts are.

Data Science: Dealing with unstructured and structured data, Data Science is a field that comprises of everything that related to data cleansing, preparation, and analysis.

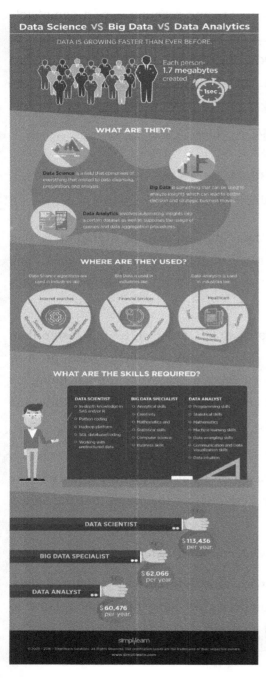

Data Science is the combination of statistics, mathematics, programming, problem solving, capturing data in ingenious ways, the ability to look at things differently, and the activity of cleansing, preparing, and aligning the data. In simple terms, it is the umbrella of techniques used when trying to extract insights and information from data.

Big Data: Big Data refers to humongous volumes of data that cannot be processed effectively with the traditional applications that exist. The processing of Big Data begins with the raw data that isn't aggregated and is most often impossible to store in the memory of a single computer. A buzzword that is used to describe immense volumes of data, both unstructured and structures, Big Data inundates a business on a day-to-day basis. Big

Data is something that can be used to analyze insights which can lead to better decision and strategic business moves.

The definition of Big Data, given by Gartner is, "Big data is high-volume, and high-velocity and/or high-variety information assets that demand cost-effective, innovative forms of information processing that enable enhanced insight, decision making, and process automation".

Data Analytics*:* Data Analytics the science of examining raw data with the purpose of drawing conclusions about that information. Data Analytics involves applying an algorithmic or mechanical process to derive insights; for example, running through a number of data sets to look for meaningful correlations between each other.

It is used in several industries to allow the organizations and companies to make better decisions as well as verify and disprove existing theories or models. The focus of Data Analytics lies in inference, which is the process of deriving conclusions that are solely based on what the researcher already knows.

The applications of each field

Applications of Data Science:

- Internet search: Search engines make use of data science algorithms to deliver best results for search queries in fraction of seconds.

- Digital Advertisements: The entire digital marketing spectrum uses the data science algorithms - from display banners to digital billboards. This is the mean reason for digital ads getting higher CTR than traditional advertisements.

- Recommender systems: The recommender systems not only make it easy to find relevant products from billions of products available but also add a lot to user experience. A lot of companies use this system to promote their products and suggestions in accordance to the user's demands and relevance of information. The recommendations are based on the user's previous search results.

Applications of Big Data:

• Big Data for financial services: Credit card companies, retail banks, private wealth management advisories, insurance firms, venture finds, and institutional investment banks use big data for their financial services. The common problem among them all is the massive amounts of multi structured data living in multiple disparate systems which can be solved by big data. Thus, big data is used in several ways like:

> ➢ Customer analytics
> ➢ Compliance analytics
> ➢ Fraud analytics
> ➢ Operational analytics

• Big Data in communications: Gaining new subscribers, retaining customers, and expanding within current subscriber bases are top priorities for telecommunication service providers. The solutions to these challenges lie in the ability to combine and analyze the masses of customer generated data and machine generated data that is being created every day.

• Big Data for Retail: Brick and Mortar or an online e-tailer, the answer to staying the game and being competitive understands the customer better to serve them. This requires the ability to analyze all the disparate data sources that companies deal with every day, including the weblogs, customer transaction data, social media, store branded credit card data, and loyalty program data.

Applications of Data Analysis:

- Healthcare: The main challenge for hospitals with cost pressures tightens is to treat as many patients as they can efficiently, keeping in mind the improvement of quality of care. Instrument and machine data is being used increasingly to track as well as optimize patient flow, treatment, and equipment use in the hospitals. It is estimated that there will be a 1% efficiency gain that could yield more than $63 billion in the global health care savings.

- Travel: Data analytics is able to optimize the buying experience through the mobile/ web log and the social media data analysis. Travel sights can gain insights into the customer's desires and preferences. Products can be up-sold by correlating the current sales to the subsequent browsing increase browse-to-buy conversions via customized packages and offers. Personalized travel recommendations can also be delivered by data analytics based on social media data.

- Gaming: Data Analytics helps in collecting data to optimize and spend within as well as across games. Game companies gain insight into the dislikes, the relationships, and the likes of the users.

- Energy Management: Most firms are using data analytics for energy management, including smart-grid management, energy optimization, energy distribution, and building automation in utility companies. The application here is centered on the controlling and monitoring of network devices, dispatch crews, and manage service outrages. Utilities are given the ability to integrate millions of data points in the network performance and let the engineers to use the analytics to monitor the network.

The skills you require

To become a Data Scientist:

• Education: 88% have a Master's Degree and 46% have PhDs

• In-depth knowledge of SAS and/or R: For Data Science, R is generally preferred.

• Python coding: Python is the most common coding language that is used in data science along with Java, Perl, C/C++.

• Hadoop platform: Although not always a requirement, knowing the Hadoop platform is still preferred for the field. Having a bit of experience in Hive or Pig is also a huge selling point.

• SQL database / coding: Though NoSQL and Hadoop have become a major part of the Data Science background, it is still preferred if you can write and execute complex queries in SQL.

• Working with unstructured data: It is most important that a Data Scientist is able to work with unstructured data be it on social media, video feeds, or audio.

To become a Big Data professional:

• Analytical skills: The ability to be able to make sense of the piles of data that you get. With analytical abilities, you will be able to determine which data is relevant to your solution, more like problem solving.

• Creativity: You need to have the ability to create new methods to gather, interpret, and analyze a data strategy. This is an extremely suitable skill to possess.

• Mathematics and statistical skills: Good, old fashioned "number crunching". This is extremely necessary, be it in data science, data analytics, or big data.

• Computer science: Computers are the workhorses behind every data strategy. Programmers will have a constant need to come up with algorithms to process data into insights.

• Business skills: Big Data professionals will need to understand the business objectives that are in place, as well as the underlying processes that drive the growth of the business as well as its profit.

To become a Data Analyst:

• Programming skills: Knowing programming languages are R and Python are extremely important for any data analyst.

• Statistical skills and mathematics: Descriptive and inferential statistics and experimental designs are a must for data scientists.

• Machine learning skills

• Data wrangling skills: The ability to map raw data and convert it into another format that allows for a more convenient consumption of the data.

• Communication and Data Visualization skills

• Data Intuition: it is extremely important for professional to be able to think like a data analyst.

Now let's talk about salaries!

Each of these professionals, data scientists, big data specialists, and data analysts, though in the same domain, earn varied salaries.

The average a data scientist earns today, according to Indeed.com is $123,000 a year. According to Glassdoor, the average salary for a Data Scientist is $113,436 per year.

The average salary of a Big Data specialist according to Glassdoor is $62,066 per year.

The average salary of a data analyst according to Glassdoor is $60,476 per year.

Now that you know the differences, which one do you think is most suited for you – Data Science? Big Data? Or Data Analytics?

If you'd like to become a complete expert in Data Science or Big Data – check out our Master's Program certification training courses: The Data Scientist Master's Program and the Big Data Architect Master's Program.

With industry recommended learning paths, exclusive access to experts in the industry, hands-on project experience, and a Masters certificate on completion, these packages will give you need to excel in the fields and become an expert.

So, what are you waiting for? Get out there, and get certified, today!

About the Author

A project management and digital marketing knowledge manager at Simple learn Avantika's area of interest is project design and analysis for digital marketing, data science, and analytics companies. With a degree in journalism, she also covers the latest trends in the industry, and is a passionate writer.

https://www.simplilearn.com/data-science-vs-big-data-vs-data-analytics-article

2.6 Data Science and Big Data: Two very Different Beasts

Creating artifact from the ore requires the tools, craftsmanship and science. Same is the case of big data and data science; here we present the distinguishing factors between the ore and the artifact.

Anaconda CON: Join us and Discover What Open Data Science Means By Sean McClure (Thought Works)

It is difficult to overstate the importance of data in today's economy. The tools we use and actions we take consume and generate a digital version of our world, all captured, waiting to be used. Data have become a real resource of interest across most industries and is rightly considered the gateway to competitive advantage and disruptive strategy.

Along with the rise of data have come two distinct efforts concerned with harnessing its potential. One is called Data Science and the other Big Data. These terms are often used interchangeably despite having fundamentally different roles to play in bringing the potential of data to the doorstep of an organization.

Although some would argue there is still confusion over the terms Data Science and Big Data, this has more to do with marketing interests than an honest look at what these terms have come to mean on real-world projects. Data Science looks to create models that capture the underlying patterns of complex systems, and codify those models into working applications. Big Data looks to collect and manage large amounts of varied data to serve large-scale web applications and vast sensor networks.

Although both offer the potential to produce value from data, the fundamental difference between Data Science and Big Data can be summarized in one statement:

Collecting Does Not Mean Discovering

Despite this declaration being obvious, its truth is often overlooked in the rush to fit a company's arsenal with data-savvy technologies. Value is too often framed as something that increases solely by the collection of more data. This means investments in data-focused activities center around tools instead of approaches. The engineering cart gets put before the scientific horse, leaving an organization with a big set of tools, and a small amount of knowledge on how to convert data into something useful.

Bringing Ore to an Empty Workshop

Since the onset of the Iron Age, Blacksmiths have used their skills and expertise to turn raw extracted material into a variety of valuable products. Using domain specific tools, the Blacksmith forges, draws, bends, punches and welds the raw material into objects of great utility. Through years of research, trial and error the Blacksmith learned to use choice gases, specific temperatures, controlled atmospheres and varied ore sources to yield a tailored product bespoke to its unique application.

With the Industrial Revolution came the ability to convert raw material into valuable products more efficiently and at scale. But the focus on scaling wasn't the acquisition of more material. It was on building tools that scaled and mechanized the expertise in converting. With this mechanization came an even greater need to understand the craft since to effectively operate, maintain and innovate at scale one had to deeply understand the process of converting raw material into products that answered to the always-changing demands of the market.

In the world of data this expertise in converting is called Data Science. The reason it takes a science to convert a raw resource into something of value is because what is extracted from the 'ground' is never in a useful form. 'Data in the raw' is littered with useless noise, irrelevant information, and misleading patterns. To convert this into that precious thing we are after requires a study of its properties and the discovery of a working model that captures the behavior we are interested in. Being in possession of a model despite the noise means an organization now owns the beginnings of further discovery and innovation; something unique to their business that has given them the knowledge of what to look for, and the codified descriptions of a world that can now be mechanized and scaled.

Conversion should Scale before Collection

No industry would invest in the extraction of a resource without the expertise in place to turn that resource into value. In any industry, that would be considered a bad venture. Loading the truck with ore only to have it arrive at an empty workshop adds little strategic benefit.

An unfortunate aspect of Big Data is that we look to the largest companies to see what solutions they have engineered to compete in their markets. But these companies hardly represent the challenges faced by most organizations. Their dominance often means they face very different competition and their engineering is done predominantly to serve large-scale applications. This engineering is critical for daily operations, and answering to the demands of high throughput and fault-tolerant architectures. But it says very little about the ability to discover and convert what is collected into valuable models that capture the driving forces behind how their markets operate. The ability to explain and predict an organization's dynamic environment is what it means to compete using data.

Understanding the distinction between Data Science and Big Data is critical to investing in a sound data strategy. For organizations looking to utilize their data as a competitive asset, the initial investment should be focused on converting data into value. The focus should be on the Data Science needed to build models that move data from raw to relevant. With time, Big Data approaches can work in concert with Data Science. The increased variety of data extracted can help make new discoveries or improve an existing model's ability to predict or classify.

Fill the workshop with the skills and expertise needed to convert data into something useful. The ore brought here will become the products that define a business.

http://www.kdnuggets.com/2015/07/data-science-big-data-different-beasts.html

2.7 Data Science and its relationship to Big Data and Data-Driven Decision Making

Two leading data science and machine learning researchers examine the relationship of data science to other important related

concepts, and to begin to identify the fundamental principles underlying data science. What will be Big Data 2.0?

Big Data Journal, Foster Provost and Tom Fawcett, Feb 2013.

ABSTRACT: Companies have realized they need to hire data scientists, academic institutions are scrambling to put together data-science programs, and publications are touting data science as a hot-- even 'sexy'--career choice. However, there is confusion about what exactly data science is, and this confusion could lead to disillusionment as the concept diffuses into meaningless buzz. In this article, we argue that there are good reasons why it has been hard to pin down exactly what is data science. One reason is that data science is intricately intertwined with other important concepts also of growing importance, such as big data and data-driven decision making; another reason is the natural tendency to associate what a practitioner does with the definition of the practitioner's field; this can result in overlooking the fundamentals of the field.

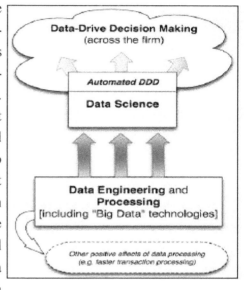

It is important (i) to understand the relationship of data science to other important related concepts, and (ii) to begin to identify the fundamental principles underlying data science. Once we embrace (ii), we can much better understand and explain exactly what data science has to offer.

Furthermore, only once we embrace (ii) should we be comfortable calling it data science. In this article, we present a perspective that addresses all these concepts. We close by offering, as examples, a partial list of fundamental principles underlying data science.

The article, part of Big Data Journal Inaugural Issue, is available at:online.liebertpub.com/doi/pdfplus/10.1089/big.2013.1508

Foster Provost is a Professor and NEC Faculty Fellow at New York University Stern School of Business.

Tom Fawcett is a leading researcher in Machine Learning.

http://www.kdnuggets.com/2013/02/data-science-big-data-decision-making-provost-fawcett.html

2.8   Evolution of the Data Scientist through the Decade: What's changed

Evolution is the truth of mankind and it's inevitable. We all are revolutionizing everyday biologically as well as technologically and so do our roles and responsibilities. Here is the summary of evolution of Data Scientist role and its hiring trends in industry throughout the decade. - **By Gaurav Vohra, CEO Jigsaw Academy**

I was invited to be a part of a panel discussion at the recently conducted Cypher Analytics Summit by Analytics India Magazine. While the topic of the discussion was 'Key skills for a data scientist", it was interesting to note that all of us (the panelists) spent a fair bit of time discussing how the skill requirement has changed over time. I think this change in skill requirement reflects the evolution that has happened in the last 10 years in the field of analytics and would make for an interesting read for anyone in the field or looking to get into the field.

Hiring Trends in 2006

I have been a part of the analytics industry for over 15 years now. I started building analytics teams back in 2005. Back then, building a new team meant hiring a bunch of statisticians, economists and mathematicians. We would hire people who had a comfort level with numbers and some basic understanding of statistics. We would then teach them business analytics. This meant a quick refresher of statistical concepts like chi-square, p-values etc. followed by training on SAS (in most cases) or R/Weka/SPSS (in a few cases).

We would then teach the new recruits to do specific analytics tasks. Marketing Analysts would learn to build market mix models or price promotion models based on the team they were part of. Financial Analysts would learn to build credit risk models or fraud identification strategies. People would focus on learning the specific task that they would be doing in their role and get started. Over time, analysts would move across teams, across clients and across domains, and this would broaden their skill set over time.

Everyone was called a Data Analyst or a Business Analyst. Similarly, there were BI analysts or Reporting Analysts or MIS Analysts who looked after the reporting piece.

Hiring Trends in 2011

Over time, businesses realized the importance of domain knowledge in analytics. The analytics industry at the time was dominated by people with strong quantitative skills that were not necessarily complemented by deep business knowledge. Analysts were working on complex analyses for products they had never used, for markets they had never been to and for customers they could not relate to. This caused obvious problems in the industry and businesses started to pay special attention to providing the right level of business understanding to the analysts. There were many changes that came about because of this.

Domain knowledge became a strong part of the analytics training. I remember the first time I took my team to visit a Wal-Mart store. They could not believe the scale of the store in terms of size and assortment. Suddenly, all those discussions about space planning and aisle management started to make sense to them.

We also started hiring more MBA graduates as well as people from a domain background. For ex: a retail analytics team will have a non-analytics person who understands the retail business very well. Analytics slowly became a domain with an eclectic mix of people – MBAs, Engineers, Physicists, even Psychology graduates.

Big Data and Analytics became the largest group. Overall engagement rates decline, but liking a post is 6.5 times more common than commenting. Machine Learning & Data Science, KDnuggets, and Data Scientists have the highest engagement levels - **By Gregory Piatetsky, KDnuggets**

Soon after my 2015 post about LinkedIn Groups Top LinkedIn Groups for Analytics, Big Data, Data Mining, and Data Science - Discussions up, Engagement down, LinkedIn - who certainly saw the same trends of declining engagement - has removed the full group statistics from public view.

The members can still see the group size, which continues to grow for most groups, but not the total number of discussions (now renamed to conversations) or comments, which continues to decline. A group member can see about 200 most recent conversations in the group; whether it takes place over 4 days or 400.

- ❖ So, what is happening to LinkedIn Groups? How fast are they growing?

- ❖ What is the rate of conversations, comments, and likes (introduced in 2015)?

- ❖ Where do groups fall in the quadrants of Active, Posting, Commenting, and Passive?

I collected the group membership on Jan 1 and Sep 30, 2016 and with the help of KDnuggets editors Prasad Pore, Matt Mayo, and Anmol Rajpurohit collected the group conversations around October 7, 2016 for 26 of the largest LinkedIn groups in Analytics, Big Data, Data Mining, and Data Science.

I also computed annual growth rate for 2015 and 2016 from Mar 30, 2015, Jan 1, 2016, and Sep 30, 2016 by simple extrapolation: annual growth = (*9-month growth*)$^{4/3}$.

Key Findings

- Overall engagement continues to decline, to 1.17 conversations per week per 1000 members, and only about 0.17 comments per week per 1000 members, but is helped by likes: 1.11 per week per 1000 members

- *Big Data and Analytics* became the largest group, replacing Data Science Central (former Advanced Business Analytics, Data Mining and Predictive Modeling)

- *Data Scientists*, *Machine Learning and Data Science*, and *Big Data and Analytics* are the fastest growing groups in 2016

- *Machine Learning and Data Science*, *KDnuggets*, and *Data Scientists* have the highest engagement levels (comments + likes)

1. Largest Groups

Here are the 10 largest groups, as of Sep 30, 2016. There were only 2 changes in the top 10 groups:

- Big Data and Analytics became the largest group, replacing Data Science Central

- Machine Learning and Data Science moved to 10th place, up from 14th, replacing Machine Learning Connection which stopped growing.

Table 1: Top 10 Largest LinkedIn Groups in Big Data, Data Science

Rank 2016	LinkedIn Group	Members Sep 30, 2016	Members Mar 30, 2015	Growth Rate 2016
1	Big Data and Analytics	253,729	120,776	75.6%
2	Data Science Central (former Advanced Business Analytics, Data Mining and Predictive Modeling)	243,988	174,362	23.2%
3	Business Intelligence Professionals	186,372	150,147	13.8%
4	Big Data | Analytics | Strategy | Finance | Innovation	173,831	128,805	32.5%
5	Business Analytics	130,534	70,326	70.7%
6	Data Mining, Statistics, Big Data, Data Visualization, and Data Science	116,307	68,539	45.2%
7	BIG DATA Professionals - Architects Scientists IOT Analytics	71,215	45,443	33.4%
8	Big Data, Analytics, Hadoop, NoSQL & Cloud Computing	62,385	33,139	31.0%
9	Data Warehouse / Big Data / Hadoop / Predictive Analytics	47,620	32,994	34.2%
10	Machine Learning and Data Science	43,483	20,876	79.5%

2. Growth

The 10 largest groups grew at a similar rate, except the top Big Data & Analytics group - see Fig 1, but the next 20 groups showed a lot more variety, with some groups like Data Scientists and KDnuggets growing fast, but many groups showing very slow growth or declining.

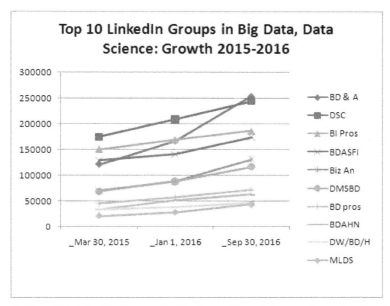

Fig. 1: Top 10 LinkedIn Groups in Big Data, Data Science: Growth 2015-2016

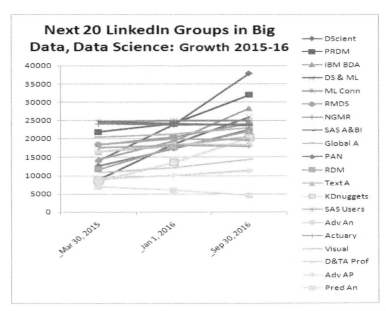

Fig. 2: Next 20 LinkedIn Groups in Big Data, Data Science: Growth 2015-2016

Table 2: Top 10 Fastest Growing (in 2016) LinkedIn Groups in Big Data, Data Science

Rank	LinkedIn Group	Growth Rate 2015	Growth Rate 2016
1	Data Scientists	102%	**86%**
2	Machine Learning and Data Science	48%	**80%**
3	Big Data and Analytics	53%	**76%**
4	Business Analytics	34%	**71%**
5	KDnuggets Analytics, Data Mining, and Data Science	85%	**71%**
6	IBM Big Data and Analytics	49%	**68%**
7	Data Science & Machine Learning	166%	**56%**
8	Pattern Recognition, Data Mining, Machine Intelligence ...	14%	**46%**
9	Data Mining, Statistics, Big Data, Data Visualization, and Data Science	39%	**45%**
10	Predictive Analytics Network	52%	**42%**

http://www.kdnuggets.com/2016/10/top-linkedin-groups-analytics-big-data-mining-data-science.html

2.9 A Tale of Two India's – a Digital Paradox

Raghav Bahl

"India is a digital paradox", **The Quint**'s Editor-in-Chief Raghav Bahl writes, in his piece for Tech Crunch, noting how unlike the media's decline in the west, Indian newspapers have grown by two-thirds in the past six years and it is predicted to stay between 12 to 14 percent for the next few years.

Despite being only a developing country, India is the seventh largest economy in the world and the fourth largest IT and tech hub. Unlike the pop culture references of a poor India, there are in fact 'two India's, with stark differences from each other.

On one hand, we see the "first India," which is currently competing to become the world's biggest Amazon, Facebook, Uber and Apple market within the next few years...On the other hand we see the "second India," which is still trying to catch-up...but whose literacy rates and GDP per capita is improving to the extent that soon hundreds of millions of tech-savvy consumers will be entering the market.

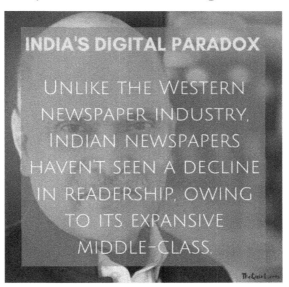

Print Media and Middle Class Readership

Quoting Freddie Dawson, Bahl writes that the ever-expanding middle class population, which interestingly falls under the category of the 'second India', is the driving force behind the Indian newspaper industry.

Although the technologically advanced Indian populations consume their news through apps and digital sites on phones or computers, the population which is lagging largely depends on traditional print media to access news.

Reading newspapers and a strong protective culture for free press dates back more than 160 years to when India was under British colonial rule. India is home to the Times of India, one of the oldest newspapers in the world, and the world's largest circulated newspaper, but it is not English-language newspapers that are pushing print press growth, but non-English vernacular papers.

Two India and Technology

According to Bahl, India currently consists of three types of news publications:

One is the vernacular publications, which are state specific and have an extensive readership.

The larger media houses run by western-educated, English-speaking directors, who have witnessed a slight dip in readership like the western media, and are looking for innovation.

The new digital media - India media houses have had the luxury to follow the course of a technological advancement, which Bahl predicts, will continue for another decade, until the middle class habitualises itself with smart phones and digital technology.

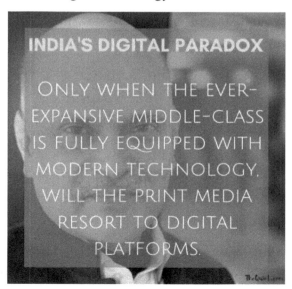

As of now, India has the world's third largest smart phone market. In 2016, India was expected to have sold 139 million smart phones, with Android devices costing less than $150.

"Rather than viewing this as a threat", Bahl writes, "Indian media companies have the luxury of viewing the slow move toward digital as a potential goldmine for which they have time to prepare."

https://www.thequint.com/india/2017/02/04/india-is-a-digital-paradox-raghav-bahl-dip-print-media

2.10 Data and innovation in the Economic Survey

The use of Big Data can however complement reforms in India's traditional statistical machinery to help generate better data and frame more informed policies.

New Delhi: This year's Economic Survey does not carry the usual statistical tables on the economy's performance, which are used widely by analysts.

This is probably because the budget has been advanced, and those tables will find place in the forthcoming volume slated for later this year. The survey seems to have compensated this by the use of Big Data and intensive data-mining of multiple datasets "to shed new light on the flow of goods and people within India".

The survey has used individual tax filings administered by the Goods and Service Tax Network to estimate state-level (both inter and intra) trade. Railway station-wise unreserved passenger traffic data provided by the Indian Railways has been used to arrive at estimates of work-related migration.

Satellite imagery has been used to calculate built-up area and estimate potential property tax collections (and hence losses being incurred currently).

Besides machine-generated large-scale data sets, even existing databases have been used more intensively. For instance, district-level estimates of the National Sample Survey Office (NSSO) statistics, which are the main source of employment and poverty/inequality statistics in India, have been used to generate insights on spatial concentration of poverty and welfare beneficiaries. Data from the Socio-Economic Caste Census (SECC) have also been put to similar use.

Ever since the start of the planning process, the official statistical machinery has largely focused on surveys almost to the point of neglecting administrative data (viz., data collected during routine administrative tasks). It is fitting that the end of the planning era should mark the beginning of a new chapter in which administrative data will be given pride of place in economic policy-making once again.

The new approach towards using diverse datasets is an important first step towards better decision-making. Take the migration data using railway traffic for example. Census-based statistics for migration are still from the 2001 census, as detailed statistics for 2011 census have not been released till now. The railway traffic-based migration data is available till 2015-16. Such data, if made transparently available on a regular basis, can give useful insights on employment and distress-related scenarios for migrant workers, which currently rely on guesstimates based on figures such as demand for jobs in the MGNREGA.

The survey has used satellite imagery for built-up areas to estimate potential property tax collections. Marrying this data with something like income tax data for India's top 50 cities and house-size census data can generate rich insights about our cities and their riches. Still, it needs to be kept in mind that Big Data alone cannot be a silver bullet for India's statistical challenges. For example, the informal sector continues to be a black hole when it comes to data. For several sectors and purposes, there are still no alternatives to better-designed and more intensive surveys.

The use of Big Data can however complement reforms in India's traditional statistical machinery to help generate better data and frame more informed policies. If the new databases are cleaned and opened (in a machine-readable format) for independent researchers to track, verify and analyze, it could usher a new era of transparency and accountability.

For a start, the finance ministry should consider opening the underlying data used in the survey in a machine-readable format.

http://www.livemint.com/Politics/hhcfeYAbw3cjPygZ8A2wKM/Data-and-innovation-in-the-Economic-Survey.html

2.11 Big Data Initiative

BDI: An R&D Perspective

By definition, **Big Data** is data whose scale, diversity, and complexity require new architecture, techniques, algorithms, and analytics to manage it and extract value and hidden knowledge from it. In other words, big data is characterized by volume, variety (structured and unstructured data) velocity (high rate of changing) and veracity (uncertainty and incompleteness).

In the Big Data research context, so called analytics over Big Data is playing a leading role. Analytics cover a wide family of problems mainly arising in the context of Database, Data Warehousing and Data Mining research. Analytics research is intended to develop complex procedures running over large-scale, enormous in-size data repositories with the objective of extracting useful knowledge hidden in such repositories. One of the most significant application scenarios where Big Data arise is, without doubt, scientific computing. Here, scientists and researchers produce huge amounts of data per-day via experiments (e.g., disciplines like high-energy physics, astronomy, biology, bio-medicine, and so forth). But extracting useful knowledge for decision making purposes from these massive, large-scale data repositories is almost impossible for actual DBMS-inspired analysis tools. From a methodological point of view, there are also research challenges. A new methodology is required for transforming Big Data stored in heterogeneous and different-in-nature data sources (e.g., legacy systems, Web, scientific data repositories, sensor and stream databases, social networks) into a structured, hence well-interpretable format for target data analytics. Therefore, data-driven approaches, in biology, medicine, public policy, social sciences, and humanities, can replace the traditional hypothesis-driven research in science.

Some of the S&T challenges that researchers across the globe and as well as in India facing are related to data deluge pertaining to Astrophysics, Materials Science, Earth & atmospheric observations, Energy, Fundamental Science, Computational Biology, Bioinformatics & Medicine, Engineering & Technology, GIS and Remote Sensing, Cognitive science and Statistical data. These challenges require development of advanced algorithms, visualization techniques, data streaming methodologies and analytics. The overall constraints that community facing are

1. **The IT Challenge:** Storage and computational power

2. **The computer science: Algorithm** design, visualization, scalability (Machine Learning, network & Graph analysis, streaming of data and text mining), distributed data, architectures, data dimension reduction and implementation

3. **The mathematical science:** Statistics, Optimization, uncertainty quantification, model development (statistical, Ab Initio, simulation) analysis and systems theory

4. **The multi-disciplinary approach:** Contextual problem solving

2.12 Big data analytics and the India equation

Updated: July 15, 2013, 07.51 PM IST

Big Data presents a huge opportunity for businesses to unfold key insights by applying principles of statistic... Read More

Big Data presents a huge opportunity for businesses; say Michael Svilar and Arnab Chakraborty.

Business environment has never been more uncertain than it is today, with severe competitive pressures, sluggish global economy and increasing customer expectations. One characteristic of these dynamics may even be more impactful than others, while at the same time offering the chance to tackle these other challenges: the exponentially increasing volume of data around businesses, both structured and unstructured.

In the last 10 years, the digital revolution and its technology driven innovations are creating a surge in especially unstructured data, coming from video streams, call center logs, smart devices, and social networks. The massive volume of data in various forms like audio, video, text, image, sensor, click-streams, geo-spatial, being generated with very high velocity, is commonly referred to as Big Data.

Big Data presents a huge opportunity for businesses to unfold key insights by applying principles of statistics, mathematics and artificial intelligence. Big Data Analytics can help discover hidden patterns and predict future scenarios that would help drive business decisions for developing innovative products, drive revenue growth, improve supply chain effectiveness, mitigate business risks and enhance customer intimacy.

Recent Accenture research shows analytics and data science have secured a spot on the boardroom's agenda. That is because organizations are recognizing there are golden nuggets of actionable insights hidden inside the vast mounds of data - insights that will help them turn business issues into outcomes and advance on what Accenture calls the "Analytics Journey to ROI". Analytics now plays an ever-increasing role in various contexts such as broad as understanding what consumers are saying about you what may be a new product opportunity or business opportunity from monitoring social networks, to personalizing offers to customers in real time, making optimal pricing recommendations, preventing network failures, mitigating disease out-breaks, intelligent city planning and management. Big Data analytics focuses on letting data be industrialized in such a way that not only drives meaningful insights in a rapid fashion and drives innovation for businesses and government.

What makes Big Data analytics even more powerful is that in many cases it enables businesses to monitor events in real-time and embed insights in real-time decision-making. Just think about getting healthcare recommendations through analytics that calculates the probability of different diseases and recommended treatments, based upon doctors written text. Similarly, leading retailers have the potential to leverage real-time footfall analytics from mobile network events, Wi-Fi data, GPS coordinates and other forms of geo-location big data to make personalized offers to customers as they travel to the store, and even while in it, based upon real time behaviors. Today city planners are experimenting with multiple forms of Big Data (e.g. Machine to Machine (M2M), street light sensors, and telematics sensors to aid government organizations in building a real-time dynamic view of an urban population and optimize the security provisioning for the city. Utility providers are leveraging sensor data related analytics to understand how operations are performing and when to do predictive maintenance.

Though the potential of analytics and Big Data is clear, one of the challenges noticed is a significant shortage of data scientists with deep analytical training in data discovery, predictive modeling, open source statistical solutions, visualization skills and business acumen to be able to frame and interpret analyses. Here, India is in an advantageous position. Over the last three decades, India has invested significantly in institutes and universities of national importance for higher education. These institutes have helped advance India's talent leadership in the field of science, math, technology, operation research, management and fundamental research. India today has one of the largest pools of analytics and data science talent in the world and has been playing a key role in supporting the analytical needs of the developed markets. But make no mistake: With the rising adoption of analytics in business, even in India the most qualified analytics professionals, data scientists, are becoming a scarce resource.

Analytics-driven business should be the new secret sauce for any organization today to drive high performance and remain competitive in the market place. Over the last decade many global corporations especially from the financial services and technology industry have initiated the analytics journey. India, with its rich talent pool, became the test bed for a few companies to pilot their initial analytics efforts. The initial success led to many global multinational corporations (MNCs) across the banking, insurance, retail, and telecom, automotive and consulting sectors to set up analytics centers of excellence either by themselves or through a trusted partner. Many of analytically driven companies like Amazon, eBay, Google, General Electric, Citibank have leveraged analytics talent existing in India. These companies have grown leaps and bounds through innovations and strategy developed using deep market insight.

To tap the analytics momentum, India now needs to build a sustainable analytics eco-system that brings in a strong partnership across the industry players, government, and academia. Some of the key actions for analytics eco-system in India would be around.

* Talent pool - Create industry academia partnership to groom the talent pool in universities as well as develop strong internal training curriculum to advance analytical depth.

* Collaborate - Form analytics forum across organization boundaries to discuss the pain-points of the practitioner community and share best practices to scale analytics organizations.

* Capability development - Invest in long term skills and capabilities that forms the basis for differentiation and value creation. There needs to be an innovation culture that will facilitate IP creation and asset development.

LATEST COMMENT

Gurinder Mohan Dua , Noida, 164 days ago

Big data is being exploited very effectively by the developed world, specially the US. This is aptly clear by the examples illustrated in the article. Disconnect is when the scenario is somehow a... Read More

* Value creation - Building rigor to measure the impact of analytics deployment is very critical to earn legitimacy within the organization.

Big Data and analytics offer tremendous untapped potential to drive big business outcomes. For organizations to leverage India as a global analytics hub can be one of the key levers to move up their analytics maturity curve.

http://www.gadgetsnow.com/it-services/Big-Data-Analytics-and-the-India-Equation/articleshow/21085728.cms

2.13 EMC-Hive India Think Tank - The power equation Big Data + Social in Governance

Aug 8, 2014 · 4:30 PM

EMC Square Offices

The role of big data + social data in influencing election decisions has been defined in the last six years since the election of President Obama in 2008. People wanted change and were not afraid to share their opinions in public conversations, and that's how person-to-person, one-on-one discussions turned from local to global and opaque to transparent on public and open social media platforms. 2012 showcased the rise of data science and big data, how media, political parties and civil society gathered opinions about issues closest to the heart, big ideas that can change and create ephemeral landscapes. Math quants and data crushers could disseminate the mounds of campaign data at their fingertips into actionable targeting information to persuade and inform people across the nation and within strategic states.

The great Indian Election of 2014 unleashed technology creativity in India and ushered the era of big data in Indian politics. Data analysis helped raise funds, rework advertisements, created detailed models for voter engagement, increasing the power of a micro-targeted strategy. New tools were created; others were commissioned to make the experience personal.

BIG DATA + SOCIAL DATA + NOW = MASSIVE INFLUENCE

The big data equation is missing how social influence, mobile data and other assets can impact the results when harnessed quickly and effectively. The potential for outside the box thinkers, creators and entrepreneurs has opened, with companies being formed to take advantage of paradigm shifts providing desirable experiences.

Come participate in the Hive Big Data Think Tank Meetup hosted jointly with EMC Corporation to network with experts and find the next big idea for your startup venture. The event will start at 5pm on 8th August 2014 and end at 8.30pm after which dinner will be served. Entry to the event is FREE and exclusively by invite only.

Program

There will be five speakers including industry leaders, startup founders and investors. Mr. R. Chandrashekhar, President, NASSCOM will preside over the event. The profile of our distinguished speakers is below:

1) R. Chandrashekhar, President, NASSCOM: Chandrashekhar has been the Chairman of Telecom Commission and Secretary in the Department of Telecommunications in the Ministry of Communications & Information Technology, Government of India since September 2010 till his retirement from Government service in March 2013. As the Telecom Secretary, he was responsible for driving several key policies and strategies covering licensing, spectrum management, National Broadband Plan, Convergence, Manufacturing, Investment, security, R&D and the National Telecom Policy 2012. He was the principal architect behind a triad of policies covering Telecommunications, Electronics and Information Technology that was unveiled in draft form by the Government of India in October 2011. M. Chandrashekhar received a M.Sc. degree in Chemistry from the Indian Institute of Technology, Bombay and a M.S. degree in Computer Science from the Pennsylvania State University, USA. He is widely travelled and has a unique understanding of cultural diversity, both within the country and across the world. He was conferred the Prime Minister's Award for Excellence in Public Administration for the year 2007-08. He has been conferred several awards including Data Quest Path Breaker of the Year Award in 2005 and Distinguished Alumnus award of IIT-Mumbai in 2010.

2) Shashi Shekhar, Chief Digital Officer: Shashi is a Digital Strategist and Innovator with nearly 18 years of experience in the Information Technology Industry. Shashi is also a well-known Blogger and Commentator on Politics and Public Policy in India. Shashi joined Niti Digital from Infosys where he spent many years focused on Product Strategy and Innovation. He assisted Mr. Narendra Modi's personal brand creation efforts through use of technology, catapulting Mr. Modi from having only regional recognition to a being a significant player on the national scene, having increased manifold the voters confidence in his ability to lead a nation.

3) Viral Shah, Co-founder and CTO of Fourth Lion Technologies: a company that is named after the hidden fourth lion representing the citizen. Fourth Lion Technologies is helping politicians discover technology tools beyond their Twitter accounts and Facebook pages, and is also beginning to work with brands in a similar way. All major political parties now work with companies to build mobile applications and crunch large data sets to formulate and execute campaigns. Shah, 34, is a computer scientist who developed technology for Aadhaar based subsidies and payments prior to starting Fourth Lion Technologies along with Shankar Maruwada and Naman Pugalia. He worked on Nandan Nilekani's much talked about election campaign, and is also the author of the open source Julia Programming Language that is becoming popular for data science and analytics.

4) S Anand, Chief Data Scientist, Gramener: Gramener is a data visualization company transforming your data into concise dashboards that make your business problem & solution visually obvious, helping you find insights quickly, based on cognitive research. Gramener offers fascinating analysis on the history of election analysis, history of every Football world cup match since 1930, review of the Indian budget reactions, etc on their website. Anand has advised and designed IT systems for organizations

such as the Citigroup, Honda, ICICI, IBM, Oracle, RBS, SAP, Tesco, etc. Anand has an MBA from IIM Bangalore and a B. Tech from IIT Madras. He has worked at IBM, Lehman Brothers, The Boston Consulting Group and Infosys Consulting. He blogs at s-anand.net

5) Karthik Shashidhar, CEO of Bespoke Data Insights: Karthik is a freelance management consultant who solves business problems using a data-driven approach. Karthik spent the last year writing a column for the Mint where he analyzed quantum of data looking at voter polls, voter turnouts, criminal candidates, exit polls and much more. His work can be viewed at http://www.livemint.com/Search/Link/Keyword/election%20metrics. He is also with the Takshashila Institution, a public policy think tank.

The Hive Big Data Think Tank brings together experts, decision makers, researchers, and visionaries from academia and the industry in: - Visualization, data infrastructure, and data science - Applications that leverage Big Data in areas such as advertising, marketing, eCommerce, CRM, security, health sciences, industrial verticals etc. We host periodic talks, panel discussions and hackathons. Join us! Come Learn, Network & Share. Brought to you by 'The Hive' this incubates funds and launches businesses that use large volumes of data for intelligent decision making.

https://www.meetup.com/Big-Data-by-The-Hive-India/events/198098092/

2.14 The impact of Big Data Analytics on Management Consulting and Human Resources in India
By *Satyakam Mohanty, CEO, Ma Foi Analytics*

Big Data Analytics start-up- Ma Foi Analytics is a part of the 20-year-old Ma Foi Group which is well known for Management Consulting and Human Resources in India. It was founded in 2012 with its headquarters at Bangalore along with offices in US, Chennai and Delhi,

Ma Foi Analytics caters to Industries like Healthcare, e-commerce, Hospitality, SME, Manufacturing, Retail and Oil &Gas.

Management Consulting, relying as it does on a combination of research-custom and syndicated, industry expertise of its experienced vertical specialists and institutional knowledge accumulated over decades of advising clients, has been an elite field where the bigger players not only continued to grow year over year but were also able to maintain high margins since the barriers to competitive entry were very high. However, Big Data has disrupted this equation.

Satyakam Mohanty

With democratization of data, access to useful information is no longer a challenge. It's what you can do with this deluge and how quickly you can do it that matters. This is where Analytics start-ups and incumbents have been quick to step in. Using a combination of Big Data technology and bleeding edge data science – artificial intelligence and machine learning based algorithms for instance; the analytics players have been able to deliver deeper insights, faster and in the process upset the Management Consulting applecart, especially with regard to Sales, Marketing and Supply Chain. Flipkart, India's leading e-tailer is a prime example of a company that has embedded big data analytics and technology deep in various aspects of business and uses it as a strategic tool to gain the competitive edge.

On their part, the Management Consulting companies haven't been sitting idle. Many have been closely following developments in the Big Data Technology and Analytics space and have set up their own Analytics wings that offer Big Data Analytics- both as a standalone offering; as well as bundled with their core consulting offerings. Accenture, for instance, has a full - fledged Analytics practice housed within Accenture Digital with a large chunk of the workforce sitting in India, many with prior experience in pure –play Analytics companies.

Human Resources: The role of the HR is to maximize the contribution of people to business goals through development and execution of the right people policies and processes. While the significance of HR can hardly be overplayed, it is equally true that while the CEO's discussions with the CFO and CSO are often based on solid data, those with the HR head, are often anecdotal. Just like Marketing, the HR of the future has to be evidence based, and organizations have started to work in this direction.

Organizations are now using social media network analysis to find the right candidates for their roles. Apart from that, utilizing historical data to identify candidates who would be a better for long term success and longevity in the organization is already a reality.

Organizations like DENTSPLY India and Johnson Matthey are using HR Analytics to drive their organizations' HR strategy. These organizations capture employee data across all locations as well as utilize Gallup data. Using analytical tools, they can design employee engagement programs based on the age, tenure and other demographics. This helps in making employees more committed to working with the company since the incentives can now be diverse and specific to what the employee requires based on his demographic profile.

Studies over the past decade have shown that a judicious use of Analytics in Human resources can help predict up to 80 per cent the employee turnover. As organizations devise evidence based people strategies, HR functions move up the maturity chain from being reactive to predictive. Big Data opens the possibilities for HR to collaborate with functions such as marketing & technology like never before. This way the

HR team adopts strategies that are business result oriented, and become true strategic partners to their organization.

http://www.cioreviewindia.com/magazine/The-impact-of-Big-Data-Analytics-on-Management-Consulting-and-Human-Resources-in-India-TNSQ8801151.html

2.15 Broad contours of DST initiated BDI programme

• To promote and foster Big Data Science, Technology and Applications in the country and to develop core generic technologies, tools and algorithms for wider applications in Govt.

• To understand the present status of the industry in terms of market size, different players providing services across sectors/ functions, opportunities, SWOT of industry, policy framework (if any), present skill levels available etc.

• To carryout market landscape survey to assess the future opportunities and demand for skill levels in next 10 years

• To carryout gap analysis in terms of skills levels and policy framework.

• To evolve a strategic Road Map and micro level action plan clearly defining of roles of various stakeholders – Govt., Industry, Academia, Industry Associations and others with clear timelines and outcome for the next 10 years.

Call for Proposal under Big Data Initiative Programme (to be opened shortly)

List of Proforma for Submission of Research Projects for Financial Support

S. No.	Description	File Format
1.	Format for Submission of R&D Projects / Center for excellence	Word

S. No.	Description	File Format
2.	Format for submitting proposals for short term Training Course/Workshop/Conference under different Big Data Initiative	Word
3.	Guidelines for Implementing Research Project	Word
4.	Progress Report	Word
5.	Project Completion Report	Word
6.	Statement of Expenditure to be submitted financial year wise	Word
7.	Format for Utilization Certificate	Word
8.	Department of Science & Technology terms & condition of the grant	Word

http://dst.gov.in/big-data-initiative-1

2.16 Taking the step forward: Government Initiatives in Analytics

APOORVA VERMA   **FEB 29, 2017**

India is the second most populated country in the world. Thus, a mine for data analysts to research, collect and analyze data. Researchers in India are an active breed, name any upcoming field under the sun and you will find research going on in that field already!

Even though researchers in astrophysics, material sciences, cognitive sciences, energy, biology, statistics, earth and atmospheric observation, bioinformatics, biotechnology, nanotechnology and many others generate a lot of data, they require advance algorithms, visualization techniques, data streaming methodologies and analytics for further development.

This momentum that big data analytics has gained in India has facilitated the launch of 'Big Data Initiative' by the Indian government1. It will aim to:

- Promote and foster big data science, technology and application in India and developing core generic technologies, tools and algorithms

- Understand the current scenario in terms of market size, different players, SWOT, etc.

- Carryout market landscape surveys to assess the future opportunities and demand for skill levels in next 10 years

- Evolve a strategic roadmap, defining the role of various stakeholders – government, industry and academia with timelines.

Talking about the Big Data initiative will not be rendered complete without the mention of BJP's Election campaign in 2014. It was one of the most data-savvy campaigns that any country has witnessed in recent times.

The IT cell of "Elect Modi Campaign" virtually connected with about 144 million people across India through Facebook, Twitter and Google plus. BJP partnered with IT and analytics firms, such as SAP, Oracle, InMobi, and PwC to get real-time updates and analysis during the elections which enabled them to react faster to any controversies in real time. Further, to drive their campaign, they planted cookies on all computers that visited the BJP website. They then extracted information about their visitors' further internet activity, for customized advertisements.

BJP had proposed to set up an Institute of Big Data and Analytics for studying the impact of Big Data across sectors for predictive science with a focus on India-specific problems, enabling businesses to invest in a wide range of issues such as national security, processing data from different languages, disseminating data to farmers about production, prices, etc.

Additionally, the Modi Government has developed various digital platforms and launched many initiatives such as MyGov, DigiLocker, Digital India, National Scholarship portal, Aadhaar card, Jan DhanYojna to connect with the citizens through websites, mobiles and smart phones and encourage citizens to be a part of discussions, suggestions and volunteering for various causes. Some of these portals, such as MyGov also keep them updated on the status of their suggestions.

Also, as a part of the "Digital India" program, common Biometric Attendance System is implemented in the government offices to collect data on the attendance of the employees.

Another example of the support of analytics is shown by the Department of Science and Technology that initiated a programme to promote Big Data Science, Technology and Applications for fostering research. They grant financial support for R&D Projects, national level Conferences/ workshops/ Seminars and for the establishment of Center for Excellence in Big Data Analytics, Predictive technologies, Cyber Security etc.

The latest to join the analytics sector is the National Payments Corporation of India with the launch of a unified payment interface that allows customers to send and receive money through smart phones WITHOUT revealing their bank account details. Transactions can be done through Aadhaar number, mobile number or virtual payment address.

Further, organizations such as Swaniti and Fourth Lion are also playing an important role. While Swaniti works with politicians by focusing on data collection and analysis, creating data dashboards and synthesizing solutions to problems at grass root levels; Fourth Lion's expertise lies in understanding how national electorates behave through InstaVaani, their quick polling tool. They may have different approaches, but both the organizations focus on analytics, building and adopting the latest technologies to provide strategies for the Indian political leaders and environment.

Even though these initiatives are encouraging, but the infrastructural bottlenecks may prove to be problematic in implementing these on ground level. However, intelligent data is the way forward and now that we have taken the first step it won't be long before we are up and ahead in the game!

http://analyticsindiamag.com/government-initiatives-in-data-analytics/

2.17 RKMVU's launches India's first Masters Level Degree Course: M.Sc. in Big Data Analytics

In collaboration with and support from Tata Consultancy Services (TCS)

Ramakrishna Mission Vivekananda University (RKMVU) at Belur Math signed a Memorandum of Understanding (MoU) with Tata Consultancy Services (TCS) to launch India's First Masters Level degree course in Big Data Analytics designed by TCS. Swami Atmapriyananda, Vice Chancellor of RKMVU and Ranjan Bandyopadhyay, Global Head – HR – BPO Services, TCS, signed the MoU in the presence of Prof. Bimal

Roy, a renowned computer scientist, Padmashree awardee and former Director of Indian Statistical Institute, Kolkata, on 23 May 2016.

Data Analytics

Current developments around the world along with the availability of the right technologies have made it possible for large amounts of data to be gathered and stored. Organizations have realized the need to utilize these large volumes of data to fuel effective and better decision making. To make the best use of this huge volume of data, it needs to be analyzed and comprehended to facilitate effective decision making. This enormous task is enabled through Big Data Analytics.

Global big data market is expected to reach USD 48.3 billion by 2018. The analytics market in India is expected to grow at a rate of 15% annually. This gigantic business need has generated a huge requirement of skilled talent to undertake such analytical jobs. Skilled manpower, educated and trained in the field of Big Data Analytics, will be required to meet this huge challenge. By 2018, the demand for those trained in this fast emerging area will reach 4.4 million globally, but only one-third of these jobs is likely to be filled. And this demand will keep increasing by leaps and bounds as years roll by.

TCS Advantage

TCS, the Industry leader in Information Technology, has envisaged a whole new long term initiative called Academia Interface Programme. One such initiative is the launch of a full-fledged two-year programme (four semesters) at the Masters level, called M. Sc. in Big Data Analytics at leading science Colleges/Universities and another programme called M.Tech. in Big Data Analytics in Engineering Colleges. With TCS's rich expertise in the field of Big Data Analytics, it foresees huge employment opportunities for professionals in this area of Big Data Analytics across several organizations globally.

M.Sc. in Big Data Analytics

This Postgraduate Programme spans four semesters. The contents will be Mathematics, Statistics, Economics and Computer Science and their applications in Big Data Analytics. The students shall learn the fundamentals of data modeling and migration, manipulation, cleansing and so on. They will lean business functions and analytics in various domains from Finance to Retail to Pharmacy etc. The fourth and last semester will be a full-time internship in Big Data Analytics at a reputed organization.

Eligibility

Please refer to the Admissions Section

Placement Opportunities

Students completing M.Sc. in Big Data programme will have huge placement opportunities in several companies thanks to growing demand for trained personnel in this emerging area. TCS itself envisages huge requirements for such professionals and will conduct campus interviews and offer jobs to eligible students who meet the recruitment norms prescribed by TCS.

Start of the Programme

M.Sc. in 'Big Data Analytics' will be started in July 2016. The first batch of students for the session 2016-18 will be completing the course in June 2018. The expected intake will be 30—35 students.

2.18 Top 10 Analytics Trends in India to watch out for in 2017

BHASKER GUPT by AIM &Analytix Labs

Analytics is by far the biggest influence in IT industry – a phenomenon evident by the rise of next-gen technology Cognitive Computing, Block chain and Virtual Reality which has at its core a valuable asset "data", and analytics quite irrefutably is the essence of it. After all, it's the whole mix of technology, data and analytics that is revolutionizing the way we work.

In keeping with our annual tradition, we present the much-researched and a carefully thought-out study carried out in association with **AnalytixLab**, a premier analytics training institute in India. We invited nominations from various organizations to identify the analytics trends that will shape the future of our industry in India for 2017. After a lot of fact-finding from the industry insiders, we bring to you the ***top 10 analytic trends*** that have had the highest impact on the analytics industry today and potentially going forward in 2017.

This year, we received an astounding **36 submissions**. A lot of new trends have hit the space, a few faded away and there are others that endured and will definitely stay. This study, now in its third year presents neatly sorted out viewpoint of the industry leaders and veterans on Top 10 Analytics Trends in India to watch out for in 2017.

Artificial intelligence becomes pervasive in business

The Cognitive age is clearly upon us— it is indicated by the fact that more than $1 billion in venture capital funding went into cognitive science in 2014 and 2015, and further supported by fact that various analysts project the overall market revenue for cognitive sciences to exceed $60 billion by 2025. As the cognitive era evolves, it will likely become another key decision making tool in the toolbox of CXOs; vital for the right applications but not entirely replacing traditional business & advanced analytics capabilities that complement the human thought process. In a nutshell, the man-machine dichotomy is not "either-or", it is unequivocally "both-and".-*Debashish Banerjee, Managing Director at Deloitte Consulting*

There is a lot of hype around "artificial intelligence," but it will often serve best as an augmentation rather than replacement of human analysis because it's equally important to keep asking the right questions as it is to provide the answers.-*Souma Das, Managing Director, India, Qlik*

Analytics of Things Continues to be a Game Changer

Internet of Things and Analytics of Things: The Indian Internet of Things (IoT) market is set to grow to $15 billion by 2020 from the current $5.6 billion. Just about every type of company seemed to have an IoT strategy in 2016. However, today, IoT is more about Data Than It Is Things. The original description of "Internet of Things," was describing a network of connected physical objects. But in 2016, it was apparent that this initial description didn't consider the importance of data or cloud computing. So now, IoT isn't about connecting billions of objects to the Internet, it is really going to be all about the data and the ability of organizations to gain insights out of all of this data. This means that getting value from data goes beyond devices, sensors and machines and includes all data including that produced by server logs, geo location and data from the Internet-*Sunil Jose, Managing Director, Teradata India*

The "Internet of Things" is exploding. It is predicted that the number of device connected would reach 50 billion by 2020. Most of these smart devices would be in factories, energy sector, health care systems, home appliances and wearable devices. The vital data so generated would enable us to track health parameters, optimize machine performance, and reduce response time for breakdowns and also save lives. In order to create real value of IoT/IIoT, the Sensors & Communications node needs to integrate with the Analytics infrastructure, else it will be a simple data collection exercise. The technologies & skills related to IoT protocols, edge analytics & real time sensor analytics will be the key differentiators for its success & adoption in the market-*Vinay Gupta, Head of Analytics at Suzlon*

Enabling real-time automated decision taking systems

There is a visible shift across many big data and analytics users to streaming and real time analytics. Businesses particularly digital advertising, ecommerce, logistics & transportation are looking to leverage ream time analytics and are heavily invested in this space. This is also apparent from the elevated adoption levels of Apache Spark Streaming, Apache Storm or Twitter's Heron-*Srikanth Sundarrajan, Principal Architect at InMobi*

Enterprises are increasingly enabling *real-time automated decision taking* systems whether to streamline operations or mitigate risk. The older rule-based systems are now being replaced by a new generation of systems powered by online machine learning and artificial intelligence – these are self-learning systems that can recalibrate in an automated manner and can be deployed on a large-scale-*Pradeep Gulipalli, Co-founder at Tiger Analytics*

Analytics is made invisible, embedded within the system

Analytics works best when it's a natural part of people's workflow. In 2017, analytics will become pervasive and the market will expect analytics to enrich every business process. This will often put analytics into the hands of people who've never consumed data, like store clerks, call-center workers2, and truck drivers-*Deepak Ghodke, Country Manager, Tableau*

Technologies that nudge us to drink water, take regular walk breaks, or inform us that our cab has arrived have become commonplace. This is not restricted to consumer facing decisions. In fact, businesses in 2016 are beginning to realize the value of this kind of data and deploy on-demand analytics to drive better decisions. They are capturing and streaming unstructured data, blending it with other data sources, deploying analytical models to unearth insights, and are using rules engines to drive applicable "nudges"-*Mihir Kittur, Co-founder, Ugam*

Fintech is growing and so is Fintech Analytics

Going by the events of the last year (2016), Fintech will clearly emerge as the most challenging as well as beneficial. The linkage of various identity proofs to uniquely identify a person and their financial footprint would be the key to the mission to drive out corruption and black money-*Dr Nupur Pavan Bang, Associate Director, Thomas Schmidheiny Centre for Family Enterprise, Indian School of Business*

Financial institutions are moving rapidly towards "digitization" and educating their customers to adopt digital channels for day-to-day activities. With eroding revenue streams, intensifying competition, and ever-increasing customers' expectation financial institutions need to explore new way of doing business. Measuring customer relationship, evaluating the customer journey and recommending right bundle of product & services at the right price in real time through technology enabled digital platform will be the vital enablers to improve customers' banking experience-*Suman Singh, Chief Analytics Officer, ZAFIN*

Rise of Self-Service Analytics

The realization that what delivers impact is not automated MLR or one-size fits all solutions, but context driven customized solutions that leverage business know-how (that probably exists deep within a company) and domain knowledge (of expert consultants with rich industry and applied analytics experience) will dawn on most business leaders in 2017-*Randhir Hebbar, Cofounder at Convergytics*

Technological advancement has led to tools for **Self Service Business Intelligence or Self Analytics**. This approach meets the needs of data producers and consumers alike, adding speed and agility to the process while protecting organizational data and the system overall with a single version of the truth-*Tejinderpal Singh Miglani, CEO, Incedo Inc*

There has been a paradigm shift in deriving business value from analytics owing to the exponential growth in the volume, variety and complexity of data. Today's competitive business environment asks for democratization of analytics with self-service capabilities to meet the time-to-insight demands. Self-service work benches, packaged analytics, dashboards, visualization frameworks and collaboration tools for data scientists (built right into the analytics frameworks) are gaining popularity. The spotlight has now shifted from IT-led reporting to business-led self-service analytics. Self-service allowing "regular" users to derive value from large data assets owned by enterprises is the way forward. Stating that, the specialists will not be redundant. In fact, there will an even greater demand to ensure that they manage and provide the entire infrastructure and a strong footing for decision making across the organization -*Jobin Wilson, Principal R&D Architect-Data Sciences, Flytxt*

Democratization and consumerization of analytics

More organizations are "democratizing" Business Intelligence (BI) and analytics to enable a broad range of non-IT users, from the executive level to frontline personnel, to do more on their own with data access and analysis via self-service BI and visual data discovery such as drag-and-drop dashboards-*Anil Chawla, Managing Director, Customer Engagement Solutions, Verint Systems.*

More data is now available to companies of all sizes. So more easy access to data within a company; sources to find external data will be a trend that I see. Companies can partner each other & leverage each other's data. One DTH company knows when you move residences & that data can help a Retailer who sells furniture or is in that catchment. I believe that in year 2017 more marketers will leverage each other's data to build more effective analytics solutions-*Ajay Kelkar, Co- founder of Hansa Cequity*

Mobile first Omni channel strategy

With increasing penetration of mobile phones, the number of mobile apps have sky rocketed. Due to the limited space on these mobile phones, consumers are engaging with apps that create value for them2. To stay relevant, the apps developers are using app analytics to understand their users' profile and transaction behaviour to fine tune their product features and offering to increase user experience and engagement. We will continue to see analytics playing a larger role to declutter the space-*Debasmit Mohanty, CEO & Founder, StratLytics*

With increased penetration of mobile, companies are taking a Mobile First approach to engage consumers, leading to progress in Mobile Analytics. With the available location and motion sensing capabilities, significant progress was made in data collection in a privacy compliant fashion to determine what, when, where, and why of the activities that consumers engage in. This data is enabling improved insight and reach for business growth and consumer experience improvement-*Amit Deshpande, Vice President, Analytic Consulting Group, Epsilon*

Leverage GeoSpatial analytics in improving business models

In 2016, we have seen "Geo spatial analytics" gain good amount of momentum in India. Geo spatial analytics refers to mapping of events to point in time locations. With a massive adoption of mobile devices across

India in the past year and businesses getting more digitized, there are lots of "time and place" data that is being collected today. Besides mobile devices, emergence of sensors with respect to smart cities in India, drones being evaluated in agricultural and construction sectors, emergence of social media in real time, we are seeing tremendous business potential in terms of leveraging **Geo spatial analytics in improving business models** and this trend will only continue to grow-*Sunil Shirguppi, Senior Vice-President – Big Data and Analytics at Happiest Minds Technologies*

In 2016, businesses found value in understanding the 'where' factor of data and the ability to query location based information or location analytics into their existing analytics. Business intelligence solutions along with geographic analysis brought forth insights that helped companies better communicate with their customers, create more targeted promotions and pursue previously unrecognized cross-selling opportunities-*Manish Choudhary, SVP, Global Innovation and MD, Pitney Bowes India*

Analytics Governance Platforms

The use of analytical models is significantly increasing across business functions (marketing, sales, risk, pricing, etc.) and business & product lines of the enterprise. They are at different stages of deployment and being used continuously by various business users simultaneously. However, post implementation of such models, businesses are not necessarily being able to track how these models are performing and not sure if they are delivering the promised value. Neither do the businesses know the inter linkage effect of all these models working together.

With the increasing use of analytical models in business decisions, consolidating them in a single technology console, monitoring the health of analytics implementations and model performance is becoming a crucial need for business leadership and regulators. This will help track the analytics performance, demonstrated ROI and avoid the risk of incorrect decisions made because of analytics. 'Analytics governance platforms' will gain prominence across all large enterprises and will become mainstream to monitor the analytics deployment through workflows. The ROI of the analytics governance platforms will be seen in the long-term and would reap the benefits of governing complex analytics environments in a single platform with more visibility to the analytics ROI-*Prithvijit Roy, CEO, and Co-founder, BRIDGEi2i Analytics Solutions*

2.19 Ten Emerging Analytics Startups in India to watch for in 2016
BHASKER GUPTA JAN 31, 2016

India is welcoming a new breed of entrepreneurs and has recently evolved to become the third largest base of technology startups in the world. With about 4,200 startups in its kitty, it all comes down to the survival of the fittest.

However, our niche being the analytics community, we consider startups from different domains such as analytics services, analytics product startups in hospitality, marketing, etc. So, here are those top 10 fighters for the year 2016 (listed in alphabetical order) that have not only shown tremendous growth but also hold huge potential for their future.

Altiscale

The Altiscale Data Cloud is a fully managed Big Data platform, delivering instant access to production-ready Hadoop and Spark on the world's best Big Data infrastructure. Altiscale is led by an experienced, renowned Hadoop team from Yahoo! including the Founder CEO, Raymie Stata, who was the former Yahoo! CTO and a well-known advocate of

Apache Software Foundation & CTO, David Chaikenand former Yahoo! Chief Architect.

With development centers in Palo Alto, Champaign (Illinois) and Chennai and sales offices in many cities, Altiscale has grown rapidly in the last few years and boasts of many marquee customers across various industries including Financial Services, Manufacturing, Healthcare, Marketing and Digital Media & Gaming.

The Altiscale Data Cloud is "always on" & secure. Their solution is always up to date with the latest production-ready releases, so the end-users can take advantage of the most recent innovation.

Dextro Analytics

Dextro Analytics helps clients take better decisions by deriving differentiating foresight and integrating customized solutions based on their revolutionary Artificial Intelligence and machine learning platform. In a short span of time, Dextro has acquired impressive clientele in North

America, South East Asia and Australia, the list including Fortune 100 companies.

Mr. Ajith Govind and Mr. Manmit Shrimali, co-founded Dextro analytics with the belief that they are re-defining the analytics and consulting industry. Dextro Analytics is building a rewarding culture with centricity on the client and employee. This is facilitated by creating unique policies which ensure continuous reward and feedback to each and every employee.

GlobCon Technologies

Glob Con Technologies is an analytics company providing cutting-edge solutions in Big Data, Customer and Marketing Analytics, Social Media, Product Strategy, Market Research, Human Capital Management, Business Intelligence and Sales Planning.

At Glob Con, we proudly position ourselves as a management consultancy with a focus on analytics to help our clients improve business outcomes. With real-time big data analytics solutions, our clients can accelerate decision-making in fast paced markets. They can also prepare for change by forecasting consumer trends using our predictive analytics package and improve their customer relations using our smart social media solutions. Our strong team of data scientists strives to provide actionable insights. With domain experts from Consulting, Finance, Retail, E-commerce, FMCG, Healthcare, Manufacturing and Sports we specialize in customizing our solutions for your specific needs. Our services come neatly packaged in easy-to-use interfaces.

Glob Con was founded by Tanmay Bhandari and Vishal G., when the two shared their love for numbers and passion for solving real-world problems with data. They share over a decade of strong analytics experience, and have earned a reputation for attacking their customer's hidden pain points. The company is based out of (but not restricted to) Mumbai. For more information, write to info@globcontech.com.

Incedo

Incedo Inc. was founded in 2011, when the technology unit of India bulls was spun out as an independent organization. With 40+

marquee clients in sales, marketing, data visualization, Interactive analytics and self-service BI, their analytics solutions are supported by a deep expertise in data management services for data collection, cleansing, consolidation and governance to ensure consistency in the use and maintenance of data.

Incedo is a Bay Area Headquartered technology firm with a track record in delivering large scale initiatives with the nimbleness, creativity and personal attention of a startup. They work with organizations in the Life Science and Financial Services verticals to implement business intelligence solutions that provide multiple perspectives and visualizations utilizing a variety of analytical tools and modeling techniques.

nFactorial

nFactorial Analytical Sciences enables enterprises to turn employee experience to customer loyalty. The company was founded by Dr. Arun Krishnan with over 17 years of experience in analytics and computing and his team has a combined experience of over 50 years across multiple organizations and countries in academia and industry.

Incorporated in 2014 in Bangalore, the year old startup is already in discussions with Healthcare, Retail, Travel, Hospitality, Banks, FMCG, BPO and IT services companies.

nFactorial's real-time solution n!Gage provides leaders and managers with actionable insights to proactively Identify burning employee and customer issues immediately, design and monitor the impact of relevant interventions in real-time as well as engage positively with employees to drive customer loyalty and revenue. The platform utilizes a performance centric model to gather employee and customer feedback on a real-time basis. Deployed in the IBM cloud, the platform is secure, scalable, reliable and customizable.

Perceptive Analytics

Perceptive Analytics is a fast-growing data Analytics Company focused on e-commerce, Retail and Pharmacy industries. Based in Hyderabad with offices in San Francisco, New York, Boston and Miami, they boast of two of the Fortune 500 clients and TATA Group Company in India.

Their CEO, Chaitanya Sagar, is an alumnus of Indian School of Business and believes in using a Five Second principle. So, no matter how many GB the data, an executive dashboard must be intelligible within 5 seconds so their customers can start using it right away. Moreover, the clients get to work on cutting edge data analytics.

They hire data scientists and those with awesome analytical and programming skills, people who love to challenge and expand your capabilities. They have a weekly "POP (Present-Over-a-Pizza) show" meeting where everyone presents their own project and gets to learn from each other!

PropheSee

Founded in November 2014 in Delhi, by three co-founders, Ishaan Sethi, Harshil Gurha and Jitesh Luthra, PropheSee is a marketing analytics SaaS platform working with brands to help them take control of their digital data & make the most educated decisions in one consolidated platform.

In the progressive data analytics arena, brands are using multiple platforms to manage their digital presence which often leads to problems around data reconciliation & a significant budget & time waste. As a consolidated tool, PropheSee leads to increased capital efficiency. Additionally, by tracking end-to-end digital data, brands can take a much more cohesive approach to digital as decision makers are able to analyze each channel in isolation as well as any effects a channel may have on another.

They have raised their SEED round from the Indian Angel Network & Stanford Angels & Entrepreneurs India, marking the latter's first investment in the country. Moreover, they were listed by SutraHR as among the 100 startups to watch in 2016.

Quantta Analytics

Founded by Malvika and Vinay Bawri, Quantta Analytics is a spatial and predictive analytics firm with offices in Palo Alto, Kolkata and Bangalore. They use analytics to answer three simple but powerful questions – who will buy from you, what will they buy from you and where will they buy it from. Clients use their services to drive revenue and reduce risk by creating synergy between their products and the customer.

Working for the energy, banking and financial, retail, FMCG, and fast food industries, they have built unique Software as a Service (SaaS) to help clients understand their data effectively.

Their vision is to lead 21st century innovation by nurturing top talent to incubate ideas that bring elegance, simplicity, and productivity to everyday life. From better functionality to beautiful interfaces, their innovations will change the way their client's work.

Repufact

RepuFact is one of the world's best Review Management and Customer Intelligence solution for the Hospitality & Tourism industry. They track User Generated Content across 125+ different internet venues and 25 global languages to extract customer reviews of all kinds, forms &languages, analyze them and give meaningful insights and quantifiable scores across various functions of the hospitality industry. This enables organizations to measure their efficiencies, evaluate standards and plan improvisation on focused parameters while engaging with the customers effectively.

The state of the art RepuFact sentiment analysis engine uses our proprietary "Natural Language Processing and Semantic Algorithms" to identify "POS Tags" (Part of Speech Tags) in a review and return a "Sentiment Value Score" for each reference & mention.

All the sentiment value scores then translate into the aggregated scores at a Department level and for relevant Key Performance Indicators. "Hospitality keyword Banks and Libraries" are derived and designed by our in-house NLP experts and a world class "Ontologies and Taxonomies" are created by data scientist for Guest Intelligence Analytics. Our average customer, a 40 room & 3 star properties have seen multiple benefits of working with us.

Scienaptic Systems

Headquartered in New York, USA and its engineering center in Bangalore, India Scienaptic Systems is a new age technology and analytics company.

Their vision is to infuse robust decision science in organizations. Scienaptic has added decades of analytics and functional experience to develop its own proprietary platform, called Ether. Built on a sophisticated big data tech stack, Ether is aimed at dramatically reducing friction in managing, exploring, modeling and lastly, distilling key actionable insights from data.

The purpose of Ether is to seamlessly enable everyday interactions between technology, business processes and humans. Scienaptic's full suite of analytics solutions is aimed at reducing end to end development time by 90% and deliver exponential increase to our customer's KPIs.

We pride ourselves in bringing together some of the best programmers, machine learning scientists and domain consultants globally available. Scienaptic founders, mentors and investors are an eclectic group of seasoned business leaders inspired by the shared vision to industrialize big data analytics and engineering at scale for businesses.

http://analyticsindiamag.com/10-emerging-analytics-startups-in-india-to-watch-for-in-2016/

2.20 Ten startups that are changing the face of Virtual Reality in India

We approached virtual reality startups in India and came up with 10 start-ups that are changing the way humans interact with computers and enriching the real world with an unrealistic approach towards videos, sound, graphics and more.

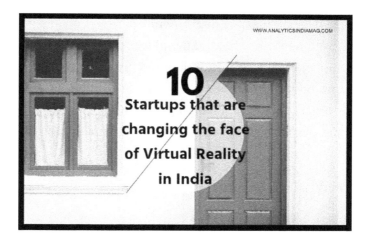

An initiative by Analytics India Magazine in partnership with **AnalytixLabs**, the focus of this study is to compare the salary trends amongst professionals, specializing in different skills and tools, while also providing an overview of the analytics salary in key Indian metropolitan cities as well as companies and across various experience levels.

Watching those sci-fi movies have sent us cold shivers and have left us with the nerve crackling experience of walking around mars, meeting Frankenstienish creatures or battling a war. Experiencing all of these as if it were real is all thanks to virtual reality. Not just movies, VR is trending down in various other sectors such as real estate, hardware, marketing and gaming, making a serious play for business relevance.

With companies such as Google, Face book, Microsoft and Samsung staking their fortune on virtual reality market, there is more than enough room for start-ups to make an impact. The global investments in AR/VR have been overwhelming with the data from tech advisor Digi-Capital showing that investments in VR touched $1.1 billion in the first two months of this year, far exceeding the $700 million invested during 2015. However, going by the data from research platform Tracxn, only nine of the 74 Indian startups in AR/VR have received funding.

While the startups struggle with various challenges such as infrastructure and network strength, the industry is booming and is evident with the companies that are adorning the list. We approached virtual reality startups in India and came up with 10 such start-ups (listed in alphabetical order) that are changing the way humans interact with computers and enriching the real world with an unrealistic approach towards videos, sound, graphics and more.

GazeMatic

Founded in the year 2015 by Karthikeyan NG & MohanRaj MS, GazeMatic prides in 'Teleport Call'. Located in Bangalore, GazeMatic is the hub of all the de-facto companies in Indian startup eco system.

Believing in the fac1t that communication in a virtual environment is going to be the new way to connect with people around the world whenever and wherever you are, they have built up "THE CALLER", a mobile application for Virtual Reality. The app is first of its kind voice caller application where you can teleport yourself when you are on a call with your friend.

Crossing a whopping 5000 downloads within the first month after releasing the product, without spending a single penny on marketing, it has more than 2000+ experience videos and the users have made 20K+ calls till now. Currently available only in Android Play store as a free app, they are all set to launch their iOS app and will also be soon on Samsung and Oculus store apps. Their breakthrough is going to be releasing the app with Live Streaming feature which will make the app literally a teleporting app.

Majority of their users are from US, UK, Germany, Russia followed by India.

Grey Kernel

'Grey Kernel' is one of India's first Virtual Reality & Advance Visualization tech start-up and their flagship product "IRA VR" is one of the most successful Virtual Reality products from India on Play store.

It has received an overwhelming response within a few weeks of the launch and currently hosts content developed In-house by Grey Kernel as well as curate from some of the Indian/International VR Studios.

Founded in 2015, Grey Kernel's first VR demo for Oculus Rift DK2 was featured among top 10 weekly downloads on Road To VR, one of the leading International VR e-journal and in a few weeks' time the company was able to pull off an International VR project. Whereas most of the Indian VR production Studios are focusing on creating Monoscopic 360 degree videos, Grey Kernel is leading the space by creating Stereoscopic/Interactive VR content & solving engineering/distribution for their clients that involves real estate, media & publishing and marketing agencies.

Meraki

Meraki was founded in November 2015 by Arvind Ghorwal, Sairam Sagiraju, Parth Choksi and Agam Garg and is one of India's first Virtual Reality content production studios for consumers as well as businesses. They create 360 degree films for events, tourism, sports, adventure, advertisements, experiential marketing, real estate, weddings, news and fiction.1

The founding team comprises of graduates from IIT Bombay and a Filmmaker which best reflects the nature of the Virtual Reality content market which is a combination of technology and creativity.

The company has made an outstanding mark within a short span since its inception and has bagged six major projects from clients such as Star Sports, Network 18, Percept Pictures and Channel V. They also continuously try and explore the immense possibilities of storytelling in Virtual Reality by producing their own proprietary content. Both, 'Strangers Again' and 'A Mumbai Summer' were well received and are now available on Milk VR.

Asia Cup, which was held in February was Meraki's one of the biggest projects in which they covered the in-stadium experiences of matches between India and Bangladesh and India and Pakistan at Mirpur, Dhaka. The India vs Bangladesh match that they captured was the world's first cricket match in VR.

SmartVizX

SmartVizX Pvt. Ltd is one of the highest funded start-ups in VR space and offers a wide range of immersive and interactive VR solutions across devices such as mobile, laptop, desktop, tablet etc. SmartVizX has been named as 'Start-up of The Week' by NASSCOM under its 10000 start-ups initiative.

Currently catering to the AEC (Architecture, Engineering and Construction) industry, the company's products VI-VIZ, ARCH-VIZ, ARCH-VIZ (Mobile) etc., offer features such as, controllable and interactive walkthroughs of entire project, view of immediate surroundings from balconies and other vantage points, actual simulation of sunlight during any particular time of the day etc. Potential customers can experience a realistic simulation, of how their future property would look like.

Developer Group, DASNAC, Rock Worth, NIIT, The Quint, Interglobe Aviation, Express Avenue and Express Group etc. are some of its clients and further plans to bring VR technology to domains as diverse as healthcare, edutainment, gaming content etc.

SmartVizX has raised an Angel Round of $ 5,30,000 from the Indian Angel Network (IAN) and Stanford Angels and Entrepreneurs. The company is already present in New Delhi, Mumbai, Bengaluru, Dubai and is in extensive talks to establish a presence in The United States.

SpectraVR

SpectraVR Studios is India's premiere full stack Virtual Reality Content Studio. Based out of Mumbai, the company was founded in 2015 and is funded by Rothenberg Ventures, a leading investor firm based out of San Francisco.

The company excels at story-telling & has built a strong team of creative directors, designers, technologists and VR enthusiasts to deliver on a wide range of services. Whether it's a live experience or creative media or animated 3D virtual reality experiences and games, SpectraVR is able to deliver quality on every platform in every vertical.

SpectraVR has already conceptualized & created over 30 VR experiences starting from December 2015, for various top brands in India such as Mercedes Benz, Maruti Suzuki, Kingfisher, Standard Chartered Bank, The Deltin Hotels, WonderLa Amusement Park, Red Chillies Entertainment for promotion of a song from their movie Dilwale, T-Series Music Company, Times Now news channel for their 'Amazing Indians' show with the Hon. Prime Minister Mr. Narendra Modi, to name a few. In addition to these SpectraVR has developed VR games around Cricket & Hang Gliding sport.

Tesseract Inc.

Tesseract Inc. is an Indian hardware company that has created the world's first 360 Virtual Reality Cameras. Its vision is to enable everybody to capture memories in 360 and VR to relive them as if they are in the same moment back again. Imagine the next IPL where Virat Kohli hits a six, and with these cameras you would be able to feel as if you are sitting next to Virat but being completely at home.

It aims to completely transform the way you record, consume and share content. And all this with hardware/software completely innovated, designed and manufactured out of India.

Their previous technologies such as Methane 360 VR are being used by companies like Make My Trip, Tistus (leading real-estate firm in Brazil), Solund House (leading real-estate firm in Denmark), Nestaway, Grabhouse and other top travel and real-estate firms in India.

Tesseract is all set to launch their consumer grade 360 Virtual Reality Camera – ViCAM later this year which is the world's smallest 360 Virtual Reality Camera.

Transcend

At Transcend their belief is going beyond limits. Founded in October 2015, at the Foothills of Shivalik ranges, Chandigarh, it comprises of a team of passion driven architects, thinkers, filmmakers, photographers, producers, technologists, R&D specialists, and developer.

With a focus on next level of interaction and storytelling, they are currently developing highly immersive VR content and applications for tourism, education, real estate, brand story, documentaries, events and education sector.

Trimensions

Trimensions is an award-winning digital services and UX design agency based in Delhi. It pioneers in both virtual and augmented reality in India and spans across different verticals including education, entertainment and enterprise.

It specializes in developing creative new approaches to train people and has ventured into 360 video production and AR for machine maintenance and VR for training simulations.

Since its inception, Trimensions has been focused on bringing exciting new technologies into the reach of the common Indian citizen and hence emphasizes on good, clear design and user experience. Offering a large variety of end-to-end services including graphic and web design, Trimensions aim to change user's perception of reality.

WOWSOME

One of the fastest growing Indian start-up in the field of Augmented Reality, WOWSOME was founded in 2015, by Vishal Reddy and Karan Bhangay. It is one of the selected portfolio company headquartered at T-Hub Hyderabad. With a growing portfolio of around 50 brands and several major publishers, they obsessively research to discover new applications for AR that will merge advertising and entertainment.

Their expertise lies in dynamic development of relevant media using Computer Vision. WOWSOME adds real time, situation based, interactive, visually stunning, and virtually unlimited digital content to environment around you by extending it to your smartphone and tablet. It works in harmony with the real world and enhances the real-life experience with relevant information.

Xenium

Xenium has been developing Virtual Reality solutions from last two years and they believe that VR empowers businesses with new visualization techniques, developers with fresh creative potential, and researchers with tools that accelerate scientific discovery. They started doing virtual reality when wireless Headgears like Oculus Rift, Samsung Gear VR were not available in the Market.

It offers a full range of products and support including the complete VR systems, custom solution design, and application development. Their virtual reality solutions are helping both enterprises and in academics by enabling innovation and enhanced communication.

Xenium is the fourth company in the world & first in India to have done a live streaming using Virtual Reality. The real-time broadcast was captured through 8 vantage points (i.e. 8 units of 360 Live Shooting Camera) and streaming done over a 10 MBS line on the Telecom Network, proving the robustness and reliability of the Telecom Network at large.

Conclusion:

While there has been a lot of buzz across Silicon Valley with the VR, India is still taking its baby steps towards this sector. According to a report by Goldman Sachs published earlier this year, the combined virtual reality and augmented reality market is estimated to reach anywhere from $80B to $182B in market size, by 2025. And with the investors, innovators and those who truly understand the DNA of VR rolling high, it is quite likely that 2016 would be the year of opportunity for VR segment in India.

http://analyticsindiamag.com/10-startups-changing-face-virtual-reality-india/

2.21 Top 10 Analytics Training Institutes in India – Ranking 2016

As part of the annual ranking process, Analytics India Magazine brings all the aspiring Data Scientists this year's 'Top 10 Analytics Training Institutes in India'. AIM has been conducting this ranking for four years now and has successfully provided insights into the analytics education world.

As part of the annual ranking process, Analytics India Magazine brings all the aspiring Data Scientists this year's '**Top 10 Analytics Training Institutes in India**'. AIM has been conducting this ranking for four years now and has successfully provided insights into the analytics education world. The journey for this study started 2 months back where each institute was analyzed minutely on various parameters to come up with the finest 10 training institutes out of the 18 nominations received by AIM.

The institutes have been ranked on 5 parameters viz Course Content, Pedagogy, External Collaborations, Faculty and Other Attributes like, Placement Assistance, Virtual Labs Events, LMS, etc. For every participating institute, each parameter was rated on the scale of 1-5 where 1 is for Worst and 5 is for Best to arrive at an overall ranking. Also, all parameters were assigned equal weights to get to the final ranking. Apart from these parameters, student as well expert feedback has been taken into consideration to arrive at this year's '**Top 10 Analytics Training Institutes in India**'.

Please note, just the training institutes offering analytics courses have been considered and universities / B-schools offering analytics programmes are not a part of this ranking.

1. Jigsaw Academy

Headquarter City: Bangalore

Cities of Operation: Global; Online training.

Year of inception: 2011

Flagship Analytics Program: Data Science with R which dovetails into Big Data Analytics

Mode of Delivery: Online Training with Virtual Classroom and Virtual Lab

Founded in 2011 by Gaurav Vohra and Sarita Digumarti – who have worked in some of the leading analytics companies around the world- Jigsaw Academy provides training in the field of analytics and Big Data. The academy has been growing rapidly year after year since its inception and has the record for training the most number of analytics professionals in India. Alumni of Jigsaw Academy are present across the breadth of analytics companies. The constant endeavour to improve their teaching methodology and have the most up to date content is what distinguishes Jigsaw Academy from other training providers.

Course Content (*Rating 4.6*): Jigsaw Academy has a unique method to deliver the best designed course content. Jigsaw Academy hires subject matter experts from the industry to build out a curriculum which is most relevant to a specific role in the industry. For example, the flagship course offered by Jigsaw Academy on Data Science with R was designed by an aero-scientist who was working at one of the world's foremost aircraft manufacturer while he was creating the course. This model ensures the course content meets the career objectives of not only aspiring students but also aspiring professionals at various stages of their careers. The course content is in-depth and comprehensive in nature enabling a trainee to be industry-ready for a particular role. Also, continuous feedback from ongoing batches to improve the course is a key differentiator for Jigsaw. They claim to have a CSAT of 4.81 on 5.

Pedagogy (*Rating 4.8*): The focus of Jigsaw's pedagogy is providing practical hands-on training to its students. Hence, in line with this pedagogical philosophy, their courses are designed in a way, that it emphasizes hands on learning by using large and actual business datasets for students to practice on the Jigsaw Lab. Case-studies also focus on practical industry problems. Strong industry exposure is also provided via multiple data science contests using datasets provided by different companies.

Faculty (Rating 4.7): 100% of the instructors at Jigsaw Academy have analytics industry experience allowing them to teach from a practical view-point. 30% of them hold a PhD. The best part is the faculty to student ratio of 1:30 which provides for better interaction and support.

External Collaborations (*Rating 4.8*): Jigsaw Academy boasts of quite a few external collaborations which include SDA Bocconi (Europe) ranked 7th Worldwide in Business & Management, IIM Bangalore, Manipal Education, SOIL and IFIM.

Other Attributes (*Rating 4.9*): Jigsaw Academy has been the pioneer for virtual labs in the analytics space in India. The institute also conducts several hackathons and webinars as part of the continuous learning experience. Jigsaw has its own LMS, the Jigsaw Learning Centre (JLC), which is robust and provides all the learning material along with case studies and assignments to students. They also have an in-house film team which include National Award winners, who ensure that the course content is not only relevant but also interesting to view and easy to learn.

*The overall rating for Jigsaw Academy is **4.76***

2. AnalytixLabs

Headquarter City: Delhi-NCR

Cities of Operation: India, USA & South East Asia

Year of inception: 2011

Flagship Analytics Program: Business Analytics 360, Advance Big Data Science

Mode of Delivery: Online and Classroom

AnalytixLabs is a training solutions firm led by McKinsey, IIM, ISB and IIT alumni. They offer a wide array of courses spanning across Data Science, Big Data Analytics and Data Visualization along with

global certifications. In addition to individual professional training, they also deliver training programs to corporate.

Course Content *(Rating 4.6)*: The crux of AnalytixLabs courses is training students for the various job roles in the analytics industry. Hence the courses are designed keeping in mind the job responsibilities of these roles and are validated by professionals from that field itself. The courses offered are at various levels starting from Beginners to intermediate to advanced level allowing students to choose based on their capabilities.

Pedagogy *(Rating 4.7)*: Providing practical training to its students is at the heart of AnalytixLabs' pedagogy. As part of this, the training includes lot of case examples close to real-life situations to get the students prepared for their jobs. Also, the institute blends all three ways of learning modes – classroom, live online and video-based for an effective training program delivery.

Faculty *(Rating 4.6)*: A lot of faculties at AnalytixLabs come with industry experience from firms like McKinsey, Deloitte, Genpact, Fidelity and Face book. On an average, the faculties have 8-10 years of hands-on experience in the field of analytics.

External Collaborations *(Rating 4.6)*: The institute has two strong external collaborations – One with Wiley for the Big Data certification and second with Data Byte Academy in Malaysia to deliver their courses and this is recognized by HR Ministry of Malaysia.

Other Attributes *(Rating 4.6)*: The institute provides complete placement assistance to its students. A team of professionals help the students right from creating their resumes to getting them ready for the interviews. AnalytixLabs provides various platforms to the candidates to install and use the software based on their course.

*The overall rating for AnalytixLabs is **4.62***

3. International School of Engineering (INSOFE)

Headquarter City: Hyderabad

Cities of Operation: Hyderabad, Bangalore

Year of inception: 2011

Flagship Analytics Program: Certificate Program in Big Data Analytics and Optimization

Mode of Delivery: Classroom

INSOFE is an institute training students and working professionals in Applied Engineering with current focus area in Data science/Big data analytics. In its endeavour to provide quality education to its students, INSOFE works towards creating their courses in a way that meet the complex industry demands.

Course Content *(Rating 4.5)*: An amalgamation of conventional methods and cutting edge technology is what defines the courses at INSOFE. As a key differentiator, INSOFE is adding value to its course by including cutting edge technologies like matrix factorization and deep learning methods. The course starts from the basic skills needed to be a data scientist and gradually moves to practical applications.

Pedagogy *(Rating 4.5)*: INSOFE's pedagogy puts weightage on 3 stakeholders -industry, universities and fellow practitioners to make their students competitive. The institute takes requirement/ inputs from its 3 stakeholders to design their curriculum.

Faculty *(Rating 4.9)*: All the faculty members at INSOFE hold a Ph. D. In fact 2 of INSOFE's mentors, Dr. Dakshinamurthy V Kolluru and Dr. Sreerama K V Murthy, have been listed among the '10 Most Prominent Analytics Academicians in India' clearly showcasing the quality of INSOFE's faculties.

External Collaborations *(Rating 4.5)*: INSOFE has tied up with companies, Soothsayer Pvt. Ltd and iCube individually to build a data science center and Intuceo, (a business user interface) respectively.

Other Attributes *(Rating 4.5)*: INSOFE has some leading name in the industry participating in its placement drive giving the students an excellent opportunity to start with. The institute has an in-house set up of Amazon cloud currently in use and is being expanded and upgraded to a much larger cluster.

The overall rating for International School of Engineering is 4.58

4. Edvancer

Headquarter City: Mumbai

Cities of Operation: Online; hence Global

Year of inception: 2013

Flagship Analytics Program: Certified Business Analytics Professional (R & SAS)

Mode of Delivery: Online

Edvancer provides training in analytics, data science & big data globally and has trained over 3,000 people till now. It is an IIM-IIT alumni venture which aims at creating an online analytics knowledge hub to meet the learning needs of all kinds of professionals interested in analytics.

Course Content (*Rating 4.4*): Industry experts are roped in by Edvancer to create/revise their course content as part of the process. The courses have been designed keeping in mind the skills sets needed to enter the analytics industry. It emphasizes on providing hands-on practical training to students with real-world case studies.

Pedagogy (*Rating 4.8*): Edvancer follows the pedagogy of 'Self-paced + Faculty support' allowing trainees to undergo training at their pace along with faculty support and guidance. Edvancer's pedagogy encourages students to interact with their trainers so the virtual classes are almost near to normal classes.

Faculty (*Rating 4.6*): Edvancer faculties are industry professionals with 5-10 years of experience and are trained extensively in the online pedagogy before they take classes. With 20% faculties having PhD, the faculty to student ratio is 1:12.

External Collaborations (*Rating 4.5*): Edvancer is a training partner for various companies like PwC, E&Y, Deloitte, JP Morgan, GE, Colgate Palmolive, L&T, Eclerx, Microsoft, Max Life, SBI Life etc. Also, the institute has partnered with Wiley, the world's largest education provider to provide a globally recognized certification in Big Data and Hadoop.

Other Attributes (*Rating 4.4*): Edvancer has a mix of big corporates and startups as part of their placement drive. Also, the institute conducts analytics hackathons and free webinars on analytics and big data to guide the trainees.

*The overall rating for Edvancer is **4.54***

5. SAS® Academy for Data Science

Headquarter City: Cary, NC, USA

Cities of Operation: Operation across 60 Countries

Year of inception: 1976

Flagship Analytics Program: SAS Certified Data Scientist

Mode of Delivery: Classroom and Live Web Classes1

Incepted in 1976, SAS is one of the oldest training institutes for analytics. SAS Academy for Data Science offers 3 programs in the field of analytics– certifications in big data, advanced analytics and data science.

Course Content (*Rating 4.2*): Experts from the analytics background are part of the team creating course offered by SAS. The programme not only focuses on providing theoretical knowledge but also hands-on practical training.

Pedagogy (*Rating 4.5*): SAS pedagogy is based on the principles of experiential learning. Also as an endeavor to provide practical training, the institute includes industry relevant projects and case studies. For each module, there is internal and continuous assessment so the trainees receive continuous feedback about their performance.

Faculty (*Rating 4.7*): 70% of the faculties at SAS hold a PhD. Also, the faculty members are experienced with an average of over 10 years of teaching and training experience. Faculty to student ratio is 1:15.

External Collaborations (*Rating 4.8*): SAS Education has academic alliances with some of the leading global universities like North Carolina State University, The University of Alabama to name a few. Also in India, SAS has partnered with various premier academic institutions like ISB, IIMB, IIML, IIMC, and NMIMS.

Other Attributes (*Rating 4.4*): SAS provides 24*7 accesses to SAS software and course materials to its trainees during the program. SAS has its own in-house virtual learning environment.

*The overall rating for SAS is **4.52***

6. Imarticus Learning

Headquarter City: Mumbai

Cities of Operation: Mumbai, Chennai, Bangalore, Delhi, Pune, Hyderabad, Jaipur, Coimbatore

Year of inception: 2012

Flagship Analytics Program: Certification in SAS & R

Mode of Delivery: Online and Classroom

Established in 2012, Imarticus is one of the Analytics professional education companies, which assists individuals and firms in meeting their human capital and skill set requirements. Headquartered in Mumbai, Imarticus has classroom and online delivery capabilities across India.

Course Content *(Rating 3.9)*: The fundamental principle behind Imarticus' course content is imparting in-depth knowledge of the analytics tools clubbed with key concepts of Data science and other related areas. Also to provide hands-on experience to the students, Imarticus provides a rigorous industry mentorship process to help them prepare on upcoming trends and challenges in the analytics industry.

Pedagogy *(Rating 4.2)*: Imarticus's pedagogy focuses on promoting constant discussion among the trainer and trainees. Also the pedagogy promotes group work among trainees and puts them under rigorous training process to build their ability to work under pressure.

Faculty *(Rating 4.3)*: Imarticus team of faculties is led by senior professionals from universities such as Columbia, MIT, and Harvard with a combined experience of technology and analytics.

External Collaborations *(Rating 4.5)*: Imarticus has quite a few external collaborations under their name. The institute is a National Skill Development Corporation (NSDC) training partner. Also it has come together with NSE to increase the awareness of the securities markets. Other collaboration includes Chartered Institute for Securities & Investment and International Institute of Business Analysis.

Other Attributes *(Rating 4.5)*: The institute has won numerous awards in the space of education. Imarticus has an excellent placement record of around 77% placements in the last few years.

*The overall rating for Imarticus is **4.28***

7. Ivy Professional School

Headquarter City: Kolkata

Cities of Operation: Kolkata, Bangalore, New Delhi, Pune & Online

Year of inception: 2007

Flagship Analytics Program: Diploma in Data Science

Mode of Delivery: Online and Classroom

Ivy Professional School (Ivy) provides Big Data Science & Analytics education in the country. They offer a wide range of courses from certification courses on Analytics to Big Data Science, SAS, R, Python, R, and Excel.

Course Content *(Rating 4.0)*: IVY's course content is designed to adhere to the industry requirements. These courses are already being used by Analytic companies for their internal training purpose proving its acceptance by industry. Other highlights being live projects and internship opportunity.

Pedagogy *(Rating 4.1)*: IVY's pedagogy is based on four pillars- See, Act, Interpret and Assess. See what the trainer demonstrates, Act on a real data set, Interpret the results to generate insights, and participants are assessed on their work. Other highlights, being availability of physical classroom in multiple cities, may be found.

. **Faculty** *(Rating 4.0)*: Ivy's core faculty team has experience with some of the leading organizations in the analytics industry and around 20% of them hold a PhD. Faculty to student ratio is 1:12.

External Collaborations *(Rating 4.5)*: External collaborations of the institute include Indian as well as global universities. Also Ivy in association with Maharishi University of Information Technology Noida has founded the School of Data Science which offers various courses in this stream. The institute is an official learning partner of companies like Genpact, Capgemini, HSBC, ITC, ICRA, and Moody's.

Other Attributes *(Rating 4.5)*: Around 85+ analytics companies participate in the placement drive of the institute. Also Ivy's cloud based virtual, Practice Sandbox, provides participants with after course remote access to the same software tools used in the course with large data sets. Ivy has its own LMS – new Adaptive Learning Management System (iALMS) to create a competitive learning environment using its unique Leader board feature.

*The overall rating for Ivy Professional School is **4.22***

8. IMS Proschool

Headquarter City: Mumbai

Cities of Operation: Institute operates in 9 cities across India

Year of inception: 2014

Flagship Analytics Program: Business Analytics Course

Mode of Delivery: Online and Classroom

IMS Proschool is an initiative of IMS Learning Resources. IMS Proschool has associated with NSE India to offer Business Analytics Certification Program. Also the institute is a partner of NSDC – National Skill Development Corporation, an initiative of Union Ministry of Finance to provide skill development training to the youth.

Course Content *(Rating 4.1)*: Joint Certification from NSE – India, IMS Proschool and NSDC makes the course offered by the institute a distinguishing one. This is coupled with hand-on training and cases studies from various domains to make the students industry-ready.

Pedagogy *(Rating 3.8)*: The pedagogy adopted by IMS Proschool is of taking inputs from both the academicians and industry people for preparing the course. Also to train students an opportunity with Capstone Project is provided to apply their learning.

Faculty *(Rating 3.8)*: The faculties at IMS Proschool come from institutions like IIMs, IITs, ISB and have over 5 years of experience in the field of analytics.

External Collaborations *(Rating 4.2)*: The institute has two very strong national level collaborations with NSE India and National Skill Development Corporation for their analytics program. Apart from this, Proschool offers Business Analytics program to quite a few educational institutions in India.

Other Attributes *(Rating 4.4)*: The institute organizes regular webinar by Industry professional on various analytic topics to give their students a feel of the industry. Also Proschool has developed its own proprietary LMS which is available on both desktop and mobile

*The overall rating for IMS Proschool is **4.07***

9. NIVT

Headquarter City: Kolkata

Cities of Operation: Kolkata

Year of inception: 2003

Flagship Analytics Program: NIVT Certified Analytics Pro (NCAP).

Mode of Delivery: Online and Classroom

Incepted in the year 2003, NIVT imparts technology training to young professionals in niche areas starting from beginner's courses to Data Analytics, Business Intelligence tool and other emerging technologies. The Institute aims to fill up the huge skill gap in the analytics industry across pan India.

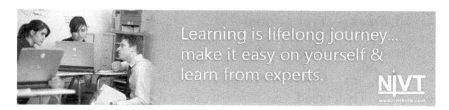

Course Content *(Rating 4.0)*: NIVT's courses aim at making its students prepared for industry roles. And to meet this objective, about 80% of the training during the course is hands-on. Also students are exposed to real time industry case studies in line with their main objective of making students industry ready.

Pedagogy *(Rating 3.7)*: NIVT provides practical training to its trainees through live project work and case studies which are more relevant in the industrial requirements. Also NIVT works on upgrading courses and delivery processes frequently to meet the ever-changing standards of the industry.

Faculty *(Rating 4.0)*: The faculties at NIVT are a mix of industry professionals and people with good amount of teaching experience in the analytics field. About 20% of faculties hold a PhD and an excellent faculty to student ratio 1:5 to provide personal attention to students.

External Collaborations *(Rating 4.1)*: NIVT is affiliated to NCVT, DGE&T, Government of India, Ministry of Labour& Employment for the ICT sector in West Bengal. Recently, the institute has collaborated with the renowned business school, United World, as their Analytics training partner.

Other Attributes *(Rating 4.1)*: NIVT makes its student's interview ready and provides analytics job related information in a timely fashion. The institute uses Blackboard, an online tool, to create Virtual Labs for collaborative learning. Also the institute organizes events, seminars and workshops on Business Analytics in various colleges.

*The overall rating for NIVT is **3.98***

10. Orange Tree Global

Headquarter City: Kolkata

Cities of Operation: Kolkata, Durgapur, Mumbai, Pune, Bangalore and Hyderabad, Gurgaon & (Chennai 2017)

Year of inception: 2009

Flagship Analytics Program: Business Intelligence and Business Analytics Program (BIBA)

Mode of Delivery: Online and Classroom

OrangeTree Global is a Business Analytics and Business Intelligence Training organization with Centers across India. The organization focuses on Business Intelligence tools like SAS, R, Python, Hadoop, Machine Learning, SPSS, and VBA.

Course Content *(Rating 3.7)*: OrangeTree Global courses are job oriented and make a student industry ready. Also mentorship by industry professionals adds value to the course content bringing in the practical aspect to make student job ready. Live projects add on to the practical approach taken by the institute.

Pedagogy *(Rating   3.6)*: The institute believes in adopting pedagogy of bottom-up approach to instill a clear understanding of expectations of analytics professionals from the industry. The institute also revises the programme annually to keep their course abreast of the changes in the industry to make it more industry relevant.

Faculty *(Rating 3.9)*: A huge number i.e., close to 60% faculties at OrangeTree Global are with PhDs. Faculties are trained by industry specialists so that they are abreast of all the industry knowledge which they can impart to the students.

External Collaborations *(Rating 4.1)*: OrangeTree Global is the official Analytics training partner for Computer Society of India. Also the institute has a tie-up with State Government of Jharkhand to offer their courses across national and state universities throughout Jharkhand.

Other Attributes *(Rating 4.0)*: OrangeTree has some of the leading companies from the industry like TCS Analytics, Genpact, HSBC Deloitte, and Fractal Analytics participating in their placement drive. Also the institute organizes hackathon and analytics related events. Virtual Labs are available to students to gain hands-on experience on analytic tools.

http://analyticsindiamag.com/top-10-analytics-training-institutes-india-ranking-2016/

2.22   10 Startups in India that are leading the race of Artificial Intelligence

Analytics India Magazine presents you a list of '**Top 10 Artificial Intelligence Start-ups**' and how each one of them is positioned differently catering to a niche area of artificial intelligence.

Artificial Intelligence has been there decades ago, but off late this field has caught pace and has been growing rapidly. Almost every organization, whether it is in the field of retail or fashion or education or banking, is trying to use artificial intelligence in a way possible to innovate and make their services user-friendly to provide convenience to their customers. AI is becoming the new face of doing business. For instance, human interaction with customers is now being replaced by chat bots.

This need for artificial intelligence by so many industries has created an environment for startups to flourish in the areas of artificial intelligence. Also the world's largest tech companies are funding start-ups in this space fueling their growth.

Analytics India Magazine presents you a list of '**Top 10 Artificial Intelligence Start-ups'** and how each one of them is positioned differently catering to a niche area of artificial intelligence.

The list of companies presented below is in alphabetic order.

AIndra Systems

AIndra Systems, incorporated in 2012, is an Artificial Intelligence based technology start-up. It is into creating Computer Vision and Machine Learning based products that address the problems of a huge magnitude in our society. With its patent-pending Face-Recognition (FR)

technology powering AIndra's smart phone based product, 'Smart Attendance Enterprise ™', it is able to deliver solutions to improve and enhance governance and productivity of various programs delivered on-the-field, for example: services like Skill training, healthcare -service delivery, financial-services, etc. in diverse remote locations.

"Drishti" AIndra's FR platform works with smartphones, laptops, desktops-with-webcam, IP-camera, tablets, etc. to authenticate the expected users/beneficiaries who are receiving certain services and verify the individual against his/her Government issued ID cards like Aadhaar Card. The SmartAttendance Enterprise(tm) works even without real-time internet connectivity using the 'Store-and-Forward' mechanism. In Healthcare, AIndra is building an affordable Cervical Cancer Screening Device with Point-of-sample collection, using their expertise in Computer Vision and Machine Learning.

Brainasoft

Brainasoft is into development of distinct and innovative AI products. Their areas of interest for software development include conversational bots, speech recognition, machine learning and human-computer interfaces. Brainasoft's flagship product i.e. Braina AI assistant is leading intelligent digital assistant software for Windows PC. Braina is used by more than 2,00,000 individuals and businesses in more than 180 countries.

Some features of Braina include speech to text dictation in third party software, play songs and videos stored locally and on online platforms such as Sound Cloud and YouTube, bring up weather information, Control PC through Android device, show news on a specific topic, learn facts from conversation and recall it when asked.

Brainasoft is soon planning to launch another innovative product like Inforobo. Inforobo will allow users to create their own AI virtual assistants and chatbot easily. Inforobo can be used for wide range of applications including customer service, device control and automation, IOT, live chat, information retrieval, website assistance etc.

Fluid AI

Fluid AI, an artificial intelligence startup, was started by brothers Raghav Aggarwal and Abhinav Aggarwal who dropped out of IIM Ahmedabad and ISB respectively to start Fluid AI.

The company's Artificial Intelligence is working in two areas. The first area is AI solutions on top of data which are able to make massively accurate predictions and take action on the same. This is helping clients undertake solutions like predicting what is the next best product to up sell a customer, what's the likelihood for a bank customer defaulting on a loan, or preventing fraud from a million transactions.

Their solution in the area of customer experience is changing the retail experience of a customer walking into a shop, bank branch or hotel lobby where they are greeted by an AI assistant smart screen. This is fundamentally changing the in-store experience allowing customers to directly interact with AI in an augmented reality environment.

Mad Street Den

Mad Street Den, headquartered in Chennai and California, is a computer vision-based artificial intelligence (AI) startup that's reimagining the future of retail. The company's first retail vertical Vue.ai is increasing business efficiencies and making shopping easier for consumers around the world.

With its team of deep tech engineers and retail experts, Mad Street Den is teaching machines to see and understand the world around them. Its technology identifies objects, people, and style preferences like colour, pattern, and texture to learn customer likes and dislikes. This personalized customer experience drives product discovery and conversions for marketplaces, brands, and online retailers around the world.

Morph.ai

Morph.ai is an AI powered B2B platform where businesses can build their own conversational services and deploy them over channels like Face book, Twitter, Slack, SMS, live-chat, in-app chat etc.

Morph.ai is building a platform that caters to all the needs of bot makers. They have pre-trained models for common use cases, reusable templates, intelligent learning from previous mistakes, storyboard to create conversation flows, integrations with multiple channels, integrations with various CRMs, dashboard for human agents to chat when AI fails.

In the consumer world, messaging is taking over the world like apps did a decade ago, presenting a huge opportunity for businesses to sell their products and services on messaging platform. Morph.ai helps business to follow the mantra "is where your users are". The users don't need to have the compulsion of installing an app to be able to use the company's services. They can buy the stuff right where they discover it. Conversational commerce removes the burden from customers and businesses and makes everything easier.

Niki.ai

Niki is an AI powered bot, which helps you complete online purchases on all your necessary services through a simple chat interface. This eliminates the need to install multiple apps and lets you make end to - end bookings on a single app. You are guided along with personalized recommendations about the service that suits you best.

Niki, backed by Ratan Tata, aspires to be a one stop destination for all your online purchasing. With a user base of over 70,000, Niki resides in Android as an App offering various services like Mobile Recharge, Utility bill payments, Cab & Bus booking, Food Ordering (Burger King) and Laundry services. Going Forward, Niki plans to be an independent platform, plugged and used on any interface, whether iOS, Messaging, Mobile OS, Wearable or otherwise.

SigTuple

SigTuple, founded by Apurv Anand, Rohit Kumar Pandey and Tathagato Rai Dastidar in 2015, uses the power of Artificial Intelligence to make Healthcare Diagnostic better. SigTuple applies the latest advances in artificial intelligence towards solving the healthcare diagnosis problem. They build algorithms which learn from medical data, and help doctors by automating disease screening and diagnosis. They enable access to these algorithms through low cost diagnostic devices and a cloud based intelligent platform.

The company's initial focus is on medical image analysis – pathology, radiology, ophthalmology – for detection of diseases and abnormalities. Their products aim to automate the manual inspection of visual data for diagnosis. This will help in improved accuracy of diagnosis by making the diagnosis process objective and standardized. Also help improve healthcare delivery by making advanced diagnostics available through low cost medical devices.

SigTuple's product Shonit (the complete peripheral blood smear analysis solution, which automates manual microscopic review of blood) is in beta usage now. Other products are in the development stage.

Skedool

Skedool.it, co-founded by Naveen Varma and DeeptiYenireddy in 2015, was started with the aim to automate repetitive everyday tasks for business executives, sales and recruiting professionals. As part of this initiative, Skedool has developed Skedool' s assistant as a blend of Artificial and Human Intelligence that quickly and accurately handles all your B2B scheduling and calendar management needs for less than 5% of

 the cost of a full time executive assistant. In addition to saving time, Skedool' s quick response time increases the conversion rate from initial outreach to getting a meeting scheduled by 40%. The company currently serves hundreds of customers including Hyperloop Transportation Technologies and Boomerang Commerce.

Skedool.it uses Natural Language Processing and Machine Learning supervised by humans to enable customers to communicate with the service via email just as they would with a human executive assistant sitting outside their office. Skedool.it is currently available for Gmail and Outlook365 and integrates with leading CRM, marketing and recruiting tools.

Staqu Technologies

Staqu Technologies Private Limited is an artificial intelligence based startup that is solving the problem of cross channel product discovery in e-commerce through the amalgamation of user experience led research and contextual research.

Staqu's products are completely research oriented and are based on deep learning, Staqu's product suite takes it a level further by using deep learning based technologies to solve existential problems customized and catering to the needs of the Indian consumers – companies and users alike.

The VGrep Suite, Staqu's flagship product suite, comprises of Visual Search, Similar Products Recommendations, Automated Attribute Generation, Fashion Trend Analysis, and Complete Look Recommendation. VGrep's Visual Search technology is a "user centric" API that can be integrated into the search engine of e-commerce companies, that lets users search for unstructured products in the e-commerce market simply by taking an image and searching for it.

vPhrase

vPhrase helps companies communicate insights in their data, in words, using AI. The company's patent pending platform, Phrazor, analyses data, derives insights and then communicates those insights, in words, in multiple languages. It automates the work of analysis and communication which is the forte of expensive domain experts and it does this at a fraction of their cost. The insights and nuances that one can explain via words cannot be explained using charts and tables alone.

vPhrase helps its clients make their internal reports easier to understand for their employees. It does that by writing personalized narratives for each employee highlighting all the important points which need attention. With vPhrase's narrative based reports, employees spend less time to understand what has happened and more time to take actions.

http://analyticsindiamag.com/10-startups-india-leading-race-artificial-intelligence/

2.23 Top 10 Analytics Courses in India – Ranking 2016

After 2 long months of in-depth and rigorous study, Analytics India Magazine is out with its annual ranking for '**Top 10 Analytics Courses in India**'. This being the fourth in the row, AIM has always been positively supporting its aspiring data scientists by providing them insights into the world of analytics education. We received 16 nominations for this study of which we have selected the finest, the best, top 10 analytics courses for all our aspiring analytics professionals.

The institutes have been ranked on 6 parameters i.e. Course Content, Pedagogy, External Collaborations, Faculty, Brand Value, and Other Attributes like, Placement Assistance, Virtual Labs Events, LMS, etc. Each participating institute has been rated on the scale of 1-5 (where 1 is for Worst and 5 are for Best) for all 6 parameters individually to arrive at an overall ranking. Equal weights were assigned to all parameters for the ranking process. Apart from these parameters, the study also considers student as well expert feedback before arriving at '**Top 10 Analytics Courses in India**' for the year 2016.

Please note, this ranking is for long term analytics programs offered by Universities / B-schools in India. This does not include training institutes for analytics.

1. PGP in Business Analytics & Business Intelligence – Great Lakes Institute of Management

- **Headquarter City:** Chennai

- **Cities of Operation:** Chennai, Bangalore, Gurgaon, Pune, Hyderabad
- **Year of inception:** 2004
- **Duration of Program:** 12 months
- **Mode of Delivery:** Weekend Classroom + Online

Great Lakes, one of the leading Business Schools in India, envisions of providing the corporate world with Business-ready Leaders. And it was in line with this vision, Great Lakes introduced their Post Graduate Program in Business Analytics (PGP-BA)to bridge the existing talent gap in the analytics industry. They have been among the first few institutes who came up with a program in Analytics.

Course Content (*Rating 4.9*): Great lakes analytics program blends Academic Excellence with Business Relevance to equip its students with skill sets required for managerial, techno-functional roles in Analytics. The curriculum is Industry Relevant which builds on the analytical foundation and industry oriented applications.

Pedagogy (*Rating 4.8*): Great Lakes adopt Blended Learning Environment (Weekend Classroom + Online) pedagogy to causes minimal disruption to work schedule. The program is designed to transform candidates to business ready analytics professionals through hands on experiential learning.

Faculty (Rating 4.8): PGP-BABI being an industry application focused course has many industry experts teaching. Around 50% of the classroom learning hours are delivered by distinguished industry experts.

External Collaborations (*Rating 4.7*): Great Lakes PGP-BABI is internationally recognized by Illinois Institute of Technology, Chicago, USA. Successful participants of the PGP-BABI program get a dual certification – a certificate from IIT, Chicago, USA in addition to the certificate from Great Lakes Institute of Management.

Brand Value (*Rating 4.7*): Founded in 2004, Great Lakes has, within a short span of 12 years, emerged as a top-ranked Business School. Great Lakes have lot of accreditations to its name. In 2014, Great Lakes were accredited by Association of MBAs (AMBA, UK) for its PGPM and PGXPM programs and became the youngest B-School in India to receive this prestigious international accreditation.

Other Attributes (*Rating 4.8*): The end-to-end career support activities are provided at Great Lakes PGPBA. Almost 66% of the PGP-BABI alumni have transitioned to Analytics roles either within their own company or in a new company.

*The overall rating for Great Lakes Institute of Management is **4.78***

2. Business Analytics and Intelligence – Indian Institute of Management (IIM B)

- **Headquarter City:** Bangalore
- **Cities of Operation:** Bangalore
- **Year of inception:** 1973
- **Duration of Program:** 1 year

- **Mode of Delivery:** Classroom; Classroom and Distance mode (online)

Established in 1973, IIM B focuses on partnering with industry and leading academic institutions, the world over to enhance the output from their courses including their analytics program Business Analytics and Intelligence

Course Content (*Rating 4.8*): The course is designed to provide in-depth subject knowledge on basic and advanced statistics in addition to learning tools and techniques. Participants are encouraged to solve case studies to understand concepts better along with a capstone assignment post each module. A real-life Industry project for a minimum of 6 months is mandatory as a part of the course to provide students with industry experience.

Pedagogy (*Rating 4.8*): IIM B implies multiple ways to make the course more industry specific and practical in nature. Their principal way of teaching is Case-based teaching and lot of practical exercises during the sessions to give a hands-on exposure to participants.

Faculty (Rating 4.9): All the faculties at the institute have a PhD showcasing the experience of their faculties. Also numerous Speakers from analytics Industry participate as guest faculty.

External Collaborations (*Rating 4.6*): IIM has external collaborations with SAS, R and Python training consultants, Qlik team for imparting technical knowledge. Also the institute has industry connect with some of the prestigious organization for promoting good Industry-Student connects.

Brand Value (*Rating 4.9*): IIMB is the only Indian business school to feature among the Top 50 B-schools on the Financial Times Executive Education 2015 Rankings and has recently topped the list of best management institutes in the 'India Ranking 2016'–the first-ever national ranking of universities by the Government.

Other Attributes (*Rating 4.5*): The institute organizes various events like conferences, workshops, and special classes in the field of analytics. The institute has Data center and analytics lab which gives access to census data and other data sources, and big data lab for participants to run through larger datasets.

*The overall rating for IIM B is **4.75***

3. Postgraduate Diploma in Business Analytics (PGDBA) – IIM Calcutta, ISI Kolkata, IIT Kharagpur (Tri-institute program)

- **Headquarter City:** Kolkata and Kharagpur
- **Cities of Operation:** Kolkata and Kharagpur
- **Year of inception:** 2015
- **Duration of Program:** 2 years
- **Mode of Delivery:** Classroom

3 institutes – IIM Calcutta, ISI Kolkata, and IIT Kharagpur have come together to offer this unique Tri-institute program in analytics. The program is a two-year full time residential program and is designed to create Business analysts and Data Scientists with skills in Statistics, Computer Science and Management.

Course Content (*Rating 4.9*): The highlight of the course is that it is a tri-institute program. Each of the three institutes focuses on separate area of business analytics, in accordance with its expertise and competence. Also there is hands-on business analytics training at a related company and continuous interaction with industry leaders throughout the course to make students industry ready.

Pedagogy (*Rating 4.9*): The curriculum across the three institutes is taught with a balanced mixture of theory and praxis. The program leverages the strengths and mutual complementarities of the three institutes.

Faculty (Rating 4.8): The students are taught by reputed faculty as well as industry leaders from each of the three institutes. Currently 51 faculties are teaching a batch of 60 students.

External Collaborations (*Rating 4.5*): The program involves interactions with industry leaders from organizations such as Microsoft, Xerox, SAS, American Express, SBI, Deloitte, KPMG, PwC, Flipkart.

Brand Value (*Rating 4.9*): All the three participating institutes are globally renowned institutes. IIT K has bagged the National IP award 2016 for Top Indian Academic institution for Patents. IIM C was the first management institute in India to be credited by AACSB, AMBA and EQUIS.

Other Attributes (*Rating 4.2*): Placement assistance is provided by a separate committee involving all the three institutes. The placements are conducted at IIM Calcutta campus

*The overall rating for this tri-institute program is **4.70***

4. Certificate program in Predictive Business Analytics – BRIDGE School of Management

- **Headquarter City:** Gurgaon
- **Cities of Operation:** Gurgaon, Noida, Bangalore

- **Year of inception:** 2013
- **Duration of Program:** The executive program duration is 51 weeks. The fresher program duration is 49 weeks1
- **Mode of Delivery:** Classroom & Online mode

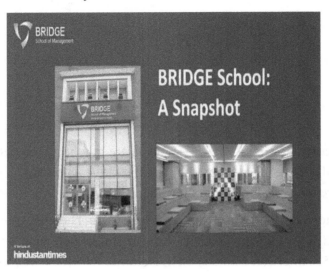

Bridge School of Management is a flagship Business School launched via a joint venture between HT Media Ltd. & Apollo Global, Inc. (USA). Bridge School offers programs in various field including Analytics (Certificate program in Predictive Business Analytics).

Course Content (*Rating 4.7*): The course is jointly offered with Northwestern University, one of the universities with leading Analytics program. Curriculum has been designed jointly by faculties of both institutes using inputs from industry practitioners in the Analytics domain to make student industry-ready.

Pedagogy (*Rating 4.6*): The program is delivered in a blended mode – classroom and Northwestern University Virtual Learning Environment – Canvas. Analytics experts from leading organizations bring in industry examples and perspective to the program adding value to the student's learning curve.

Faculty (Rating 4.4): 50% of the Analytics faculty from Northwestern and Bridge School are either PhD or Research Scholars (pursuing PhD). Also analytic industry experts participate in delivering core lectures to the analytic students.

External Collaborations (*Rating 4.4*): Bridge School has an exclusive academic collaboration with Northwestern University School of Professional Studies. Also Bridge School is a Registered Educational Provider for Project Management Institute.

Brand Value (*Rating 4.6*): Backed by India's media leader HT Media and Global Education group-Apollo Global (USA), BRIDGE School leverages best-in-class knowledge, expertise and technology for an innovative learning environment and industry relevant programs.

Other Attributes (*Rating 4.5*): Bridge's career management services team networks with the industry, academia and the students to lead the entire placement process. The institute hosts Hackathons to train their analytics professionals

*The overall rating for Bridge School of Management is **4.53***

5. Executive Program in Business Analytics – MISB Bocconi and Jigsaw Academy

- **Headquarter City:** Mumbai
- **Cities of Operation:** Powai, Mumbai
- **Year of inception:** 2014
- **Duration of Program:** 10 months
- **Mode of Delivery:** Classroom and Online

Jigsaw Academy was founded in 2011 by Gaurav Vohra and Sarita Digumarti to provide quality training in the field of analytics and Big Data. Executive Program in Business Analytics is their flagship course.

Course Content (*Rating 4.4*): The course is a healthy mix of Analytics and Big data. It focuses on live proprietary case studies in Big Data and Analytics to give hand-on experience to students.

Pedagogy (*Rating 4.5*): The pedagogy adopted is to strike a balance between work and study with a blend of online and offline classes.

Faculty (Rating 4.6): This certification program includes distinguished faculty from SDA Bocconi, Milan and industry experts apart from in-house faculties

External Collaborations (*Rating 4.6*): Jigsaw has partnered with IIMB for Big Data analytics course training and content development. Also it offers content for all analytics electives taught at SOIL in addition to teaching for the same.

Brand Value (*Rating 4.4*): Jigsaw has become a preferred choice of students, universities and companies for their data science training requirements. And its alumni base of over 40,000, students worldwide speaks about its brand value in the education industry.

Other Attributes (*Rating 4.4*): Jigsaw provides complete placement assistance and also has virtual labs and LMS facility for its students.

*The overall rating for Jigsaw Academy is **4.48***

6. Post Graduate Program in Business Analytics – Praxis Business School

- **Headquarter City:** Kolkata
- **Cities of Operation:** Kolkata and Bangalore
- **Year of inception:** 2007
- **Duration of Program:** 9 months
- **Mode of Delivery:** Classroom

Praxis Business School was early to recognize the need for trained analytics resources and introduced the first one-year full-time analytics program in the country in 2011, their flagship course being PGP in Business Analytics.

Course Content (*Rating 4.6*): The Course aims at equipping students with the tools, techniques and skills to enable a seamless absorption into the domain of Analytics and grow into the roles of Data Scientists. The program is co-created and co-delivered with Knowledge Support from PwC and ICICI Bank.

Pedagogy (*Rating 4.5*): Praxis adopts a pedagogy which his practical in nature. Students during the course are exposed to a set of near real world projects. Faculty use data available from Kaggle competitions to create assignments for students and their solutions are benchmarked against global leader boards.

Faculty (Rating 4.5): 65% of the faculty members teaching analytics subjects are associated with Analytics organizations . Also guest faculty from Praxis knowledge partners, namely ICICI Bank and PwC are part of the teaching process.

External Collaborations (*Rating 4.3*): Praxis has quite a few external collaborations 9PWC, ICICI Bank, Abzooba Inc, Ericsson Global Services, IBM Watson Labs, Modelytics) with industry professional to deliver certain special analytics classes during the course.

Brand Value (*Rating 4.2*): Praxis Business School has been the pioneer in bringing in full time education program in the field of analytics. And the program has received overwhelming response from the students and the industry. It initiation has now been followed by several institutes launching program in analytics.

Other Attributes (*Rating 4.5*): Praxis has a formal placement process to generate quality opportunities for internships followed by final placements.

The overall rating for Praxis Business School is **4.43**

7. Post Graduate Program in Data Science, Business Analytics and Big Data (PGP-DS-BA-Big Data) – Aegis School of Business, Data Science & Telecommunication

- **Headquarter City:** Mumbai
- **Cities of Operation:** Mumbai, Pune
- **Year of inception:** 2002
- **Duration of Program:** 11 months, 9 months of training (3 terms each of 3 months) + 2 months of Internships
- **Mode of Delivery:** Classroom, Online, Hybrid Model

Aegis School of Business, Data Science & Telecommunication offers various programs in 25 countries to top executives from top IT/Telecom firms. In 2015 Aegis joined hands with IBM to offer high end courses in the field of Data Science, Business Analytics, Big Data, and Cloud Computing & Mobility. Their flagship program being PGP-DS-BA-Big Data.

Course Content (*Rating 4.2*): Aegis's analytics program in association with IBM is designed with the help of leading Data Scientists to meet the Data Scientist's skills and competencies framework. A wide range of core and elective courses are offered to provide freedom to participants to design the program suiting to their and industry needs.

Pedagogy (*Rating 4.5*): Aegis focuses on making its students industry-ready and this is reflective in their pedagogy. The institute brings together the current software content, real-world industry experiences and hands on exposure to give the participants a practical exposure in the field of analytics.

Faculty (Rating 4.3): This program is delivered by Data Scientist engaged in real-life Data Science and Big Data Analytics projects from around the world with 45% of faculties having a PhD.

External Collaborations (*Rating 4.5*): Aegis has collaborated with IBM to offer high end courses in the field of Data Science, Business Analytics, Big Data, Cloud Computing and Mobility. MTNL, a leading Govt. of Indian telecom service provider, is Aegis' Infrastructure partner in Mumbai.

Brand Value (*Rating 4.3*): The focus of Aegis is on technology and analytics is a perfect extension to it. Aegis offers various programs in 25 countries to top executives speaking high of its brand value.

Other Attributes (*Rating 4.7*): Career Management Center (CMC) at Aegis facilitates all students' paid internship and final placements. Also Aegis and IBM have set up an IBM Business Analytics and IBM Cloud Computing Lab to help students and faculty members enhance their analytic skills.

*The overall rating for Aegis School of Business, Data Science & Telecommunication is **4.42***

8.   Certificate Program in Business Analytics – NarseeMonjee Institute of Management Studies (NMIMS), Bangalore

- **Headquarter City:** Mumbai
- **Cities of Operation:** Bangalore
- **Year of inception:** 2009

- **Duration of Program:** 12 months
- **Mode of Delivery:** Classroom

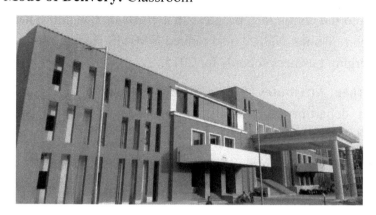

Incepted in 2009, NMIMS Bangalore, is active in the area of Executive education and runs General Management and Analytics program (Certificate Program in Business Analytics) focused on working professionals.

Course Content (*Rating 4.2*): The course content aims at preparing working executives for a career in Analytics by training them on basic, advanced and application focused courses. The curriculum design and program structure is prepared in consultation with Analytic Board of Governors, a body consisting of eminent professionals from industry.

Pedagogy (*Rating 4.4*): The courses are delivered through lectures, case discussion, lab sessions, assignments, group tasks and projects. The participants are evaluated through home assignments, projects and exams.

Faculty (Rating 4.5): Faculty for the program consists of permanent and visiting faculty members with 60% having PhD. Visiting faculty members are Analytics professionals from various organizations.

External Collaborations (*Rating 4.5*): NMIMS Bangalore has collaboration with SAS Institute for providing SAS tools and conducting Workshops in various areas of Analytics.

Brand Value (*Rating 4.6*): Ed-universal has ranked NMIMS Bengaluru as 14th in General Management in Central Asia, which is a testimony to the continuous progress that NMIMS Bangalore has made in a short span of time. NHRD also ranked NMIMS Bengaluru amongst the top 5 emerging business schools for 2015.

Other Attributes (*Rating 3.9*): The institute has a full-fledged placement department consisting of a placement director and 5 staff members to assist students.

The overall rating for NMIMS Bangalore is 4.35

9. PG Diploma Program in Data Analytics – IIIT Bangalore & UpGrad

- **Headquarter City:** Mumbai (UpGrad), Bangalore (IIIT-B)
- **Cities of Operation:** Online hence Global (UpGrad), Bangalore (IIIT-B)
- **Year of inception:** 2015 (UpGrad), 1999 (IIIT-B)
- **Duration of Program:** 11 months
- **Mode of Delivery:** Online

UpGrad, founded by media stalwart Ronnie Screwvala, is an online higher education platform providing industry relevant programs. The International Institute of Information Technology, Bangalore focuses on education and research in IT.

Course Content (*Rating 4.0*): UpGrad and IIIT-Bangalore have collaborated1 to develop this online 11-month Program in Data Analytics. The program offers the right blend of statistics, technical and business knowledge to ensure that participants learn exactly what the employers need.

Pedagogy (*Rating 4.1*): The teaching style adopted is case-led, wherein faculty and industry experts use a series of industry relevant examples to teach complex analytics concepts.

Faculty (*Rating 4.2*): IIIT-Bangalore and UpGrad faculty are majorly from the analytics domain with 67% having a Phd. Also industry experts are involved in designing and executing the program as they bring in industry perspective.

External Collaborations (*Rating 4.0*): The program has established flagship partnerships with Analytics Leaders like Uber, Genpact, and Gramener. Further, the program has been built in collaboration with 30+ Analytics industry experts from leading corporations.

Brand Value (*Rating 4.2*): UpGrad's brand value is reflective in its partnership with 50+ companies like Star TV, Disney, Google, and Microsoft to develop program content and provide mentorship to students. IIIT-B, with its model of education, and industry interaction, has grown in stature over time to become an institution of considerable repute in academic as well as corporate circles.

Other Attributes (*Rating 4.0*): UpGrad and IIIT-Bangalore will be providing placement assistance. A Virtual Cluster for the Big Data course is set up for participants.

*The overall rating for UpGrad is **4.08***

10. Business Intelligence and Big Data – IMT Ghaziabad

- **Headquarter City:** Ghaziabad

- **Cities of Operation:** Ghaziabad

- **Year of inception:** 1980

- **Duration of Program:** 11 weeks

- **Mode of Delivery:** Classroom

IMT Ghaziabad is a fully autonomous university and offers several post graduate, doctorate and executive education programmes in management.

Course Content (*Rating 3.8*): The course gives you a blend of industry knowledge, concepts and experiential learning through collaborative teaching by industry experts.

Pedagogy (*Rating 3.9*): The pedagogy will be a mix of lectures, experience sharing, real life case discussion, assignments and industry/research based projects. The course is focused on strategic issues with cases as the primary vehicle for learning.

Faculty (Rating 3.7): Faculties include a mix of in-house and industry exports with 98% of in-house faculties having PhD.

External Collaborations (*Rating 4.0*): IMT has many industry associations and international collaborations. IMT has 50+ International collaborations towards various academic modules co-teaching and joint learning.

Brand Value (*Rating 4.3*): IMT Ghaziabad is an institute that has been there for long and is recognized for the courses its offers and for the quality of students that come out of the institute to build their names in industry.

Other Attributes (*Rating 3.9*): Students opting for this course are provided with placement support. ICDM, a data management conference is organized by the institute.

*The overall rating for IMT Ghaziabad is **3.93***

http://analyticsindiamag.com/top-10-analytics-courses-india-ranking-2016/

2.24 Ten Super Exciting Data Science / Machine Learning / Artificial Intelligence based startups in India

NSS, DECEMBER 9, 2016

Introduction

Data technologies have been around for some time now. But, increase in data generation and availability of servers on the cloud has enabled an entire generation of startups working on ideas which were unthinkable a few years back. The change in landscape is aptly summarized by the quote below:

Whenever I see data today, I think OPPORTUNITY

At Analytics Vidhya, we love startups and we love data! So, mixing the two provides us with the heady mix which we thrive on. That is where this article was born. Today, we will look at 10 exciting startups in the Analytics / Data Science / Machine Learning / Artificial Intelligence based in India, which are looking to disrupt the world in coming years.

Framework to shortlist the startups

This list has been curated based on certain parameters, which act as indicators for success of startups. The parameters on which startups have been evaluated are:

The founding Team – This includes the diversity of the founding members, their educational background and their past experiences.

The Sector / Market – The industry in which the startup plays and the opportunities that it can leverage in that market.

Investment – Whether the startup has raised funds, the amount and quality of funding received.

Recognition – This includes the mentions and awards the startup has received.

Growth / Traction – Takes into account revenue growth and the clients.

List of Companies

1. Edge Networks

Incorporated in 2012 by Arjun Pratap, Edge Networks dreams to change the way HR industry works right now. With an ever increasing number of job seekers, the process of finding a right match for a particular job profile today has become extremely cumbersome. With Data Science and Artificial Intelligence at its core, Edge Networks has developed their product HIR Ealchemy to match people with the required job. The solution

provided by them facilitates talent acquisition, internal workforce optimization and talent analytics. Edge Networks was featured in Nasscom's Emerge 50 2016 list.

2. Fluid AI

What if I tell you, there is a company out there which is working to convert any screen into a gesture controlled AI powered assistant? Then be it in malls, banks etc. these screens will be able to address you when you approach a product kept next to it just like a human staff does? Fluid AI is one such company which is on the verge of a revolution for personalization in Finance, Government, Web and Marketing. Founded in 2009 by two brothers Abhinav Aggarwal and Raghav Aggarwal, Fluid AI is leading the virtual customer assistance market. It aims to cater to various sectors to mimic human interaction with the customer & help reduce operational cost for a company. Fluid AI serves clients like Vodafone, Toyota, Deloitte, Emirates, NBD, Barclays, Rolls Royce, Accenture and Axis Bank. This is one company that you must keep an eye on.

3. Flutura

Every now & then we see new analytics startups trying to generate insights from structured and unstructured data. But Flutura

founded by Derick Jose, Srikanth Muralidhara and Krishnan Raman is different. Flutura believes in *actions* and not *insights*. Flutura works on M2M model via its product **Cerebra** where it collects data on thousands of data points of various different machines. And it then leverages these data points to convert it into actionable strategies like pre-scheduling repairs for machines, order spare parts, etc. This model increases the life of machines, saves cost on operational loss and increases efficiency. Flutura has been recognized as one of the Top 20 Most Promising Big Data Companies globally by California-based Tech magazine, CIO Review and was also recognized by TechSparks2013 as one of the Top 3 startups out of India.

4. Heckyl

Trading is an uncertain world and the best example of Butterfly Effect. Any small incident in some part of the globe can result in huge gains or losses in the trading industry. What if there was a way to keep track of all these news, people emotions, trending sentiments, etc. all in a single place that can optimize your trading strategy?

Founded in 2010 by four former Merrill Lynch executives Abhijit Vedak, Jaison Mathews, Mukund Mudras, SomSagar, Heckyl is

 revolutionizing the trading industry for brokerage firms, short-term traders, investors and fund managers. Heckyl does this through its integrated trading terminal which also provides visuals and heat maps of sentiments and market data to help traders find the right trading opportunities.

Some of the clients are Angel Broking, Sharekhan, MotilalOswal. Heckyl is a Mumbai based startup.

5. Mad Street Den

You plan to buy a red knee length floral dress from some online fashion websites and what you get in return is either a red dress, a red short dress and every other combination but not the one you had wanted.

This is where Mad Street Den's flagship product Vue.ai comes in which relies heavily on Machine Learning and Artificial Intelligence. Vue.ai provides visual search using captured photos, targeting customers through emails and messages with their own style preferences. The e-commerce companies can customize their homepages according to the preferences of their customers along with automated tagging of products. The interesting  feature of Mad Street Den's algorithms is the use of neuromorphic principles which facilitate organic learning using less data.

Mad Street Den was founded by couple Anand Chandrasekaran and Ashwini Asokan in 2013 with from their office in Chennai.

6. Niki.ai

Founded in 2015 by Sachin Jaiswal, Nitin Babel, Shishir Modi and Keshav Prawasi, Niki.ai aims to be the one-stop solution for a customer's order. The startup leverages natural language processing and machine learning technologies to converse with customers over a simple chat interface, and places their orders with their partner businesses within seconds.

The startup, in August, launched its Face book Messenger bot. With an Android app and now Nikibot, Niki helps people in India hail a cab, order food, and pay for laundry or the electricity bill, among other things. The bot lets users pay for services directly in chat via Paytm without having to leave Facebook Messenger.

The company works on a channel partnership model and generates revenue for every order processed on its platform. It is now also working with brands to provide those chatbots for their use case and application.

Niki.ai has Ratan Tata as one of its backers and is a must app to try at once.

7. ShopR360

Founded in 2015 by RajulTandon and Pranav Bhruguwar ShopR360 provide video analytics solutions to malls, retailers, hypermarkets and quick service restaurants.  Their technology enables to distinguish staff from customers and easily integrates with existing CCTV infrastructure at no additional cost. Their solutions help to increase staff productivity, map customers journey in retail stores, measure footfall, bounce rates and dwell times. As a result, increase conversion rate and help in strategic placements of products in stores.

ShopR360 uses a combination of Wi-Fi/Bluetooth sensors, CCTV and Optical Character Recognition. ShopR360 featured in Nasscom's Emerge 50 list of 2016.

8. SigTuple

In a nation where there is an enormous shortage of trained medical practitioners, SigTuple founded by ex-American Express Employees Tathagato Rai Dastidar, Rohit Kumar Pandey, Apurv Anand in 2015 took up the task to assist medical practitioners in fast diagnosis of diseases using Image processing and Classification with AI and Machine Learning at its core. SigTuple aims to build affordable medical diagnosis solutions using a microscope, a cellphone app and cloud-based engine for analysis and reporting.

SigTuple is backed by Flipkart founders and Accel Partners.

9. SocialCops

In their own words- Socialcops are on a mission to confront the world's most critical problems using data. Their platform helps in driving healthcare policy, smarter cities and education outcomes.

Socialcops' offers three products – Collect, Search and Visualize. Collect is an android app where human sensors feed data into it on a regular basis. This is currently being employed in places like Jharkhand for purposes where no data exists. Through

Search, data collected can be structured and sort through at a very fast pace. Visualize helps in making decisions from the collected data.

Today, SocialCops is working on to improve the healthcare segment of India by acting as data aggregator at grass root level.

Socialcops in lieu of their contribution to make the world a better living place have been mentioned in Fortune 40 under 40 and Forbes 30 under 30.

10. VPhrase

Vphrase, founded by Neerav Parekh in 2015 is a Natural Language Processing company with PHRAZOR as its product which can convert and structured content such as graphs into words as if they were written by

a human analyst. VPhrase is on the verge of an innovation in terms of reports that are prepared and consumed by the employees of companies. PHRAZOR can generate automated reports, write articles, weather reports. The possibilities are endless. The thing that makes VPhrase all the more exciting is its capability to analyze graphs and create a word report in multiple languages.

VPhrase is backed by seed funding platform Venture Catalysts.

End Notes

It has not been long for AI and Machine Learning in India. Yet, various exciting Startups have been incorporated which are pushing the boundaries of technology and human comfort meanwhile solving real world problems. Apart from the 10 above startups, there are many more startups in analytics industry which are waiting to leave a mark. If you are aware of a company which is pushing boundaries of AI, share with me in the comments below.

I hope you enjoyed reading this article as I much as I did writing it. I would like to know your thoughts on the above startups, share your opinion in the comments below.

You can test your skills and knowledge. Check out **Live Competitions** and compete with best Data Scientists from all over the world.

https://www.analyticsvidhya.com/blog/2016/12/10-super-exciting-data-science-machine-learning-artificial-intelligence-based-startups-in-india/

2.25 Big Data and the Internet of Things don't make business smarter, Analytics and Data Science do

Big Data does not convert data into actionable information. Big Data does not create value. But Data Science does, and it does not have to be complex or expensive, or even big. - **By Michael O'Connell, Chief Analytics Officer at TIBCO.**

I recently wrote an article on this topic that was published in Tech In Asia. The article focuses on Big Data applications in the Asia Pacific region. I am speaking at Strata Singapore on December 8. Here is a shortened version of the article. Tech In Asia is a great site – check out their community.

For the past few years, Big Data and the Internet of Things (IoT) have been driving the digital revolution toward the "smart everything."

While North America is projected to hold the largest share of the Big Data market, the Asia Pacific region is the fastest-growing Big Data market. Beyond Big Data implementations at the enterprise level, planners and politicians on the largest scale are looking to Big Data to facilitate the creation of "smart cities."

In its "Smart Cities in Southeast Asia" report, PwC highlights the factors that are driving this approach.

"Urbanization," it says, "is increasing at a rate that will likely result in significant tension; with demand outstripping resource supply, urban planning is becoming critical."

The report states that one critical way that cities will remain live able is to evolve, through the use of technology, into a so-called "smart city." This will call for the generation, collection, storage, and analysis of massive amounts of data across power, transport, water and sanitation, and telecoms. The cost, however, will be huge – the Asian Development Bank estimates that between 2010 and 2020 the region would require almost US$600bil in investments across these four sectors.

The basic idea behind Big Data and IoT is that everything consumers and businesses do is now leaving a digital trace – which can be turned into smart insight. While this is a great vision, the most important part of the process is often not appreciated, i.e. making actionable information out of the raw data.

Qiao Li, Senior Market Analyst, Big Data and analytics at IDC Asia Pacific observes: "One in three organizations in the region find it difficult to build business case or measure ROI while leveraging BDA solutions, and we see organizations are becoming more pragmatic in justifying business cases and starting small in their BDA journey."

What businesses need to understand is this:

Big Data does not convert data into actionable information. Big Data does not create value. But Data Science does, and it does not have to be complex or expensive, or even big.

Data Science is not just about data scientists, it's about business acumen and passion.

Data Science is a three-legged stool that combines business acumen, data wrangling and analytics to create extreme value. Focusing on the hard science skills such as statistical methods is a common mistake when actually; developing the knowledge about a particular business and wrangling the relevant data are often the most important skills to bring to the table.

It's one thing to know how to play with numbers, but it's more important to understand what insights these numbers reveal on the business, and what actions to take based on these insights. Experience and business knowledge plays a role, as well as curiosity and passion. Sometimes the best results come from unlikely people just because of their desire and persistence.

Driving Insights to Actions with Analytics -

Turning Data into Insights, and Insights into Action is a multi-step process:

1. Ask the right question by deciding which specific business problem to tackle. Make sure you are focused and spend every minute on high value business problems.

2. Sourcing and accessing the appropriate data sources. Organic big data are cheap and non-intrusive, but often not representative to the business problem. Seeking out the best, most representative data is a key initial task.

3. Clean and transform these data sources. Massaging available data to address the business problem is time-consuming but crucial. The best analytics methods can't make up for poor quality data.

4. Clearly define the response variables and explanatory features that inform the business problem. Crisp definition of variables and features is central to deriving actionable insights.

5.   Prepare visualizations and dashboards highlighting the key response variables and features so that everyone can quickly derive insights on the business issues.

6.   Create predictive models and rules that encapsulate the insights for ongoing analysis and action.

7.   Publish the dashboards, models and rules for ongoing use across the business.

8.   Refresh with source data as often as practical for the business problem at hand. Some data don't change very fast and/or can't be auctioned right away. In other cases, we can drive action intraday or even in the moment.

9.   Define alerts and notifications so that appropriate stakeholders are informed when there are opportunities or threats on the business.

Each of these steps is rooted in common sense, and keeping intensely focused on the business problem at hand. With this kind of focus, data science drives significant value across industries and functional areas. For business problems where data are in motion, we can get all the way through these 9 steps and drive extreme value to the business. Some examples include:

- Omni channel customer engagement and appropriate offers while customers are transacting on a website
- Order fulfillment and inventory restocking based on demand, inventory and purchases
- Proactive machine management and maintenance to prevent/address failures and enhance machine productivity
- Oversight of transactions for fraud and compliance
- Logistics and transportation optimization and routing
- Price optimization based on updating demand and conditions.

The sheer volume of data strains comprehension – according to Entrepreneur.com, by 2020, every person online will create roughly 1.7 megabytes of new data every second of every day, and that's on top of the 44 zettabytes (or 44 trillion gigabytes) of data that will exist in the digital universe by that time.

Confronted with this tsunami of data, the key to avoiding wasted investment, misguided conclusions, and even terminal panic, is quite simply the application of data science and common-sense business skills to extract value and information from all the available data; and thereby to drive business strategy, tactics and operations through refreshed information; and with relevant business context, in the moment.

Original post Reposted with permission.

Bio: Michael O'Connell, Ph. D., is the Chief Analytics Officer at TIBCO Software, developing analytic solutions across a number of industries. He has been working on statistical software applications for the past 20 years, and has published more than 50 papers and several software packages on statistical methods. Michael has Ph.D. in Statistics from NCSU (1992) and is Adjunct Professor of Statistics there.

http://www.kdnuggets.com/2017/01/big-data-iot-business-smarter-analytics-data-science.html

2.26 AI, Data Science, Machine Learning: Main Developments in 2016, Key Trends in 2017

PyCharm: Python IDE for Developersget it now.

By Matthew Mayo, KDnuggets

2017 is here. Check out an encore installation in our "Main Developments in 2016 and Key Trends in 2017" series, where experts weigh in with their opinions.

At KDnuggets, we try to keep our finger on the pulse of main events and developments in industry, academia, and technology. We also do our best to look forward to key trends on the horizon.

Over the past few weeks, we published a series of posts outlining expert opinions in data science, machine learning, artificial intelligence, and related fields. See these previous iterations below:

- **Machine Learning & Artificial Intelligence: Main Developments in 2016 and Key Trends in 2017**

- **Big Data: Main Developments in 2016 and Key Trends in 2017**

- **Data Science & Predictive Analytics: Main Developments in 2016 and Key Trends in 2017**

In an encore post of this series, we bring you the collected responses to an amalgam question -- including experts from all of the previous posts' fields -- while adding a second dimension this time around.

1. "What were the main developments in AI, Data Science, Machine learning in 2016 and what Key Trends do you expect in 2017?"

2. "How can we get more women involved in this field?"

Without further delay, here is what we found.

Jennifer Chayes, Distinguished Scientist & Managing Director, Microsoft Research New England and Microsoft Research New York City – "I'd like to thank one of my researchers, Alekh Agarwal, for great input here".

Main developments in 2016:

- Reinforcement Learning: Many advances were made on the empirical side, notably AlphaGo. Also remarkable was the number of new platforms for testing RL methods, including Project Malmo from Microsoft, Universe from OpenAI, Deep Mind Lab from Google, and Torch Craft from Face book. There were major contributions from Microsoft Research NYC: On the practical side, the Decision Service is the first deployable system for RL: arxiv.org/abs/1606.03966; on the theory side, the Contextual Decision Process https://arxiv.org/abs/1610.09512 is the first statistical foundation for RL with contextual policies.

- Fairness Issues: Of note, there were several works trying to quantify what it means for fairness to be a part of algorithm design, see e.g. the 2016 FATML workshop: www.fatml.org/schedule/2016.

- Physics and AI: My collaborators and I have developed a non-equilibrium statistical physics explanation of the "unreasonable effectiveness" of learning (shallow) neural nets: www.pnas.org/content/113/48/E7655.full?sid=e1bedfb2-c8ab-441c-bcd2-dbdd7005721c, which we are working to extend to DNNs.

Trends for 2017:

- Reinforcement learning: More advances, particularly spurred by the release of the new platforms in 2016.

- Physics and AI: The development of new algorithms for deep neural nets, including more principled algorithms with better performance, based on non-equilibrium physics ensembles.

- Non-convex optimization: Over the last few years, there has been increasing understanding of when and how we can solve non-convex problems in ML. Expect to see additional breakthroughs here in the next year or two.

Getting more women involved in the field:

The way to increase the number of women in AI, ML and data science is two-fold. First, we must expand the definitions of the fields to include their interaction with the other sciences, including the biological and social sciences. A prime example of the contribution of the social science approach to AI is development of new field to make ML fairer, accountable and transparent (FATML), a community in which many of the leaders are women. Second, we need to establish networks among the women who are already in the fields. A great example is Women in ML http://wimlworkshop.org/, an organization co-founded ten years ago by four women in ML who were rooming together during the 2005 NIPS conference. The first WiML workshop took place at NIPS 2006 with almost 100 participants. WiML 2016 had almost 600 participants, which was roughly 10% of NIPS. The networks established through WiML tend to keep women in the field and in particular to expose them to new opportunities.

Jill Dyche, Vice President, SAS Best Practices -

Natural language - Writing this feels like an anachronism, since I was working with a natural language processing back in the early 1990s. Some smart folks at a company called AICorp had figured out how to pose English questions to a database. A program would parse the question into words that would be referenced against an established lexicon that could be used to automatically translate the request into SQL. Thus the question, "What were last year's revenues for Widget x compared to the prior year's?" would reliably (though not necessarily quickly) return an accurate answer.

As you can imagine, this opened up a whole new world to business users accustomed to waiting for programmers to email them datasets that they would then be forced to pick through, often extrapolating the right answer.

Flash forward to an hour ago when I just asked Alexa to dim the lights in my office. As consumers become more comfortable using commercially available natural language functions - "Okay, Google" - the ability to combine natural language, voice recognition, and advanced analytics will continue to offer promising new capabilities.

Now, where are my keys? "Alexa...?"

I both appreciate and dread this question. Why? Because my knee-jerk response is to answer in a way that separates women from men.

But then again, in the tech world women are separated from men, both physically (more women work in the service sector, more men have offices with doors) and metaphorically. So, I'll stand by my knee-jerk answer: Offer women communities. After all, there are fewer of us around, so it's much harder to find other like-minded colleagues who share our experiences. (This phenomenon is even more prevalent in the minority and LGBTQ communities.) We yearn to hear from women who have overcome what we're grappling with now, to hang out and learn together. And we want to hear from men—especially from men in power—about how to widen the circle. Bring us together and acknowledge we're a sub-group who wants to participate, be better, and help our companies thrive. Invite more of us to the recruiting table, and into the board room. show that revenues will rise—and thus so will our numbers.

Ian Goodfellow, Research Scientist at OpenAI -

1. What were the main developments in AI, Data Science, Machine learning in 2016 and what Key Trends do you expect in 2017?

One of the largest trends of 2016 was the mainstreaming of reinforcement learning, beginning with AlphaGo's victory. We've begun to see machine learning move from datasets to environments, beginning with OpenAI Gym and culminating in OpenAI's Universe and DeepMind Lab.

Adversarial training has become very popular during the past year, with Yann LeCun describing it as the best idea in machine learning in the last ten years. "Adversarial" was a more common word in ICLR 2017 submission titles than "reinforcement," "variation," "convolution" or "unsupervised."

On the commercial side, we've seen NVIDIA's stock soar, numerous deep learning startup acquisitions, and the rise of far more players in the autonomous driving space.

In 2017, I think we can expect to continue to see an influx of people and dollars into the field. The deep learning hardware market will become more competitive and more complex, with new specialized hardware taking on GPUs. Companies that were not traditionally associated with machine learning will build machine learning teams to streamline their business.

As the field grows, researchers will be able to diversify and populate previously niche areas, like AI safety, machine learning security and privacy, and economic effects of AI.

2. How can we get more women involved in this field?

This is a complex issue and I will comment on just one aspect of it where I have some experience. This year OpenAI ran the first-ever Self-Organizing Conference on Machine Learning. We made a major effort to boost participation from groups that have traditionally been underrepresented in machine learning, and we learned a lot in the process. For conference organizers, I can definitely suggest having a good code of conduct (we used one created by the Ada Initiative) that ensures everyone will feel welcomed. We also found that it's very important to do a lot of outreach. We sought out several people from underrepresented groups and explicitly invited them to the conference.

We found that people from underrepresented groups were less likely to be able to attend (due to not being able to get time off from work, obligations to care for family members, etc.) so this extra effort was necessary to have a more balanced conference. Finally, we gave out travel grants to members of these groups who want not to be able to attend otherwise. Overall, we feel that these efforts greatly improved the conference for all participants.

Nikita Johnson, Founder, RE•WORK -

1. At RE•WORK events over the course of 2016, both unsupervised learning and reinforcement learning became a more prominent feature in talks and discussions, startups taking part to the industry leaders in the field. I'm sure this will continue to advance further over the next year. In 2017, I am expecting to see further advancements in applying deep learning to understand and predict videos, working towards summarizing what happens in a video clip.

2. It's a subject we are all aware of at RE•WORK as we are currently an all-female team! To try to get more women involved in the field, we have created a series of 'Women in Machine Intelligence' dinners to provide a welcoming and supportive environment for women to present their latest work to their peers, but also for women to attend to meet other women working in the field. The attendees are always a mix of large established companies, startups and researchers, to provide an interesting networking environment for women looking for inspiration, new job roles, or new collaborative partners at the event. We'll continue to grow these types of events in 2017 and hope to see yet more women becoming role-models for the next generation interested in AI and data science!

Zachary Chase Lipton, PhD student in the Computer Science Engineering department at the University of California, San Diego; contributing editor at KDnuggets, blogger at Approximately Correct -

So much has happened in 2016, it's hard to say where to begin. On the industry side, I would say that 2016 was the year that data science went beyond analytics. For a long time, machine learning academics have had big ideas about intelligent agents making real-time decisions in real-world settings. And we've had some experimental success and fancy mathematics to support these ideas. But when you looked at industry, most people have clung to more mundane "analytics" applications. In this shallow view, machine learning algorithms are useful mainly for data visualization, building dashboards, basically decision support. For many years, a small cadre of major players like Google, IBM and Microsoft has integrated machine learning into live systems. But it's been rare. Over the last year, we've seen story after story of ML powering self-driving cars, neural machine translation, personal assistants, and more. I expect these trends to continue.

As in any year, research tended to lead practice, even within companies. While the major developments in live products all relied on supervised learning, this paradigm has several frustrating limitations. First, supervised learning models conditional probabilities P(Y|X), assuming data is observed, but not tampered with. Supervised learning tells us about correlation, but not causality. It tells us nothing about what might happen to Y when we *take an action*, i.e., P (Y|do(X)). Another limitation of supervised machine learning is that our most effective algorithms (deep learning) tend to rely on thousands or millions of labeled examples.

From a research perspective, I saw 2016 as a year in which the primary focus of the applied machine learning community shifted beyond supervised learning. Two developments stand out: deep reinforcement learning (DRL) and generative adversarial networks (GANs). While these ideas have roots in papers from 2013 and 2014, respectively, this year each gave birth to a large community of dedicated researchers. Deep reinforcement learning weds the representational power of deep neural networks with the reinforcement learning paradigm, in which an agent optimizes a policy to increase the reward signal it receives. While the methods were made famous on games like Atari and Go, we're now starting to see more research on deep reinforcement learning for practical applications. Generative adversarial networks are a creative new approach to unsupervised learning, developed by Ian Goodfellow. Initially GANS were used primarily for generative modeling, but new papers extend them to tasks like auto-encoding and semi-supervised learning.

Looking forward to 2017, I see a few big trends. For one, there's a sense in industry and academia that dialogue systems may be the next big area to fall. With recent progress in speech recognition and sequence tagging, the major primitives are already in place. We should note, there are still some big open questions. What should the objectives of an artificial interlocutor be? But for constrained domains, I expect rapid progress. I also expect to see more advanced efforts to apply DRL to real-world problems. A final prediction is that machine learning will start to realize its promise in the medical domain. For some problems, like radiology, the basic technology should already be in place and the remaining hurdles may mostly be HCI and regulatory issues. For other problems, like predicting treatment response, I expect to see researchers start to think seriously about reinforcement learning for medicine.

The lack of women and traditionally underrepresented racial groups in machine learning, and computer science broadly is a question I think about constantly. I'd like to help in any way I can. And yet I'm also aware that as a Caucasian man, there may be certain limitations on my ability to be a leader in this movement. Perhaps the biggest thing we can do is to give the women who are entering this field and embarking on their careers every possible opportunity to succeed. I think this includes some amount of affirmative action. It also includes being critical of the selection criteria we use. If CS departments prioritize students with many years of programming experience, this could reinforce the discrimination that keeps women out of CS in high school.

Another thing we can do is support the organizations that are already working well. Women in Machine Learning (WiML) is a fantastic group that has organized workshops co-located with NIPS. Companies and universities should sponsor their events and support the great work they do to promote women in our field and showcase their work. This year, I attended as the co-author of a paper by my collaborator at UCSD, SubarnaTripathi. As stark as the demographic numbers seem, I'm optimistic about gender diversity in machine learning. Already, there are so many prominent ladies at the top of the field that everyone, regardless of gender, can look up to. Anima Anand Kumar, Joelle Pineau, Jennifer Chayes, Finale Doshi-Velez, Anca Dragan, Fei-Fei Li, Suchi Saria are a few that pop out at me. Among my peer group I've also been grateful to learn a lot from Been Kim, Hanie Sedghi, SubarnaTripathi, and my collaborator on approximatelycorrect.com, Victoria Krakovna.

Hilary Mason, Founder at Fast Forward Labs -

At Fast Forward Labs, we do apply machine learning research and data science advising for a variety of clients with interesting opportunities. This means I have a few different perspectives on the interesting developments in the field.

From a purely algorithmic perspective, I'm very excited about probabilistic programming, and how it is becoming useful for combining human knowledge with data to learn something rigorous about the world. I'm also optimistic about the continued pace of expanding possibilities for using neural networks, particularly in constrained compute environments or for complex NLP problems.

From an application perspective, we're still at the very beginning of meaningful automation. In 2017, we'll see significant automation in very narrow domains. I expect much of this will be for high-value problems, so think of finance and medicine, not consumer applications, just yet.

Finally, there's a ton of interesting work happening around the practice of data science, machine learning, and AI. What does it mean to be a data scientist? What kinds of processes do we need to effectively explore data and tie those into meaningful products? How do we build new on ramps into the field? What will data science even look like in ten years, and what tools do we need to build to get there?

One of the things that I love about working in data science is that people come to the practice from a variety of different backgrounds, both academically and culturally, and that makes working in data science richer than other, more rigidly defined, disciplines. Diversity isn't just a matter of gender, either. Nor is it a pipeline problem. There's a textbook of content that could go here, and I'm hardly an expert, but this is just common sense: If you want to see more diversity in the set of people working in data science and machine learning, offer opportunities to a more diverse set of people. They'll be amazing. And when you invite them into your environment, do your best to make it welcoming.

Michael O'Connell, Chief Analytics Officer, TIBCO -

Some key developments in 2016 included:

- More emphasis on "representative data", rigorous analytics and data science to identify insights and understand business issues.
- Mainstreaming of machine learning and predictive analytics for business, customer and engineering applications.
- Rise in deep learning, beyond the big internet companies, especially for some specialized applications e.g. fraud in the banking system.
- Continued rise in engineering analytics – especially in IIoT applications, where anomaly detection is foundational.

- Significant uptick in "systems of insight", where insights from analytics are transformed in to notifications, alerts and actions on the business.
- Continued migration to governed data discovery across the corporate landscape – providing self-service, but with guidance and best practices; along with performance, governance and security.
- Beginnings of hybrid cloud adoption with scalable tenant resources and contextual routing, along with hybrid data and elastic compute engines.

For 2017, I see more action in all these areas, especially in "systems of insight" – turning insights from visual and predictive analytics in to actions. This includes real-time streaming analytics for rapid intervention and action, at moments of truth in business processes. I also see less of a boundary between data preparation and visual analytics, as data wrangling and insight discovery become more intertwined.

My TIBCO Data Science team currently comprises ~40% women. I've made no deliberate attempt to favor women in the hiring process. On analysis, I've been drawn to the work ethic, passion, productivity and professionalism of the women on my team.

I like the dynamic of men and women on my team. It mirrors our day to day world, and I think it helps bring forth a rich spectrum of ideas. My team is also heterogeneous on age, race, industry background and skills across stats, computing, data, viz., software development and presentation. The entire team enjoys the mentoring and collaboration across these dimensions.

Data Science requires strength in analytics, computing, data and business. It's enormously satisfying to see these dimensions addressed across the team in virtual, collaborative work streams; creating value, impact and action in our software, solutions and customer deployments.

Elena Sharova, Computer scientist with specialization in machine learning; Data scientist in financial risk measurement -

In my view 2016 has been a very good year for AI, Data Science (DS) and Machine Learning (ML). Firstly, the breadth of industries and areas where AI, DS and ML are being applied has seen considerable growth. From art and literature to science and business, I am seeing new applications almost on a daily basis. Secondly, the awareness of this field and its potential has greatly increased, more and more people are looking to study it, or change career. Finally, 2016 has delivered timely lessons of caution about the degree of reliance on models.

The key trends in 2017 should continue along the same lines: finding new areas for application and increased emphasis on validation of modeling assumptions.

As in Computer Science or other technical fields, it may take some time to achieve a good gender representation. However, I am convinced that DS and ML will attract more women in the near future. This is because a successful data scientist requires skills such as storytelling and an eye for detail which often come naturally to women. Again, the breadth of application will ensure that female data scientists can pick a niche, like data journalism or data science applications in psychology and sociology, if they choose to do so. I have personally been inspired by both female and male role models, and as long as we maintain supportive and collaborative work and study environments, the gender misbalance will go away.

Tamara Sipes, Principal Data Scientist at Optum/UnitedHealth Group -

Key Trends:

i) I see the data science productivity tools such as the R caret package or DataRobot and similar as gaining more popularity. These allow data scientists to quickly test a variety of methods, parameters, as well as sampling techniques and compare them based on a predetermined evaluation comparison.

ii) There are many indicators that Deep Learning and Ensemble Modeling will continue to be utilized more in the day to day applications, not just in data science competitions.

iii) Dealing with streaming data and evolving or changing data will likely be the focus in the near future as well. The models built on historical data that has since evolved need to be refreshed and fine-tuned accordingly.

Including women: We can start by reaching out to middle and high school level students and building up from there. Mini seminars or motivating talks by well-established female data scientist or researches in the field would be my recommendation.

http://www.kdnuggets.com/2017/01/ai-data-science-machine-learning-key-trends.html

2.27 Data Science, Predictive Analytics Main Developments in 2016 and Key Trends for 2017

Key themes included the polling failures in 2016 US Elections. Deep Learning, IoT, greater focus on value, ROI, and increasing adoption of predictive analytics by the "masses" of industry. **By Gregory Piatetsky, KDnuggets.**

We recently asked some of the leading experts in Data Science and Predictive Analytics for their opinion on the most important developments of 2016 and key trends they expect in 2017.

See also a previous post Big Data: Main Developments in 2016 and Key Trends in 2017. A summary of AI & Machine Learning Main Developments and Key Trends will be published next week.

Some of the key themes that emerged are the polling failures in 2016 US Presidential Elections, Deep Learning, IoT, greater focus on value and ROI, and increasing adoption of predictive analytics by the "masses" of industry.

Here is what the experts thought on Data Science, Predictive Analytics Main Developments in 2016 and Key Trends in 2017.

<u>Kirk D. Borne</u>, the Principal Data Scientist at BoozAllen, PhD Astrophysicist, Top Data Science/Big Data Influencer -

In 2016, I saw several significant data science-related developments, including,

- greater emergence of the **citizen data scientist** accompanied by a growth in self-service tools for analytics and data science;

- **deep learning** being applied across a variety of use cases (including text analytics)

- emergence of AI-driven chatbots in customer call centers and customer service touch-points;

- more demands from organizations to see real ROI and benefits from big data and data science, with a focus on "proofs of value" instead of "proofs of concept"; and

- Machine intelligence becoming a significant component of processes, products, and technologies across a broad spectrum of use cases: connected cars, internet of things, smart cities, manufacturing, supply chain, prescriptive machine maintenance, and more.

In 2017, we expect to see greater expansion of edge analytics use cases: machine learning embedded with sensors or close to the point of data collection -- the machine learning may be invoked via APIs or in processors close to the data collector or integrated into the sensor chip architecture itself. The patterns, trends, anomalies, and emergent phenomena (BOI: Behaviors of Interest) that are discovered close to the edge will enable better and faster predictive and prescriptive analytics applications in many domains: cybersecurity, digital marketing, customer experience, healthcare, emergency response, engine performance, autonomous vehicles, manufacturing, supply chain, and more.

Tom Davenport, Distinguished Professor at Babson College, co-founder of the International Institute for Analytics, and a Senior Advisor to Deloitte Analytics -

2016 Developments

- **Decentralization of analytics groups**: After a period of consolidation, organizations began to decentralize analytics to business units and functions, in many cases attempting to retain some degree of enterprise coordination.

- **Combinations of proprietary and technologies**: Many large corporations are making use of proprietary and open source analytics and big data technologies-often combined within a single application.

- **Fragmentation of cognitive technologies**: Large, monolithic cognitive technologies have been broken into a series of single-function APIs that can be combined to form complete systems.

- **Fuzzy quantitative roles:** Quantitative analysts, data scientists, and developers of cognitive applications have become less distinguishable; clear roles and titles are a thing of the past.

2017 Trends

- **Operational cognitive applications**: Cognitive will move from "science projects" to operational applications.

- **Questioning of model assumptions:** <u>Polling failures</u> in the 2016 presidential election will lead more managers to question the assumptions behind analytical models.

- **Classification of cognitive tools:** More organizations will understand and classify the different cognitive tools available to them and apply them to appropriate business problems.

- **Push for transparency:** Owners of strategic and regulated machine learning applications will push for greater transparency in those applications, and will eschew less transparent algorithms.

<u>Tamara Dull</u>, Director of Emerging Technologies at SAS -

This year's "big data" event was the <u>U.S. election</u> cycle because it brought the big data/data science/predictive analytics discussion to the Public Square. Granted, these weren't the terms most folks were using, but in the U.S., we experienced data up-close-and-personal: its' role, its' uses and misuses, its' interpretations and misinterpretations, and its' insights, right and wrong.

As data continues to pervade every aspect of our professional and personal lives, courtesy of the Internet, both the private and public sectors will be pressured to ensure that the collection, use, and analysis of data is safe, secure, and <u>ethical</u>. If a company doesn't get it right, they will cease to exist.

<u>John Elder</u> , founder and chairman of Elder Research, US largest analytics consultancy -

A year ago, Science magazine gave a "runner-up scientific breakthrough of 2015 award" to a study that attempted to <u>replicate 100 top experiments</u> published in psychology journals a few years previous. But researchers were only able to replicate 39. Bad as this is, it is feared to be much better than the track record for Epidemiology, where those published medical "discoveries" appear to be right only 5-35% of the time. Most of the problems of finding **spurious correlations**, I believe, are due to bad data science. Replacing outdated significance formulas with re-sampling procedures such as <u>Target Shuffling</u>, would better calibrate how likely random results could arise as strong as the apparent discovery, given the vast search performed by the researcher and the mining software. New criteria would be needed for publication worthiness, but results would be much more reliable, saving massive resources, and even lives.

<u>Anthony Gold bloom</u>, Co-founder and CEO of Kaggle, the leading Data Science competition platform -

Companies like Airbnb, Climate Corporation (now Monsanto) and Opendoor are great examples of how data science can have a big impact. They have built strong data science teams that impact decisions across their companies in 2017, we'll see those companies lead the way in adopting tools and processes that solve some of the big pain points in doing data science: particularly sharing and **collaborating** on data science workflows and pushing models into production. In 2016, the hot topics in academic research moved from deep neural networks to **<u>reinforcement learning</u>** and generative models.

In 2017, we should start to see some of these techniques used for pragmatic business use cases. Some of the promising areas for reinforcement learning include algorithmic trading and ad targeting.

<u>http://www.kdnuggets.com/2016/12/data-science-predictive-analytics-main-developments-trends.html</u>

2.28   Machine Learning & Artificial Intelligence: Main Developments in 2016 and Key Trends in 2017

As 2016 comes to a close and we prepare for a new year, check out the final installment in our "Main Developments in 2016 and Key Trends in 2017" series, where experts weigh in with their opinions - **By Matthew Mayo, KDnuggets.**

At KDnuggets, we try to keep our finger on the pulse of main events and developments in industry, academia, and technology. We also do our best to look forward to key trends on the horizon.

We recently asked some of the leading experts in Big Data, Data Science, Artificial Intelligence, and Machine Learning for their opinion on the most important developments of 2016 and key trends they 2017.

To get up to speed on our first 2 posts published outlining expert opinions, see the following:

- **Big Data: Main Developments in 2016 and Key Trends in 2017**

- **Data Science & Predictive Analytics: Main Developments in 2016 and Key Trends in 2017**

In the final post of the series, we bring you the collected responses to the question:

"What were the main Artificial Intelligence/Machine Learning related events in 2016 and what key trends do you see in 2017?"

Common themes include the triumphs of deep neural networks, reinforcement learning's successes, AlphaGo as exemplar of the power of both phenomena in unison, the application of machine learning to the Internet of Things, self-driving vehicles, and automation, among others.

We generally asked participants to keep their responses to within 100 words or so, but were amenable to longer answers if the situation warranted. Without further delay, here is what we found.

Yaser Abu-Mostafa, Caltech (in consultation with Professor Hsuan-Tien Lin and Professor Malik Magdon-Ismail)

2016 and 2017 are an exciting time for **Machine Learning**. There are two trends that have been accelerating. First, the showcases that prove ML to be an extraordinarily powerful technology; the recent successes of AlphaGo and inhuman encryption are compelling examples. Second, the expanding reaches of ML applications -more complex tasks, more domains, and more acceptance of ML as the way to exploit data everywhere. The Google / Microsoft / Face book / IBM AI partnerships are there for a reason.

Xavier Amatriain, VP Engineering at Quora -

2016 may very well go down in history as the year of "the Machine Learning **hype**". Everyone now seems to be doing machine learning, and if they are not, they are thinking of buying a startup to claim they do.

Now, to be fair, there are reasons for much of that "hype". Can you believe that it has been only a year since Google announced they were open sourcing **Tensor Flow**? TF is already a very active project that is being used for anything ranging from drug discovery to generating music. Google has not been the only company open sourcing their ML software though, many followed lead. Microsoft open sourced CNTK, Baidu announced the release of Paddle, and Amazon just recently announced that they will back MXNet in their new AWS ML platform. Face book, on the other hand, are basically supporting the development of not one, but two Deep Learning frameworks: Torch and Caffe. On the other hand, Google is also supporting the highly successful Keras, so things are at least even between Face book and Google on that front.

Besides the "hype" and the outpour of support from companies to machine learning open source projects, 2016 has also seen a great deal of applications of machine learning that were almost unimaginable a few months back. I was particularly impressed by the quality of Wavenet's audio generation. Having worked on similar problems in the past I can appreciate those results. I would also highlight some of the recent results in lip reading, a great application of video recognition that is likely to be very useful (and maybe scary) in the near future. I should also mention Google's impressive advances in machine translation. It is amazing to see how much this area has improved in a year.

As a matter of fact, machine translation is not the only interesting advance we have seen in machine learning for language technologies this past year. I think it is very interesting to see some of the recent approaches to combine deep sequential networks with side-information in order to produce richer language models. In "A Neural Knowledge Language Model", Bengio's team combines knowledge graphs with RNNs, and in "Contextual LSTM models for Large scale NLP Tasks", the DeepMind folks incorporate topics into the LSTM model. We have also seen a lot of interesting work in modeling attention and memory for language models. As an example, I would recommend "Ask Me Anything: Dynamic Memory Networks for NLP", presented in this year's ICML.

I could not finish this review of 2016 without some mention of advances in my main area of expertise: **Recommender Systems**. Of course, Deep Learning has also impacted this area. While I would still not recommend DL as the default approach to recommender systems, it is interesting to see how it is already being used in practice, and in large scale, by products like YouTube. That said, there has been interesting research in the area that is not related to Deep Learning. The best paper award in this year's ACM Recsys went to "Local Item-Item Models For Top-N Recommendation", an interesting extension to Sparse Linear Methods (i.e. SLIM) using an initial unsupervised clustering step. Also, "Field-aware Factorization Machines for CTR Prediction", which describes the winning approach to the Criteo CTR Prediction Kaggle Challenge is a good reminder that Factorization Machines are still a good tool to have in your ML toolkit.

I could probably go on for a couple of pages just listing impactful advances in machine learning in the last 12 months. Note that I haven't even listed any of the breakthroughs related to image recognition or deep reinforcement learning, or obvious applications such as self-driving cars or game playing, which all saw huge advances in 2016. Not to mention all the controversy around how machine learning is having or could have negative effects on society and the rise of discussions around algorithmic bias and fairness.

So, what should we expect for 2017? It is hard to say given how fast things are moving in the area. I am sure we will have a hard time just digesting what we will see in the NIPS conference in a few days. I am looking forward to many machine learning advances in the areas that I care the most about: personalization / recommendations, and natural language processing. I am sure, for example, that in the next few months we will see how ML can tackle the problem of fake news. But, of course, I also hope to see more self-driving cars on the roads and machine learning being put to good use for health-related applications or for creating a better informed and more just society.

YoshuaBengio, Professor, Department of Computer Science and Operations Research, Université de Montréal, Canada Research Chair in Statistical Learning Algorithms, etc. -

The main events of 2016 from my point of view have been in the areas of deep **reinforcement learning, generative models,** and neural machine translation. First, we had AlphaGo (DeepMind's network which beat the Go world champion using deep RL). Over the whole year, we have seen a series of papers showing the success of generative adversarial networks (for unsupervised learning of generative models). Also in the area of unsupervised learning, we have seen the unexpected success of auto-correlation neural networks (like the Wave Net paper from Deep Mind). Finally, just about a month ago we have seen the crowning of neural machine translation (which was initiated in part by my lab since 2014) with Google bringing this technology to the scale of Google Translate and obtaining really amazing results (approaching very significantly human-level performance).

I believe these are good indicators for the progress to be expected in 2017: more advances in **unsupervised learning** (which remains a major challenge, we are very far from human abilities in that respect) and in the ability of computers to understand and generate natural language, probably first with chatbots and other dialogue systems. Another likely trend is the increase in research and results of applying deep learning in the healthcare domain, on a variety of types of data, including medical images, clinical data, genomic data, etc. Progress in computer vision will continue as we see more applications, including of course self-driving cars but I have the impression that in general the community is under-estimating the challenges ahead before reaching true autonomy.

Pedro Domingos, Professor of computer science at UW and author of 'The Master Algorithm' -

The main event of 2016 was AlphaGo's win. Two areas where we might see substantial progress in 2017 are **chatbots** and **self-driving cars**, just because so many major companies are investing heavily in them. On the more fundamental side, one thing we'll probably see is increasing hybridization of deep learning with other ML/AI techniques, as is typical for a maturing technology.

Oren Etzioni, CEO of the Allen Institute for Artificial Intelligence. He was a Professor at U. Washington, founder / co-founder of several companies including Fare cast and Decide, and the author of over 100 technical papers -

The tremendous success of AlphaGo is the crowning achievement for an exciting 2016. In 2017, we will see more reinforcement learning in **neural networks,** more research on neural networks in NLP & vision. However, the challenges of neural networks with limited labeled data, exemplified by systems like Semantic Scholar, remain formidable and will occupy us for years to come. These are still early days for **Deep Learning** and more broadly for Machine Learning.

Ajit Jaokar, #Datascience, #IoT, #MachineLearning, #BigData, Mobile,#Smartcities, #edtech (@feynlabs + @countdowncode) Teaching (@forumoxford + @citysciences) -

2017 will be a big year for both **IoT** and **AI.** As per my recent KDnuggets post, AI will be a core competency for Enterprises. For IoT, this would mean the ability to build and deploy models across platforms (Cloud, Edge, and Streaming). This tie continuous learning to the vision of continuous improvement through AI. It also needs to new competencies as AI and divots converge.

Neil Lawrence, Professor of Machine Learning at the University of Sheffield -

I think things are progressing much as we might expect at the moment. **Deep learning** methods are being intelligently deployed on very large data sets. For smaller data sets I think we'll see some interesting directions on model repurposing, i.e. the reuse of pre-trained deep learning models. There are some interesting open questions around how best to do this. A further trend has been the increasing press focus on the field. Including mainstream articles on papers placed on **Arxiv** that have not yet been reviewed. This appetite for advance was also present last year but I think this year we've seen it accelerate. In response I think academics should probably become a lot more careful about how they choose to promote their work (for example on social media), particularly when it is reviewed.

Randal Olson, Senior Data Scientist at the University of Pennsylvania Institute for Biomedical Informatics -

Automated Machine Learning (AutoML) systems started becoming competitive with human machine learning experts in 2016. Earlier this year, an MIT group created a Data Science Machine that beat hundreds of teams in the popular KDD Cup and IJCAI machine learning competitions. Just this month, our in-house AutoML system, TPOT, started ranking in the 90th percentile on several Kaggle competitions. Needless to say, I am confident that AutoML systems will start replacing human experts for standard machine learning analyses in 2017.

Charles Martin, Data Scientist & Machine Learning Expert -

2016 has been the watershed year for **Deep learning**. We have had a year with **Google Tensorflow**, and the applications keep pouring in. Combined with say Keras, Jupyter Notebooks, and GPU-enabled AWS nodes, **Data Science teams** have the infrastructure on-demand to start building truly innovative learning applications and start generating revenue fast. But they may not have the talent? It is not about coding. It is not an infrastructure play. It is very different from traditional analytics, and no one really understands Why Deep Learning Works. Still, let's face it, it is all Google and Facebook talk about! And the C-suite is listening. In 2017, companies will be looking to bring best-of-breed Deep Learning technologies in house to improve the bottom line.

Matthew Mayo, Data Scientist, Deputy Editor of KDnuggets -

The big story of 2016 has to be the accelerated returns we are seeing from deep learning. The (not solely) neural network-based "conquering" of Go is likely the most prominent example, but there are others. Looking forward to 2017, I would expect that the continued advancements in **neural networks** will remain the big story. However, **automated machine learning** will quietly become an important event in its own right. Perhaps not as sexy to outsiders as deep neural networks, automated machine learning will begin to have far-reaching consequences in ML, AI, and data science, and 2017 will likely be the year this becomes apparent.

Brandon Rohrer, Data Scientist at Facebook -

In 2016 machines read lips more accurately than humans (arxiv.org/pdf/1611.05358.pdf), type from dictation faster than humans (arxiv.org/abs/1608.07323) and create eerily realistic human speech (arxiv.org/pdf/1609.03499.pdf). These are the results of exploring novel architectures and **algorithms. Convolution Neural Networks** are being modified beyond recognition and combined with reinforcement learners and time-aware methods to open up new application areas. In 2017, I expect a few more human level benchmarks to fall, particularly those that are vision-based and thus amenable to CNNs. I also expect (and hope!) that our community forays into the nearby territories of decision making, non-vision feature creation and time-aware methods will become more frequent and fruitful. Together these make intelligent robots possible. If we are really lucky, 2017 will bring us a machine that can beat humans at making a cup of coffee.

Daniel Tunkelang, Data science, Engineering, and Leadership -

The biggest story of 2016 was **AlphaGo** defeating Lee Sedol, the human world champion of Go. It was a surprise even to the AI community, and it will be remembered as the tipping point in the rise of deep learning. 2016 was the year of deep learning and AI. Chatbots, self-driving cars, and computer-aided diagnosis have unlocked the possibilities of what we can do by throwing enough GPUs at the right training data. 2017 will bring us successes and disillusionments. Technologies like TensorFlow will commodify deep learning, and AI will be something we take for granted in consumer products. But we'll hit the limits of what we can model and optimize. We'll have to confront the biases in our data. And we'll grow up and realize that we're nowhere close to general AI or the **singularity**.

http://www.kdnuggets.com/2016/12/machine-learning-artificial-intelligence-main-developments-2016-key-trends-2017.html

2.29 How to Build a Data Science Team

Posted by Ronald van Loon on February 3, 2017 at 6:00am

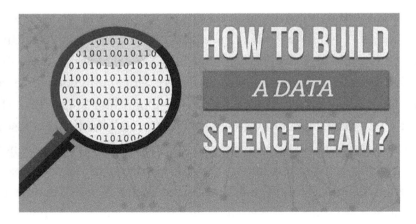

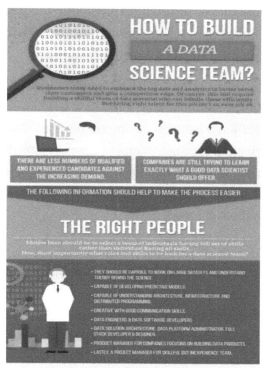

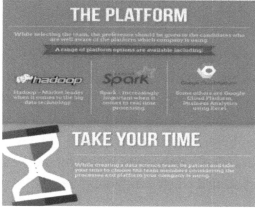

Businesses today need to do more than merely acknowledge big data. They need to embrace data and analytics and make them an integral part of their company. Of course, this will require building a quality team of data scientists to handle the data and analytics for the company. Choosing the right members for the team can be difficult, mainly because the field is so new and many companies are still trying to learn exactly what a good data scientist should offer. Putting together an entire team has the potential to be more difficult. The following information should help to make the process easier.

The Right People

What roles need to be filled for a data science team? You will need to have data scientists who can work on large datasets and who understand the theory behind the science. They should also be capable of developing predictive models. Data engineers and data software developers are important, too. They need to understand architecture, infrastructure, and distributed programming.

Some of the other roles to fill in a data science team include the data solutions architect, data platform administrator, full-stack developer, and designer. Those companies that have teams focusing on building data products will also likely want to have a product manager on the team. If you have a team that has a lot of skill but that is low on real world experience, you may also want to have a project manager on the team. They can help to keep the team on the right track.

The Right Processes

When it comes to the processes, the key thing to remember with data science is agility. The team needs the ability to access and watch data in real time. It is important to do more than just measure the data. The team needs to take the data and understand how it can affect different areas of the company and help those areas implement positive changes. They should not be handcuffed to a slow and tedious process, as this will limit effectiveness. Ideally, the team will have a good working relationship with heads of other departments, so they work together in agile multi-disciplinary teams to make the best use of the data gathered.

The Platform

When building a data science team, it is also important to consider the platform your company is using for the process. A range of options are available including Hadoop and Spark. Hadoop is the market leader when it comes to big data technology, and it is an essential skill for all professionals who get into the field. When it comes to real-time processing, Spark is becoming increasingly important. It is a good idea to have all the big data team members skilled with Spark, too.

If you have people on the team that do not have these skills and that do not know how to use the various platforms, it is important they learn. Certification courses can be a great option for teaching the additional skills needed, and to get everyone on the team on the same page.

Some of the other platforms to consider include the Google Cloud Platform, and business analytics using Excel. Understanding the fundamentals of these systems can provide a good overall foundation for the team members.

Take Your Time

When you are creating a data science team for the company, you do not want to rush and choose the wrong people and platforms or not have quality processes in place. Take your time to create a team that will provide your company with the quality and professionalism it needs.

http://www.datasciencecentral.com/profiles/blogs/how-to-build-a-data-science-team

2.30 Top 10 Big Data Trends 2017

2016 was a landmark year for big data with more organizations storing, processing, and extracting value from data of all forms and sizes. In 2017, systems that support large volumes of both structured and unstructured data will continue to rise. The market will demand platforms that help data custodians govern and secure big data while empowering end users to analyze that data. These systems will mature to operate well inside of enterprise IT systems and standards.

1. Big data becomes fast and approachable

Image: https://cdns.tblsft.com/sites/default/files/800x800_1.jpg

Options expand to speed up Hadoop

Sure, you can perform machine learning and conduct sentiment analysis on Hadoop, but the first question people often ask is: How fast is the interactive SQL? SQL, after all, is the conduit to business users who want to use Hadoop data for faster, more repeatable KPI dashboards as well as exploratory analysis.

This need for speed has fueled the adoption of faster databases like Exasol and MemSQL, Hadoop-based stores like Kudu, and technologies that enable faster queries. Using SQL-on-Hadoop engines (Apache Impala, Hive LLAP, Presto, Phoenix, and Drill) and OLAP-on-Hadoop technologies (AtScale, Jethro Data, and Kyvos Insights), these query accelerators are further blurring the lines between traditional warehouses and the world of big data.

2. Big data no longer just Hadoop

Purpose-built tools for Hadoop become obsolete

In previous years, we saw several technologies rise with the big-data wave to fulfill the need for analytics on Hadoop. But enterprises with complex, heterogeneous environments no longer want to adopt a siloed BI access point just for one data source (Hadoop). Answers to their questions are buried in a host of sources ranging from systems of record to cloud warehouses, to structured and unstructured data from both Hadoop and non-Hadoop sources. (Incidentally, even relational databases are becoming big data-ready. SQL Server 2016, for instance, recently added JSON support).

In 2017, customers will demand analytics on all data. Platforms that are data and source-agnostic will thrive while those that are purpose-built for Hadoop and fail to deploy across use cases will fall by the wayside. The exit of Platfora serves as an early indicator of this trend

Further reading: UNCOMMON SENSE: THE BIG DATA WAREHOUSE

3. Organizations leverage data lakes from the get-go to drive valueimage:

A data lake is like a man-made reservoir.

First you dam the end (build a cluster), then you let it fill up with water (data). Once you establish the lake, you start using the water (data) for various purposes like generating electricity, drinking, and recreating (predictive analytics, ML, cyber security, etc.).

Up until now, hydrating the lake has been an end in itself. In 2017, that will change as the business justification for Hadoop tightens. Organizations will demand repeatable and agile use of the lake for quicker answers. They'll carefully consider business outcomes before investing in personnel, data, and infrastructure. This will foster a stronger partnership between the business and IT. And self-service platforms will gain deeper recognition as the tool for harnessing big-data assets.

Further reading: MAXIMIZING DATA VALUE WITH A DATA LAKE

4. Architectures mature to reject one-size-fits all frameworks

Hadoop is no longer just a batch-processing platform for data-science use cases.

It has become a multi-purpose engine for ad hoc analysis. It's even being used for operational reporting on day-to-day workloads—the kind traditionally handled by data warehouses.

In 2017, organizations will respond to these hybrid needs by pursuing use case-specific architecture design. They'll research a host of factors including user personas, questions, volumes, frequency of access, speed of data, and level of aggregation before committing to a data strategy. These modern-reference architectures will be needs-driven. They'll combine the best self-service data-prep tools, Hadoop Core, and end-user analytics platforms in ways that can be reconfigured as those needs evolve. The flexibility of these architectures will ultimately drive technology choices.

5. Variety, not volume or velocity, drives big-data investments

Gartner defines big data as the three Vs: high-volume, high-velocity, high-variety information assets. While all three Vs are growing, variety is becoming the single biggest driver of big-data investments, as seen in the results of a recent survey by New Vantage Partners. This trend will continue to grow as firms seek to integrate more sources and focus on the "long tail" of big data. From schema-free JSON to nested types in other databases (relational and NoSQL), to non-flat data (Avro, Parquet, XML), data formats are multiplying and connectors are becoming crucial. In 2017, analytics platforms will be evaluated based on their ability to provide live direct connectivity to these disparate sources.

Further reading: VARIETY, NOT VOLUME, IS DRIVING BIG DATA INITIATIVES

6. Spark and machine learning light up big data

Apache Spark, once a component of the Hadoop ecosystem, is now becoming the big-data platform of choice for enterprises.

In a survey of data architects, IT managers, and BI analysts, nearly 70% of the respondents favored Spark over incumbent MapReduce, which is batch-oriented and doesn't lend itself to interactive applications or real-time stream processing.

These big-compute-on-big-data capabilities have elevated platforms featuring computation-intensive machine learning, AI, and

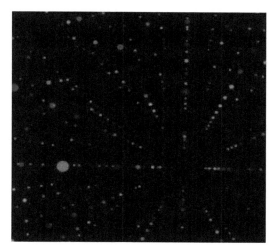

graph algorithms. Microsoft Azure ML in particular has taken off thanks to its beginner-friendliness and easy integration with existing Microsoft platforms. Opening up ML to the masses will lead to the creation of more models and applications generating petabytes of data. As machines learn and systems get smart, all eyes will be on self-service software providers to see how they make this data approachable to the end user.

Further reading: WHY YOU SHOULD USE SPARK FOR MACHINE LEARNING

7. Convergence of IoT, cloud, and big data create new opportunities for self-service analytics

It seems that everything in 2017 will have a sensor that sends information back to the mother ship.

IoT is generating massive volumes of structured and unstructured data, and an increasing share of this data is being <u>deployed on cloud services</u>. The data is often heterogeneous and lives across multiple relational and non-relational systems, from Hadoop clusters to NoSQL databases. While innovations in storage and managed services have sped up the capture process, accessing and understanding the data itself still pose a significant last-mile challenge. As a result, demand is growing for analytical tools that seamlessly connect to and combine a wide variety of cloud-hosted data sources. Such tools enable businesses to explore and visualize any type of data stored anywhere, helping them discover hidden opportunity in their IoT investment.

8. Self-service data prep becomes main stream as end users begin to shape big data

Image: <u>https://cdns.tblsft.com/sites/default/files/800x800_8.jpg</u>

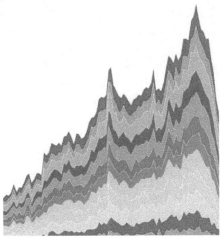

Making Hadoop data accessible to business users is one of the biggest challenges of our time.

The rise of self-service analytics platforms has improved this journey. But business users want to further reduce the time and complexity of preparing data for analysis, which is especially important when dealing with a variety of data types and formats.

Agile self-service data-prep tools not only allow Hadoop data to be prepped at the source but also make the data available as snapshots for faster and easier exploration. We've seen a host of innovation in this space from companies focused on end-user data prep for big data such as Alteryx, Trifacta, and Paxata. These tools are lowering the barriers to entry for late Hadoop adopters and laggards and will continue to gain traction in 2017.

Further reading: WHY SELF-SERVICE PREP IS A KILLER APP FOR BIG DATA

9. Big data grows up: Hadoop adds to enterprise standards

Image: https://cdns.tblsft.com/sites/default/files/800x800_9.jpg

We're seeing a growing trend of Hadoop becoming a core part of the enterprise IT landscape.

And in 2017, we'll see more investments in the security and governance components surrounding enterprise systems. Apache Sentry provides a system for enforcing fine-grained, role-based authorization to data and metadata stored on a Hadoop cluster. Apache Atlas, created as part of the data governance initiative, empowers organizations to apply consistent data classification across the data ecosystem. Apache Ranger provides centralized security administration for Hadoop.

Customers are starting to expect these types of capabilities from their enterprise-grade RDBMS platforms. These capabilities are moving to the forefront of emerging big-data technologies, thereby eliminating yet another barrier to enterprise adoption.

Further reading: THE

10. Rise of metadata catalogs helps people find analysis-worthy big data

Image: https://cdns.tblsft.com/sites/default/files/800x800_10_0.jpg

For a long time, companies threw away data because they had too much to process.

With Hadoop, they can process lots of data, but the data isn't generally organized in a way that can be found.

Metadata catalogs can help users discover and understand relevant data worth analyzing using self-service tools. This gap in customer need is

being filled by companies like Alation and Waterline which use machine learning to automate the work of finding data in Hadoop. They catalog files using tags, uncover relationships between data assets, and even provide query suggestions via searchable UIs. This helps both data consumers and data stewards reduce the time it takes to trust, find, and accurately query the data. In 2017, we'll see more awareness and demand for self-service discovery, which will grow as a natural extension of self-service analytics.

https://www.tableau.com/resource/top-10-big-data-trends-2017

2.31 The Demand for Big Data Scientists in India will grow in 2017: Report

Big-Data: Rita G Chauhan - Jan 5, 2017

A new report from Bengaluru-based Simplilearn.com predicted the job opening boost in big data industry in 2017. New trends in big data technology trends will affect different industries and therefore demand for big data professionals will also increase.

In 2016, 'big data' was the new buzzword in the Indian technology space. It is expected that this momentum will remain continue in 2017 as the industry is booming fast in India. Multiple startups emerged in this segment and now they are offering tremendous jobs for big data professionals for ensuring success. "In 2017, demand for data scientists in India will grow hugely.

I expect the need to greatly outweigh the supply, with one lakh jobs available globally, but only 200,000 people are equipped with the skills needed. The sexiest job in the 21st century requires a mixture of multidisciplinary abilities and suitable candidates must be prepared to learn and develop constantly," said Ronald Van Loon, big data thought leader and advisory board member at Simplilearn.

The Simplilearn's report titled 'The India Big Data Job Market Report' also uncovered the list of top cities with highest job openings in this segment. It mentioned Bengaluru as the top city for big data jobs with holding 40 per cent share of the total job market. Other cities with a high demand for big data professionals are Pune, Delhi, Hyderabad, Mumbai and Chennai.

Fast Growing Market

Recently IDC also revealed a report related to the growth of the big data industry. According to IDC, "The Big Data industry will grow with a CAGR of 23.1 per cent in the period of 2016 – 2020." It is estimated the total market touch USD 57 Billion by 2020 all along double digit CAGR for infrastructure, software and services. According to IDC, infrastructure comprises of storage infrastructure, networking and computing etc. and all this will grow with 21.7 per cent CAGR. Software encompasses of information management, software applications, discovery and analytics and all this is expected to grow with a CAGR of 26.2 per cent. On the other hand, services segment includes support services and related infrastructure and software. It is expected to grow with 22.7 percent CAGR.

In general, big data refers to large sets of data that can be analyzed to reveal patterns and trends, specifically in the context of human behavior and interactions. Kashyap Dalal, Chief Business Officer, Simplilearn.com said, "Though there is huge demand for talent in the sector, there is a gap in demand and supply as two-thirds of data analyst jobs are yet to be filled."

The report of Simplilearn's recognizes the boost in demand for big data professionals to Indian IT service companies that are re-directing and bidding for new-age digital projects in big data and cloud computing.

Big Data Startups Raised Funding

The most prominent Indian big data startup is Bengaluru-based Mu Sigma, which raised $211 million from investors MasterCard, Sequoia Capital and General Atlantic and is valued around $1.5 billion. Other startups in this space that raised funding in 2016 were Bridgei2i, Realbox Data Analytics, Fractal Analytics, Scienaptic, and others. CollegeDekho,

OYOFit, Oliveboard are some other startups serving in the Big Data Analytic industry. Like 2016, 2015 was also the great year for big data analytics startups with more than $260 million funding generation by numerous startups.

AUTHOR: Rita G Chauhan

She enjoys writing about business ideas, startups, business services and helpdesks for startups who face challenges and always hunt for informative writing pieces online. You can check out about her works online especially at Franchise India website. She has also written for various article sites like Ezine Articles and Articles Base etc. She contributes blogs on different topics for websites; BlogSpot and word press for SEO and online promotion purposes.

http://www.indianweb2.com/2017/01/05/demand-big-data-scientists-india-will-grow-2017-report/

2.32 Big Data, Data Analytics to Play Vital Role in Financial, Banking Services

By J Deepthi Nandan Reddy | Express News Service | Published: 11th December 2016 | Last Updated: 11th December 2016

HYDERABAD: Big data and data analytics are going to play a big role in financial and banking services post demonetization, as most of the financial transactions are set to go online.

Though banks, Non-Banking Financial Companies (NBFCs) and other companies dealing with financial services are already using data analytics, its importance is set to grow by leaps and downs in the new scenario.

"We have recently tied up with a data analytics firm to assess the creditworthiness and intent of the borrowers. We are confident that data analytics will help us in great way in the upcoming days to make correct decisions," said Shankar Vaddadyi founder and director of i-lend.in, a peer to peer lending company, based out of Hyderabad.

Lending companies like i-lend believe that by analyzing the digital footprint of a person, his attitude, preferences, financial status, societal status and other core information can be gleaned and ascertained. The stress on big data and data analytics has become so pronounced that some financial companies have been giving more importance to data analytics than CIBIL score.

"Banks do not give loans to a person if his CIBIL score is less and they follow it absolutely. But sometimes a person might default on a loan due to various unavoidable reasons even though he is genuine. Data analytics can provide even better insight than CIBIL score about a person's creditworthiness. And the results arising out of data analytics will have accuracy of more than 90 percent," explains MadhavaTurumella, CEO of Cove Venture, a data analytics company.

Besides banks and NBFCs, government departments like Income Tax Department, Registration Department and law enforcing agencies are already using data analytics. This trend is only set to increase on a huge scale post demonetization, thus creating new opportunities and market for companies involved in big data and data analytics.

"Already we have been using data analytics detect insurance related frauds. Post demonetization our job is set to become easy and more accurate, as most of the financial transactions are set to go online and people inadvertently leave digital footprints," added R Raghavan, CEO of Indian Insurance Bureau.

http://www.newindianexpress.com/cities/hyderabad/2016/dec/11/big-data-data-analytics-to-play-vital-role-in-financial-banking-services-1547915.html

2.33 2017: Digitization of Medical Sector Is Good for Our Health

By Team MMM on January 9, 2017

A recent survey by Do plexus, India's largest and fastest growing community of doctors revealed that 83% of physicians preferred online medical learning as it removes demographic barriers and is convenient.

In this day and age, there's hardly an industry left untouched by technology. In the medical sector, technological innovations are facilitating better and faster diagnoses, optimal resource utilization, reduction in errors and a positive change in the way care is delivered. Healthcare digitization and advanced medical technologies are making possible a more affordable, data-driven personalized care from a remote setting. This is contributing to better outcomes for all stakeholders of the healthcare ecosystem. Here's how key medical innovations are affecting the various healthcare entities.

Picture courtesy: Wikipedia Commons

Patients

Wearable devices are rapidly transforming the way healthcare is delivered to patients. Body patches have been developed for continuous monitoring of heart rates and body temperature, among other parameters.

Sensors are being created to read biomarkers for gauging the levels of *stress* in a person and synchronizing them with blood pressure and pulse rate to determine the state of anxiety. Based on the results, the patient is given personalized insights into his/her specific stressors and the right relaxation techniques are suggested. This is how technology is driving a shift from treatment towards prevention.

A key benefit of wearable technology and integrated IT systems is that it is making possible for care to be given to patients, wherever they are. Such remote monitoring reduces patients' visits to clinics and their overall medical expenses. This is a boon to those suffering from chronic illnesses.

Clinicians

Medical technology has equipped doctors with tools for a more accurate diagnosis and delivery of healthcare. Innovations like Augmented Reality (AR) have the potential to bring in a paradigm shift in the existing healthcare practices. AR healthcare apps can give surgeons precise, real-time, 3D views of the surgery site, vastly improving accuracy and surgical outcomes. AR can also be used in medical education to enable learners get a much-better understanding of the human anatomy.

A chief factor changing healthcare is the industry's rapid digitization. Doctors are increasingly going online to source information that will help them deliver the best treatment and care possible.

A recent survey by Docplexus, India's largest and fastest growing community of doctors revealed that 83% of the physicians preferred online medical learning as it removes demographic barriers and is more convenient.

Online networking platforms like Docplexus are empowering doctors like never before by making available a great deal of information on medical advances, medico-legal issues, healthcare policies and best practice standards. They also act as a channel for doctors to engage with peers and seniors and collaborate towards better medical outcomes. Online CMEs and KOL interactions keep clinicians updated on the latest developments in life sciences.

"Data science and machine learning equip pharma companies to improve their drug development process. They improve the outcomes of clinical trials and enable accurate predictive analyses leading to the creation of the most effective drugs."

Pharmaceutical Companies

Data science and machine learning equip pharma companies to improve their drug development process. They improve the outcomes of clinical trials and enable accurate predictive analyses leading to the creation of the most effective drugs.

AR can be used to provide drug information to doctors and patients in an innovative way. Patients are in no position to decipher complex drug descriptions and find themselves distanced from knowing how exactly the pills they take work inside their bodies. Doctors too, not skilled to interpret complex statistical data of clinical trials that is presented to them in textual format. Their extremely busy schedules make things more challenging.

Pharma can use digital technology to convey drug information to their targeted audience through a mix of audio, video and text. This can be done by establishing more digital touch points with the target segment. A digital connect equips pharma with crucial data that can be analyzed to understand their market's needs and develop the right kind of drugs. It lends them unique insights into their customers' behaviours and preferences. They can personalize their offerings and measure the impact of their strategies. Docplexus offers its pharma client's great value through its expertise in digital marketing comprising the right content strategy, the latest software architecture and a structured analytics and feedback loop.

To conclude, technology is reshaping the medical sector like never before. It is poised to craft a new era characterized by faster, better and more efficient healthcare, dramatically improving global patient outcomes in the near future.

2.34 Data Science Comes of Age
Tue, 10/01/2017 - 09:50 by Steve

As traditional at the start of the New Year, many are taking the opportunity to propose some predictions for how 2017 might unfold. The independent innovation charity Nesta has boldly published ten predictions for trends, social movements and technological breakthroughs that it believes will dominate the year ahead. Although focused on the UK, these imaginative possible futures are just as applicable to many other regions of the world. Underpinning these predictions is a reliance on data and, more specifically, a dependency on greater data skills from all sectors of the economy.

The Nesta predictions are fascinating as they range from the purely technical such as blockchain (which will grow) and the internet (which will fragment), too much broader social movements and transformations such as social engagement – between people, and institutions – and diverse creative practices. What cuts across these, and is indeed a prediction in its own right, is the need for individuals at all stages in their lives and careers to acquire the new skills necessary to enable all of this to materialize.

What is also clear when we examine the future is that the organizations and practices that exist today are changing. This transformation is happening because of the impact of digital technologies and the ensuing shift in business models and revenue streams. We can see it in all sectors, from aerospace to food and from manufacturing to entertainment. We have already seen the shape of new organizational structures in the form of the digital start-ups that have flourished in recent years. These start-ups have grown and evolved into thriving enterprises that have maintained their lean startup philosophy but adapted to the challenges of growth and maturity.

The EU-funded EDISON project has been considering the data-related skills and competences individuals need in this new era, and how best to address the growing demand from organizations for individuals at all levels to be suitably equipped to thrive in the digitized economy. The challenge is that both work and the research environment are transforming into interdisciplinary environments, so data-related skillsets must be harmonized to foster collaboration. The EDISON project has collected these skills and competences under the umbrella of Data Science partly as a term for the experts who will acquire a broad range of Data Science specialism, but also to recognize the needs of the many who will focus their careers on traditional roles, as well as those embracing new, as yet undefined, roles, all of which will require varying degrees of specialism in data-related skills.

Data Science therefore becomes, to some extent, the common language of the information-led economy with all of us benefiting from a greater awareness and confidence in communicating in a data-centric world. The EDISON project has created a framework, EDISON Data Science Framework (EDSF), which presents the skills and competences, job profiles, knowledge and even a model curriculum for Data Science. The project team are now refining this framework and expanding the support resources to enable more sectors and fields to benefit. In order to achieve this, the team would welcome involvement from those with interests in teaching, training, learning and operating in the data science profession. One way of doing this would be to donate some of your valuable time to complete a survey that will enable the team to tailor the existing work to the needs of the broadest possible audience.

The future is uncertain, as it always has been, but embracing and understanding the wealth of data that we are creating about our world offers the potential for all of us to increase our understanding of the world and improve the decisions that we all make about this future.

http://edison-project.eu/2017-data-science-comes-age

2.35 Data Science Trends to Look Out for in 2017

Machine Learning is here to stay, with more firms following Google and Facebook in the race to attract the best machine learning experts and Data Scientists. We also see a merger of IoT and Data Science. Read on for more trends.

By Andrew Dipper

The world of data science, big data and IoT (Internet of things) is continuing to grow and adapt at an astronomical rate. Businesses are slowly able to piece together more information from different sources, meaning that they can make more sense of their data. Using data has become more and more important in creating new business opportunities and growth. Companies are still discovering the potential of utilizing data and the importance of monetizing that data in some form to benefit the business. Here's what we can expect to see from the data science industry in 2017 – and how it might affect you.

Changes in data science qualifications

It's been described as "summoning the demon" by Tesla's Elon Musk, but machine learning is here to stay. Amazon, Face book and

Google have all entered the artificial intelligence race in recent years and in 2017 more businesses will look to attract the best machine learning data scientists to strength their departments.

But competition for jobs could get a lot tougher too. Don't be surprised to see machine learning become mandatory for a career in data science from 2017 as more universities incorporate AI into their curriculums. If you want to stay ahead of the curve, there are a number of AI and machine learning certifications at your disposal. While these come at a high price – normally at least $10,000, give or take –there are numerous training courses on Coursera or edX that are free or at a low cost.

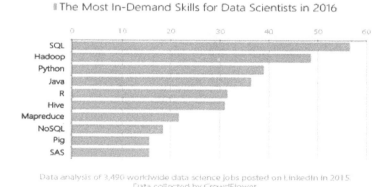

The Most In-Demand Skills for Data Scientists in 2016

Data analysis of 3,490 worldwide data science jobs posted on LinkedIn in 2015.
Data collected by CrowdFlower.

In terms of the other skills you need to succeed in data science, strong technology and coding knowledge, particularly using R or Python – but experience with SAS and MATLAB are also beneficial.

You also need to be comfortable working with relational databases, so SQL is incredibly important. In 2015 SQL was listed as the most important skill to have from a study of 3500 LinkedIn job listings. Hadoop, Python and Java were also prevalent.

IoT and data science merges

Despite a few key differences, data science and IoT are often seen as two sides to the same coin. In 2017, the two industries will come even closer together, with data scientists looking to access data from devices in real-time and to perform advanced analysis – or be used to decide.

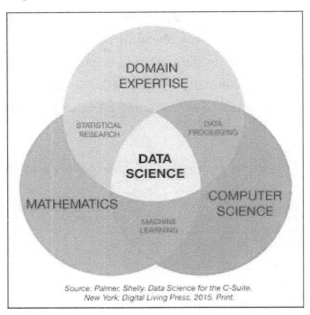

Source: Palmer, Shelly. *Data Science for the C-Suite.*
New York: Digital Living Press, 2015. Print.

So how does that work out in the real world? Think about it like this. soon, you won't need keys to enter your home. As you approach the front door, it will sense your presence and automatically unlock itself for you. Then, as soon as you leave the house, it will ask all the non-essential energy units in the house to turn off – in turn saving the homeowner money.

This may sound like something you'd see on the Starship Enterprise but we should start seeing these relationships really take shape in 2017 – and you need to make sure you have the skills to jump on these projects.

As well as AI, data science for IoT means you should be able to work with RIL (radio interface layer) across a variety of devices, edge processing, real-time processing and deep learning.

The rise of big data technologies

We've already seen this grow astronomically in 2016, but in the next year budgets for big data technologies will rapidly increase as it becomes more widely accepted amongst businesses. Most companies have already identified that they need to improve this area of business, which will, in turn, lead to more data scientists being needed to handle the masses of extra data they have to access.

If you're looking to forge a career in data science, knowledge of big data and data frameworks are essential. You want to specifically look at Apache Hadoop, HDFS, Hbase, Spark, Storm, Solr, and Kafka.

A healthcare industry led by data science

Data science has already been invaluable in improving the outcomes of epidemics and predicting patient behaviour. In 2015, data scientists helped predict further West Nile virus outbreaks in the United States, with 85% accuracy. And earlier this year, a team of scientists developed a model that can predict the likelihood of bats carrying Ebola. Expect data science usage in the healthcare industry to grow further in

2017 as healthcare professionals look for ways to improve day-to-day needs and save lives.

TRANSFORM HEALTHCARE THROUGH
EFFECTIVE USE OF INFORMATION

With the rise of electronic healthcare records the amount of data at our disposal is at an all-time high. While massive amounts of data have its benefits and drawbacks, there are many lucrative opportunities for scientists looking to decipher this data in 2017. If you're looking for an emerging market to work in, this is it.

http://www.kdnuggets.com/2016/12/data-science-trends-2017.html

2.36 Big Data Analytics- Big Security

Ratan Jyoti: **Chief Information Security Officer (CISO), Ujjivan Financial Services**- Published on February 5, 2017

Big Data Analytics is and can be most effective fortifications against cyber intrusions. Accurate, speedy and effective information can help us in lessening of critical time from detection to remediation and thus proactively defend and protect your information and infrastructure. If we call the Intrusion Detection and Prevention System as First generation of the Security System, the second generation belongs to Security Information and Event Management (SIEM) which were without the data analytics. The third generation belongs to Big Data Analytics based Security Information and Event Management (SIEM) which is typically the Next generation SIEMs and are heavily relying on Big data and its analytical capabilities. A Big Data security analytics ecosystem can give firms enhanced visibility into their users, applications, network and information. Following are some of the usage of Big data which if utilized suitably will make differences:

1.   **Real Time Transaction and Fraud Monitoring**

For last few decades the Card and delivery transaction frauds have been challenge for banks and payments systems. Fraud detection on a real-time basis is one of the most visible application of big data analytics and data mining and as s a result the real-time Risk Based transaction monitoring have become feasible. Many Fraud Risk Management (FRM) solutions rely upon the Big data capabilities and the best part is that they are still evolving.

2.   **Improved Security Analytics and advanced Security Operation Centre**

The Big Data Analytics unleashes fresh capabilities of security analytics. Security Operations Centers (SOCs) have traditionally relied on trademarked Security Information and Event Response Systems (SIEMS) for their security analytics proficiencies. New security analytics capabilities have evolved because of Big Data Security Analytics which helps in real-time alerts, real time anomaly detection, real time correlation etc. at amazing speed.

3.   Big data analytics and building threat intelligence

Cyber Threat intelligence is all about empowering Cyber Security decision-making and response. Most of the organizations today ignore some or many security alerts or events as they are overwhelmed by the deluge of events and alerts. Question remains are they ignoring something that they shouldn't? Are they inviting possible breach? What is the tradeoff – possibly automated system which can suppress false positives or unconnected information and thus answer is the accurate Threat Intelligence. Although use of big data analytics is already evident in the way of Threat Intelligence but I foresee a level of maturity in this area.

4.   Cloud Security with Big Data analytics

Data breaches and theft can be disastrous and if this cloud based data theft or breaches as it can cause significant loss to business and reputation because they handle enormous amount of data and information. Because of shared resources it is even more vulnerable as weakness of one shared resources can impact all other. Techniques like "attribute based encryption "and big data analytics can help in providing the security to the cloud emphatically. Anomaly and behavior change can be detected using "feature extraction".

Big data analytics and its application can help in preventing and detecting threats at an early stage, using more erudite pattern analysis and correlating multiple sources in no time.

https://www.linkedin.com/pulse/big-data-analytics-security-ratan-jyoti?trk=hb_ntf_MEGAPHONE_ARTICLE_POST By Vardaan - Sep 11, 2015

http://www.indianweb2.com/2017/01/05/demand-big-data-scientists-india-will-grow-2017-report/

2.37 Preparing for a 'Cloud'y Year- Top Cloud Telephony Trends for 2017

<u>AMBARISH GUPTA</u> 01/02/2017

2016 has been the springboard year for Cloud communications. Over the past 12 months, Cloud communications has gained a significant momentum, which will continue well into 2017 as enterprises migrate additional applications to the cloud and feature real-time communication applications. With massive business uptake and exponential growth, several industry reports have forecast this growth trend to be on track in 2017 as well. Given that cloud communications are benchmarked for rapid evolution soon, here are a few of cloud telephony trends that might prove to be a shot in the arm for the cloud communications industry in the upcoming year:

The Progressive Role of Public Cloud Services

From private clouds to public clouds, organizations are making a rapid transition after realizing the amount of savings it generates in terms of time and cost. Organizations are rapidly migrating onto public cloud services to meet all business requirements, be it emails, documents, business applications, or unified communication systems. This offloads the responsibility of day-to-day maintenance and management of the IT setup to cloud-based service providers, and frees up their internal IT teams to focus on business-critical innovations and drive additional revenue streams for enterprises. The steady progress of the global public cloud market can be gauged from its consistent annual growth of 22 percent, growing from $87 billion in 2015 to a projected $146 billion in 2017.

Web-based Communications

With 2017 poised to be the year of web communications, we will witness several integrations between web-based interfaces and communication technology. Numerous emerging technologies are already eliminating the need for plug-ins, hardware, or proprietary technology by enabling communications features and functions to be natively embedded into websites and web-based applications. By promoting interconnectivity between all supported devices, these integrations will allow organizations to exponentially increase the outlay of their communications infrastructure without heavy investments.

Cloud Communications & CRM (customer relationship management)

Intelligence is a buzzword in today's technological arena, and 2017 will see more companies benefitting from evolved voice communications. By integrating their communications infrastructure with customer databases, organizations will be able to create intelligent communication networks that place consumers at the heart of any interaction. This will not only drive better productivity for a business, but will also significantly enhance its customer experience quotient. Furthermore, businesses will rewrite more applications and shift it completely to the cloud platform to optimally utilize the elasticity of cloud communications.

Hybridization of Cloud Platforms

While public cloud platforms and third-party providers help to significantly cut down on the costs, they also bring in a high risk of compromising sensitive and secured information. As a result, most CIOs are looking towards adopting a hybrid model with the help of Hyper converged infrastructure (HCI). It offers reintegrated storage resources that creates small, isolated pockets of information and helps to run cloud implementations faster. In fact, HCI solutions are considered the foundation for any private cloud development.

Greater Pro-activity and Improved Response Times

Technology has improved response times and facilitated a proactive business approach. Increasing sophistication in communications technology and its integration with CRM systems will allow enterprises to drive more growth, achieve greater scale, improve customer service, and generate better returns. Productivity will no doubt shoot up because of improved response times, as will the end-user service satisfaction.

Data Utilization

Data has emerged as the new 'gold' for the global business landscape, and 2017 is expected to further underline the impact of properly utilizing data. Gartner predicts that as many as 25 percent businesses will create the leadership role of Chief Data Officer (CDO) to specifically oversee information management and value extraction from available data to enable highly informed and accurate decision-making.

Conclusion

Communication technologies have evolved in step with a fast-changing business ecosystem, and are providing organizations with a competitive advantage when it comes to accomplishing both long-term and short-term objectives. As more day-to-day functions migrate onto a digital platform and remote workforces continue to rise, there will be a greater convergence between tech and the way businesses currently work. Businesses that understand this changing paradigm and adopt cloud-based communications into their everyday functioning early will eventually be optimally positioned to achieve long-term success.

By **Ambarish Gupta**: **Ambarish Gupta is the Founder and CEO of Knowlarity- a Cloud Telephony company focused on SME in emerging markets. Previously, he was a Consultant at Microsoft, before which he had served as a Senior Associate at McKinsey And Company.**

http://www.iamwire.com/2017/01/top-cloud-telephony-trends-2017/146884

2.38 Guide for Library Links on Digitization, Preservation, Curation and Data Management: Big Data / Data Science

This LibGuide provides resources and assistance to libraries and other organizations embarking on, or involved in, digitization projects, curation and data management (which includes data science/big data, data / text mining, dataset & other resources)

- Toggle Dropdown
- Digital Curation & Resources
- Data ManagementToggle Dropdown
- Science Toggle
- Resources Toggle
- Articles/Reports/LibGuides
- Digital Libraries / ETDs / Scholarly Repositories Toggle Dropdown
- Research Process
- Wits Library

Definitions

- Big Data - What is it?
- Big data - Wikipedia, the free encyclopedia
- Data Science: An introduction
- Definitions of Big Data | Opentracker - Digital Analytics
- Five first steps to creating an effective 'big data' analytics program
- Understanding Big Data | Opentracker - Digital Analytics
- Undefined By Data: A Survey of Big Data Definitions (Jonathan Stuart Ward and Adam Barker)
- What does Big Data mean?
- What is big data (Big Data)? - Definition from WhatIs.com
- What is big data analytics? - Definition from WhatIs.com
- What is big data as a service (BDaaS)? - Definition from WhatIs.com
- What is big data management? - Definition from WhatIs.com
- What is data mining? - Definition from WhatIs.com
- What is Data Science?
- What is data science? - Definition from WhatIs.com
- What is Hadoop? - Definition from WhatIs.com
- What is predictive analytics? - Definition from WhatIs.com

Guidelines

- Big Data
- Guide to big data analytics tools, trends and best practices
- Layman's Guide to the Big Data Ecosystem (2014)

Trends in Big Data

- Big Data Trends - Forbes
- Trends in Big Data: A Forecast for 2014 | CSC

Managing Big Data

- Big Data: The Management Revolution - Harvard Business Review
- Managing Big Data
- What is big data management? - Definition from WhatIs.com

Best Practices

- Best Practices For Managing Big Data - Forbes
- Guide to big data analytics tools, trends and best practices

Tools and Analytics for Big Data

- 'Big data' analytics spawns a revolution
- 7 top tools for taming big data | Business Intelligence - InfoWorld
- 16 Top Big Data Analytics Platforms - InformationWeek
- 50+ Open Source Tools for Big Data |
- Big Data-Startups | The Big Data open source tools
- Big Data Analytics: What it is and why it matters?
- Big Data Analytics | Pentaho Software for Big Data
- Big Data Analytics | Talend
- Big Data Toolkit
- Former Yahoo data chief: Analytics is the future of 'big data'
- IBM Big Data and Analytics
- In-memory analytics tools pack potential big data punch
- New Mobile 'Connect Insight' Data Analytics Tool for Higher Education Leads McGraw-Hill... -- AUSTIN, Texas, March 3, 2014 /PRNewswire/ --
- Open Access Data Protocol (Science Commons)
- The Value of High-Performance Analytics

Big Data / Data Science

- 7 Biggest Business Benefits from Big Data
- The Awesome Ways Big Data Is Used Today To Change Our World | LinkedIn

- Beyond Big Data – The New Information Economy
- Big Data" The Key Skills Businesses Need
- Big Data - the next frontier for innovation, competition and productivity
- Big Data : The 4 Layers Everyone Must Know
- Big Data: The Eye-Opening Facts Everyone Should Know
- Big Data basic concepts and benefits explained - TechRepublic
- The Big Data Conundrum: How to Define It? | MIT Technology Review
- Big Data Startups
- Big Data Trends Briefing: Digital Cream London 2013 | E-consultancy
- Big Data White Paper
- Data Science and Prediction
- Harnessing the power of big data | Local Leaders Network | Guardian Professional
- How Big Data Liberates Research
- How to manage big data and reap the benefits
- The key word in "Data Science" is not Data, it is Science
- New Multistakeholder Initiative: "My Data Belongs To Me" | Intellectual Property Watch
- Putting Big Data in Context | Innovation Insights | Wired.com
- Sendhil Mullainathan: What Big Data Means For Social Science (HeadCon '13 Part I) | Edge.org
- The size of Big Data matters, and also what you do with it
- Staying Ahead of the Big Data Curve
- Survey Demonstrates The Benefits Of Big Data - Forbes
- Tackling Global Problems with Big Data (Chatham House)
- Ten Practical Big Data Benefits | Stories | Data Science Series
- Tom Davenport's Guide to Big Data - Forbes

- What is Big Data Analytics? Technology and Benefits Defined - Webopedia.com
- Why Big Data is the new competitive advantage - Ivey Business Journal

Data Science Resources

- Data Science Resources
- Data Scientists Talk

Big Data and Higher Education

- 6 ways Big Data is changing higher education - eCampus News | e-Campus News
- At MIT, Weighing Balance of Privacy and Big Data - Higher Education
- Big Data and Higher Education [Infographic] - datascience@berkeley
- Big Data MOOC Research Breakthrough: Learning Activities Lead to Achievement - EdTech Researcher - Education Week
- Keeping Up With... Big Data | Association of College & Research Libraries (ACRL)
- Recent Big-Data Struggles Are 'Birthing Pains,' Researchers Say - Research - The Chronicle of Higher Education
- Researchers develop tools to access 'scholarly big data' – FierceBigData
- The Rise of Big Data in Higher Education (Webinars)
- Where Do Big Data and Higher Education Intersect? - Edudemic
- Why Big Data is a Big Deal for Higher Education | EDUniverse

Videos/Vimeos

- Big Data

- Cognitive Analytics | Artificial Intelligence | Tech Trends 2014 | Deloitte
- Guide to big data analytics tools, trends and best practices

Tutorials on Big Data

- Video| Big Data / Hadoop Tutorial For Beginners -Parts 1 thru 8 (62,000+ Views) | DATA SCIENCE REPORT - TODAY!

Online Courses in Big Data in Education

- Big Data in Education | Coursera

Articles/Blog items

- 3 lessons in big data from the Ford Motor Company — Tech News and Analysis
- 10 Things Statistics Taught us about Big Data
- The Awesome Ways Big Data Is Used Today to Change Our World
- The Best Big Data Quotes of All Times
- Big Data - Deal with The Negatives to Enjoy the Positives | Enterprise CIO Forum
- Big Data - The Chronicle of Higher Education
- Big Data - Wits - IT's a journey
- Big data: are we making a big mistake?
- Big data: are we making a big mistake? - FT.com
- Big data: hype or transformation? - KMWorld Magazine
- Big Data: New Opportunities and New Challenges
- Big data: The next frontier for innovation, competition, and productivity
- Big data can transform learning – as long as lecturers take control
- The Big Data Conundrum: How to Define It? | MIT Technology Review

- Big Data meets big data
- Big Data Orientation | Opentracker - Digital Analytics
- Big data sparks cultural changes - FT.com
- Big Data Weekly: Social media analytics + (Hadoop) ETL back in the spotlight | SiliconANGLE
- The Big Deal About Big Data and What It Means for IT And You - Forbes
- The Big in Big Data relates to importance not size
- A brief history of open data -- FCW
- Crunching Words in Great Number - Technology - The Chronicle of Higher Education
- Data privacy change could be a bitter pill | News | Times Higher Education
- Dealing with Big Data
- Dealing with Big Data - November issue of Software Magazine - News –XtremeData | Big Data Analytics
- Discovery success linked to big data and the cloud, says Rio Tinto
- Does anyone really understand big data? | ZDNet
- Google Flu Trends: The Limits of Big Data
- The Growth of 'Citizen Science' - Technology - The Chronicle of Higher Education
- How to manage big data and reap the benefits
- Infographic: The 4 Vs of Big Data
- Is big data a big deal?
- Making Sense of Big Data in the Petabyte Age
- Most data isn't "big," and businesses are wasting money pretending it is – Quartz
- The new technologies needed for dealing with big data | PandoDaily
- The Promise of Big Data

- Research SA - The Big Data Revolution
- SA readies for big data storm
- Trends in Big Data: Three Ways to Reap Big Rewards
- Understanding Big Data
- Understanding big data leads to insights, efficiencies, and saved lives | Harvard Magazine Mar-Apr 2014
- What's Up with Big Data Ethics? - Forbes
- What's the Deal with Big Data? | TechViews
- Who owns Big Data? – TechRepublic
- The wrong way: Worst practices in 'big data' analytics programs

Technical Reports

- The Global Information Technology Report - Rewards & Risks of Big Data (2014) (World Economic Forum)

White Papers on Big Data

- Kroes wants White Paper on Big Data
- NESSI White Paper, December 2012

OA Journals

- Big Data & Society OA Journal
- Critical Questions for Big Data - Information, Communication & Society - Volume 15, Issue 5
- International Journal of BigData (IJBD, The First Open Access Journal on Big Data) (ISSN: 2326-442X), New York, USA
- Journal of Big Data

E-Books on Big Data

- IBM Understanding Big Data
- Understanding Big Data: e-book | The Big Data Hub

http://libguides.wits.ac.za/digitisation_preservation_and_digitalcuration/BigData

Chapter 3: Big Data and Data Science Application by Government of India

3.1 How Big Data is improving Lives for the Better in India

MALHAR BARAI, 19 SEPTEMBER 2016

Last year, Big Data was still at a very nascent stage in India. And very few industries could make sense out of it. Fast forward to today, we see not only industries but also various governments trying to leverage big data.

What has changed in a year?

The technology has changed by leaps and bound. And so is the understanding about big data and the power it can give to industries and governments.

In India, our first brush on a large scale was around the elections.

During that time, we often heard stories on how political parties were looking at information at booth level and trying to gauge the mood of the nation. Information suddenly became a potent tool within political circles and we are now seeing a lot more activism around it.

Post that, we are seeing advancement in technology and more usage by the government as well as brands driven by actionable insights derived for big data.

How big data is improving lives in India

AADHAR: The first example I would like to cite is about the massive government exercise in the form of AADHAR. That project has enabled the government to reach out to the citizens directly, thus helping them in transferring various government benefits directly to their accounts – DBT, MNREGA, bio-metric attendance, etc.

AADHAR is touted as the world's biggest biometric database and has been an oft-cited example of best usage of big data. Earlier, we often heard about corruption while doling out benefits to citizen, having a direct channel to transfer benefits, such cases are rarely heard now. AADHAR indeed has helped the citizens as well as the government in plugging the leakages.

Traffic management using big data

Namma Bengaluru is another example. Recently, the traffic department announced the setting up of a command centre. This centre monitors the feeds from various cameras at major junctions. In technical terms, this feed is a form of big data given its volume and velocity. The centre analyses feed data and have automated signals at few of the junctions, thus enabling traffic to move smoothly.

The long-term benefits would be – apart from saving on time to reach your destination - enormous savings on fuel given the volume of traffic. Take that into account and imagine the savings the government will have in its fuel bills.

Automation in manufacturing sector

Working in a tech organization, I see a lot of manufacturing companies asking for automation of various tasks. In layman terms, we are seeing disruption in the manufacturing sector driven by the need of faster and cheaper roll out of products. The sector is handling this need by looking at big data gained from various manufacturing processes and improving forecast, testing and production. For price sensitive markets like India, such automation and optimization of processes by relying on big data is helping bring down the product price, thus driving consumption.

Consumerization of big data

Finally, on the consumer side of business, I would like to quote Myntra app-only approach, though it didn't succeed the way it should have. The aim was to track the app usage, gather data and understand consumer behaviour. This would have helped them send customized deals and improve sales.

An eye into future

'Smart' City implementation

The government is talking a lot about smart cities and has drafted a list of cities they would like to convert into 'smart' city. What exactly does that entail?

For starters, we have seen how the massive urbanization is crippling lot of present day cities. To mitigate that, the government is setting up a cluster that would be futuristic, but at the same time much of the services will be governed by a digital grid. This grid will be capturing data related to civic and personal amenities – birth, death, water, sewage, electricity, etc., thus eliminating all or most of the physical touch points. The data thus generated will help the government in allocating appropriate resources for business continuity as well as personal well-being.

Smart homes

We are already looking at few 'smart' homes where your devices have the capability to track usage and are interconnected. So, based on the data usage, you might have your coffee ready when you wake up, water warm for you to bath, a toast at an optimum temperature, the room temperature optimized by the time you're back from work, etc.

That would be the power of big data when you wake up tomorrow, and with India investing in 'smart' cities much of this could be a reality before you can anticipate.

So, here's to the future of tomorrow!!

Disclaimer: The views and opinions expressed in this article are those of the author and do not necessarily reflect the views of Your Story.

https://yourstory.com/2016/09/big-data-improving-lives-india/

3.2   Data Sciences Can Save India and here is why
VISHAL KRISHNA, 27 JUNE 2016

India produces data of more than 1 billion people. But all this data is used for the benefit of an organization or an institution. Sometimes, this data is not even the real reference point for solutions to be provided because they are produced to suit the needs of a corporate. In a country where we are creating the best analytics talent – for the world – there is enough room for individuals to be used in crunching data that matters for the country. However, several stakeholders must come together and use data sciences to provide predictive and prescriptive outcomes for every industry vertical. Why can it save India? The better we use our data, the better for policymakers to understand industry.

Take the example of a simple thing like the incidence of usage of the drug "Metacin" in the suburbs of Kandivali and Borivali in Mumbai. A platform collating and understanding this data can tell you that these are stock market traders working in South Mumbai, who pick up the medicine in suburbs in the North. This allows a drug company to plan their distribution better and the insurance industry to plan policies around the associated lifestyle diseases. Or these traders can be just told to stop worrying and save themselves the bother.

There is data from banks, agriculture, healthcare, and from manufacturing, which can be managed by consortiums created by these stakeholders. These stakeholders are the very institutions or companies that run the industry. But to what end? It is a means to make the country accountable and offer transparent services to citizens and businesses.

Let us say why we need data platforms by vertical and then this data set should function on a larger horizontal platform. For example, when smart phone vendors say that there are 250 million units sold in the country, what does it mean? It means nothing till we find out what kind of consumption activity entails from using these phones. The consortium in this case would be the telecom operators, the e-commerce companies, the retailers, and smart phone manufacturers. This data platform not only functions as a platform, where different parties share information monthly, but double times as a data cruncher for understanding trends. This is a technology and services play, and needs investments from all the stakeholders. However, the investments in technology will be less than $20 million because things will be provisioned on the cloud – in a datacenter – and the money will be sunk in to manage data scientists. The only investment will be in the data transfer pipe, which requires integration between the datacenters of stakeholders and the machines managed by the data consortium.

We are far away from reality. The data available in this country is like the exit poll data in television channels, which are never right. Perhaps the only real live data set being used in this country is the Bombay Stock Exchange and the National Stock Exchange, which is why the world respects the country's stock market movement.

How the lack of right data affects the promise of big data in India

Doing it the Aadhaar way?

However, there is hope because the Aadhaar database – built by the Unique Identification Authority of India – will become a game changing platform to deliver services to people in India. Even the Unified Payments Gateway is a single platform to allow payments in this country without middlemen. Come to think of it, these are data platforms powered by technology.

Imagine insurance and healthcare data on a single unified platform to improve medical care. Where should we begin to create such a database and whom do we entrust this data to? The merits of such a system are tremendous. Surely, when we can collect identities of Indian citizens through Aadhaar, it is possible to get other forms of data on to a platform.

If we look at Google's objective, it wants to organize the world's data and provide it universally. A similar objective can be replicated and used for India, provided there can be some transparency ensured in security and delivery of services. Let us look at healthcare and SMBs to prove the case.

Healthcare data

There is production data from pharmaceutical companies, and there is medicine-administered data in hospitals along with data pertaining to insurance paid. Bringing this ecosystem together is considered the most difficult process. But, a policy making it mandatory to get these institutions to create a consortium is a necessity. Such a platform would be like an automobile standard for connected vehicles (which is collection of all world's leading automobile companies) or in this case this would be a connected healthcare platform to understand the incidence of the disease by region or a suburb.

Registered stakeholders upload the data of medicine produced and consumed, diseases treated and the insurance paid on a daily basis. The customer data is irrelevant here, but the macro data can generate patterns that can become actionable.

The opportunity to understand diseases treated, and the medicines that have been aiding better health of citizens, can set off a healthcare revolution. It can bring healthcare prices down. The patient gets the right medicine, better priced and customized insurance, and the hospitals get rewarded for providing better care.

Obama care or the Affordable Care Act in the US is based on this premise. It asks stakeholders to transform themselves with technology and aid change through new clinical and financial strategies to make healthcare affordable. Data is a central driver of accountability here.

In India's case, the data can become a readily available sample for medical research. Unfortunately, the coming together of these three stakeholders –pharmacy companies, hospitals and insurance companies – remains a barrier because there is no financial gain for them. Here is why they have to do it.

According to the IFC, an estimated four billion people earn less than $3,000 a year (or approximately $8 a day) form the base of the pyramid (BoP). BoP populations are chronically underserved when it comes to basic necessities – especially healthcare. Despite challenges of access, the BoP population represents a significant unfulfilled demand. The BoP healthcare market in Asia is estimated at around $95.5 billion.

Corporate/SMB data for banks

According to Zinnov, the consulting company, there are 50 million SMBs in India that contribute to 65 percent of the country's GDP. 21 percent of these are manufacturing companies situated in 1,200 SMB clusters. Today, banks have no way of telling which of the companies can be funded.

About 40 percent of these companies depend on financing from friends and family. Most of the debt capital raised from banks stems from their personal relationships rather than sound business metrics. Can there be a platform for this? Perhaps the Confederation of Indian Industry should become the custodian of all data of these companies. It should then create a platform that allows banks to access information on SMBs and then decide the potential of the business as well as the risks involved in funding them. The filings in the Registrar of Companies can be made mandatory too. These filings are treated as a pain today and rightly so because of the drudgery in the system with regard to taxes. What we have been successful at as a nation – especially in companies' – is to dodge the tax man because even the tax man is unreasonable.

The transformation in this case is to keep all the political and bureaucratic elements away from this platform. The platform itself should not become a harassment tool. Instead, banks – along with the platform – can assist SMBs to raise capital, take risks, and provide opportunity for growth.

Streamlining this industry can add more jobs, and improve access to talent capital and technology. Banks can truly reduce their non-performing assets and make their balance sheets robust. They can even change modes of funding from a collateral-based system to a convertible debenture or equity model.

India needs to employ 300 million youth by 2030. Manufacturing can provide at least 30 percent of these jobs and SMBs can prosper with data being captured on a common platform. The industry can truly compete with knowledge sharing rather than working in isolation.

Similar data platforms can be created to protect consumers, improve civic services and more importantly provide better education to make people employable. It is not an impossible endeavour to execute such a change because the data is already being generated. It just needs someone to gather, collate, and make sense out of it. To add food for thought, today, the US can know more about India than India itself because all of the country's social, consumption, and trade data stored in foreign datacenters. It is about time we use data sciences to change ourselves and not let others change us for them.

https://yourstory.com/2016/06/data-sciences-save-india/

3.3 Why Data Science matters and how to approach it for your Digital Transformation

Posted by: JO and DADO **July 3rd, 2015 in** Articles **17241 Views 0**

Big Data is one of the biggest buzzwords of the past few years. Here's a great quote about it:

"Big Data is like teenage sex. Everyone says they're doing it, hardly anyone really is, and nobody knows what they're doing."

Those of you who are familiar with our Digital Transformation methodology know that we like things *a little more pragmatic*, so here is how you should start using data as a backbone of your business.

The why

Every industry has digital challengers that are outperforming the competition. They all use data as a core ingredient of their business strategy, and they do so from the start.

Airbnb for example hired its first Data Scientist when the team had just 7 people in an apartment. It's important to bring data scientists in projects from the start, not later on once things turn out to be a mess.

Uber has its own #UberData blogposts, in which they explain some of their data projects in detail. This not only shows their accomplishments, but they also use these posts to attract data scientists to come work for Uber.

P.S. if you get a kick out of this, Uber is hiring for lots of roles, including the Science Team!

Netflix set new standards for personalization in its streaming service. They mapped out very well which aspects of the business can be optimized through data and also have a clear view on what role it will play in the future of the company.

If you want to compete with digital challengers, data needs to be treated as one of the crucial drivers of transformation in your business. The battle simply can't be won without it. At this point however, few businesses have teams of data scientists in place that take care of all data sources and analyze them to create business opportunities. This gives companies that use data well a large competitive advantage.

The how

We see 5 main reasons why few companies are accomplishing stuff with their data:

1. No clear data architecture
2. A lack of a data strategy
3. Missing clear ownership
4. Not having enough quality data
5. Putting data in a silo

1. No clear data architecture

As many business processes are virtualizing, more and more data sources are popping up. Think about CRM systems, client service systems, social media platforms, mobile apps, in-store data, website analytics, collaboration tools, sales platforms, etc. These platforms are generating new data streams, are you using these?

The very first step to use data to your advantage is setting up clear data architecture to build an overview of all the different data sources. Define which types of data should be tracked, linked or combined to drive business value.

2. A lack of a data strategy

One of the biggest mistakes is monitoring and mining a plethora of data, without having a clear idea what the actual output should be. So why hire data scientists if you don't even know what you expect from them?

You need to define clear objectives, here are the most common ones to inspire you:

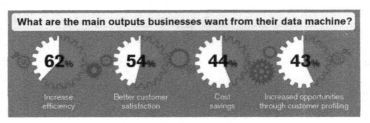

Source: Experian Data Quality

3. No clear ownership

An architecture and strategy are the fundamentals. To put things into practice you need to appoint the right people. You need a team with ownership over your data, because we all know that everyone is too busy and managing the data of a company is not a side job, it's more than a full-time job if you really want to take it serious.

Data Scientists are a new profile for most companies, and they are hard to find as this is a domain which is just starting out. Here is how Netflix is recruiting a Senior Data Scientist.

4. Not enough quality data

According to Experian Data Quality, 86% of businesses suspect their data might be inaccurate in some way. 44% says incomplete data is their biggest problem and 41% says the biggest problem is outdated information.

This doesn't just happen overnight, there are 4 reasons why your data may be inaccurate: Human error, poor internal communications, a lack of a data strategy and a lack of resources. Find the problem and solve it at the source, or cleaning up your data will only be a temporary measure but a huge investment.

"DJ Patil, the recently appointed Chief Data Scientist of the White House, summarizes the data problem well, noting that "you have to start with a very basic idea: Data is super messy, and data cleanup will always be literally 80 percent of the work. In other words, data is the problem." ~*Source:* Techcrunch

5. Putting data in a silo

Last but not least: setting up a data science team that is working in a silo, not horizontally serving the different business units, will turn the outcome into an isolated data-crunchers story. We believe that data scientists should be incorporated into the cross-departmental team of the Chief Digital Officer to make it succeed.

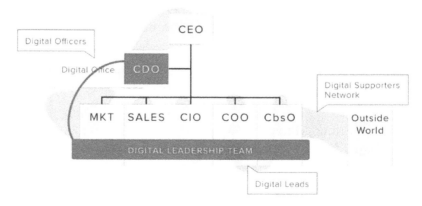

Whatever business you're in, we hope you understand the importance of incorporating data into the core of your business activities.

Don't let the opportunity pass by! Our book on Digital Transformation might help you to get started on the strategy part.

http://www.digitaltransformationbook.com/why-data-science-matters-and-how-to-approach-it-for-your-digital-transformation/

3.4   How Data Analytics Can Help Modi Government Catch the Demons of Demo

Aashish Chandorkar - Jan 09, 2017, 12:43 pm

The government will have heaps of complex transaction data from the post-demonetization months.

Here's how it can leverage data analytics capabilities to track down those who may have tried to game the banking system.

When Prime Minister Narendra Modi made the demonetization announcement on the night of 8 November, it started an administrative chain reaction focused on squeezing money launderers, promoting less-cash economy and of course remonetizing the banking system. As the all-important 30 December cutoff for depositing demonetized currency notes ended, the focus has shifted to the next logical steps. The government and the Reserve Bank of India (RBI) will now have to work on computing tax liability for those who declared their cash and deposited their holdings in the banks and on busting money launderers who tried to game the constantly changing and readjusting demonetization rules in November and December.

The maturing of financial services technology over the last few years has also coincided with increasing global threats of crime and terrorism, which need movement of money. Over the last couple of decades, global regulators have been trying to keep up with money trails which fund global crimes, tax evasion through tax havens, and the routine day to day conversion of unaccounted wealth to legitimate assets which happens in every economy to varying degree.

Money laundering as a concept is hardly alien to the banking systems worldwide. Peter Reuter in his 2004 book *Chasing Dirty Money* explained the three-step process of money laundering: Placement – putting the illicit wealth in the financial system, layering – creating a maze of financial transactions to create an illusion of legitimacy to their placed wealth, and integration – using these transactions to legalize the illicit wealth.

India has its own set of rules in the money laundering space, primarily governed by the 2002 Prevention of Money Laundering Act, which has since been modified a few times. Banks in India have to comply with a host of regulatory provisions, which include know your customer (KYC), filing cash transaction reports (CTRs) for reporting flow of cash in and out of the banking system, and filing suspicious transaction reports (STRs) for any suspect pattern of transaction activity in bank accounts. These provisions try to catch patterns, which correspond to one or more of the three steps Reuter characterized as laundering.

Indian financial system has several players – foreign banks, public sector banks, private banks, cooperative banks, rural banks, credit cooperatives, and the specialized non-banking financial corporations. The technology capability, understanding of operational risk, regulatory appreciation and general understanding of financial fraud varies in a big way across these myriad institutions. Globally, the financial engineers have demonstrated their ability to always outpace financial regulators in the last decade, and India is perhaps no exception. In this operating environment, a sudden jolt with nationwide systemic impact like demonetization was always going to expose the weaker innards of financial services.

Yet, the government and the RBI are now faced with the task of finding fiscal upside as well as catching potential tax offenders. The key to success may lie not in the hallowed precincts of North Block in Delhi or in the RBI headquarters in Mumbai. The Financial Intelligence Unit (FIU) of the Ministry of Finance (MOF) and the RBI may have to work jointly with the several data analytics companies spread in various information technology (IT) cities to attain their dual objectives through 2017.

The FIU and the RBI will be saddled with heaps of complex transaction data from the post-demonetization months. The data volumes for November and December 2016 will be obviously much higher than usual. And buried deep inside these datasets will be the answers government is seeking. This is where data analytics capabilities like pattern matching, linking accounts to individuals, creating 360 degree views of customers, analyzing long time series data, and linking transactions to tax returns will come in handy. Thankfully for the government, these skills are aplenty in the Indian technology industry, apart from the homegrown capability with the FIU and the RBI.

Data analytics can come in handy in various ways for the government beyond scrutinizing the CTRs and STRs filed by the banks. Some of the areas to dive deeper into are as follows.

First, match cash transactions to account profiles: This is a low hanging fruit where the bank data can directly throw red flags. Checking *Pradhanmantri Jan Dhan Yojana* accounts, their funding dates, and deposit and withdrawal patterns in the last two months should be the first port of call. There is a lot of anecdotal evidence in media around misuse of these accounts by money sharks, either for a fee or just by threatening the account holders.

Second, check for new activity. Analytics can be used to determine the number of new accounts opened against a specific identifier like Permanent Account Number (PAN). There may also be a chance that fraudsters may have opened multiple accounts to deposit small amounts using different government identity cards and not seeded PAN in all of them. Using data with the Income Tax department on passport or Aadhaar to link individual IDs to trace such accounts should be explored. Once a linked database is available, the same can then be used to find transactions like depositing small sums of cash in multiple accounts in primary or secondary holder capacity.

Third, analysis of past pre-demonetization data: It will be critical to interpret cash movement in accounts as well as entire bank branches in November and December against the activity levels in the last few months. The government has already asked for April to October cash movement data from the banks. Bank branches which have suddenly shown manifold rise in cash movement could be liable to be scrutinized in their entirety. This can be achieved by using a combination of algorithms like time series, clustering and regression to pin point fraud.

Fourth, checking remittances: There could be situations where demonetized cash moved out of India through *hawala* route and corresponding net of fee money transfers made back to Indian accounts against dubious trade papers. Scrutinizing remittances, which are complex exercise given the intermediaries involved in any global money movement, will be critical.

Fifth, too many inward electronic payments in an account: Launderers may have enrolled several accomplices trusting them with small sums of money, which can then be transferred from the agents to the principal electronically. If there are bank accounts with unusually high inward RTGS/NEFT payments bunched together in the last few or next few weeks, it should raise a flag.

Sixth, using credit instruments: A potential laundering activity could be to use credit instruments like credit cards with unusually high sums deposited in these accounts to be used later.

Seventh, profiling bank branches: While a prudent banking IT system will have restrictions or clear trails on backdated transactions and adjustments, it is fair to assume that there could be loopholes known to some bank employees or smaller banks may not have good IT systems and controls in place. Scrutinizing bank branches with more than usual STR activity or abrupt changes in complexity of STRs will be handy.

Eighth, creating a 'related account' view: If multiple accounts (e.g. of relatives or family connections) have made repeated payment transactions (e.g. deposit in one account, then distribute the money across accounts), creating a view of such related accounts will be important. This may be the most common way of structuring illegal money in the banking system. Techniques like geospatial analysis on bank branches in a given PIN code can be employed

Ninth, matching Income Tax data to bank data: This is perhaps the most crucial aspect of demonetization analytics, to link income patterns to transaction patterns. The bank account data – at least in theory – is already available with the I-T department. The challenge will in unearthing either incorrect income or incorrect bank data and linking the two using PAN information. Any steps taken in this area will also have to ensure that government does not cross the red lines of tax terrorism – a fear which has been routinely expressed by various commentators in media and periodically acknowledged by various government officials themselves.

Tenth, matching trade invoices cash transactions and positions: This is perhaps the most complex and most productive area for tracing illegal wealth. Trade invoices, along with property, gold, art, and cash, form the main source of black money in India. The government will have to balance its promise of not digging too much in the past when it comes to small businesses with the need for busting big offenders. Matching patterns in trade invoices, cash in hand, and related banking transactions especially taking a historical view against the fourth quarter 2016 view can unearth a lot of muck. But it is not clear how much political capital does government want to spend in this area in the immediate future.

This is also a good time for analytics firms to sharpen their market offerings and for the governments to institutionalize technology driven compliance. There can be no better use case for the "Make in India" initiative too. This government is definitely the most technology friendly regime India has ever had. Will it make a push to tap the wide talent base India has to accomplish important political and economic objectives?

Only time will tell, but given the resolve the Prime Minister has shown in pushing the policy boundaries in the last few months, no one should bet against it.

https://swarajyamag.com/economy/how-data-analytics-can-help-modi-government-catch-the-demons-of-demo

3.5 Data and Innovation in the Economic Survey

The use of Big Data can however complement reforms in India's traditional statistical machinery to help generate better data and frame more informed policies.

New Delhi: This year's Economic Survey does not carry the usual statistical tables on the economy's performance, which are used widely by analysts.

This is probably because the budget has been advanced, and those tables will find place in the forthcoming volume slated for later this year. The survey seems to have compensated this by the use of Big Data and intensive data-mining of multiple datasets "to shed new light on the flow of goods and people within India".

The survey has used individual tax filings administered by the Goods and Service Tax Network to estimate state-level (both inter and intra) trade. Railway station-wise unreserved passenger traffic data provided by the Indian Railways has been used to arrive at estimates of work-related migration.

Satellite imagery has been used to calculate built-up area and estimate potential property tax collections (and hence losses being incurred currently).

Besides machine-generated large-scale data sets, even existing databases have been used more intensively. For instance, district-level estimates of the National Sample Survey Office (NSSO) statistics, which are the main source of employment and poverty/inequality statistics in India, have been used to generate insights on spatial concentration of poverty and welfare beneficiaries. Data from the Socio-Economic Caste Census (SECC) have also been put to similar use.

Ever since the start of the planning process, the official statistical machinery has largely focused on surveys almost to the point of neglecting administrative data (viz., data collected during routine administrative tasks). It is fitting that the end of the planning era should mark the beginning of a new chapter in which administrative data will be given pride of place in economic policy-making once again.

The new approach towards using diverse datasets is definitely an important first step towards better decision-making. Take the migration data using railway traffic for example. Census-based statistics for migration are still from the 2001 census, as detailed statistics for 2011 census have not been released till now. The railway traffic-based migration data is available till 2015-16. Such data, if made transparently available on a regular basis, can give useful insights on employment and distress-related scenarios for migrant workers, which currently rely on guesstimates based on figures such as demand for jobs in the MGNREGA.

The survey has used satellite imagery for built-up areas to estimate potential property tax collections. Marrying this data with something like income tax data for India's top 50 cities and house-size census data can generate rich insights about our cities and their riches.

Still, it needs to be kept in mind that Big Data alone cannot be a silver bullet for India's statistical challenges. For example, the informal sector continues to be a black hole when it comes to data. For several sectors and purposes, there are still no alternatives to better-designed and more intensive surveys.

The use of Big Data can however complement reforms in India's traditional statistical machinery to help generate better data and frame more informed policies. If the new databases are cleaned and opened up (in a machine-readable format) for independent researchers to track, verify and analyze, it could usher a new era of transparency and accountability.

For a start, the finance ministry should consider opening up the underlying data used in the survey in a machine-readable format.

A new methodology is required for transforming Big Data stored in heterogeneous and different-in-nature data sources (e.g., legacy systems, Web, scientific data repositories, sensor and stream databases, social networks) into a structured, hence well-interpretable format for target data analytics. As a consequence, data-driven approaches, in biology, medicine, public policy, social sciences, and humanities, can replace the traditional hypothesis-driven research in science.

Big Data does not convert data into actionable information. Big Data does not create value. But Data Science does, and it does not have to be complex or expensive, or even big.

Data Science is a three-legged stool that combines business acumen, data wrangling and analytics to create extreme value. Focusing on the hard science skills such as statistical methods is a common mistake when; developing the knowledge about a particular business and wrangling the relevant data are often the most important skills to bring to the table.

Fast Growing Market

Recently IDC also revealed a report related to the growth of the big data industry. According to IDC, "The Big Data industry will grow with a CAGR of 23.1 per cent in the period of 2016 – 2020." It is estimated the total market touch USD 57 Billion by 2020 all along double digit CAGR for infrastructure, software and services. According to IDC, infrastructure comprises of storage infrastructure, networking and computing etc. and all this will grow with 21.7 per cent CAGR. Software encompasses of information management, software applications, discovery and analytics and all this is expected to grow with a CAGR of 26.2 per cent. On the other hand, services segment includes support services and related infrastructure and software. It is expected to grow with 22.7 percent CAGR.

In general, big data refers to large sets of data that can be analyzed to reveal patterns and trends, specifically in the context of human behavior and interactions. Kashyap Dalal, Chief Business Officer, Simplilearn.com said, "Though there is huge demand for talent in the sector, there is a gap in demand and supply as two-thirds of data analyst jobs are yet to be filled."

The report of Simplilearn's recognizes the boost in demand for big data professionals to Indian IT service companies that are re-directing and bidding for new-age digital projects in big data and cloud computing.

3.6 Use of Big Data in Government's Overarching Policies and Reforms

January 17, 2017 Divya Bharathi G, Prasanth Reddy Burramukku

Introduction

It is by now no surprise that we live in a world of data. Of late, big data has been the hottest buzzword across all industries. It's one of those things big companies and startups constantly talk about when people ask what "the next big thing" will be. Data is produced in greater quantities and by more sources than ever before and analyzed faster and with greater sophistication than was imaginable just a few years ago. Every day, new tools are created to turn raw data into information, and information into visual representations. The reach and applicability of big data seem limitless.

Around 40% of the world population has an internet connection today. In 1995, it was less than 1%. The number of internet users has increased tenfold from 1999 to 2013. The first billion was reached in 2005.Currently 3.6 billion people use internet and more than 4.9 billion use mobile phones to communicate. With so many technology and internet enabled devices all around data is being produced at unprecedented levels globally. Many innovations have been made toward expanding the technological capacity to generate, store, and analyze data from multiple sources and for a multitude of purposes. Individuals, firms, machines, and government agencies produce data at unprecedented rates. Some 2.5 quintillion bytes of data are produced every day, and approximately 90 percent of existing data was produced in the last two years alone. The ever increasing data footprint provides a range of possibilities for usage by government.

Researchers are being carried out to determine whether big data could help governments improve policy design and service delivery. Strengthening policy and promoting investments in big data and cloud computing areas offer potential tools for "changing production patterns, generating quality employment, creating local value-added, and enhancing the region's competitiveness and integration into global markets.

Methodology

Earlier much effort was put in by the government to gather, store and analyze large amounts of information. Many governments and firms have been collecting large amounts of data about their citizens or customers to better understand their preferences and provide better services and products. Big Data can significantly change the way public services reach citizens.

For instance, when a 5.9 earthquake hit near Richmond, Virginia on August, 2011, residents in New York City read about the quake on Twitter feeds 30 seconds before they experienced the quake themselves. People are more connected than ever and increasingly empowered. Citizens expect to get the information they want, when they want it, and in whatever way they want to access it. In the past few years, digital technology i.e. online portals, mobile apps, self – service kiosks etc. has unleashed a tsunami of information on the government and changed the dynamic of its relationship with citizens. New expectations require governments to be ready to receive, process, share and deliver information and services anytime, anywhere and on any device. Enter Big Data. Big Data provides the opportunity to transform the business of government by providing greater insight at the point of impact and ultimately better serving citizenry.

For Public sector organizations that are ahead of the curve on Big Data adoption, the greatest benefits lie in improved performance and productivity, transparency and risk assessment and policy decision making and operational intelligence.

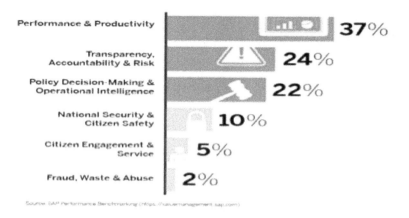

So, the next time an earthquake strikes a city, its citizens might have already been forewarned and evacuated to shelters. That's the promise of Big Data for government.

Government collects all sorts of data from the public; it has access to birth data, death data, area of country, security data. In real time Big Data can be of great use to the government in formulating and altering the policies of the country. Important role of big data in transforming the face of various sectors is in the following way.

Taxation:

Many developing economies today face taxation challenges which include tax evasion, low collection rates, and weak tax administration. Tax evasion and income tax fraud are the main problems that are to be identified and addressed. Tax data includes business transactions, invoices, property details etc. Countries like Brazil, China, and the United

States have used big data to formulate, improve, and manage tax policy and administration in diverse environments. Tax authorities have been using innovative technical solutions to implement sophisticated fraud detection strategies using socio-demographic data and taxpayers' behavior predictive analytics using big data. Tax administration system makes extensive use of big data solutions that use multi- and cross-referencing to verify business information which makes it very difficult for people to find the loopholes in the system. All these data analytics can help in prevent people from evading tax, which results in more national income thereby higher growth

Climate Change:

With many of the countries ratifying the Paris Agreement in October, 2016, it is the duty of the country to ambitiously fight against the climate change. Big Data can adversely help our country in achieving the climate change goals. By getting data on a continuous basis from all the factories and industries in the country, the government can impose stricter rules and taxes on the factories which are polluting the most. This data can also help government in devising barriers to entry for companies implementing the technologies which are not complying with the ambitious pollution standards.

Big Data can also help government predict the weather conditions and thereby drought or famine in advance and can accordingly ease the regulations on import of food and other groceries to prevent inflation.

Smart Cities:

Smart Cities AwasYojna Mission was launched by Prime Minister Narendra Modi in June 2015. A total of ₹980 billion has been approved by the Indian Cabinet for development of 100 smart cities and rejuvenation of 500 others. Smart cities can fundamentally change our lives at many levels such as less pollution, garbage, parking problems and more energy savings. Despite the path to implementation is full of the challenges, big data and the Internet of Things (IoT) have the power to drive the implementation. Big data and the IoT are going to work with other software and hardware to lead the vision of smart city to fruition.

How can big data contribute to smart cities?

• The traffic will be measured and regulated with the help of RFID tags on the cars. The RFID tags will send the geo location data to a central monitoring unit that will identify the congested areas. Also, the citizens will always know via their smart phones and mobile devices the exact status of public transportation and its availability.

• Even garbage collection will generate data. Residents who dispose of garbage will need to use a chip card in the containers. Garbage trucks will not collect and dispose garbage anymore. Each house will have garbage disposal units and garbage will be sucked from them to the garbage treatment centers which will dispose it in an environment friendly way. The garbage will have used to generate power for the city.

• The smart energy grid can measure the presence of people in a particular area in a particular moment and can accordingly adjust the street lights. For example, the smart grids will ensure that areas that are scantly populated will automatically have some of the street lights turned off. This will result in a lot of energy savings.

- Big data can help reduce emissions and bring down pollution. Sensors fitted in the roads will measure the total traffic at different times of a day and the total emissions. The data can be sent to a central unit which will coordinate with the traffic police. Traffic can be managed or diverted along other less congested areas to reduce carbon emissions in a particular area.

- Parking problems can be better managed. Cars will have sensors attached which can guide the car to the nearest available parking lots.

Big data can also help government in understanding the requirement of infrastructure in various parts of the country and thus can help it plan the usage of resources efficiently.

Defense Sector:

When the government has access to security data like how many soldiers are present in the border areas, coastal areas and hilly regions, it also knows the number of penetrations from terrorists in different regions, it can see in real time, the current assigned soldiers and assigned equipment and their use. Through all this information collected through drones, sensors etc., the government can formulate a plan for research and development of particular weapons, and same for training soldiers for desired tactics. The Military generals can update the strategy in real time and device policies which can make the defense sector function efficiently. With the real time tracking of military activities of the neighboring countries, government can effectively allocate its resources to counter the strategies devised by the opponents.

Citizen Security:

Big data helps in reducing crime and achieving other citizen security goals. Data will make life more secured for the citizens. For example, children playing in the parks will wear bracelets with sensors which will allow the children to get tracked in case they go missing.

Conclusion:

For a developing nation like India, investing in big data can be very instrumental in helping it reach the growth targets. With the help of predictive analytics, big data can help the nation to plan and use its resources efficiently. It can help the government in better governance and track its growth effectively. Big data analysis will give the country a boost in its development plans and a step closer to its strategic goal.

References:

1. http://www.opengovasia.com/articles/big-data-helps-indian-government-collect-more-tax

2. http://www.businessinsider.in/Big-Data-Is-One-Of-The-Biggest-Buzzwords-In-Tech-That-No-One-Has-Figured-Out-Yet/articleshow/40554353.cms

3. https://publications.iadb.org/bitstream/handle/11319/7884/Big-Data-in-the-Public-Sector-Selected-Applications-and-Lessons-Learned.pdf

4. http://www.mondaq.com/x/475484/tax+authorities/Big+Data+And+The+Seismic+Shift+Happening+In+The+Tax+Sector

5. https://www.google.co.in/search?q=big+data+in+public+sector&espv=2&biw=1366&bih=662&source=lnms&tbm=isch&sa=X&ved=0ahUKEwij6LXd-LTRAhXBL48KHZOSD70Q_AUIBygC#imgrc=_

Authors Name:

Divya Bharathi G, NMIMS, Mumbai & Prasanth Reddy Burramukku, NMIMS, Mumbai

3.7   CAG Readies to Meet Big Data Challenges Sri Shashi Kant Sharma Inaugurates Centre for Data Analytics

Press Information Bureau, Government of India, Ministry of Finance 06-September-2016 17:23 IST

The CAG's Centre for Data Management and Analytics (CDMA) is going to play a catalytic role to synthesize and integrate relevant data into auditing process. This was stated by the Comptroller and Auditor General of India while inaugurating the Centre here today. He said the CDMA will help to enhance the efficiency and accuracy of evidence in the audit process and will be a game changer in the field of public audit.

A brainchild of Sri Shashi Kant Sharma, the CDMA aims to build up capacity in the Indian Audit and Accounts Department in Big Data Analytics to exploit the data rich environment in the Union and State Governments. Sri Sharma had anticipated the challenges posed by such developments in the Government and realized opportunities arising from data analytics. This initiative focuses development of in-house capacity covering the entire workforce working under him. Sri Sharma also indicated that this was only the first milestone in the field of Big Data Analytics. He also hinted that the Centre will be located in a separate building once an appropriate location is identified.

Prior to the setting up of the Centre, the CAG brought out a Big Data Management Policy for the Indian Audit and Accounts Department. A Task force was set up to study the policy document and recommend its implementation. The Task Force in May 2016 recommended setting up this Centre. The Centre is to be equipped with latest analytic tools and infrastructure to assist and guide the Data Analytic Groups constituted in all audit offices of CAG across the country through setting up the data management protocols and steering the data analytic capacity of the department. This initiative of CAG of India puts it amongst the pioneers in institutionalizing data analytics in government audit in the international community. CAG of India is also a member of an international project on 'Data Analytics' under the Working Group on IT Audit of International Organization for Supreme Audit Institutions.

DSM/BSC/SJ/RSJ/MCJ

http://pib.nic.in/newsite/PrintRelease.aspx?relid=149570

3.8 How Big Data Analytics Can Help in Making the Most of Data from Demonetization

By administrator: Posted on January 18, 2017

Sandeep Lodha

Demonetization, the necessary evil, is touted to flush out black money from our economy. But to accomplish this, the government has to leverage on Big Data analytics to build an intelligent data capturing mechanism by integrating various data sources, writes Sandeep Lodha, Director, Net web.

Firstly, let's address the elephant in the room. Was demonetization the best way to capture data to unearth black money? It was not necessary, but getting quality data and actionable results from the data would otherwise have taken a very long time. Filtering the data more or less decides the pace of the system. Has big data generation received a boost from the demonetization drive? I would say a sure shot "yes", for two reasons: (1) we were able to get about 85% of cash into the banking system and record the inflow. (2) Cash is the lifeblood of the black economy. Black money is usually held in form of cash before it takes other forms like real estate or gold. It will get increasingly difficult for black money generators to repeat the act of hoarding black money.

Despite these measures, people are still trying to play with the system. But they don't realize how they're leaving a trail of digital footprints of their foolhardy attempts. Let us take an example. When the government allowed the exchange of old currency notes with new notes to a limit of ₹2000, there have been cases where people have made the exchange multiple times through various banks using the same ID or a different one, subsequently crossing the limit imposed. But it's a matter of time till authorities uncover these activities once the data is gathered at a central location. Based on several parameters, the government will be able to identify the total amount exchanged by each individual during the provision period of exchanging currency. To those who are fearlessly trying these antics, I would simply say – "ignorance is bliss". And those who opine that black money will continue to regenerate; I would say it looks difficult to do so without leaving a footprint. This would be a war that data scientists will wage against them, being armed with the most lethal and definitive tool called Data. Taxmen will now have a new army, much more definitive conclusions and a huge appetite to process data that was earlier not within their reach.

Another aspect I would like to discuss is the collection of data which are in islands. It is reassuring to note that most of them are in control of the central government. If I have to name a few important ones, they are:

1. **AADHAAR** – This is the Indian government's unique identification program which is linked to different institutions, ID cards and forms of identifications. It is supposed to be one of the most reliable forms of identification since it includes biometric identifiers which are unique to individuals. This helps the government maintain linked data from activities such as banking, income tax, vehicle registrations, mobile subscriptions, property registrations and even travel. The government can track every individual's income and expenditure which is currently not possible through other IDs. Today, the AADHAAR program has more than 90% of the population enrolled and is gaining more prominence by the day. With several points of authentication and identification built in, and with the centralization of data, this will be the easiest and richest source of data. AADHAAR already has a Big Data system powering at the back end.

2. **Passport Details** – Another source of information is passport and immigration data which is online and centralized. This helps the government track foreign travels. And with the help of the OCI card, they have information available on the overseas citizens of India.

3. **Driving Licenses** – These are largely controlled by the respective state government. Although, most licenses issued today are digitized, there is still a need to incorporate data into a central database. This information is important as it is used as an effective identity proof for certain transactions. That being said, it might become redundant once driving licenses are linked to AADHAR, but until then it's a rich source of data.

4. **PAN Number** – The Permanent Account Number (PAN) is largely used as identification for Income Tax payers and is controlled

by the central government. In another effort to flush out black money, the RBI has come up with a new regulation to link the PAN to bank accounts, non-banking financial transactions etc. which is a good subject of analysis for the government. The income tax department already has a reasonable amount of analytics capability.

5. **RBI** – The RBI perhaps has the largest repository of financial information in the country with data on banks, financial institutions, foreign exchange and currency. This is an extremely useful area to mine data.

6. **Banks** – Data from bank transactions would be of immense use as almost all banks are now digitized and have centrally located servers as well. There might be some challenges in getting this information at a central location, but I don't foresee a big issue.

7. **Land records** – These are largely held by the state government, and offer an opportunity to plan its next level of attack against black money in real estate. Linking it with AADHAR will pose some major challenges and roadblocks for black money hoarders.

8. **GST** – Once implemented, the government will have precise details of goods and services bought and sold in the system. It does have some complexities with central and state GST components, but will be completely digital and track able. With the GST registration proposed to be linked to PAN, this interconnect will facilitate effective data exchange and track every transaction to a minuscule level.

There are many more sources but even if a part of the list mentioned above is taken into account, the system of tracking things would be remarkable.

The bottom line is, these huge chunks of data islands will need an efficient Big Data system to store them centrally. A good team of data scientists will be required to continuously work towards finding answers to questions raised by the government and taxmen. Even security and other related concerns will find answers for themselves - for example, financing of terrorism and other subversive activities. Eventually, the patterns will be identified and system alerts will be triggered to effectively control any illegal activities that beset the system. Is this too difficult to achieve? It will not be easy, but given the government's sheer determination, it's a small cost with big long-term gains. I also believe it's time the Indian government created the official post of Chief Data Scientist of India, who would shape policies and practices to harness the power of Big Data that holds such great potential for the future of this country.

At this juncture, I am excited from a data enthusiast's point of view. Although, the government is silent on what it plans to do with the data captured, I am hooked to every bit of information that counts. Lastly, when I read that the government is planning to bring millions of people in the tax net, I was wondering if Big Data is already at play there. I'm thrilled to see Mr. Nandan Nilekani involved, and I'm confident that we're in safe hands with a visionary and data enthusiast like him advising the government. I was delighted with the statement he made – "From data poor country we are turning into data rich country".

Author Bio: Sandeep Lodha is the Director of Net web Pvt. Ltd, Singapore*. As a data scientist, he leads the big data solutions team at Net web – a provider of servers, workstations, storage, high performance computing and big data solutions. Lodha's journey with data analytics started in 2011 when he spearheaded various big data & HPC projects for Net web Technologies. He is a frequent keynote speaker on big data, data science, and HPC at international conferences and meetings, and has written various articles on the application of HPC and big data across industry sectors.*

http://hpc-asia.com/how-big-data-analytics-can-help-in-making-the-most-of-data-from-demonetization/

3.9   Demonetization: Five Ways in Which Big Data Analytics Can Trace Black Money in India

GUEST   NOVEMBER 30, 2016

After the Indian government banned Rs. 500 and Rs. 1000 currency notes, the economy has taken a hit. While the jury is still out as to whether the move is a good one or not, it has created trouble for common people. Additionally, the exchange of such a huge number of notes is a Herculean task, with millions holding the currency, of which 85% of the monetary value is held in higher denominations.

The measures are supposedly to curb black money and root out corruption from the economy. However, modern technologies such as Big Data Analytics can make it possible to trace black money painlessly and unearth the trail in five simple ways.

o   Currency notes have a country identifier, denomination, unique serial number, and a mechanism for counterfeit prevention. These are all essential details of a currency note that can be captured easily and in real time. Every time an authorized transaction is conducted through a proper channel, all the details can be captured and the notes can be traced to the end user or account holder.

o   Cash counting and currency detection machines are used in banks and financial institutions. Those machines can be equipped with sensors to detect and store serial numbers of currency notes that are run through them. With manifold increase in the number of affordable sensors that collect and transmit data, new possibilities are continuing to emerge. These advancements can help financial institutions capture more detailed data in real time at reduced costs and from areas that were previously inaccessible. This would basically result in a data tsunami with extremely high volumes of data being generated and collected.

o   Big Data tools are ideal for huge and complex data sets— something that wasn't possible with traditional data-processing methods. Data analytics can process such humongous data sets to uncover hidden patterns and unknown correlations, leading to the discovery of meaningful trends and tips. Financial institutions can leverage it to describe transactions, predict financial fraud, and improve detection and surveillance. Mathematical and statistical tools and algorithms decipher trends (where are the currencies coming from?) and make predictions (possible locations where the cash hoarding may take place).

o   Analytics tools can provide insights into monetary malpractices and detect currency corruption using the present infrastructure; thus, obviating the need to take drastic measures or purchase new technology or equipment. Existing infrastructure can be innovated to meet requirements. With the development of new Analytics tools and advanced storage capabilities, it is easy to assess the flow of currency. Since there would be no time lag, investigative agencies could constantly monitor any suspicious flow of currency in real time.

o   Analytics tools may be calibrated to factor in several other parameters such as the geographical location, serial numbers, individual account, etc. Using the data, meaningful information can be retrieved and every transaction can be traced to the account holder or to the last person.

"Tools such as Big Data can be effective in collecting information about financial misappropriation. The data provided by banks can be analyzed to find unusual activity in currency flow, whether at an individual or a regional level," said Shashank Dixit, CEO, Deskera, a global leader in cloud technology that has developed its own Big Data tool.

(Disclaimer: This is a guest post submitted on Techstory by the mentioned authors. All the contents and images in the article have been provided to Techstory by the authors of the article. Techstory is not responsible or liable for any content in this article.)

Image Credits: rtve.es

About the Author:

Technology Evangelist, avid blogger and enthusiast, is basically a storyteller at heart. With more than 10 years of experience in journalism, MuqbilAhmar has enjoyed his stints with other media like TV, magazines, and Web. When not surrounded by startup and tech stories, he likes to dig for inspirational ones. He writes on Cloud, Big Data, IoT, startups, SMEs, Enterprises, Technology, ERP, CRM, and everything under the sun—viewed from the prism of new era tech. An M. Phil from JNU has made him liberal and tolerant. Music and food are his passion which keeps him going, apart from buzzing off whenever the opportunity arises. You can tweet him at @muqbil_ahmar or connect through LinkedIn and Facebook.

http://techstory.in/demonetization-black-money/

3.10 Data Analytics Post Demonetization in India

The demonetization of ₹500 and ₹1000 banknotes was a policy enacted by the Government of India on 8 November 2016.

The announcement was made by the Prime Minister Narendra Modi. PM Modi declared that use of all ₹500 and ₹1000 banknotes would be invalid from midnight and announced the issuance of new ₹500 and ₹2000 banknotes in exchange for the old banknotes.

The government claimed that the demonetization was an effort to stop counterfeiting of the current banknotes allegedly used for funding terrorism, as well as a crack down on black money in the country. The move was described as an effort to reduce corruption, the use of drugs, and smuggling.

(Source: https://en.wikipedia.org/wiki/Indian_500_and_1000_rupe e_note_demonetisation)

This led to huge lines of people outside banks and ATMs to withdraw new notes for daily needs and depositing cash to exchange notes f older denominations.

This also leads to a huge data analytics opportunity for data science to serve treasury and tax departments of India. The following data points would be of particular scrutiny for Indian data scientists helping or om contract to Indian Govt.

1. **Fraud**– This would examine data points where inactive and dormant bank accounts suddenly had a huge inflow of cash. This data would be further matched and merged with income tax records using PAN CARD as a matching and AADHAR CARD too. Additional matching keys would be Name, Date of Birth, Address

2. **Terrorism** – Terrorism in India is specific to a few geographic areas like Jammu and Kashmir and Naxalite areas. These could be further analyzed for fine tune of unusual currency patterns

3. **Cashless modes for laundering money** (Anti Money Laundering)- Plastic Money and Mobile apps saw a huge upsurge for

transactions. This could be further used for additional sources of information since KYC norms of Telecom need Identification and so do Bank Accounts.

4. Specific sectors- Land (real estate), Jewelery and other high value, high ticket items can be scrutinized

Overall data will be huge, so choosing the right database combination as well as the analytic (including especially Big Data Spatial Analytics) could be key to help the current PM 's ambitious vision to transform India's economy.

https://decisionstats.com/2016/11/30/data-analytics-post-demonetization-in-india/

3.11 Demonetisation: Data Analytics Could Have Traced Black Money in India
By Muqbil Ahmar 23 Nov 2016, 14:48

Parliament has come to a standstill, millions are queued up at banks and ATMs and there is a raging debate in the nation about the government's drastic step of banning of Rs 500 and Rs 2000 currency notes. The measures are supposedly aimed at controlling black money, ensuring transparency, and annihilating graft from the economy. Whatever be the intention, one thing is sure—the exchange of currency by a billion people would be a Herculean task—millions hold the currency, with 85 percent of the money in circulation held in those high denominations.

However, rather than resorting to such steps, there are new technologies that can be leveraged to trace black money without having the population pay such an absurdly huge price and inflicting lesser pain to the people. Big Data Analytics can unearth black money being circulated in the Indian economy. The new-era technological tools indicate monetary malpractices in real time. They detect currency corruption through the existing infrastructure only.

All currencies and notes have a country identifier, a denomination, a unique serial number, and a mechanism to prevent counterfeiting. There are cash counting machines in banks and financial institutions that can be equipped with currency detection, along with improved tools that would store serial numbers of notes that are run through them at a central repository. All that data though huge for any mechanized system would be easily tackled by Big Data which has been invented to tackle such huge data sets.

"Big Data and Analytics can be effective in collecting information about financial fraud. The data that is provided by banks can be easily analyzed to find out if there is unusual activity in currency flow at an end point or the person using the currency, no matter whether it is happening at individual or regional level. Mathematical models and algorithms would indicate the approximate location of stashed money after the Big Data is run through the tools," said Shashank Dixit, CEO, Deskera, a leader in cloud business software, which has developed its own Big Data Analytics tool.

The tools analyze complex and unwieldy data sets. This wasn't possible earlier with conventional data-processing methods. The tools process the Big Data to uncover unknown correlations and hidden patterns. Financial institutions and banks can leverage the meaningful trends and tips to scrutinize suspicious transactions, improve detection and surveillance, and predict and prevent financial fraud.

Mathematical and statistical tools and algorithms pick up trends (the direction of currency flow) and predict fraud and tax evasion (possible locations of currency hoarding).

The Data Analytics tools can also be recalibrated to factor in several other parameters such as geographical location, transactions in individual accounts, serial numbers of currency notes in circulation, etc. This would eventually lead to the collection of meaningful information which can trace each and every transaction to the account or account holder.

With *over 10 years* of experience in the field of journalism, the author is a technology evangelist and avid blogger.

Publish date: November 23, 2016 2:48 pm| Modified date: November 23, 2016 2:48 pm

http://tech.firstpost.com/biztech/demonetisation-data-analytics-could-have-traced-black-money-in-india-349194.html

3.12 Big Data Can Drive India from 'Cashful' To 'Cashless'

By: Sunil Jose | Published: December 5, 2016 7:15 PM

India's demonetization drive is the largest ever undertaken anywhere in the world. The government's intention is to mop up huge amounts of idle cash, much of it unaccounted and undeclared wealth and channelize it into the formal banking system thereby increasing liquidity, reducing inflation and of course, reducing the dependence on cash-only money.

What Prime Minister Modi definitely achieved was in military parlance referred to as 'shock and awe' – an outcome of the use of overwhelming power and spectacular displays of force to paralyze the enemy's perception of the battlefield and destroy its will to fight. The success or failure of demonetization can be debated by both sides but that is only one part of the argument. The psychological effect of this is (and something of greater relevance) that the physical dependence on cash will reduce and India will march towards a more transparent, inclusive and cashless economy, which is most welcome.

Digitization and big data analytics will make it more difficult to get away with under-declaration of wealth and income, help increase tax revenues and also plug existing loopholes in the system. (Source: Reuters)

'Transparency' is welcome and because herein lies the story of tax evasion, money laundering and a parallel economy which, according to economists could be almost 50% of the formal economy. So, transparency should be seen in the light of India's income tax collections. Only about 3% of Indians pay income tax (as per latest data released). As this number has slowly inched up, the total income tax collections have risen nine-fold to Rs. 2.86 lakh crores in 2015-16, from Rs. 31,764 crores in 2000-01. Compare this with the amount that has been put into the banks so far – between November 9 till November 17 (till when data is available) approximately Rs. 4 lakh crores were deposited with the government estimating that a total of Rs. 10 lakh crores will be deposited by December 30, 2016. That's almost 4 times the annual income tax collections of 2015-16. Of course, this is not all black money and only some of this will go into the government's coffers. But assuming even a 10% tax gain from this deposit result in the government netting 1 lakh crores (or over US$ 14.5 billion) in tax income.

The demonetization exercise should actually be seen as an iceberg. Most of what is being reported is basis what is visible. But the core benefit lies in what will accrue over time – which brings me back to the issue of transparency. Going forward, the intended fallout is about the treasure trove of data that the government gleans from this exercise, which will enable it to widen the tax net. Assuming even if an additional 1 crores citizens are coming into the tax net; it has the potential of doubling the tax base and significantly increasing collections.

Big Data Analytics to the rescue!

Economists and other experts believe that the so-called 'black cash' represents only about 10% of the 'black wealth' of the country – the rest being invested in gold, property, business or offshore. So, what happens to the 90%? That is the real story. That is what India tax sleuths will need to unearth while also tracking those who will continue generating black wealth. Can this be done? And if so, how?

One of the first things to enable this is the digitization of the economy, facilitated by a cashless economy linked to PAN and Aadhaar cards of every Indian. This will be the foundation to enable the government to monitor money movement taking place within and outside India. In a digitised economy, every transaction will leave its own trail, however miniscule. Millions of transactions undertaken every day will therefore throw-up insightful data that will form the bulwark of information for the government to track.

This is where big data and analytics will come into play – helping form patterns that can be recorded and help identify activities that are suspicious and unscrupulous and reveal the profiles of those behind such transactions. Big data analysts and data scientists will link this emerging data with existing information already with the tax and other departments or relevant ministries including customs and excise, property registration bodies, courts, police and phone records, district authorities, utilities, net banking transactions (linked to digital wallets and credit cards) etc., unearthing even more data of relevance to highlight unorthodox or revealing financial insights. This will help identify not just individuals but also companies and other entities involved in tax evasion, money-laundering, identity thefts or other illegal / anti-national activities. For instance, then if a person is not filing the requisite tax or evading tax but their expenditure on their personal car, monthly utility bill or property ownership is very high the tax department will now be able to correlate this data using advanced analytics and nab the defaulter. At the same time, such information will also enable them to work on enhancing services for the taxpayers and assist in resolving tax return refunds and customer service issues effectively.

To enable this and get the data mining underway, records will need to be digitised and interconnected between municipal authorities, law enforcement agencies, government agencies and ministries both at the centre and state – making for an impenetrable net of data and information. Much of this is already underway. Only once this is done will the true outcomes of the intended benefits of demonetisation actually start coming into play.

Indian Tax Agencies have already embarked on the Advanced Analytics project called "Project Insight". Objective of this project is to develop a comprehensive platform for effective utilization of information to promote voluntary compliance, deter non-compliance and to impart confidence that all eligible people pay appropriate tax. Primarily this system will be used to widen and deepen tax base, detect fraud and leakage of revenue, support investigations and provide insights and inputs for policy making.

Digitisation and big data analytics will therefore make it more difficult to get away with under-declaration of wealth and income, help increase tax revenues and also plug existing loopholes in the system. The converse is also true – money launderers will become smarter and more sophisticated, using technology lawyers and accountants to hide their wealth. Nevertheless, things will be more difficult. As the saying goes – 'when the tough get going, the going gets tough!'

The author is Managing Director, Teradata India.

http://www.financialexpress.com/economy/big-data-can-drive-india-from-cashful-to-cashless/464972/

3.13 Demonetization – A Heady Cocktail Served with Big Data & Analytics the Hangover Continues
Posted on December 22, 2016

It looks like the Indian Income Tax department is all set to have a ball on New Year's Eve and beyond into 2017. With interesting data being captured silently all through the years and especially after the unforgettable evening of November 8, 2016; the insights generated relentlessly are all set to make Big Data Analytics services the hero of the story of exposing unaccounted money in the system.

Demonetization in India; it seems is going to be a long and interesting epic. The plot thickens as the determined central government keeps giving interesting twists and turns to the saga, with shocking announcements every other day. Well, shocking for some, interesting for most!

And we all remember how it all began soon after the Diwali celebrations had ended.

But, what really is interesting to know is that slowly and silently the infrastructure has been put in place to give a boost to the citizen centric services, enhancing the citizen experiences and putting critical data on the fingertips of lawmakers, government agencies and the sorts.

The banks accounts being linked with the Aadhaar cards or the PAN card itself makes the transactions visible to the Income tax department since long before demonetization and enables it to take prudent steps today with the help of technology.

BI & Big Data make their mark everywhere, every industry thought of. With visionary leaders taking upon the task of running a country as professionally as running an enterprise itself; these technologies become an affair to remember for enterprises and the country too. Unexpectedly; BI & Big Data, the pulse of new age, become critical tools in this complete revamp of the country in providing insights to the Income Tax Department to identify the evaders from the genuine lot.

What would surely have been a practically impossible task without technology support in place; scrutinizing accounts, the movement of funds and of course generating the pointers to abnormal activities is all set to be possible as a completely revamped and rigorous exercise from the New Year's Eve onwards as promised by the central government.

A New Year's Eve Date – BI Big Data and the Regime

It was about time, that the administration identified the bottle necks to bring the system back on track. The signs were everywhere pointing to a single solution. Contemporary technology to methodically set out creates new age workflows and procedures.

- The government agencies and several bodies keep collecting organized data over the years but without a comprehensive platform to analyze and interpret it this was a fruitless exercise.

- The volume of the Government to Citizens, G2C & Citizens to Government, C2G transactions change the very definition of large; making it impossible to manage without efficient technology support.

- Critical data lies unused as it is tough to interpret such a large-scale volume and analyzing the data stored becomes a challenge because of complicated workflows and processes followed by the governing agencies.

- The data sources are varied and interconnecting the dots makes it a highly complex & intricate task.

- Citizens across the country and the various hierarchical government agencies expect to avail information at times they want, in the way they fashion, in a self-service mode.

- The reports produced from various systems need to be co-related and offer the complete picture to the key people.

- The lengthy processes in generating information from the data collected become threatening bottle necks in decision making and executions.

Making Sense of the Big Data with the Endless Vs

A sure shot way of turning challenges brought forward by these signs had to be Big Data Analytics Services, converting huge volumes of disparate data into actionable information for the governing agencies making BI and Big Data interdependent and indispensable. The multiple Vs of data captured throughout this vast country, harnessed by Big Data & Analytics makes this a story worth telling.

The Challenges of Big Data

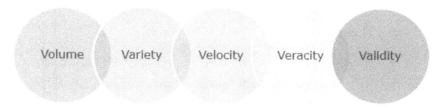

Volume

With the large volumes of data generated by individual & corporate transactions on systems like banks, land & property deals, tax and more the amount to be analyzed is massive.

Variety

Forms of data both structured and unstructured generate from data sources like spreadsheets, databases, emails, devices, PDFs, and more poses challenges for storage and is also trying to analyze and make sense.

Velocity

The velocity at which data flows in from sources like transactions, machines, human interactions, communication networks, websites, mobile devices is not only huge, it is unimaginable.

The real-time insight into these huge data sets is achieved by BI.

Veracity

The deviation in data that is being stored and mined is very significant to the problem being analyzed by BI and needs to be handled with great care.

Validity

This big data veracity couples up a new problem of the correctness and accuracy of data and purposefulness for the intended use. Most certainly, correct data is a key to make the right decisions. Appropriate storage and processing defines the validity of such data and BI solutions need to reconfirm the correctness of the data to be put to use.

In a Nutshell

Technologies ensure continual improvements in the governing experiences as well as citizen experiences. With futuristic good governance practices shaping up slowly and steadily, Big Data consulting in India is projected to become the backbone of good governance with a marked digital transformation.

The BI & Big Data Advantages to the Governing Bodies

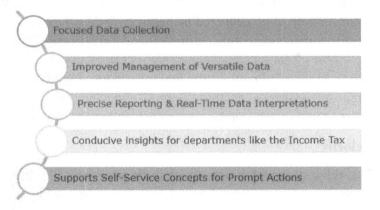

- Focused Data Collection
- Improved Management of Versatile Data
- Precise Reporting & Real-Time Data Interpretations
- Conducive insights for departments like the Income Tax
- Supports Self-Service Concepts for Prompt Actions

India waits for 2017 with a hope for the change waiting to happen. It was about time.

http://blog.spec-india.com/demonetization-heady-cocktail-served-big-data-analytics-hangover-continues/

3.14 Niti Aayog Brings in Big Data Big Gun to Track Fraud in Jan Dhan A/Cs

Yogima Seth Sharma &Prachi Verma Dadhwal *New Delhi*

It's not the income tax department, but a team of Big Data experts sitting in a corner room at the Niti Aayog which is scanning the post-demonetization deposit deluge in Jan Dhan accounts to identify the fraudulent ones.

Depending on the success of this exercise, the team may also scrutinize all bank accounts for unusual transactions after demonetization, a senior government official said.

Pulak Ghosh, a data analytics expert who teaches at Indian Institute of Management-Bangalore and advises a UN Big Data project, is leading the team at the Aayog, the official told ET. He is part of the government think tank's data analytic cell, being overseen by Avik Sarkar, an officer on special duty to Aayog vice chairman Arvind Panagariya. IIM-B confirmed Ghosh's assignment at the NITI Aayog. "While it is right that Professor Pulak Ghosh has been roped in by NITI Aayog, he is unavailable for comment as he is currently traveling on work, "a spokesperson said in an emailed response to ET's queries.

In Big Data, huge amounts of information are machine analyzed to reveal patterns, trends and associations. Data analytics is still a very niche area in India, especially in government work.

"The knowledge of Big Data and analytic for checking fraud in banking is very relevant. For large systems, big data and analytics is needed, "TV Mohandas Pai, former board of member at Infosys, said, endorsing the move.

The government official said the analytic cell of the Niti Aayog was seeking access to transaction networks of all banks to analyze the data and look for deposits and withdrawals which were aimed at laundering black money.

Jan Dhan accounts had seen huge inflows since demonetization.

While `646 crores had come into 32 lakh such accounts between October 2 and 30, the inflows swelled by `29,000 crores to `74,321 crores between November 2 and 30, with most of the deposits happening after November 8. This has raised suspicion that the accounts had been used for money laundering. The Pradhan Mantri Jan DhanYojna was launched in 2014 to increase the coverage of formal banking. Accounts under it have a deposit limit of `50,000.

Sensing their misuse following demonetization, RBI restricted withdrawals from such accounts to `10,000 a month. By the end of December, the amount in these accounts fell to `71,036 crores. Since scrutinizing the data would be a humongous task, the work was assigned to Ghosh's team at Niti Aayog.

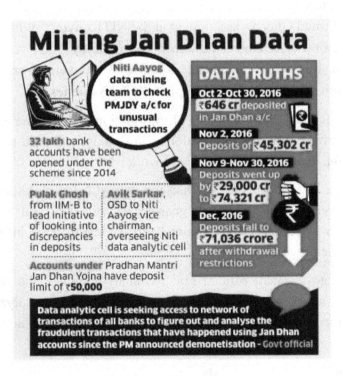

Prior to IIM, Ghosh was a professor at Georgia State University and Emory University. He is serving also in advisory group on Big Data at UN Global Pulse. He is a fellow at the Centre for Advanced Financial Research and Learning, promoted by RBI. "Big Data research is of great importance these days because of Internet of Things applications where one is expected to collect a huge amount of data from interconnected sensors, "IIT-Delhi Director V Ramgopal Rao said.

Don't Mix Up Roles

Niti Aayog is a think tank, not a law enforcement agency. That job of enforcement is best left to the income-tax department that is empowered under law to probe tax evasion. There is no reason why the tax department cannot hire data analytics firms to mine information. Interference, if any, in law enforcement functions will become messy and lead to needless harassment of taxpayers.

http://epaperbeta.timesofindia.com/Article.aspx?eid=31818&articlexml=
Niti-Aayog-Brings-in-Big-Data-Big-Gun-24012017015017

3.15 Big Data Analytics Will Help Bridge India's Tax Gap. Here's how!

1 Jan 2017 in Category (is): Posted on Categories <u>**HEADLINES**</u>

India's performance on the 'Tax Revenue as a % of GDP' parameter is by far the lowest within the BRICS economies. Estimates peg the effective taxpayers in India to less than 4-5% of its population.

The current government has shown emphasized focus on increasing tax base and tackling black money through policy interventions like demonetization, GST roll out, tax agreements, Benami Property Act, etc. These initiatives will allow the revenue departments to develop a data supply chain i.e. capture and store data at an unprecedented scale, and speed. This data can be supplemented with data generated through digital transactions, JAM (Jan Dhan, Aadhaar & Mobile) trinity, and data from across industries.

However, having this data alone will not help unless there is a focused approach towards making this data intelligent and generate insights. With skills and manpower constraints across tax departments, the challenge will remain in identifying tax evasion and / or fraudulent behavior non-intrusively. The ability to identify miss-declarations and frauds has historically been dependent upon the experience of the tax investigators, which has often led to biases and has occasionally resulted in poor citizen experiences.

WAY FORWARD

It is here that a big data and advanced analytics platform can play a critical role in integrating and exploiting the multiple data sources to help tax departments in efficient discharge of their responsibilities and bridging the tax gap. This will not only help them build integrated views of tax filers and individual tax submissions but also empower them to respond in a more targeted way, thereby using resources optimally. The platform can yield better outcomes right from registration of business to filing returns, risk profiling of taxpayers, identifying scrutiny cases, returns assessments, post-filing audits in real time to better servicing and improving experience of taxpayers. It will also empower the respective departments in confronting tax malpractices like circular trading, hawala dealing, input tax credit (ITC) over-claims, sales under-declarations, transfer pricing manipulations, etc.

As these malpractices are constantly evolving, the platform will help identify data patterns that may not otherwise be discernible to human analysts. For example, the platform can help unearth complex business relationships, identify circular trading and hawala dealers that merely exist on paper and issue fictitious invoices to enable customers to claim credit on the basis of these fictitious invoices. This is achieved by running algorithms and models to cross reference the purchases as submitted by dealers against the corresponding information of sales as submitted by them, which otherwise would have been extremely cumbersome given the nature of data, data volume and data quality.

It's important to note that the advanced analytics approaches provide ultra-early detection, reduce false positives and empower authorities to run scenario models enabling them in better policy formation and planning. These would result in speedy and near real time analysis of information, which would create facility to handle more cases with ease and be more effective.

So why hasn't this been done often enough, you might ask? Implementation by no means is as straight forward as it sounds. Key business considerations around different connotations of the same term, differences in jurisdictional applicability of an `entity', to name a few, would need to be built into the models before any meaningful analysis can be carried out. The solution needs to reward the honest taxpayers and motivate others to file appropriate returns. For all this to fructify, there needs to be a strong push from tax departments for data sharing, embracing advanced analytics and partnering with experts to help build the right capabilities. A few progressive government departments have commenced their journey and started to reap the benefits.

http://sciencejunction.in/big-data-analytics-will-help-bridge-indias-tax-gap-heres-how/

3.16 Income Tax Department to Use Big Data to Scrutinize Bank Accounts

8 Dec, 2016 **in** *Big Data* **by** *Support*

On 8th Nov-16, when honourable Prime Minister of India Narendra Modi began his first ever televised address to the nation, there was great curiosity among the people to know what it was all about. But suddenly there was a shock to the nation when PM announced that from the same day the Rs.500 and Rs.1000 currency notes would be discontinued to track black marketers and the black money they carry. He also announced that anyone having money in these denominations can get them exchanged or deposit them in their accounts with some limitations that were also declared.

Now the question arises – How is the government or IT department going to track the black money that has been deposited and how will they segregate black money holders from genuine tax payers? With more than 1.25 Billion populations and 100s of millions bank accounts, it is a big question that how IT department will find out discrepancies? Similar to Software Industry Income Tax department is also going to use latest and hottest technology BIG DATA.

It is practically impossible for IT officials to manually compare tax/account data with the data that it is collecting from banks. Big Data Analytics is being used to look into the inconsistencies which will then be thoroughly inspected by tax officials. This is the first time that our government will use Big Data analytics on such a large scale to sieve through personal taxes.

The Big Data tools won't be just used to collect details about the money being deposited by individual but it will also be used to gather information like tax paid by the individual in past years (could be decade), corporate tax that his company has paid, number of employees he has in his company and if they have also deposited any money recently and other tax related data. If discrepancies are observed, these Big Data tools will raise red flags / alerts. This would help tax officials to finally come to conclusion regarding his genuineness or being a black marketer and then they could issue notices to individuals based on this after December 31.

As Big Data can handle huge volumes of data in the range of PBs or 100s of trillions records, it will help IT professionals to scrutinize the Transactions / Account details / Tax information efficiently and quickly.

Let us hope the government gets success in their mission to find out black money holders and BIG DATA will do miracle in "Modifying the nation".

Let's hope that Achhe din aanewaale hain…

3.17 Tax Department Leans on Big Data Analytics to Mark Out Multiple PAN Holders

Income tax department will analyze the voluminous data available post demonetization for checking relationships between PAN holders.

To plug tax loopholes, the income tax (I-T) department will use Big Data analytics to track down evaders by collecting information such as common address, mobile number and e-mail to establish relationship between their multiple PANs. The department, with support from private firms, will analyze the voluminous data available post demonetization for checking relationships between PAN holders.

The managed service provider (MSP), which the I-T department plans to hire, will design and operationalize analytical solution that will help collating data, matching it and identifying relationships as well as clustering of PAN and non-PAN data, an official said.

The analytical solution would help the department gather data received from banks, post offices and other sources for linking of information and identification of duplicate details. It will also identify records with errors or other defects for resubmission.

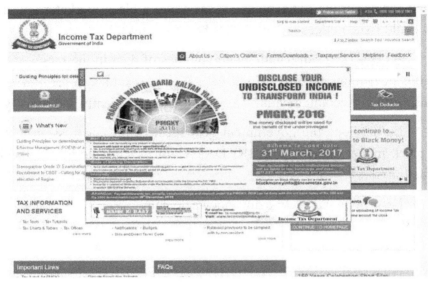

The analytical solution would help the income tax department gather data received from banks, post offices and other sources for linking of information and identification of duplicate details.

"The data quality errors and defects will be communicated to the reporting person or entities, say, banks or post offices for correction and improving data quality," the official added.

The data integration and matching of the PAN based demonetization information with that of I-T databases such as tax returns, TDS, third-party reporting, tax payments, would be used to build a comprehensive profile for the taxpayer. It will help identify link between PAN holders on the basis of relationships (business association, asset and transactional association) available in various databases, the official said, adding that the analytics will do clustering of PAN-linked demonetised data using identified relationships as well as common address, mobile number, e-mail and bank branch.

Also, it will cluster non-PAN demonetized data using common name, address, mobile number, e-mail and bank branch. Taxpayer segmentation on the basis of taxpayers' status, type of ITR form used, nature of business, taxpayer segment, age of the individual and compliance history will also have to be prepared. It wills priorities demonetization data based on taxpayer segment, relationships, clusters, rules and risk matrix.

"Different types of interventions (send e-mail, SMS, outbound call, letter, notice, verification and investigation) can be selected for taxpayer priority and segment," the official added.

http://www.livemint.com/Politics/oQ0KWChGcW0Dcco3CS39dM/Tax-department-leans-on-Big-Data-analytics-to-mark-out-multi.html

3.18 Tax Official Use Big Data and Analytics to Combat Black Money Menace

Tech savvy Tax Officers use Big Data and Analytics to fight black money: In a first for the Government of India (GOI), the Income Tax department will reportedly use big data analytics to comb through personal bank deposits money holders. The move has reportedly been adopted to streamline the task of IT officials since it is impossible to go through all the bank details and compare it with tax-related data.

As per reports, the analytics tool was used in the past for corporate tax reporting. Now, for the first time it will be used on a massive scale to rule out any in discrepancies found in personal taxes and records.

How will the analytics tool work?

- According to news reports, the big data analytics tool will match the tax returns filed by people, tax related data and tax paid by people who own companies.

- All the data (such as how much money was deposited by individuals) will be parsed from banks

- Any discrepancies observed in tax records will be red flagged

- Based on the alerts, IT officials will issue notices to individuals post December 31

The move is largely seen as an effort to separate tax payers from black money holders. It comes close on the heels of Prime Minister Modi's landmark demonetization drive that caused a nationwide stir. In a similar move earlier in the year, the IT department had fired a salvo to banks and post offices to submit details of high value cash deposits in banks and post offices.

http://analyticsindiamag.com/tax-official-use-big-data-analytics-combat-black-money-menace/

3.19 Tax Officials Are Using Big Data Analytics to Crack a Whip on Black Money Hoarders

BI INDIA BUREAU 0DEC 7, 2016, 11.36 AM

The Income Tax department has become tech-savvy and is using analytical tools to assess personal bank deposits to crackdown on black money. The tax officials are using big data analytical tools for the first time to keep an eagle's eye on personal accounts. Earlier, such tools were used only for corporate tax.

"It's practically impossible for tax officials to go through all the data obtained from banks and compare it with other tax-related data. Analytics is being used to look at discrepancies. This would then be scrutinized by experienced tax officials," a person close to the development told ET.

Through this big data analytical tool, the tax officials can scan through tax returns filed by individuals, companies, etc. In case of irregularities, these analytical tools raise red flags. Tax officers could then issue notices to individuals based on this after December 31.

Talking to ET, another person close to the development, said, "What the analytics tool can throw up is not just the cash deposited in banks by an individual, but details of the income tax paid over the years, corporate tax paid by his company, number of employees he has and whether they too have deposited money recently. Every detail of the individual's tax history can be known."

Under the bill to amend Section 115BBE of the Income Tax Act, deals with unexplained deposits in banks will be taxed. According to the amendment, tax officers can now tax such deposits at 60% (plus cess) as against 30% earlier. The new tax law is applicable from April 1, this year.

http://www.businessinsider.in/Tax-officials-are-using-big-data-analytics-to-crack-a-whip-on-black-money-hoarders/articleshow/55849137.cms

3.20 How Big Data Enables a Successful Implementation of Demonetization in India

On the evening of 8th November, the people of India were on the receiving end of a big surprise – a surprise with positive intentions. But it was a big one, nevertheless. The Government of India enacted a policy that made ₹1000 and ₹500 notes no longer valid as legal tender money.

Just after the announcement, all the ATMs, and cash deposit machines were filled with people either depositing or taking out their money. After that came the long queues in front of banks and again in ATMs, due to the severe cash crunch and the fixed cap on the amount that can be withdrawn or deposited.

The government made their intentions clear that this was the best way to curb the black money present in the economy and also root out the corruptions or terrorist activities that were being boosted by this black money. It is believed that 85% of the currency notes in circulation will be replaced and this has led to different views. Here, I'll let the experts in economics do the talking. But, one thing that is for sure, without technology this would have been a very hard thing to accomplish.

New age technologies like e-wallets, smart phones, internet of things (IoT) and big data analytics have come to the rescue; to contain the chaos that could have ensued. Though one can argue that it is only a luxury of the rich, there is a counter argument that the future is bright.

However, there is one significant technology and its presence cannot be seen by the people immediately; but it can be one which changes the whole game towards the positive direction. It's Big Data Analytics. One can be even brave enough to say that it will be one of the major players. Big data has become like gold in this digital age and it offers huge opportunities. If you want to cash on this opportunity, there is still time to learn big data and grow in this field.

Here are some of the ways how big data analytics can play an important role in the successful implementation of demonetization:

- Uncover hidden transactions – Big Data Analytics is the process of examining large data sets to uncover hidden patterns. This can be very helpful in examining the patterns of transactions to understand if there are any fraudulent activities. Government financial institutions can take the help of big data analytics to check if there is a sudden flow of transactions that seems irregular and this will help to crack down on black money hoarders.

- A helping hand for the tax administration – With the demonetization move, there is a deluge of work for the tax administration. It is difficult to handle such huge amount of data to look for irregularities. It has become the proverbial "searching for a needle in a haystack" situation at present. This is where big data analytics can play a role in mining the data and analyzing it for any discrepancies. With many policies that are already present like TDS (tax deduction at source), TCS (tax collection at source), PAN for high volume transactions and financial agencies (banks, credit card companies, etc.) reporting high-volume transactions to IT department, it has become even easier.

- Check corruption and terrorism – One of the reasons for the government to opt for demonetization was to check the unaccounted money that goes into terror activities. Terror activities in India are geographically-specific and with the help of big data analytics, the unusual currency patterns in those areas can be focused on a microscopic level.

Corruption is also another evil deeply associated with black money. With digitalization and along with the help of big data analytics, it will be possible to curb corruption. The flow of money can be trailed with the help of big data analytics and this will reveal the patterns associated with it. Cash counting machines and other machines that are associated with handling cash can be equipped with sensors or data gathering tools, which will help in getting information regarding the flow of cash.

We can see that big data can play a great role in the successful implementation of demonetization to flush out the black money out of the economy and to put a check on fraudulent transactions.

https://datafloq.com/read/big-data-analytics-implementation-demonetization/2499

3.21 Data Analytics Post Demonetization in India

Ajay Ohri: Experienced Data Scientist: November 30, 2016

The demonetization of ₹500 and ₹1000 banknotes was a policy enacted by the Government of India on 8 November 2016.

The announcement was made by the Prime Minister Narendra Modi. PM Modi declared that use of all ₹500 and ₹1000 banknotes would be invalid from midnight and announced the issuance of new ₹500 and ₹2000 banknotes in exchange for the old banknotes.

The government claimed that the demonetization was an effort to stop counterfeiting of the current banknotes allegedly used for funding terrorism, as well as a crack down on black money in the country. The move was described as an effort to reduce corruption, the use of drugs, and smuggling. (Source: https://en.wikipedia.org/wiki/Indian_500_and_1000_rupee_note_demonetization)

This led to huge lines of people outside banks and ATMs to withdraw new notes for daily needs and depositing cash to exchange notes for older denominations.

This also leads to a huge data analytics opportunity for data science to serve treasury and tax departments of India. The following data points would be of particular scrutiny for Indian data scientists helping or on contract to Indian Govt.

1. **Fraud-** This would examine data points where inactive and dormant bank accounts suddenly had a huge inflow of cash. This data would be further matched and merged with income tax records using PAN CARD as a matching and AADHAR CARD too. Additional matching keys would be Name, Date of Birth, Address

2. **Terrorism -** Terrorism in India is specific to a few geographic areas like Jammu and Kashmir and Naxalite areas. Deposits and exchanges in these areas could be further analyzed for fine tuning of analysis and unusual currency patterns

3. **Cashless modes for laundering money** (Anti Money Laundering) - Plastic Money and Mobile apps saw a huge upsurge for transactions. This could be further used for additional sources of information since both KYC (Know Your Customer) norms of Telecom need Identification and so do Bank Accounts.

4. Specific sectors- Land (real estate), Jewelery and other high value, high ticket items can be scrutinized

Overall data will be huge, so choosing **the right database** combination as well as the analytic (including especially **Big Data Spatial Analytics**) could be key to help the current PM's ambitious vision to transform India's economy.

The right database should be based on volume, velocity and variety of data AND security (you don't want your neighbouring countries to know this information)

Algorithms like k-means clustering (for data reduction) processed in parallel on a Big Data Spark or other technologies in a private secure Government of India cloud could be some solutions.

Spatial visualization should help with visualizing state, district and bank branch level information. Social Network Analysis can help pinpoint fraudulent deposits by relatives.

Again, analysis based on multiple sheets of Excel won't really help here.

https://www.linkedin.com/pulse/data-analytics-post-demonetization-india-ajay-ohri

3.22 Leveraging Data in Real Estate – The New Beginning

By Fatima Bohra - Jul 25, 2016

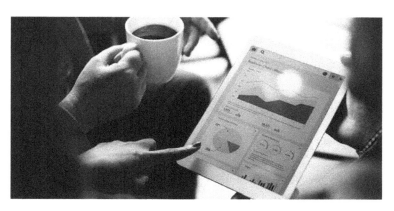

Data is the new, new fizz in the real estate domain, not only does it plunger the pace in retail market but also alters the strategies of real estate, to create quite a big impact on the marketing scales. But what actually matters is how the companies use the power of data smartly, to leapfrog other companies in this present high-time race.

Data and Real life

Data is now an integrated part of the real world, data is everywhere, it's the basis of our modern economic world; ramping from common individual to large enterprises and firms- data is there. Big Data comes with numerous benefit slots for every other sector; however, it's very conceptual with real estate, while still being an uncharted territory amongst the leaders of this domain.

Data Analysis, gateway to a whole new world!

To be exact, Data is everything which merges up our work procedure, how it is done, what it is all about and why it is done! Strictly speaking, Real estate does not involve handling much of data; it keenly focuses on the 'Consumer picture' out in the market portrait. Real estate with the help of Data, analyses discrete data patterns to pick up decisions to raise better productivity with a multiplicative factor. Data in whole, comprises of a single database, easily accessible to a retailer or the company itself, which in case of real estate is coupled directly to the leveraging so as it raises the potential of that firm more realistically by showcasing a complete view of mortgaged and estimated prices before clients, hence eliminating doubts and hassles about the correct pricing of a project. REstate is one such start-up working in the same domain. With funding from UAE based Global venture capital equity firm Idein Ventures, REstate is looking forward to structuring the real estate market in India; by providing real estate developers brand name to land to their finding and financing, and hence thumping its impression in the world of real estate. It claims to use data and research before constructing anything, so that the best possible building is constructed which gives the highest return based on the market needs.

REstate, headquartered at Bangalore and Hyderabad and with a well-built team is growing notably in its current offline profile, also has a technology driven exclusive Land Bank that uses data analysis and market research to deal with all stakeholders- landowners and builders.

Leveraging the Data

Data is more about its orientation towards an agent itself and leveraging is all about making the data transparency in each process effective, so as to specialize with detailed analysis to lure a bigger sector of customers. Data, right now, is trying to uphold the roots of real estate involving advanced analysis and customization aiming at engagement with comparatively a larger section of retailers, customers etc. Leveraging of such Data can be done in following ways - here are some examples to show the potential of using data in real estate which some companies are doing:

1. **Traffic Data:** If before building a residential or commercial complex in an area, a developer looks at the traffic data in the area and finds out how the traffic will play out, an analysis can be done on the kind of people who would be willing to work/live in the area. The entire building plan can change based on what the traffic data says.

2. **Neighborhood Data:** Pricing of a property is not just dependent on the land which it stands on, but also on the kind of people present on the property and the kind of people present around the property. Hence, appropriate pricing for any construction can be justified only by having a detailed analysis of the neighborhood, with all data related to the income level of people around and a median of the same, the distribution chart of the kinds of jobs people are in, the distribution for the age groups of people living in the neighborhood, play a very important role, especially for residential construction.

3. **Combination of Traffic and Neighborhood Data:** Now this is where the power of algorithmic conclusions comes into play. The above-mentioned data is not enough in knowing the price or cost or the type of construction needed on any land and there are tons of other parameters which need to be considered. And sometimes, a combination of some of those parameters (sometimes those permutations can run into millions) should also be given importance to

conclude some aspects with respect to the said data. If traffic in the late evening – 8 pm to 10 pm- is very high on the roads surrounding the area, but the people living there are mostly from government jobs background, you are in a position to conclude that most of the traffic is from outsiders and the place has an affinity to attract people from outside the locality. This is a simplistic dumped down assumption to convey the point.

Future with Data Analysis in Real Estate

With data assimilating completely in a technical world, it now seems easy for a manufacturer, retailer or a company to endorse its sales and products. And Real Estate is no different. though traditional developers are still not giving the data the importance it deserves, players and developer brands like REstate are coming up to give a new meaning to real estate development. The future is bright and data will play a major role in cleaning and improving real estate, and creating a much stronger and transparent real estate domain.

http://www.indianweb2.com/2016/07/25/leveraging-data-real-estate-new-beginning/

3.23 How Big-Data to Be A Big Part of India's Weather Insurance in the Year 2016

By Suman Chaudhary - Jan 5, 2016

Big Data analysis has become a crucial part of business planning in the recent times. Gathering extensive information through innovative technological means and analyzing it has enabled companies and governments to not only operate efficiently but build sustainable strategies for the future. The ability to combine and calculate data has given corporations the ability to gain valuable insights about different aspects which impact profitability of ventures. Big Data has proved instrumental in spurring sectors such as Agricultural Insurance and Risk Management. Companies can now analyze data and implement more sustainable strategies thus minimizing risks.

For your information, 'Weather insurance' is an indemnity for losses that may arise due to abnormal weather conditions. These abnormal weather conditions can be events such as excess of rainfall, shortfall in rainfall or variations in temperature, wind speeds and humidity.

Weather Insurance and risk management has come as a boon to agriculture in India. The Agricultural sector employs the largest share of India's workforce but has seen its GDP share deplete gradually in recent times (17% as of 2014). Sustainable weather insurance schemes and damage control planning in case of blights and droughts have helped both farmers in fields and brands in markets achieve a more risk free and viable environment. Manufacturers like PEPSICO and Bayer Inc. have been able to collaborate with farmers in order to tackle agricultural hazards and increase yield of their raw material resources. Risk management firms through big data analytics have been able to provide security against unforeseen climatologically based risks for corporations. They help farmers improve soil quality, revive from natural disasters, and gain adequate knowledge and resources for a better produce.

Ushering in of big data analytics in India has now been made easier through the very affordable cloud storage services initiated by global tech giants like IBM, Microsoft and Amazon. Storage of data in cloud is a convenient way to make collection, access and analysis of big data across sectors a reality in India.

The advent of the Internet of Things has taken technological collaboration and information sharing to the next level. A large network of hardware that can efficiently capture and share information has made researches much easier and thorough than ever before. IOT broadly refers to a network of multiple devices that share info through a cloud based application. An IOT framework has been established by globally acclaimed IT giant IBM which has made big data analytics much more efficient and commercially viable. This technological advancement has facilitated implementation of big data a reality across different sectors in the country. Another positive innovation witnessed in the field comes in the form of some very hi-tech and complicated microprocessors platforms established by international vendors like Raspberry that have made available easy integration of IOT network with a cloud based storage. With the accessibility to a cloud based internet of things platform, gathering information on climatic changes, upcoming weather phenomenon, tracking rains, improving soil quality as well as comfortably assisting farmers at the grass root level has become faster and more successful than ever before.

Smart IT services like, land surveying, remote sensing and GPS tracking has enabled corporations to aim for better produce and has helped insurance companies better assess situations. Big data analytics has been instrumental in helping more than 500,000 farmers across the country to efficiently deal with natural calamities. It has also enabled a surge in crop insurance across the country, taking the weather insurance sector for Rs.

300 Crores to Rs. 5000 Crores in less than 10 years. This trend is set to continue and with IOT and cloud based storage the sector is projected to show a rapid growth in both harvest and financial sustainability.

Firms like Weather Risk Management Services Ltd. (WRL) have been able to put these technological innovations in place and design strategies in collaboration with both government entities like SIDBI and Ministry of Agriculture and private corporations to better safeguard businesses. Research companies like WRL provide crucial data to assess ongoing and upcoming situations as well as integrate their technological prowess with big companies.

With such expertise and added 'big data' enabled prowess, weather insurance and risk management has greatly improved the industry scenarios in the recent times. Steps taken by technological pioneers like IBM and Microsoft to make big data analytics more achievable at a global scale will not only make sectors stable, it is likely to improve the condition of millions involved in agriculture around the country. With the help of resourceful platforms for IOT, the process of integration of big data analytics in business planning is set to significantly improve operations and performance across sectors leading to increased sustainability. Researchers have projected this trend to continue to restructure business approach in different sectors in 2016, making IOT a reality in India.

This article is authored by Mr. Sonu Agrawal, Founder and MD, Weather Risk Management Services Ltd. (WRL)

http://www.indianweb2.com/2016/01/05/how-data-analytics-to-be-a-big-part-of-weather-insurance-in-the-year-2016/

3.24 Big Data, Data Analytics to Play Vital Role in Financial, Banking Services

By <u>J Deepthi Nandan Reddy</u> | Express News Service | Published: 11th December 2016 02:29 AM | Last Updated: 11th December 2016 03:54 AM | **A+A A-** |

HYDERABAD: Big data and data analytics are going to play a big role in financial and banking services post demonetization, as most of the financial transactions are set to go online.

Though banks, Non-Banking Financial Companies (NBFCs) and other companies dealing with financial services are already using data analytics, its importance is set to grow by leaps and downs in the new scenario.

"We have recently tied up with a data analytics firm to assess the creditworthiness and intent of the borrowers. We are confident that data analytics will help us in great way in the upcoming days to make correct decisions," said Shankar Vaddadyi founder and director of i-lend.in, a peer to peer lending company, based out of Hyderabad.

Lending companies like i-lend believe that by analyzing the digital footprint of a person, his attitude, preferences, financial status, societal status and other core information can be gleaned and ascertained. The stress on big data and data analytics has become so pronounced that some financial companies have been giving more importance to data analytics than CIBIL score.

"Banks do not give loans to a person if his CIBIL score is less and they follow it absolutely. But sometimes a person might default on a loan due to various unavoidable reasons even though he is genuine. Data analytics can provide even better insight than CIBIL score about a person's creditworthiness. And the results arising out of data analytics will have accuracy of more than 90 percent," explains Madhava Turumella, CEO of Cove Venture, a data analytics company.

Besides banks and NBFCs, government departments like Income Tax Department, Registration Department and law enforcing agencies are already using data analytics. This trend is only set to increase on a huge scale post demonetization, thus creating new opportunities and market for companies involved in big data and data analytics.

"Already we have been using data analytics detect insurance related frauds. Post demonetization our job is set to become easy and more accurate, as most of the financial transactions are set to go online and people inadvertently leave digital footprints," added R Raghavan, CEO of Indian Insurance Bureau.

http://www.newindianexpress.com/cities/hyderabad/2016/dec/11/big-data-data-analytics-to-play-vital-role-in-financial-banking-services-1547915.html

3.25 Big Data for Anti-Poverty Programmes: A Politically Embedded View

9 Jan 2017 Author: Silvia Masiero Category: Centre for Service Management

The idea of *datafication*, intended as rendering many non-quantified processes into data, has become ubiquitous in business intelligence. Mayer-Schonberger and Cukier (2013) refer to big data as "a revolution that will transform how we live, work and think", since data have transitioned from the role of optional asset to that of programmatic lens to see the world and frame it. Given the pervasive nature of datafication, it makes sense to examine its social and developmental implications, asking whether and how it can affect the ways in which anti-poverty action is conducted on a world scale.

I began collecting data on the computerization of anti-poverty schemes; in particular food security measures, in south India in 2011, and

wrote my PhD thesis on this. Since then I have conducted multiple rounds of fieldwork, to monitor the evolution of the Indian anti-poverty system from back-end digitization to biometric recognition of users. My interest in datafication emerged from the observation that data became, over time, an integral part of the making of the nation's anti-poverty policy.

Silvia Masiero

Digitization vs. Datafication

One important question is on the effect of big data on the social safety nets designed for the world's poor. These nets, known as anti-poverty programmes, are devised to protect the poor and vulnerable against livelihood risks. These programmes range from food security to employment guarantees, health insurance, and anything that constitutes a primary need for below-poverty-line citizens, and are widely diffused across developing nations. With the advent of the Internet and mobile money, such programmes have already been pervaded by diverse forms of digitisation.

However, datafication of anti-poverty programmes is radically different from digitization at large. If digitization refers widely to the adoption of digitalism in existing processes, datafication is a process in which data of beneficiaries become the basis for administering the programme. It involves systematization of citizens' data into databases that collects all relevant information. This allows recognising entitled citizens, telling for example those below the poverty line from those who are not, and assign entitlements accordingly, such as food or cash transfers.

Aadhaar: Datafying India's Anti-Poverty System

Examples of anti-poverty programme datafication abound worldwide. For example, cash transfer programmes across Africa are moving to mobile money, assigning entitlements on the basis of user data. Perhaps the most powerful example of this is that of India, where the Unique Identity Project, or *Aadhaar* (meaning "foundation"), proposes to collect the biometric data of all residents, storing them in a central database. The Aadhaar project is the biggest biometric project worldwide, and provides a unique 12-digit number to all those who enroll, capturing their 10 fingerprints, iris and photograph.

The purpose of this form of datafication is that of simplifying delivery of social services, enabling rapid identification of those entitled. With Aadhaar, biometric details are linked to citizens' data, hence a fingerprint is enough to access subsidized food grains or other benefits. This is hailed worldwide as an example of best practice in information and communication technology (ICT) for development, and one that can turn citizens' data into means for more effective anti-poverty action. But as it emerged from my research, the reality may be more complex than that.

More specifically, my research on Aadhaar reveals two points on the datafication of anti-poverty programmes. First is their technical rationale, aimed at producing more effective and accountable food security systems. Second are the political consequences that the new data architecture produces.

A Politically Embedded View

The technical rationale lies in fighting *exclusion* errors, which exclude entitled users from service provision, and *inclusion* errors, meaning inclusion of the non-entitled. Aadhaar's datafication discriminates the poor from the non-poor, so that a non-entitled citizen cannot receive social safety benefits. It also gives users an identity, so that poor citizens without documents can have access. Nevertheless, this effect is sometimes blocked by malfunctioning ICTs, resulting in below-poverty-line citizens being prevented from accessing their entitlements, resulting in technology-induced disempowerment rather than in the desired systemic improvement in service delivery.

But political consequences are visible too. Aadhaar has the function of transforming India's anti-poverty agenda, based on subsidies for the poor, into a system in which cash will be directly transferred to them. This embodies the Central Government's intention to do away with subsidies, substituting them with a free-market system based on bank accounts. This has the potential to dismantle India's current social policy, while many poor citizens – unbanked and suspicious of market intervention – report being in strong favour of subsidies instead of cash.

As a result, the main argument made in my research is that datafication does much more than streamlining existing anti-poverty programmes. Entrenched in extant social policies, it can deeply transform their inner architecture, as Aadhaar is doing with India's system of social security. As big data become increasingly incorporated in anti-poverty systems worldwide, it is hence important to appraise this phenomenon through a politically embedded lens, asking whether and how datafication is actually expanding poor people's entitlements.

I will give a seminar titled *The Affordances of Big Data for Poverty Reduction: Evidence from India* at the UNESCO Chair in

ICT4D on 2 February 2017, 1pm to 2pm. The seminar will be hosted by Royal Holloway University of London, Queen's Building, QB136. If this work interests you, it will be my honor and pleasure to hear from you, I am contactable at all times at s.masiero@lboro.ac.uk.

This Blog post was written by Dr Silvia Masiero, a Lecturer in International Development at the SBE, a member of the Centre for Service Management (CSM) and an affiliated member of the UNESCO Chair for ICT4D. Silvia can be contacted via S.Masiero@lboro.ac.uk

http://blog.lboro.ac.uk/sbe/2017/01/09/big-data-for-anti-poverty-programmes-a-politically-embedded-view/

3.26 68% of Indian businesses ready to thrive in a digital world: Microsoft study

Nandita Mathur TOPICS: INDIAN BUSI

Microsoft Asia Data Culture Study polled 940 C-Suite executives from medium-to-large companies across 13 Asian markets, including India.

Photo: iStock

About 90% of respondents in India feel that data culture should be driven top down with a formalized role in the leadership team to drive successful adoption of data strategy. Enterprises in Asia are convinced about the need to be data-driven, but not all believe they have the right digital strategy, a survey found. About 88% of business leaders in Asia agree that it is important for their businesses to be data-driven for agility.

However, 57% believe they still do not have a full digital strategy in place. In comparison, 68% in India believe they have a full digital strategy in place today. The India-specific data was shared by Microsoft on Wednesday and is part of the findings of the Microsoft Asia Data Culture Study 2016.

The study polled 940 C-Suite executives from medium-to-large companies across 13 Asian markets including India. Respondents were surveyed on their organizations' digital and data strategy, and readiness for the digital economy.

TOP 5 BARRIERS TO ADOPTING A DATA CULTURE

RANK	INDIA'S TOP 5 BARRIERS	ASIA'S TOP 5 BARRIERS
1	Data security	High costs
2	High costs	Data security
3	Fragmented IT investments	Lack of digital skills in the workforce
4	Leadership Prioritisation	Fear of change
5	Company Culture	Securing funding

About 90% of respondents in India feel that data culture should be driven top down with a formalized role in the leadership team to drive successful adoption of data strategy. Most business leaders felt that data culture should be led by the chief digital officer, and the chief data officer.

The study also ranks data visualization, IoT (Internet of Things), cloud data storage, predictive data analytics and real-time analytics as the top five data capabilities that businesses will require in the next 12 to 18 months. These capabilities are clearly aligned to how they see their data culture evolving to meet their needs. When it came to leveraging IoT, Indian business decision makers are more focused on smart R&D, followed by security management, and safety monitoring as their top priorities.

TOP 5 BENEFITS OF EMBRACING A DATA CULTURE

RANK	INDIA'S TOP 5 BARRIERS	ASIA'S TOP 5 BARRIERS
1	Ability to make real-time decisions	Ability to make real-time decisions
2	Improve customer satisfaction and retention	Efficiency in operations
3	Compete more effectively against disruptors Improve processes	Improve processes
4	-	Better business continuity
5	Create new revenue streams Transform business operations	Improve customer satisfaction and retention

The survey points out some key issues that Indian businesses need to address to realize their full potential as data-driven organizations:

1. Building infrastructure for data agility is a key imperative for Indian businesses

—89% in India agreed that they need to drive an agile data-driven business. However, they think their capabilities in infrastructure are inadequate (compared to 88% in Asia).

—62% in India said that their data is accessible across mobile devices today.

—67% felt confident that their existing data infrastructure is scalable with business growth.

—72% of respondents in India use data to predict future trends.

2. Data governance plan, data security policies and collaboration are the priorities of Indian businesses

—89% in India felt that data driven collaboration across the organization needs to be enabled (compared to 87% in Asia).

—70% of the respondents polled in India were confident they have a clear data security policy that would prevent unauthorized leakage and threats.

—71% of the respondents in India claimed they have a clear data governance plan to guide ownership, storage and use of data.

3. Indian businesses want to create an analytical workforce

—77% respondents in India agreed on the importance of having a data-savvy workforce (compared to 84% in Asia).

—74% in India (Asia average is 42%) felt they have employees who have the relevant skills to combine data to help identify business outcomes.

—74% of organizations polled in India have invested in training to enhance their employees' data skills.

The study thus highlighted the confluence of cloud, mobility and data is changing the way companies do business with their customers. This is resulting in new demands that make it necessary for every business to transform to a digital and data-driven business.

http://www.livemint.com/Industry/Wrp7Nd7XShnwSqFck0ZzdN/68-of-Indian-businesses-ready-to-thrive-in-a-digital-world.html

3.27 Cashing in This Diwali & Halloween with Big Data & Analytics

Posted on October 28, 2016

Crazy times are here again with the celebrations across the globe. Shopping, gifting, travelling, touring, sight-seeing and dining out like there is no tomorrow; pure fun & frolic.

Shopping & last minute visits to the stores just before festive times can turn into a nightmare for shoppers. The rush, the pressure and the arguments mount for many. For others, it can be pure fun and loads of excitement simply because they are better planned, know exactly what they want and what would please them.

Booking tickets, making reservations for holidays & even simple reservations for dining out become absolutely silly with frantic calls & clicks to grab the best.

It is in fact completely crazy times for many businesses.

- Retailers & Malls
- Logistics
- Travel Companies
- Hotels
- Transportation

That is exactly when Big Data Analytics services come to rescue! Big fun in holidays for all!!! Gathering data all year around to help derive the most accurate analysis for the businesses for every customer, for every market; online or in the stores to make to the perfect suggestions to customers keeping them engaged and of course predict what is expected to help the businesses combat the madness.

Leveraging Big Data

Since the customer can easily compare multiple vendors at a touch or a click, businesses understand that loyalty is fickle and digital purchases make it even tougher. Knowing what puts off the visitors becomes as important as marketing & sales for businesses.

What Hassles the Visitor

- Products out of stock
- Tickets & bookings sold out
- No free shipping
- Longer times for delivery
- No self-service options available

Leveraging Big Data Analytics services in conjunction with a well thought of plan makes fruitful strategizing possible to keep the customers happy. With practical technology like the beacons which grab the attention of patrons of various businesses, mobile technologies, social media and the improving infrastructure; Big Data Analytics Solutions become the Pulse of the New Age Data.

Big data is at work everywhere there are visitors in the holiday frenzy; in malls, in shops, at tourist destinations, at restaurants or at hotels.

Big data silently captures data from social media, online stores and also the useful apps; round the clock and accurately, becoming the best deal around for travel or instrumental in partnering with the tiny beacons to offer better guest engagement as also complementing retail analytics with beacons.

Insights Offered by Big Data & Analytics for Holidays & Beyond

The data gathered all through the year offer critical insights to be leveraged during the festive times for big time sales in form of coupons, offers and other loyalty approaches.

The Insights

Information about Customer Profiles

Gifting Vs Personal Purchasing Predictions

Sentiment Analysis & Mood Analysis

Predictive Modeling for Strategizing Business & Pricing

Increasing Efficiency of Operations by predicting workforce requirements

Strategizing with Big Data Analytics services to Cash in during the Holidays

With strong insights, strategizing sales during the festive seasons become more methodical and a logical strategy evolves.

• Peak holiday time predictions for customer to know what would be expected
• Preferences
• Behavior

- Demands
- Combat traffic & visits to avoid out of stock or sold out situations
- In-store
- e-Commerce
- Plan inventory & logistics to match the demands expected
- Customize products & promotions as per the markets & specific geographies
- Personalized marketing through apps and social media
- Multichannel marketing to enable a seamless experience across devices
- Dynamic suggestions for adapting shelf displays & online displays to catch the pulse of the visitors
- Enable cross selling by accurately analyzing what the customer might want specially to go the current behavior as well as past history

Big Data & Analytics as a Service

Understanding the need to keep focus on core expertise, various businesses adopt DaaS – Data as a service model to keep a tab of critical data and generate relevant insights. DaaS captures and integrates multiple categories of data from various touch points all-round the year.

- Basic Data
- Data gathered & aggregated from multiple data sources to arrive at demographics and market related patterns
- This data set becomes the long term target data set
- Offline – Online Data Combination
- This approach is use for interrelating offline & online transactions to arrive at patterns and conclude user preferences and choices
- Data of this kind is of great use for personalized marketing, on boarding and planning campaigns

- Real-time Data
- Instrumental in analyzing with an as it occurs approach, real-time data becomes vital in cross selling with purchase intent analysis
- Real time data is at the core of offering relevant and unforgettable user experiences

In a Nutshell

The many advantages offered Big Data Analytics companies can no longer be denied and businesses recognize these to make the most of the holiday season.

The Advantages

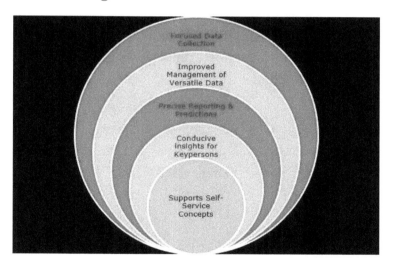

Big Data most certainly value adds to the enterprises in handling & analyzing extremely high volumes of data coming in from diverse sources. The sales boost, especially during the holiday season realized because of the integration of Big Data & Analytics into the enterprise workflow is tremendous as critical data is being effectively captured and analyzed like no other could have.

https://blog.spec-india.com/cashing-diwali-halloween-big-data-analytics/

3.28 Intel & DST - Innovate for Digital India Challenge 2.0

CHALLENGE 1.0

On April 24, 2015, in an unprecedented move, and one that has since become a framework for public-private partnerships, Intel & Department of Science and Technology ("DST"), the `Intel & DST - Innovate for Digital India Challenge', supported by MyGov and Department of Electronics and Information Technology ("DeitY") and anchored by CIIE, IIM-A.

The Challenge was launched to drive local ingenuity and encourage the creation of intuitive, easy to use products and solutions that enable and drive access to services imperative for development. 1,913 ideas were received across healthcare, agriculture, education and other sectors.

The Challenge received support from our Honourable Prime Minister, Mr. Narendra Modi and mentorship from eminent industry experts. The top 10 teams were felicitated by Mr. Ravi Shankar Prasad, Minister Communications & IT and Mr. Pranab Mukherjee, Hon'ble President of India.

The Challenge ended on April 2016 with the announcement of top three teams were granted INR 2 million as equity investment

In 2014, the Government of India unveiled a far-reaching, visionary blueprint of a Digital India, one where country has a Digital Infrastructure as a utility to every citizen, Governance and Services on demand, and Digital empowerment of citizens.

The Digital India vision has nine pillars that outline how India can be propelled to its next phase of growth by harnessing technology where every citizen has access to education, healthcare, and services remarkable for a nation's inclusive growth and development.

The Digital India vision of the Government seeks to empower every citizen with the benefits of technology by enabling digital transformation. Intel is committed to fulfilling this vision by not just creating a culture and ecosystem of innovation, but to steer innovation towards solving India's problems.

In this light Intel & the Department of Science & Technology, Government of India ("DST"), have come together again to foster a new wave of disruptive innovation that empowers citizens and transforms India by announcing the Intel & DST – Innovate for Digital India Challenge 2.0 ("Challenge"). This Challenge will benefit from the continued support of MyGov and Ministry of Electronics and Information Technology ("MeitY") and will be anchored by T– Hub Foundation, among India's largest incubators.

Challenge 2.0: Journey of India's Digital India Vision

In 2014, the Government of India unveiled a far-reaching, visionary blueprint of a Digital India, one where the country has a Digital Infrastructure as a utility to every citizen, Governance and Services on demand, and Digital empowerment of citizens.

The Digital India vision has nine pillars that outline how India can be propelled to its next phase of growth by harnessing technology where every citizen has access to education, healthcare, and services remarkable for a nation's inclusive growth and development.

Intel Inside® Digital India

India faces tremendous challenges that stem from, among other things, a lack of pervasiveness of knowledge and technology across the geographical expanse of the country.

Ensuring a well-connected India with access to broadband in the farthest corner; digital literacy; and availability of solutions that enhances every citizen's livelihood are the primary measures to be taken for Digital India.

Intel has been working with the Government and eco-system to scale digital literacy throughout the nation under Intel's Digital Skills for India initiative, through which Intel is committed to train 5Mn people with digital literacy skills by the end of 2015. From **secured and managed digital infrastructure** in Data Centers for storage, connectivity, data transfer, and analytics; **Accessible, Affordable Computing Devices & Solutions** with High Performance Computing devices; to **Skill Development & Capacity Building** through the various initiatives and programs, Intel is accelerating Indians with its innovations and making India digital.

Innovation for India & Skills for India

Intel has been fostering innovation since inception. Driven by Moore's Law, it has been initiating various programs that create huge economic value and drive social advancement for over two decades in India.

The milestones achieved are reflected in the success of Intel® International Science and Engineering Fair that had over 180 winners, 18 of them received the honour of having minor planets named after them; Intel® Higher Education Program, which promotes innovation and entrepreneurship, and has reached 235,000 students and 4,500 faculties across 550 institutions so far; and Intel® PhD Sponsorship program that looks forward to enhancing the quality of research in the nation.

Skills for India

Intel is enabling the citizens of India to be digitally literate. The programs designed to equip them with digital skills include Intel® Teach Program that has trained over 18 lakh teachers in India to use technology for the past fifteen years; Intel® Learn Easy Steps that helped in spreading digital literacy to 38 lakh people under National Digital Literacy Mission, which is co-founded by Intel; and Intel® Digital Skills Training Application, which is comprised of Digital Literacy, Financial Inclusion, Healthcare and Cleanliness in 5 Indian languages. Intel has also launched an initiative, in association with Bharat Broadband Network Limited*, that aims at imparting digital literacy to key resource persons in the first 1000 Panchayats under the National Optic Fiber Network* roll-out in India.

http://innovatefordigitalindia.intel.in/

3.29 Mygov, Intel & DST Announce the Top 10 Innovators from Intel & DST – Innovate for Digital India Challenge 2.0

The #IFDI Challenge 2 has the continued support of MyGov and Ministry of Electronics and Information Technology ("MeitY") and is anchored by T– Hub Foundation, one of India's largest incubators.

The #IFDI Challenge 2 received 797 entries that aim to create a Digital India through innovative solutions and solve existing problems faced by her citizens. Out of these, 20 shortlisted participants presented ideas to a panel of experts and at the end of this phase, top 10 selected teams entered the accelerator phase wherein they are eligible to receive grants of up to Rs. 3 lakh and mentoring to build Minimum Viable Products ("MVPs") based on Intel® architecture.

The top ten innovations in #IFDIChallenge2 center around Smart City, Agricultural Solutions, Healthcare and Sustainability.

The accelerator phase includes a residential week-long boot camp at T-Hub, Hyderabad led by GBI, T-Hub and USMAC with mentoring from experts such as Pradeep Lokhande (Rural Marketing) and Ashish Deshpande (Design Thinking) as part of Intel led #Let's Talk Innovation series of webcasts and Intel technical specialists. Teams will build their MVPs out of their locations with virtual team management and mentoring by a panel of experts from Government, Intel, T-hub, Industry and GBI. This phase will culminate with a Demo Day at Hyderabad on 9th February, 2016 wherein teams will present their prototypes to a panel of experts. At the end of this phase, top three teams will be identified to move into the next round of the #IFDI Challenge 2. Engineering support and product kits are provided by T-Hub, Intel and Intel-trained engineers and it also includes access to Intel India Maker Lab in Bengaluru.

We are extremely proud to present the top 10 entries of the #IFDI Challenge 2 and look forward to disruptive innovations that impact millions of Indians. The battle of innovations towards the vision of a Digital India begins now!

Congratulations to the Top 10 teams of #IFDI Challenge 2!

Oizom Instruments Pvt. Ltd.	Jainam Mehta	Ahmedabad	Smart City
Gayam Motor Works Pvt. Ltd.	Sriharsh B	Hyderabad	Sustainability / Renewable
AllizHealth	Chinmoy Mishra	Pune	Healthcare Solutions
Iotrek Technology Pvt. Ltd.	Piyush Vishwakarma	Delhi	Smart City
NeuroTech	Nitin Vasanth	Kochi	Healthcare Solutions
INICU and ICHR	Harpreet Singh	Delhi	Healthcare Solutions
E-DeWeeder	Nitin Saluja	Chandigarh	Healthcare Solutions
Banyan Sustainable Waste Management Pvt. Ltd.	Mani Vajipey	Hyderabad	Sustainability / Renewable
Waste Ventures India	Roshan Miranda	Hyderabad	Sustainability / Renewable
Thyrometer	Varsha Singh	Chandigarh	Healthcare Solutions

http://innovatefordigitalindia.intel.in/top-ten-two-thousand-sixteen.html

3.30 Modi Government Using Big-Data & Social Media to Assess Public Mood and Trending Issues

By <u>Kirti Sharma</u> - Jul 27, 2016

The Modi government came to power two years ago in 2014, thanks to an aggressive campaign done by Modi himself and his party Bhartiya Janta Party (BJP). There is no denying the fact that a considerate amount of BJP's success goes to the digital and social media campaigning route that it adopted back in the year 2014 and the amazing way in which it used the big data. Well, even after two years of being elected one thing is absolutely clear, Modi and his party's fondness for social media (and Photoshop) has only gained by heaps and bounds with time.

One such example is the Prime Minister's Office (PMO) using big data analytics to process the citizen's sentiments and ideas through the mygov.in crowd sourcing platform. Along with this, the Modi government is also quite active on social media as it helps them get an overall picture of the citizen's concerns and expectations on government work.

According to information disclosed by a <u>news piece</u>, the Modi government is making use of quite a large professional data analytics team to filter and process all the key points that rise in debate on the platform mygov.in and also assesses popular public mood about important issues from social media networking sites such as Face book and Twitter. All the key findings from the mygov.in platform and the social media networking sites is then put together in special reports, along with concrete actionable measures. The Ministers are then requested to take into account all the findings of the report and take actions accordingly, especially on 19 key policy challenges that include job creation, energy conservation, expenditure reforms, skill development and famous government initiatives such as Clean Ganga, Clean India, and Digital India.

It is but natural that as the platform will gain more and more traction, scalability will be become a central issue. India currently occupies the second position in terms of world population and is most probably going to jump to first position by surpassing China by the year 2050. In fact, Modi has been politely asking and pursuing the Indian communities in Australia and America to make their contributions to mygov.in. According to experts, seeing the pace with which the platform is flourishing, a couple of years down the line, the platform will see an active contribution of about 30-50 million people.

Some experts see the PMO's use of big data in the project as a roadmap for democracy in the 21st century world. One of the biggest challenges that the governments face nowadays is how to be relevant to its citizens. If all the citizens of the nation are given the opportunity to collaborate, it will provide the administrators a grip over the nation's important needs rather than losing the message midway between the numbers of layers of bureaucracy.

In the west, most of the government treats their citizens as consumers, which is basically very upsetting and completely a wrong way to go. There is a need to understand that while a consumer pays the bills and cribs, a citizen on the other hand interacts in a different manner and owns up to his actions.

The current times are witnessing a criminal under-utilization of data by the federal departments. One of the biggest challenges that the big data faces with the governments is that it shouldn't supersede their ideologies and beliefs. In fact, statistics can be manipulated and twisted in order to give more fodder to ideologies. But, once it is pushed beyond correlation and into causality, data can become a major driving force.

One of the reasons that makes mygov.in platform highly distinguishable from others is the fact that it isn't just minting out data, but also transforming this data into actionable insights for helping out the Indian ministries.

In the current scenario where people are feeling extremely disconnected, disappointed and far from their governments, the Modi government's big data card could actually be a winner and revolutionize the way democracies function in the current century.

http://www.indianweb2.com/2016/07/27/indian-government-using-big-data-revolutionize-democracy/

3.31 Arun Jaitley to Address Auditors General of Commonwealth Nations

By: PTI | New Delhi | Published: March 21, 2017 2:42 pm

The 23rd conference will be attended by 52 commonwealth countries and 9 British Overseas Territories.

Finance Minister Arun Jaitley (File)

Finance Minister <u>Arun Jaitley</u> will tomorrow address the auditors general of the commonwealth nations and British overseas territories. The 3-day conference that opened today is being held in India for the first time, hosted by Comptroller & Auditor General (CAG). Representatives of the participating nations will look into the scope of leveraging technology in public audit as well as share experiences on environment audit.

The 23rd conference will be attended by 52 commonwealth countries and 9 British overseas territories. "While some of these countries feature in most developed countries of the world, there are several which belong to Least Developed Countries (LDCs) and Small Island Developing States (SIDS)," a finance ministry statement said. The auditing organizations in these countries come together every three years to discuss the challenges before them. The last conference was held in Malta in 2014.

About 80 delegates from 37 countries are expected to participate in the conference. There will be 24 heads of Supreme Audit Institutions (SAI), the statement said. CAG, under Shashi Kant Sharma, is a pioneering SAI in the field of data analytics and use of technology in public Auditing. CAG also heads the International Working Group on

Information System Audits and provides technical assistance to various audit institutions of other countries in use of technology and conducting IT audits.

Similarly on Environment related subjects, several CAG reports on water pollution, waste management, renewable energy and compensatory a forestation have been lauded nationally and internationally, the statement said.

http://indianexpress.com/article/india/arun-jaitley-to-address-auditors-general-of-commonwealth-nations-4578818/

3.32 How Big Data Is Revolutionizing Indian Railways to Ease the Pain of Getting Tatkal Ticket

If we talk about the most comfortable means of transport in India, then without a thought we would say "Railways" or the "Train". Yeah, that's right; the journey through train is considered the most comfortable yet cheapest means of transport.

Let's get back to earlier days when the first train journey happened in 1853. The first train journey took place between Bori Bunder (Bombay) ad Thane in which a fourteen carriage long train was drawn by 3 locomotives. The journey covered a distance of 21 miles.

Over the last 160 years, Indian railway has encountered drastic change. It has created a niche for itself for being the second largest rail network in the world with 115,000 km of track and 19,600 odd trains. Indian railways have in its service more than one million people and carries over 23 million people every day.

Railway is losing its touch

It's a bitter fact that railway is losing its Midas touch gradually. The appearance of low fare airlines and betterment of roadways as well as preference for buses and other vehicles for smaller routes has created an intense competition.

Indian Railways has also been under the radar for its e-ticketing system. The IRCTC site is one of the most frequently visited site, but the navigation is far from being streamlined. The IRCTC website still looks like a site created in early 2000s due to frequent server errors and sluggish speed.

And, the always being on one's top critical list, the "Tatkal ticket booking system" is like a disease, which cannot be cured. The process of getting a Tatkal ticket via Indian Railway's sluggish system is the most complicated yet stressful task ever. The server seems going in coma just a few seconds before 10 AM, and resurrect when every seat has been booked.

Solution to Railway's Sluggish Performance

Now the question that pops out is what can be done in this regard to prevent slow speed and pull it back on the track?

Here, the one and only solution to this problem is Big Data.

If you think from a customer's point of view, then the most apparent concern is ease of ticket booking. With reliable yet steadfast big data tools, it's indeed possible to tackle more customers logging on the site. These customers should also avail a hassle-free experience while booking tickets online.

Measures to simplify it also include analyzing the most frequented routes by passengers and facilitating them the required details hardly in ten seconds and getting an E-wallet option for all the account holders.

Data analytics will chomp historical transactions for a particular customer and pre-empty the train & seat numbers chosen by the customer, hence saving valuable time for those who travel a lot and often choose same trains or coaches.

Tweaking the Tatkal Mechanism

The mechanism of Takal ticketing has to be twisted in terms of technology implemented. With thousands of users logging in on the site at the same time, it's obvious that the system handles such shocks without being crashed. The in-memory ability of such cases has to be increased so that the transactions do not roll out in critical Tatkal hours.

Steps taken by Indian Railways to Improve the Situation

Well, the good news is that Indian Railways have been working on this problem since long time back and now have taken certain steps to improve the scenario. They are about to employ CRIS (Centre for Railway Information systems) for giving a face lift to the IRCTC website. The CRIS based their latest technology on Pivotal GemFire, which is a distributed in-memory database a division of Pivotal Big Data Suite.

The resulting system was checked for a month & then officially introduced in July 2014. The system has brought improvements to the stats considerably, with the load limit going up to 10000 from 2000 per minute. Time taken to book a ticket has been cut down by great fraction and the user verification is done from in-memory data.

Yet, there is a lot of improvement still pending. Tatkal tickets aren't a cup of coffee to get while working with the sluggish speed of

IRCTC website. The duty is on the authorities to not to let it fade away, and get Indian Railways back on the track that it should be.

So, we hope that the next stoppage of Indian Railways would be the **Big Data**.

http://www.madridsoftwaretrainings.com/how-big-data-is-revolutionising-indian-railways-to-ease-the-pain-of-getting-tatkal-ticket.php

3.33 Analytics Sector Will Figure among World Top Three: Nasscom

Jun 24, 2016: Published By: The Hindu

Rapid growth expected: Former Nasscom chairman B.V.R. Mohan Reddy with CEO of Fractal Analytics, Srikanth Velamakanni, addressing a press conference on the sidelines of Big Data and Analytics Summit-2016, in Hyderabad on Thursday.

The sector is witnessing a rapid growth on the back of increased demand for cloud-based and predictive analytics solutions.

The National Association of Software and Services Companies (Nasscom) is confident of India's big data and analytics sector figuring among the world top three in the next three years. The premier industry body also maintains its outlook of the sector posting an eight-fold revenue growth, to reach $16 billion by 2025.

The sector, which clocked revenues of $2 billion last fiscal, is witnessing a rapid growth on the back of increased demand for cloud-based and predictive analytics solutions by BFSI (banking, financial services and insurance), retail, telecom and healthcare industries.

Given the emphasis of user-industries on drawing insights from data and growth opportunities available to service providers, the number of entities in the sector is on the rise. As many as 100 firms were added in 2015 taking the total to 600.

Addressing a press meet as part of a two-day Big Data and Analytics Summit-2016 that opened here on Thursday, vice-president, industry initiatives, K.S. Viswanathan said Nasscom was pursuing a multi-pronged approach focused on skill development, thought leadership, products and platforms for the benefit of the sector. The summit was being held in the backdrop of a need for a strong eco-system. While the opening day saw Nasscom launching an online social collaboration platform for analytics professionals, Friday would see companies discussing skills and capabilities required as part of an effort to frame a curriculum for colleges. Nasscom's BPO Forum member and CEO of Fractal Analytics, Srikanth Velamakanni, said the future was in analytics and BPOs should adopt Artificial Intelligence to stay ahead than becoming a victim of the curve.

Former chairman of Nasscom B.V.R. Mohan Reddy said the digital-connected world, low cost of bandwidth as well as sensors and computing becoming affordable are the factors contributing to growth of big data and analytics.

Hyderabad in race

One of the support measures under consideration is setting up of a Centre of Excellence for Big Data and Analytics.

According to Mr. Viswanathan, an announcement regarding the location of CoE is expected from the government shortly. Several progressive State governments have expressed a desire to host the facility that will be developed on a public private partnership mode on the line of the first CoE (for IoT) in Bengaluru, whose inauguration is scheduled early next month.

Stating that Hyderabad was "one of the hot contenders" for the facility, in which Union Department of Electronics and IT, the respective State government and industry would be stakeholders, he said the CoE would focus on building capability matrix, skilling and research.

http://www.fractalanalytics.com/news/analytics-sector-will-figure-among-world-top-three-nasscom

3.34 Big Data Analytics Sector in India to Reach $16 Billion by 2025: Nasscom

Posted By RSRIT on Jul 1, 2016

In the arena of data science, a lot has yet to be discovered. The time frame is such that it is helping professionals open up new dimensions of the concept regarding data analytics, and it is creating a huge sensation among nations across the globe.

It is known to everyone that data science is very effective in giving your business a new level, and make your trade different from the rest. The National Association of Software and Services Companies have mentioned that by the year 2025, India is going to experience manifold growth in the sector of data science in terms of eight dimensions.

Nasscom has declared that the Indian data science sector which has already made it among the top ten markets of data analytics all across the world is going to have a hike in its development in terms of profit from the current position of $2 billion. The organization has clearly set a goal of making India surge to the top three of markets. The organization has been nurturing a positive attitude towards the phenomenon. They feel that in any case, this will be a great venture for India to develop its economy.

The Vice President of Nasscom, K.S. Viswanathan had said that the sector of data analytics is a fast-growing arena. Where, the demand of the big businesses relates to the idea of data handling appropriately. The

Vice President also said that the sector had the scope to see growth by the following five years. He stated that the growth would be at the rate of compounded annual growth rate (CAGR) of about 26 percent. According to his words, it was also added that India shall be enjoying a 32 percent share in the world market.

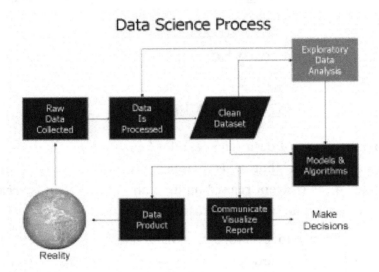

Nasscom also declared that there are a number of analytic companies and organizations in India, which add up to about 600 including 400 of the firms being newly established. About 100 of the companies were established in the year 2015. Therefore, it is clear that in the couple years that passed, an estimated worth of $700 million start-up funding had been observed in the country. This implies that the advancement of Indians on the data science platform has seriously taken momentum. The Vice President has also adjoined that the data analytics companies have succeeded in making India as the evolving place for data science solutions across countries. Big data is looking forward to the development in its way of conduction of processes in all the sections of industries such as retail, telecom, BFSI as well as healthcare.

The industry of data analytics has over 90,000 employees in different firms. Over the consecutive five years, the industry would require recruiting a huge number of manpower. The development of the sector is so fast that the need for people, which shall work for the companies is a big factor. The former chairman of Nasscom has added that the industry would focus on the development of skills in the sector. Artificial intelligence, along with algorithms that enhance deep learning have enriched the machines to work on tasks, which require profound expertise.

http://www.rsrit.com/blog/2016/07/01/big-data-analytics-sector-in-india-to-reach-16-billion-by-2025-nasscom/

3.35 Nasscom Sees India among the Top 3 Destinations for Analytics By 2025

By Pranjal Kshirsagar / 30 Jun 2016, 14:55

The National Association of Software and Services Companies (Nasscom) recently concluded the fourth edition of its Big Data & Analytics Summit 2016 in Hyderabad. The focus of the Summit was driving business outcomes and customer experience by way of leveraging analytical services and products.

Growing at 8 times the current levels, the analytics industry is expected to reach $16 billion from the current level of $2 billion. There are over 600 analytical firms in India, out of which approximately 400 are startups and are positioning India as an emerging hub for analytics solutions for industries across the globe. The Big Data and analytics industry is witnessing a rapid growth driven by increased demand for cloud-based (SaaS) and predictive analytics solutions by industries such as BFSI, retail, telecom, and healthcare.

Big Data is not a textbook concept any more – it touches each and every organization, big or small, in some way. Exponential growth of the number of devices, paired with the deluge of unstructured data – in the form of social media interactions, video or text – has ensured that. Being able to tap into this data and act on the insights is a key differentiator between digital attackers and the laggards. The key to the future in leveraging big data technologies lies in the ability to harness its use in addressing complex problems.

Nasscom notes that this rapid rise of analytics is reflecting in job creation across verticals and functions with skills from analytics, business and technology. With over 90,000 analytics professionals in India across HR, marketing, risk and security, healthcare, and verticals like retail and finance, the industry is witnessing the emergence of specialized roles like data architect, data strategist, data visualization analyst and change manager, among others.

"Multiple opportunities are emerging across business verticals and are opening up large opportunities for companies in data, infrastructure, software and analytics. Of special importance is emergence of custom visualization software, development of algorithms for predictive analytics, cloud based services and Machine to Machine learning. The growth trajectory shows that India will soon emerge as big data and analytics hub of the world," added BVR Mohan Reddy, Former Chairman, Nasscom and Founder and Executive Chairman at Cyient.

KS Viswanathan, VP at Nasscom believes India is already among the top 10 destinations for analytics and can feature in the top 3 in the world by 2025. He believes organizations today are realizing the power of Artificial Intelligence (AI) and investing in utilizing these algorithms in all aspects of their business. The industry will start exploring artificial intelligence and deep learning algorithms for analytics and radically change product delivery to create new markets and engagement models.

Speaking to Tech2 at the Summit, Viswanathan says that finding the right talent to address this analytics revolution is also an aspect that cannot be ignored. He feels finding tools for analytics is the easier part.

But leveraging the tools to make models and then driving insight from there is the bigger challenge that only the right people can resolve.

Tags: <u>Analytics</u>, <u>Artificial Intelligence</u>, <u>big data</u>, <u>machine learning</u>, <u>NASSCOM</u>, <u>Startups</u>

<u>http://tech.firstpost.com/biztech/nasscom-sees-india-among-the-top-3-destinations-for-analytics-by-2025-323172.htm</u>

3.36 Indian Analytics Sector Set to Grow 8 Times

By D. Govardan   Jun 23 2016, Chennai   Tags: News
govardand@mydigitalfc.com

More than 600 analytical firms are positioning India as an emerging hub across globe.

The Indian analytics industry is set to grow eight times to touch $16 billion, from the present $2 billion by 2025. More than 600 analytical firms in the country, including around 400 startups, are positioning India as an emerging hub for analytics solutions for industries across the globe, says software industry body, Nasscom.

The big data and analytics industry is witnessing a rapid growth by increased demand for cloud-based (SaaS) and predictive analytics solutions by industries such as BFSI, retail, telecom and healthcare. Big Data has now also gone beyond disruptive, with exponential growth of the number of devices, paired with the deluge of unstructured data through social media interactions, video or text, having ensured that, Nasscom said in a statement. This rapid rise of analytics is reflecting in job creation across verticals and functions with skills ranging from analytics, business and technology. With over 90,000 analytics professionals in India across HR, marketing, risk and security, healthcare and verticals like retail and finance, the industry is witnessing the emergence of specialized roles like data architect, data strategist, data visualization analyst and change manager, among others.

"Multiple opportunities are emerging across business verticals and are opening up large opportunities for companies in data, infrastructure, software and analytics. Of special importance is the emergence of custom visualization software, development of algorithms for predictive analytics, cloud-based services and machine-to-machine learning. The growth trajectory shows that India will soon emerge as big data and analytics hub of the world," BVR Mohan Reddy, former chairman, Nasscom and founder and executive chairman, Cyient said, while speaking at the Big Data and Analytics Summit, organized by Nasscom and inaugurated in Hyderabad on Thursday.

"India is today amongst the top 10 destinations for analytics and our aspiration is to be amongst the top 3 in the world by 2025. Nasscom is partnering with its members to build a multi-pronged approach that encompasses skill development, thought leadership, products and platforms, to realize this vision," said KS Viswanathan, vice president, Nasscom. Artificial intelligence and deep learning algorithms have advanced rapidly to enable the development of machines that can now do tasks that require deep expertise and skill. The best companies at present are realizing the power of AI and investing in utilizing these algorithms in all aspects of their business. Industry will start exploring artificial intelligence and deep learning algorithms for analytics and radically change product delivery to create new markets and engagement models.

http://www.mydigitalfc.com/news/indian-analytics-sector-set-grow-8-times-023

3.37 Nasscom Aims to Make India a Force in Big Data, Analytics

KV KURMANATH

Aiming high Former Nasscom Chairman BVR Mohan Reddy (centre) with Fractal Analytics CEO Srikanth Velamakanni and Nasscom

Senior VP Sangeeta Gupta are at a press meet in Hyderabad, on Thursday NAGARA GOPAL.

IT lobby targets $4 billion revenues in three years; launches e-community to build ecosystem

HYDERABAD, JUNE 23: With a view to making India one of the top-3 global destinations for big data and analytics in the next three years, Nasscom has launched an online community to pep up the analytics industry in the country as part of its Mission 'Three-by-Three'.

The National Association for Software and Services Companies (Nasscom) aims to take the industry revenue to $4 billion from the present base of $2 billion over the three-year period.

Terming it a 'Three-by-Three' campaign, KS Viswanathan, Vice-President (Industry Initiatives) of Nasscom, has said that the industry is growing at a CAGR (Compound Annual Growth Rate) of 26 per cent. "We expect that the growth rate will continue in the next nine years to cross the $16-billion mark by 2025, giving us a market share of 32 per cent in this space," he told reporters on the sidelines of the fourth edition of the 'Big Data and Analytics Summit' here on Thursday.

India has about 600 firms operating in this space. "The demand for analytics is growing significantly as more and more devices are connected and Artificial Intelligence is transforming the technology space. That about 100 new start-ups have come up in 2015 alone shows the potential," he said.

Online community

In order to build a supported ecosystem, the association has launched an online community for all the stakeholders in the analytics space. The online community will help stakeholders discuss the issues, challenges and opportunities to grow the industry.

About 20 analytics firms are going to meet under the aegis of Nasscom and discuss the professional proficiencies that they require. They are to come out with a set of recommendations on the kind of skill sets they will require.

"We have identified seven job skills in the big data and analytics space. We are in the process of talking to engineering colleges to upgrade the curriculum in order to equip students with big data and analytics skills," said former Nasscom Chairman BVR Mohan Reddy.

He, however, noted that the industry needed to build resources internally for the moment, from its existing staff base.

Analytics Centre

Hyderabad has emerged as a strong contender for the establishment of a Centre of Excellence for Big Data and Analytics.

Nasscom hopes that an announcement will soon be made on the Centre of Excellence. The centre's mandate will be to drive research in the analytics space and strengthen the ecosystem.

(This article was published on June 23, 2016)

http://www.thehindubusinessline.com/info-tech/nasscom-aims-to-make-india-a-force-in-big-data-analytics/article8765282.ece

Chapter 4: Data Science Application by Private Sectors

4.1　Aditya Birla Financial Services Group Picks Teradata EDW to Gain More Business and Customer Insights

Newsletter: ETCIO | Updated: April 20, 2016, 12:47 IST

Teradata solution will enable ABFSG to create a single source for data and insights for its entire business, across multiple group companies and will help to gain a better understanding of customers across the financial services businesses and improve services

Teradata, a big data analytics and marketing applications company said that the Aditya Birla Financial Services Group (ABFSG), a leading non-bank financial services group has expanded its Teradata Enterprise Data Warehouse (EDW) project to better support their customer centricity vision.

ABFSG selected the Teradata Data Warehouse platform and revamped the Teradata Financial Services Data Model (FSDM) implementation. This follows their earlier commissioning of the Teradata Data Warehouse solution to help produce reports and provide information for all sales, marketing, and customer-service-related business units for its life insurance and asset management business, Birla Sun Life Insurance Company and Birla Sun Life Asset Management Company in 2009.

ABFSG faced challenges in bringing together all relevant data from nine different companies and delivering actionable analytics and management information systems (MIS) reports from a single place. This led them to evaluate analytics solution providers in the market. The organization realized that a Teradata solution expansion would give them the ability and agility to increase competences and capabilities, providing quicker turnaround and informed insights for better decision-making.

The Teradata solution will enable ABFSG to create a single source for data and insights for its entire business, across multiple group companies. The solution will help ABFSG to gain a better understanding of customers across the financial services businesses and help provide better, more relevant and timelier service to their end customers.

""We were looking for a technology partner with proven expertise, an understanding of our business, and one that offered solutions that could be scaled up to meet future demand. Teradata has proven to be the best fit and we are certain that they are future ready," said G. V. Gopalakrishnan, COO - Financial Services, Aditya Birla Group.

Further, "ABFSG recently established a central analytics team to handle risk analytics and we are planning to leverage the platform to do all the data mining and other advanced analytics on the Teradata solution," added Gopalakrishnan.

"We have in fact started doing some analytics related proof of concepts which, when live, will help serve real-time analytics enabling us to acquire more customers and reach new segments of customers. The upgrade has more than lived up to our expectation because processing time has now come down by 30-40%," he informed.

ABFSG selected the Teradata Data Warehouse, with its ability to start small and grow according to requirements, to fuel its business intelligence (BI) and customer relationship management (CRM) initiative. Scalability was a critical factor as they were looking at a five-year growth of up to 27 Terabytes of data which meant they could support more Lines of Businesses (LoBs) without spending extra money. Teradata's FSDM provided ABFSG with an enterprise-wide blueprint for their data and a structure to help manage their information as well as get a single-source view of transactional, financial and risk management data.

In terms of results, maximizing customer value through democratization of data across different departments and functions and then operationalizing it has been a major differentiator at ABFSG.

This has helped deliver cost savings, including improved consolidated reporting, reduced external audit fees, improved product pricing and improved campaign ROI. The company also sees benefits in terms of storage savings and processing improvements, along with the extra competences and services they can now offer customers.

Additionally, IVR and customer-care call-centre operations are two areas where ABFSG has used web services to leverage Teradata. The solution has helped their team members to make more accurate calculations and decisions.

"It is indeed a pleasure to be working with a customer like ABFSG who is completely focused on providing better services and experiences for their customers. ABFSG chose our solutions as they consider them to be the best in the market in terms of not only technology and functions but also with regard to return on investments," said Sunil Jose, Managing Director, Teradata India.

"Adopting Teradata solutions has helped them understand their business data better, paving the way for further business expansion along with enhanced customer engagement," added Jose.

http://cio.economictimes.indiatimes.com/news/big-data/aditya-birla-financial-services-group-picks-teradata-edw-to-gain-more-business-and-customer-insights/51906625

4.2   Microsoft Showcases the Power of Analytics and Machine Learning to Transform Businesses and Drive Inclusive Growth

MUMBAI, India, November 8, 2016: Posted August 8, 2016 by Firozgar Hansotia

Bengaluru, August 8, 2016: Microsoft India today inaugurated the first edition of Machine Learning & Data Sciences (ML&DS) Conference in India. This two-day conference is aimed at exploring the tremendous possibilities with Big Data, Machine Learning, Artificial Intelligence and Open Source technologies to enable a rich set of platforms, intelligent apps, services and experiences to accelerate economic growth, empower people and drive real impact. The conference will host 600 participants, including data scientists, students, developers, government elites, start-ups, cricketers and Microsoft experts, who will share new insights and showcase powerful solutions that are driving digital transformation for organizations and communities in India and worldwide.

Joseph Sirosh, Corporate Vice President of Data Group at Microsoft, while delivering the keynote at the conference, said, "Cloud based services for Machine Learning and Big Data, together with the Internet of Things (IoT) have the potential to revolutionize every aspect of our lives, viz., sports, healthcare and education and even our government. At Microsoft, our ambition is to democratize the access to these technologies so that software developers can build, innovate and transform the world with them. I am thrilled to be part of the first ever Machine Learning and Data Science Conference in India, and I am looking forward to showcasing unique platforms such as the Cortana Intelligence Suite that are helping customers harness the power of Artificial Intelligence."

Demonstrating the wide-ranging possibilities of data analytics, Microsoft also unveiled an Azure Machine Learning based approach for calculating target scores in weather-interrupted T20 cricket matches. It uses machine learning, applies advanced analytics to past data and existing mathematical formulation to derive the outcome. The approach is now available as a Jupiter notebook in Microsoft's Cortana Intelligence Gallery for software developers to build on and improve using existing data across multiple areas such as playing conditions, weather and cricket grounds.

https://ncmedia.azureedge.net/ncmedia/2016/08/IMG_9704.jpg

From Right – Shamya Dasgupta – Senior Editor, Wisden India; Aakash Chopra – former Indian cricketer; Meetul Patel – General Manager, Microsoft India; Javagal Srinath – former Indian cricketer and Joseph Sirosh – Corporate Vice President – Data Group, Microsoft at the Microsoft Showcase for Machine Learning and Data Sciences in Sports at Bengaluru. The showcase discussed the growing impact of technology on sports and the role Microsoft's Machine Learning can play in accurately calculating target scores in weather-interrupted T20 cricket matches. It also discussed possibilities of how Machine Learning can transform sports management and administration including monitoring health condition on the field, predicting injuries and taking pre-emptive action.

Speaking about the conference, **Anil Bhansali, Managing Director, Microsoft India (R&D) Pvt. Ltd.**, said, "At Microsoft, we see tremendous possibilities to partner in India's digital transformation with our transformative technologies, our offerings and local cloud services. Microsoft's capabilities and pioneering work in the field of machine learning in India is helping bring efficiencies in the fields of agriculture, healthcare and education. We are also pleased to extend the benefits of machine learning to the sports fraternity by offering a platform for software developers in India to create solutions that could change the approach to sports administration and sports management. This really shows the expanse of impact this technology can have on varied segments and communities."

Machine Learning is one of Microsoft's key focus areas and one in which the company is making significant inroads, both in terms of research and development breakthroughs as well as translating the outcome of its work into real customer impact. To boost the state's education ecosystem, Microsoft is working with the Government of Andhra Pradesh on a machine learning based model to analyze and predict drop outs and take preventive action. It has engaged with L. V. Prasad Eye Institute to build a predictive model that helps predict regression rates for eye operations, enabling doctors to pinpoint the procedures needed to prevent and treat visual impairments. To aid digital agriculture in Andhra Pradesh, Microsoft has partnered with ICRISAT to provide powerful cloud-based predictive analytics to empower farmers with crucial information and insights to help reduce crop failures and increase yield, in turn, reducing stress and generating better income.

The first day of the conference will feature an overnight hackathon for students and early-stage developers to build cool, intelligent applications that take advantage of Microsoft Cognitive Services. Top participants will get a unique opportunity to pitch their ideas to top Indian VCs, faculty and Microsoft executives. In addition to the hackathon, the event will also feature demo booths showcasing the exciting capabilities of

Microsoft Machine Learning platform and Application program interface (APIs) powered solutions in the field of healthcare, education, agriculture, and how start-ups and businesses are using it to drive transformation and create opportunities. Over the course of the two days, the conference will feature over 30 technical sessions, tutorials, demos and more that will showcase Microsoft's innovation in this field.

About Microsoft India

Founded in 1975, Microsoft (Nasdaq "MSFT") Microsoft is the leading platform and productivity company for the mobile-first, cloud-first world, and its mission is to empower every person and every organization on the planet to achieve more. Microsoft set up its India operations in 1990. Today, Microsoft entities in India have over 7,000 employees engaged in sales and marketing, research and development, and customer services and support across ten cities – Ahmedabad, Bangalore, Chennai, Delhi, Gurgaon, Hyderabad, Kochi, Kolkata, Mumbai and Pune.

https://news.microsoft.com/en-in/microsoft-showcases-the-power-of-analytics-and-machine-learning-to-transform-businesses-and-drive-inclusive-growth/#sm.00000s46f7zpaleppsh3qnq6rfvf5#EkgxmUYXdmcvAJwI.97

4.3 GE Digital: Driving the Next Industrial Revolution through Analytics

RICHA BHATIA: DEC 27, 2016 0

It is one of the most revered industrial giants in the world, anchored in Boston and operating from around the world with businesses in aviation, energy, healthcare and many others and now GE Digital. GE Digital is at the core of company's transformation into Digital Industrial. And how! By connecting streams of machine data to powerful analytics and people, providing industrial companies with valuable insights to manage assets and operations more efficiently. A transformation that now makes it a 'Digital Industrial'; combining company's rich expertise in industry with new technology talent at locations like the new state of the art digital hub in Bangalore. Based in Whitefield, the 200,000 sq. feet facility is the largest digital hub for GE. The company recently announced that it will create job opportunities for technology talent and plans to add over 1000 positions in the coming two years' time. The **Digital Hub** is part of a network of technology centers that GE has, spread out across San Ramon, Detroit, New Orleans, Glen Allen, Budapest, Riyadh and Bangalore.

Pradeep Menon, Vice President, Analytics and Data Domain,
GE Digital India in an exclusive chat with AIM

If you thought GE's legacy was just industrial-focused, the US conglomerate proves you wrong with its complete reinvention. In an exclusive chat with **Pradeep Menon, Vice President – Analytics and Data Domain**, GE Digital tells *Analytics India Magazine* what led to the birth of Predix and how it is built on bedrock **of analytics**. He also spoke about why GE took on the **role of digital** and its bullish plan to be among the **most noted analytics captives** globally. *AIM* got an exclusive look at the spanking new facility outfitted with cutting edge office & workspace technologies. "Organizations in today's world have to move towards a digital reality. It is more an imperative, than an option and GE Digital is GE's answer to that and the latest startup in the 124-year-old company. And to make it successful, we will be bringing in the best talent available into our hubs with a renewed focus on diverse talent at leadership and analyst levels" shared Menon, over the twenty-minute long interview.

In fact, GE Digital is unlike any other GE office, which underscores how GE the multinational wants to **reinforce its status as the premiere digital industrial company**. The **digital efficiency** is evident not just in services delivered but in the office across the board. For example, *AIM* observed employees can locate their colleagues across floors over a Digital Bridge app, or jump into a video conference just by the conference room identifying them through their phones or laptops.

Well, GE is not entirely abandoning its industrial heritage either. GE is bringing the Industrial Internet to life by connecting machine sensors on a network and allowing them to communicate with each other. GE combines decades of experience building innovative industrial machines with cutting-edge data science and analytics expertise today. In fact, Predix, the **"cloud-based operating system for the industrial internet of things"** is driving the global economy, connecting heavy machinery, industrial equipment and helping derive real-time insights from them. "By 2020, Predix will be processing a million terabytes per day. World-class talent and software capabilities help us drive digital industrial transformation for big gains in productivity, availability and longevity. Industrial is something that GE is very familiar with and an area that we are well known for, so there is a lot of knowledge we can use in building these applications," explains Menon.

4.4   Driving Digital Transformation with Data Science

Immense amounts of data are flowing into and out of today's businesses, but it's often difficult to know how to turn this data into actionable insights. Data science has incredible potential for businesses of all types to create models that find patterns in this data and use them as the basis for transformative software. From location sensor data and customer loyalty programs to predictive analytics that improve the customer experience, employee engagement, and operational efficiency, a world of possibility awaits organizations that can crack the data science code.

Unlocking new opportunities with data science

No matter what industry you're in, data science can play a major role in helping to digitally transform your business—a goal to which more and more organizations aspire. CIO defines digital transformation as "the acceleration of business activities, processes, competencies, and models to fully leverage the changes and opportunities of digital technologies and their impact in a strategic and prioritized way." But more than just acceleration, digital transformation is about the need for businesses to outpace digital disruption and stay competitive in a rapidly evolving business environment. Without doubt, data science needs to be a fundamental component of any digital transformation effort. Often described as a new frontier, "Big Data" is widely thought to have the potential to transform industries and to up-end business models that have been in place for decades. By looking for patterns in data and creating software that can regularly and reliably turn that data into actionable insight, data science can give companies an advantage that is difficult or even impossible for competitors to match. This opportunity is why so many businesses are adopting data science; but as with all game-changing technologies, the main driver is already shifting toward necessity. Customer demand and other factors, like technology itself, are changing the concept of what's possible and making it imperative for companies to keep up. Here are four technologies that illustrate this reality.

1.   Machine learning—Technology now makes it possible for software solutions to learn and evolve. Software with machine learning capabilities can produce different results given the same set of data inputs at different points in time, with a learning phase in between. This is a

major change from following strictly static program instructions, like the models from the 1990s.

2.   Omni-channel architecture—Because customers shop across channels and classes, decisions made in one class or channel have an impact on products in other classes and channels—whether it's pricing, promotions, staffing, inventory, or assortment decisions. With omni-channel architecture, all your channels stay in alignment.

3.   Cloud—Companies are increasingly taking advantage of the elastic nature of the cloud and deploying this technology for the flexibility, agility, and affordability it provides. Cloud-based applications can provide your people with real-time access to information from anywhere in the world at any time. By replicating the same environment across the globe, multiple global environments remain in sync, and response time is optimized. Most importantly, because applications in the cloud are always current, always available, and highly scalable, the cloud makes continuous innovation an achievable objective.

Data science needs to be a fundamental component of any digital transformation effort.

4. Network visibility— In a global economy, network visibility is essential; however, most systems today are only able to give you half of the picture. You can track where products are within your virtual "four walls" or outside of them within your network of suppliers. But getting a fully integrated picture has historically been challenging. Cloud-based collaboration platforms capable of automating hundreds of processes on a global scale are rapidly changing the definition of "visibility," with companies on the cutting edge of this technology standing to make great gains. Three principles for use -

All this technology produces vast amounts of data. How do you use all the data from these and other new technologies to make better decisions and improve operations? The answer is "by making it accessible, meaningful, and actionable". Follow these three principles, and you'll be on your way:

1.   Make data consumable—Data science models—and the data they produce—must be easily consumable by the average user. You shouldn't need a PhD to benefit. Having access to easily consumable, real-time insights and visualizations of complex sets of data can unlock new opportunities and revenue streams—and help improve customer relationships and your bottom line.

2.   Make data adaptable—Models should be self-learning and highly automated, so users can get the most from them. The models must learn and evolve, so the data you get are relevant to your users today and in the future. The models and data also need to be accessible through your existing enterprise platforms, so everyone can easily get to them.

3.   Make data transparent— "Black box" solutions that hide their functions from users or that can't be re-used across your technology ecosystem are no longer acceptable. When users can't justify, or explain why they accepted a solution's recommendation, they stop using it. Your users must be able to drill down to understand where the data behind the recommendation originated. When users understand the recommendation as well as the reasons for that recommendation, their experience is more meaningful; preparing your industry for a digital transformation.

Data scientists at Infor® Dynamic Science Labs create models that find patterns in this mass of data and work with developers to build these models into Infor software. Infor Dynamic Science Labs is a group of scientists, mathematicians, economists, and engineers who are driving the next generation of enterprise software. They're creating software that is smart, self-learning, and focused on the future. They work with customers and product managers to identify industry-wide challenges and then solve those using elegant but understandable scientific methods.

Some of the areas Infor Digital Science Labs are working in

1. CRM science

As part of the digital transformation driven by data science, Infor Dynamic Science Labs is building a CRM science engine that digests the immense volume of data flowing into your organization and advises you on what to do next. The engine predicts which customers are most likely to purchase; what they are likely purchase next; and whether they are at risk of leaving. For industries where sales people reach out to individual customers, Infor Dynamic Science Labs is building a smart sales assistant tool. The sales assistant identifies which customers are the best leads for new revenue. It creates profiles on each customer, so that the sales person is aware of each customer's recent interactions and purchases. And, using the next likely purchase algorithms, the sales assistant identifies which products are mostly likely to be purchased next by a customer and why. Finally, the solution offers churn prediction, so you can identify your at-risk customers and work to prevent losing them. For distributors with counter sales locations, the CRM sales assistant can alert the checkout staff to remind customers about likely purchases that they may have forgotten. If a contractor is buying replacement parts to fix a piece of equipment, for example, perhaps the sales person can suggest follow-on pieces or specific tools that could make the job easier—or save the contractor a second trip.

For retailers, CRM science can be used in a different manner. For example, instead of giving a customer who's checking out a coupon to use on their next visit, with opt-in loyalty programs, customers can receive coupons and recommendations as soon as they set foot in one of your stores or outlets. In the old way of doing things, customers might only receive a coupon for their next purchase when they're at the register, checking out. By sending them coupons and promotions when they're already in the store, you don't have to wait for that next visit for them to spend. CRM science can also enable you to allocate staff to store departments based on the next likely purchases of the people currently in your store, so you can match up the right sales people with the right customers. Or, if you know there are areas of the store where customers always have questions, you can be sure to have those areas staffed. Whether you're a retailer, distributor, or manufacturer, when your sales people have additional information about a customer, they can provide the best service and help increase your revenue.

2. Real-time supply chain monitoring and optimization

In the digital world where we now live, maintaining visibility into your global supply chain is essential to avoid costly delays and inventory shortages. Delays in Shanghai or Long Beach, for example, can affect operations all over the world. Traditional supply chain management tools have relied on analysts building complex, specific models to estimate shipment durations and arrival times. With increased computing power and global supply chain data collected by GT Nexus, a cloud-based global supply chain management platform, Infor can more accurately model supply chain timelines automatically, eliminating the need for costly manual models and allowing you to detect disruptions in real-time and mitigate them. The GT Nexus network connects global companies to their partners, both onshore and offshore, and provides real-time visibility into order and shipment status, so brand owners can optimize their supply chain for greater agility, faster turns, and lower costs. By combining machine learning with a Big Data analytics platform, you can better understand which delays are normal variations and which are true system-wide disruptions—like strikes or natural disasters. Because you can continuously monitor the data feed in real-time, you don't need to think about it. The platform will notify you if there is a problem, and give you a range of solutions. Your analytics system can then surface those delays and send you an alert.

When there is a disruption, you can dive into your affected shipments and see what the impact is for each of them. When you are integrating data across your entire business—you can develop a deeper understanding of what is truly important to you:

■ How do these disruptions affect your business downstream?

■ Which shipments are more important than others?

■ What is the optimal tradeoff between faster shipping times and additional cost? Using this deep knowledge about your business, you can get real-time suggestions on how to mitigate disruptive events in a way that is best for your business. That way you can secure alternate transportation before others can—like reserving rail chasses or truck capacity before it runs out. The data collected by GT Nexus not only helps you to detect disruptions, it allows you to confidently chart a course around these bottlenecks in your supply chain. When your employees have better information, they are more aware of potential problems and can plan accordingly.

3. Location-based inventory analytics

RFID tags and similar technologies have become much more affordable in recent years, allowing retailers, distributors, and manufacturers to potentially tag and search every piece of inventory in their stores or warehouses. Combined with sensors that identify the location of each tag, this technology allows you to collect a wealth of data that gives you real-time insights into the location of every item in your inventory. In retail, you can use sensor data to assess the fit of items based on what is left behind in fitting rooms—learn what items people try on but never buy and determine whether there's a fit problem, for example. You can use this information to correct the style design, or to stop producing items that aren't selling and avoid unnecessary markdowns.

Location data can also be used to create an optimal store layout. You can figure out what people pick up and put down and where certain items do best. You can also use consideration data to determine cannibalization and recommend assortments. What if one product is replacing another? You can determine which product makes the most sense for your business to carry. RFID and other sensors also create a lot of valuable insights about your warehouse inventory, as well. You can obtain accurate inventory levels without wasting valuable employee time counting. You can track each item in your warehouse to find misplaced items. Not only do you waste time having your employees look for lost items, but you can also miss out on sales. By tracking the movement of the inventory in your warehouses, you can also optimize the location and storage of your inventory—and find new opportunities to make your business more efficient.

By combining machine learning with Big Data analytics, you can better understand which delays are normal variations and which are true system-wide disruptions. With Infor Dynamic Science Labs, you can transform the way you do business. We're using predictive analytics, mathematical modeling, optimization, forecasting, and more to help customers identify opportunities. Using data science, we can create and validate solutions that can improve your decision-making—so it's easier for your customers to do business with you.

http://www.infor.com/content/executive-briefs/digital-transformation-science.pdf/

4.5   From Data Science to Data Stories: Bridging the Gap to Digital Transformation (Highlights)
Katya Vladislav leva, Data Stories (Evolved Analytics)

Predictive analytics and data science are gaining importance and proven impact despite the hype. Surprisingly, the data science universe and the business universe keep coexisting without too much overlap. We claim that data-driven solutions will see a greater success in business and industry only when they are understood and internalized by domain experts (not just data scientists), and when domain experts take ownership of the solutions. This can only happen if predictive analytics outcomes are communicated to domain experts in human language with a narrative. Otherwise, they have little chance to be sustainably deployed.

Digital transformation and data-driven strategy are proven to increase EBITs, but are assumed to require epic efforts in terms of upfront investment and unique talent acquisition. Budgets are almost always spent on collecting the data with little to no plans on what to do with it later, which makes the transformation incomplete. Interestingly, the technology exists to turn all of this data into immediate actions without epic efforts and with existing human capital. Data stories' claim is that turning data science into data stories is the missing ingredient in completing the data-driven transformation and making it an enjoyable.

This video is a short version of the presentation given at MATLAB EXPO. To watch the full-length video, see the link in the "Other Resources" section below.

https://www.mathworks.com/videos/from-data-science-to-data-stories-bridging-the-gap-to-digital-transformation-highlights-121423.html

4.6   The role Big Data plays in Digital Transformation

Daniel Newman , CONTRIBUTOR, *I research, analyze and discuss all things Digital Transformation:* Opinions expressed by Forbes Contributors are their own.

Access to big data has changed the game for small and large businesses alike. Instead of using small focus groups and general demographics to extrapolate target market activities, modern companies can now access specific information—and lots of it—about employees and customers, helping fine tune marketing and sales, and drive increased ROI. Big data can help businesses solve almost every problem with a working, research driven solution.

But, for many organizations, "big data" is a scary term. Where does the info come from? How do I translate such a massive and ever changing data set into usable information? I've found the key to successfully leveraging big data in order to support digital transformation strategy is to start slowly.

Big Data and Digital Transformation

Digital transformation helps companies embrace a culture of change and remain competitive in a global environment, but, when companies decide to go digital, the process is a little bit like losing weight ('tis the season!). You can't go on a diet for a few weeks and expect fast or lasting results. Losing weight has to be a lifestyle change, and so does incorporating big data into your business strategies.

Big data allows companies to make meaningful, strategic adjustments that minimize costs and maximize results. If you know what consumers and employees are doing currently, you can create projections for what they will do in the future, and start implementing changes to address their needs and your goals. A digital transformation isn't complete unless a business adopts big data.

Image: Flickr

Identifying Goals

Some enterprises read or hear about the types of data other companies use in their own digital strategies. This should never provide yours with a starting point for pursuing big data applications. Every business is unique, and needs to look strategically at both short- and long-term goals.

Identify the biggest challenges you face in the marketplace today. With a list of goals and challenges, companies can start to break down big data into usable insights that will drive success. Start small, and avoid using non-specific goals—such as "maximize the bottom line." Instead, try to overcome pointed challenges and meet objectives to:

- Improve or change the customer experience.
- Improve employee workflow for better productivity.
- Identify customer pain points in the digital world for marketers to focus on.
- Retain customers.
- Reduce costs.

Find the Right Data Sets

You can find useful data both in-house and in the marketplace. You're CRM and ERP tools offer significant insight into consumers and employees, and leveraging that data often only requires knowing how to structure a report. You can also use social media management systems and online tools such as Google Analytics to monitor consumer behavior and brand interactions. Use the focus of your goal to inform the data sets you use to address the problem.

If you can identify one metric that will influence your approach to a goal, find and use it first. As more questions surrounding that initial goal arise, continually look for new data sets that can provide the information you need to make informed decisions. Avoid guessing or only relying only on logic to optimize your strategies, and look for tools that will provide you with the reports needed to make a sound judgment call.

Maximizing the Benefits for Any Business

You don't have to be a data analyst or employ one to start using big data. Many tools and platforms exist today that can help you take data sets, manipulate them, and present them in an orderly fashion for your team to evaluate and use. Often, finding valuable information requires generating a simple report that provides you with an overview of your current impact, trends, or projections.

If your enterprise still has a hard time understanding how big data can streamline a digital transformation, I'd advice taking a few continuing education classes, attending a seminar, or hiring a consultant. Once you have access to the tools and know how to interpret the data, your company has everything it needs to start gaining momentum and make a successful digital transformation. Stay competitive in the marketplace in 2016 with a strategy to incorporate big data into your business operations.

https://www.forbes.com/sites/danielnewman/2015/12/22/the-role-big-data-plays-in-digital-transformation/#5642eaf475d3

4.7 Realizing the Potential of Big Data and Analytics

Daniel Newman, **CONTRIBUTOR**, *I research, analyze and discuss all things Digital Transformation*: Opinions expressed by Forbes Contributors are their own.

It's not what you know. It's what you *do* with what you know. That's something companies worldwide will be learning—for better or worse—in the coming year when it comes to big data.

Gurus among us have proclaimed 2017 will be the year big data goes main stream. If you're anything like me, you may be wondering if that has already happened and if not, why? Even many teenagers I know use Google Analytics to monitor their daily "brand." The truth is 2017 marks an even more meaningful shift when it comes to using data in business. For the first time, it will drive business operations, rather than simply reflecting performance. That's a powerful proposition for those who use analytics effectively. On the flip side: It could be absolutely devastating for companies who are falling behind.

Shutterstock

If you're worried your business may have missed the big data boat, you're in good company. According to the Harvard Business Review, a majority of today's businesses are "nowhere close" to recognizing the value analytics can bring. The reasons are all-too familiar: Lack of vision, lack of communication, lack of an actual plan. The good news: you *can* do something about it. Below are just a few things to keep in mind as you assemble—or re-assemble—your strategic big data plan.

Find a Champion

Like most big changes in any company, management plays a huge role in how quickly their companies will adopt—and adapt—to it. If you are planning to introduce or enhance your analytics platform, establish supporters and mentors in every sector of the company. After all, data is never central. From your front-line customer service team to your top senior executives, the decisions you make based on results and reporting will reach every single layer of your company—including YOU.

Whether gathering data on the front end or making big decisions in the C Suite, every single person in your organization must buy in to the value analytics brings. If not, you run two major risks. First, you could end up with dirty data, which is worthless when it comes to making good, solid business decisions. Second, you could amass tons of amazing data insights that are never utilized by your executive teams. Consider creating a dedicated communication campaign surrounding analytics to ensure full-scale penetration and success.

Create a System for Success

One of the biggest mistakes many companies make is not having a system in place to support their analytics efforts. Who is managing it? Reporting on it? Gathering the information? Inputting the data? How often do they do it? How often do they report it? And what's about post-collection? Who analyzes the information, and how? If you haven't outlined these processes, your data will never pay. Get those systems and dedicated employees in place on the *front end*, before your information gathering even starts.

Indeed, most of us know having an outdated database or pipeline is one of the easiest ways to put a nail in our business' coffin. The same can be true for your analytics system. MNP notes many companies don't even know what types of data they have—let alone whether that data is accurate. If nothing else, your data needs to be pure. That means someone needs to be accountable for keeping it that way. Not sure who that person is? Hold off on making any decisions surrounding your analytics program until you do.

Establish Clear (And Simple) Goals

If you don't know what you're trying to find, you'll never find it. Make time to answer questions like: How will we measure success, effectiveness, and value? And even more importantly, *what will we do with the information when we find it?*

Keep your goals simple, at least initially. The amount of information flowing our way at any given moment can be overwhelming. In fact, in 2015, IBM noted the world creates 2.5 quintillion bytes of data every single day. Even more startling: at the time, the company estimated 90 percent of the world's data had been created in the last two years alone. Imagine what we're producing now! This kind of data flow can lead to "paralysis by analysis." It can turn us into deer caught in the proverbial headlights of "data overwhelm." To help, try to avoid overly complex analytical goals. Start slow, and learn to trust your data through clean, clear results before taking on overly-complicated initiatives.

Embrace Change

When used effectively, analytics do far more than validate your company's path to success. They can offer a new pathway to *successful change*. If you aren't open to using them to their fullest, you may as well sit out of the game—just be ready to get left behind!

Indeed, change isn't just coming, *change is here*—whether we like it or not. Analytics have the power to disrupt nearly every part of today's economy, changing everything from how we run our businesses to the type of businesses we run. big data is here to stay. Embrace its potential! It could lead your company to unimaginable levels of success.

Daniel Newman is CEO of Broadsuite Media Group, principal analyst at Futurum and author of Building Dragons.

https://www.forbes.com/sites/danielnewman/2017/01/31/realizing-the-potential-of-big-data-and-analytics/#4ce532c4709a

4.8   Microsoft India Projects itself as Open Source Champion, Says AI is the Next Step

VISHAL KRISHNA, 20 FEBRUARY 2017

The company announced that it is building the world's largest artificial intelligence platform

At *.ai Intelligent Cloud, a conference hosted by Microsoft India in Bengaluru on Monday, the company said that Big Data, Cloud, and intelligence have changed the way machines compute services for human beings. It also announced that it was building the world's largest artificial intelligence (AI) platform.

"Cognitive services will change IT applications in the future. Services can become intelligent with machine learning and we are providing APIs to startups for computer applications like vision, speech, language, knowledge and search," says Sandeep Alur, Microsoft Lead Evangelist.

The company also positioned itself as a champion of open source technologies, with over 16,000 contributions made on GitHub, an open source internet hosting service. Large corporate like Google are in the game too. They joined the .Net Foundation technical steering group, which was launched by Microsoft.

Microsoft, in return, joined the Linux Foundation. While this global exchange of knowledge is well-founded, today everyone wants to know what AI is all about.

Analysts at Gartner tell *Your Story* that today most neural networks are still in the realm of machine learning, which means outcomes, can be predictive. Computer science experts will say that AI comes with reasoning power, which means machines, can fool you into believing they are human.

That said, several software engineers are going after building computers that can create predictive outcomes for services. Say, a machine can tell when a part could fail and will inform the customer about going to the dealership to replace the part. Let us also say you call a BPO and a chatbot using voice technologies, which will guide you through a query better than any human. Says Alur of Microsoft.

"Today, building a bot means maintaining several source codes. But we have created a framework for bots with one source code."

Research firm Markets & Markets says the AI market could be $16 billion by 2022.

Bot frameworks can change the way BPOs function and change their outcomes.

However, the point is that while all these frameworks make it easy with a lot application channels, saying that we are in the realm of AI is a wrong argument. However, the push that Microsoft offers, to go towards AI with machine learning, is something to watch out for.

Let's look at the numbers. If we look at all the system integrators, starting from Accenture to Infosys to TCS to Wipro, their revenues from platforms that offer AI or machine learning is less than 10 percent.

"Data is critical and we can build models that can become critical for predictive planning," says Anish Basu Roy, CEO of Shotang.

Several startups that *Your Story* spoke to believed that machine learning was today called AI. "Everything that is F of X is considered AI, when all we are building is an intelligent machine," said founders of a couple of startups who did not want to be named.

Representatives of the Indian startup ecosystem in the room were extremely robust. Over 200 of them were present and most of them were in the realm of data analytics, cognitive sciences and predictive maintenance. Somehow, the feeling was that they were here to witness Satya Nadella's talk with Nandan Nilekani.

https://yourstory.com/2017/02/microsoft-india/

4.9   Industries of the Future: The Race for Robotics, Genomics, Analytics, Cyber security and Digital Transactions
MADANMOHAN RAO, 18 OCTOBER 2016

Exponential technology growth is transforming the world in ways never seen before, opening up new entrepreneurial opportunities while also causing wrenching socio-economic change. The new book *The Industries of the Future* points out examples, trends and success factors in sectors ranging from robotics and cyber security to genomics and analytics (see also my review of the book *No Ordinary Disruption*).

As Senior Advisor for Innovation to the US Secretary of State, author Alec Ross traveled to over 40 countries. He is a Distinguished Visiting Fellow at the Johns Hopkins University and serves as an advisor to investors, government and industry. In 2000, he and three colleagues co-founded the social venture One Economy.

The 305-page book is a good mix of storytelling and economic analysis, backed up by 40 pages of reference citations. I have clustered some of the startups and innovative organizations in these booming sectors in Table 1, followed by brief overviews of each of the five sectors.

Table 1: Innovation by sector

Sector	Startups and innovators
Robotics	Deep Mind, Raven, Aldebaran, Grishin Robotics, Singular team, Motoman, Honda ASIMO, Tokai RIBA, KAIST JEROS, African Robotics Network
Genomics	Base Health, Synthetic Genomics, Human Longevity Inc., Broad Institute, PGDx, Beijing Genomic Institute
Digital transactions	Square, Stripe, AliPay, M-Pesa, BitCoin, Xapo, Crypto METH
Cyber security	Cloud Flare, Proof Point, Fire Eye
Big Data, Analytics	Standard Treasury, Palantir, Open Ag Data Alliance, Health Map

Robotics

The word 'robot' was first coined by Czech sci-fi writer Karel Capek. The 'singularity' – the point when AI surpasses human intelligence – could come by 2023 (Vernor Vinge) or 2045 (Ray Kurzweil). 'Weak' AI (in specific functions) is advancing exponentially, but 'strong' AI (human-like cognition) is growing only linearly. While much attention focuses on robots doing human tasks, they may soon be doing things impossible for humans.

Robots are well suited to a wide range of tasks – dangerous, dirty, dreary, as well as context-sensitive, spatially dexterous and judgment-focused. Robots have high cap-ex but relatively low op-ex, as compared to routine tasks requiring high human op-ex (salaries) but low cap-ex (training). Robots can free humans to do more productive things, but there will be labour and cultural repercussions on society as robots impact blue-collar as well as white-collar work.

Smart cars may help reduce accidents caused by the 'four Ds' – distraction, drowsiness, drunkenness and driver errors, but issues of trust and the 'human touch' still remain. **"The driverless system will have to prove to be nearly perfect before it scales,"** cautions Ross.

Trends to watch include robot-assisted surgery, educational robots (eg. for autistic children), cloud robotics for connected learning (breaking free from the confines of in-circuit memory and logic), materials such as air muscle, and small components for nanobots.

Japan leads the world in robotics, industrial as well as eldercare, followed by China, the US, Korea and Germany (in terms of robot sales). Japan is home to the longest-living people on the planet and has the largest population of the elderly. It is also tough on immigration. The country has a favourable cultural predisposition towards robots, thanks to Shinto animist beliefs, and is reinventing robotics the way it reinvented cars in the 1970s and consumer electronics in the 1980s.

Examples include Toyota's 'female' nursing aide Robina and her 'brother' Humanoid; Honda's ASIMO (Advanced Step in Innovative Mobility) healthcare companion; RIKEN's RIBA (Robot for Interactive Body Assistance) caretaker, which can even lift humans; and AIST's PARO, a robot seal pet. Robots will be that rare technology that reaches elders first.

Other examples include Korea's jellyfish-eliminating robot swarms, Panasonic's hair washing robot (for salons and hospitals), Motoman's waiter robots, and Manchester airport's robot janitors. China is also investing heavily in robotics as it faces labour cost competition from other countries like Vietnam.

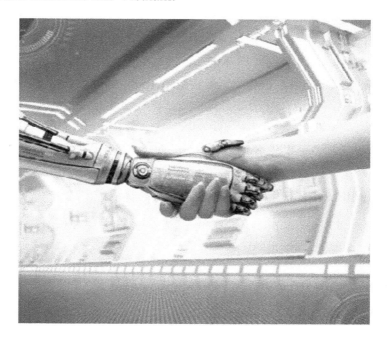

Genomics

Genomics, the next trillion-dollar industry, took off in the mid-1990s, and the cost of genome sequencing dropped a million-fold in 10 years. Genomics can help detect and treat cancers at early stages, target genes that cause depression and suicidal behaviours, and even lead to 'designer babies.' Individualized drugs could be as important a change in medical practice as the introduction of anesthesia in the 19th century.

Other related developments include 'medical hacking' to unearth new insights into the human brain, aggregated databases to advance research into autism and Parkinson's disease, the creation of products to slow down the process of ageing (Human Longevity Inc.), and even bringing extinct species back to life (Revive and Restore Project).

The Beijing Genomic Institute is now the largest genomic research centre in the world, with more sequencing machines than all of the US. China is becoming the third-largest producer of science and engineering academic articles (after the EU and US).

Digital advancements in the medical field also include mobile health. For example, Medic Mobile uses a smart phone light and camera to diagnose malaria and tuberculosis in Africa; Med Africa apps help Kenyans with symptom diagnosis and doctor appointments; the Eye Netra device and app assist eye doctors with remote diagnosis; and medical analytics could be off shored to parts of the world with the requisite skill sets.

Codification of money markets and trust

Digital algorithms are redefining the way trust has been negotiated between citizens, companies and governments. Just as the internet disrupted the information, communication and commerce industries in its first 15 years, it may now disrupt banking, law and accountancy.

Platform creation is the new wealth, and this will also lead to concentration of wealth in the market leaders and their regions, Silicon Valley being a prime example. There will be legal and socio-economic repercussions in terms of wage levels and worker protection laws.

eBay first helped traders trust total strangers on a massive scale; marketplaces for services have extended this model (see my book review of *Peers, Inc*). Uber is worth more than double the value of Hertz and Avis combined, and can dominate related sectors like delivery. AirBnB is worth more than twice as much as Hyatt, allowing people to travel cheaper and longer, and now even offers castles for rent.

Square is helping small businesses and consumers transact, redefining offline local experiences, and even building new consumer profiles for potential loans based on spending pattern analysis. Approximately 25 percent of Kenya's GNP flows through the M-Pesa network, which offers payment and loan services as well as salary payments. Zain Zap promotes mobile remittance services. LinkedIn founder Reid Hoffman has also invested in Xapo, which has built a network of underground vaults storing private keys and cryptographic materials.

In terms of crypto currency, BitCoin is the leading player, based on P2P trust networks, public ledgers, and distributed blockchains with embedded history. New governance structures and firms will emerge, analogous to the rise of DNS for internet communication.

Cyber security

We seem to have moved from an era of 'Cold War' to 'Code War' with the rise of cyber-attacks on confidentiality, availability and integrity. The cost of cyber-attacks has crossed $400 billion a year, more than the GDP of 160 countries. Cyber security could be a $120 billion market by 2017.

The Shamoon-Distrack attack brought down IT services and business activity in Saudi Aramco and RasGas. A payments system attack on retailer Target cost it billions of dollars in market value. DDoS attacks have brought down independent news sites in Hong Kong and websites of Estonian banks.

North Korean sites attacked Sony Pictures' emails and data after a movie about a fictitious assassination plot against their leader. The Twitter account of Associated Press was hacked in 2013, and false news circulated. Many companies and countries have had trade secrets stolen online.

Unfortunately, cyber risks will continue to increase in frequency, scope and methods, thanks to the rise of IoT (hackers and malicious thing-bots in connected cars, wearables, grids). Barriers to entry for cybercriminals are much lower than for other types, but many companies continue to implement security as an afterthought.

Startups will be a growing source of insights and solutions for implementing cyber security. "Cyber security is going to be very similar to Silicon Valley startup and acquisition patterns," says expert Chris Bronk. This field is becoming a steady source of well-paid employment as well.

"Liberty without security is fragile, and security without liberty is oppressive," cautions Ross, pointing to the tradeoffs that people will have to negotiate. Security will be a combination of public good administered by the government and private good purchased in the marketplace.

Data: The raw material of the information age

Digital storage became more cost-effective than paper systems for the first time in the 1990s. Ninety percent of the world's digital data has been generated over the last two years alone. Increases in data gathering and computing power have turned analytics into 'both a microscope and telescope' for sense-making and forecasting. Big Data and analytics are transforming everything from supply chains and agriculture to advertising and elections.

The quality of automated translation is improving thanks to more data, more computing and better software; users can flag correct and incorrect translations in real-time. This can lead to the loss of jobs for translators, but can also accelerate globalization through better understanding of multiple languages.

Precision agriculture in the digital age can help farmers with what to do, as well as when and where, as exemplified by Monsanto's Field Scripts recommendations and Field View App. Agriculture firms will have to continue to acquire the most promising startups to stay ahead of the curve, says Ross.

Countries like India can gain much from smart farming. **"No other country has suffered more from a lack of farm modernization than India,"** says Ross. There have been 300,000 farmer suicides in the past 20 years, and 25 percent of the world's hungry live in India (190 million).

In the financial world, fintech startups are forcing large institutional banks to invest in their own technology overhauls. "Engaging with the startup and venture capital community forces us to think about innovation in a different way, more revolution than evolution," says David Reilly, tech executive at Bank of America.

Zac Townsend, founder of startup Standard Treasury, sees banks as data companies. But traditional banks have antiquated data systems, which has made them inefficient and un-innovative in storing value, moving value and pricing risk in real-time.

During the 2012 US presidential campaign, the Obama campaign sometimes tested 18 variations of a single email to see which was most effective for fundraising. Data modeling, summarization and visualization have helped Palantir manage massive and often messy data for the security and securities industries.

However, defining and defending data privacy will become a major issue. "Technology is transforming us into brilliant fools," warns critic Leon Wieseltier. Data ownership, quality and processing needs to come under intense scrutiny.

There are huge differences between the 'always off' generation of earlier times and the 'always on' generation of today and the future. A big challenge today is work-life balance, and knowing where to draw the line between public and private personas.

Globalization

In addition to the above tech trends, one chapter in the book addresses geographic dimensions of innovation. Many countries have tried to create their own versions of Silicon Valley, but without much success, especially when it comes to ambition, meritocracy, culture and labour-market characteristics.

Pockets of excellence are emerging around the world, such as cyber security in Russia and Israel, Industry 4.0 in Germany, e-society in Estonia, and hybrid development models in Singapore, China and India. "The single most successful country of the last half-century is South Korea," says Ross.

Openness of society and opportunities for women entrepreneurs are important success factors in the long run. The 'girl geek' phenomenon in Indonesia is a good example of women entrepreneurship in a society that has embraced Islam.

"China and India are both grappling with the growing need for openness in their own ways," says Ross; Brazil is also struggling to get its model right. "India is a country increasingly defined by technology, global services and a fast-growing middle class," he adds, pointing to the Aadhar initiative as a potential game-changer (see my book reviews of *China's Disruptors* and *Recasting India*).

"The progress of women in Chinese society over the course of decades is one of the major reasons it is the economic power it is today," says Ross. "Infrastructure is super-developed in China but under-developed in India," observes economist Nouriel Roubini. India also needs to commit itself to primary education for all citizens.

"Africa's entrepreneurs are now changing the face of the continent, fueling development and creating a new class of globally competitive businesses," says Ross, pointing to Grainy Bunch, iCow, Andela Fellows and Apps4Africa as examples . But on another continent, Argentina is being held back by 'control freak economics.'

Economic returns in these future industries will be unevenly distributed. Many people around the world are feeling under siege, and feel that it is harder to get ahead. "Many people will gain. Some will gain hugely. But many will also be displaced," Ross cautions.

New forms of social anxiety and fraud are arising, and new ways to cope will have to be devised by individuals, families, societies and countries – ranging from competitiveness to parenting. The global mindset, cultural curiosity, inter-disciplinary skills and multi-cultural fluency will be key requisites for success. "Ironically, in a world growing more virtual, it has never been more important to get as many ink stamps in your passport as possible," Ross jokes.

"Future growth depends on empowering people. Innovation and globalization have created opportunity the likes of which has never before existed," Ross sums up.

https://yourstory.com/2016/10/industries-of-the-future/

4.10 15 Indian Big Data Companies to Watch Out for in 2015
EMMANUEL AMBERBER, 5 FEBRUARY 2015

As the data we generate every micro-second grows and accelerates at a rapid velocity, the requirement for making a business decision is shifting from hindsight-based decision making to a foresight-based approach. Companies are banking upon Big Data and analytics. According to an industry report by NASSCOM – in partnership with BlueOcean Market Intelligence, the analytics market in India could more than double from the current $1 billion to $2.3 billion by the end of 2017-18.

In a nut shell, here are three things that Big Data can do for your business:

1. **Improve your top line through unprecedented personalization at scale.** It can do this by *helping you acquire new customers, retaining and up-selling to your existing customers and through customer support services.*

2. **Improve your bottom line through unprecedented efficiency at scale.** *The ability to timely tell how long a SKU has been out of stock matters. If suppliers can find out the SKU level they can quickly take decisions to restock.*

3. **Improve governance through unprecedented monitoring at scale.** *At US President Obama's recent visit to India, the government installed 15,000 CCTV cameras. When there is not enough man power to watch all the streams the government can use Big Data to take unstructured data of video streams and run pattern matching algorithms to identify happenings based on certain set-parameters.*

Bangalore-based Mu Sigma, started by Dhiraj Rajaram in 2004, has been the category creator in this space and is already estimated to be a billion-dollar-worth entity. And there are several more in the space from India.

Here are 15 Indian Big Data companies to watch out for:

1. Heckyl: TechSparks 2011 Winner Company in financial data analytics space. Founded by Mukund Mudras, SomSagar, Abhijit Vedak and Jaison Mathews.

2. Sigmoid Analytics: A TechSparks 2014 company, based out of Bangalore, Sigmoid is in the area of real-time Big Data warehousing, streaming and ETL (extract, transform and load) on Apache Spark. They have a technology infrastructure which companies can use to store their data in a desired format, perform operations on it and generate insights.

3. Flutura: Mines Big Data to perform analytics and gives hidden insights from huge chunks of machine generated data for global oil

and gas majors to bring in efficiency and safety. Flutura was founded by Krishnan Raman, Derick Jose and Srikanth Muralidhara.

4. Indix: Computes real-time data to give product insights for decision makers on an intuitive dashboard. Founded by Sanjay Parthasarathy, the company has its product engineering center based out of Chennai.

5. Fractal Analytics: Helps companies in predictive analytics and decision sciences to understand, predict and shape consumer behavior through advanced analytics, harmonize data, tell visual stories and forecast business performance.

6. Crayon Data: An algorithms called the White Box, Simpler Choices, takes massive data, cleans it up and presents only actionable insights to banking, hospitality and, telecom sectors. It was founded by Srikant Sastri, Suresh, Shankar and Vijay Kumar.

7. Germin8: It is a leading Data Analytics company that helps brands with social media measurement and monitoring solutions by analyzing conversations in real time. The Mumbai-based company was founded in 2007 by Raj Nair and his son Ranjit Nair.

8. Aureus Analytics: With its platform called ASAP (Aureus Statistical and Analytics Platform) it produces insights by mining enterprise data. Aureus was founded by technology professionals Anurag Shah, Ashish Tanna and Nitin Purohit.

9. **Dataswft:** A product of Bizosys Technologies Pvt. Ltd, it has a customized search engine that can decode technical information and return search queries within milliseconds. It was founded by Sunil Guttula, Abinasha Karana and Sridhar Dhulipala.

10. C360: Corporate 360 Pvt. Ltd provides IT sales intelligence data services to enterprises. The startup was founded by college dropout Varun Chandran. Prior to founding Corporate360, Varun was working as sales and marketing executive with the likes of SAP, Oracle, Dell and

NetApp. C360 is based in India and Singapore. Another similarly located Big Data company is Antuit holdings, which raised $56 million from Goldman Sachs and Zodius Capital.

11. Metaome: It is a health care Big Data company focused on life sciences, founded by Kalpana Krishnaswami and Ramkumar Nandkumar. Metaome's products DistilBio **a free version** web-based graph search and **enterprise version** platform that accrues a variety of data from difference sources (laboratory data management systems, private and public databases) and makes it structured to help in identifying a pattern.

12. Frrole: It is a Social intelligence startup with a media and brands focused offering, which allows its customers to integrate real-time Twitter data into their digital properties and TV shows. The startup was founded by Amarpreet Kalkat, Nishith Sharma and Abhishek Vaid.

13. **Bridgei2i:** It focuses on user-centric applications of Big Data. Founders are Prithvijit Roy, Ashish Sharma, Pritam Kanti Paul.

14. **Formcept:** Focused on making data analysis accessible to everyone; founders are SureshSrinivasan and Anuj Kumar.

15. PromptCloud has been founded by Prashant Kumar. Prompt Cloud is a DaaS (Data-as-a-Service) platform; it crawls the web sphere for data extraction and has been founded by Prashant Kumar.

In addition, there are more companies we have not listed that are doing impressive things in the market. DataWeave gives access to curate datasets through APIs. Guavus offers Data analytics solutions. Valiance uses data science for businesses.   Latent View and Vcubec are Big Data consultancy companies. Please share the names of your favorite Big Data and Analytics Company in the comment section.

15 Big Data trends to watch out for in 2015 (*Infographics courtesy: Aureus Analytics*)

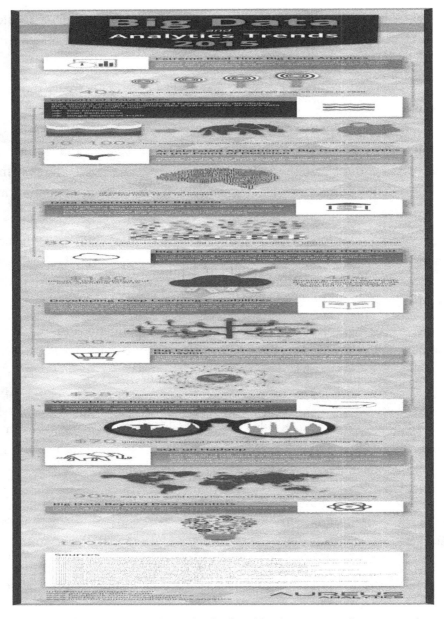

https://yourstory.com/2015/02/indian-big-data-companies-startups/

Chapter 5: Big Data Applied in Agriculture

5.1   Launch of Digital India: A programme to transform India into a digitally empowered society and knowledge economy

Submitted by <u>e-Agriculture</u> on Wed, 29/07/2015 - 17:43

<u>e-agriculture Strategy</u>

1 July saw the launch of the Digital India initiative, by the country's Prime Minister, Narendra Modi. This ambitious umbrella initiative encompasses many diverse areas of government in its goal of transforming India into a digitally empowered society and knowledge economy.

The <u>presentation which accompanied the event</u> emphasizes three key aspects of the initiative - i) Digital Infrastructure as a Utility to Every Citizen ii) Governance & Services on Demand and iii) Digital

Empowerment of Citizens. The presentation explains the nine pillars upon which Digital India is based. For those in the agricultural sector, the key pillar appears to be number 5 - Electronic Delivery of Services - which describes "Services for Farmers" such as real time price information, online ordering of inputs and online cash, loan, relief payment with mobile banking.

Indeed, reports online describe that Prime Minister Modi and his cabinet have already given the green light to development of an Online National Agriculture Market to oversee online trading and ensure smooth processing of transactions, which would possibly also include storage and transportation of farm produce following their online sale.

The move appears to be generally welcomed, yet some bloggers (such as this article published on Vibhor Sinha blogs) caution that it is ambitious and successful implementation will certainly pose a number of challenges.

http://www.e-agriculture.org/news/launch-digital-india-programme-transform-india-digitally-empowered-society-and-knowledge

5.2   Challenges in the Adoption of ICTs for Rural sector - Learning from Nano Ganesh ICT in India

Submitted by Santosh Ostwal ... on Thu, 24/11/2016 - 20:02

e-agriculture Strategy

This blog intends to throw light on the concerns and the challenges faced by the ICT manufacturers or service providers as well as the ICT users.

Technology, along with an appropriate business model, plays a vital role in empowering the rural population. Especially in case of ICTs for the rural sector, there are frequent new arrivals, trends, innovations and products but many of them lack the last mile execution-operation-maintenance model. The rate of innovative ICT evolution is too high as compared to the rate of field adoption due to so many imposed challenges.

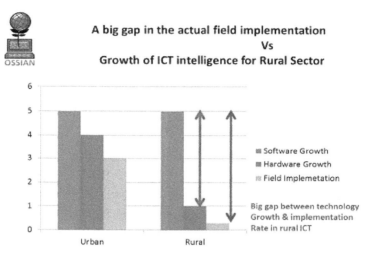

Y axis numbers are units just for understanding the comparison

Challenges for the ICT manufacturers or service providers

They face difficulties in accessing the rural population for marketing, promotion, demonstration, installation and post-sales support. They struggle a lot for building the trust about their technology consuming heavy expenses and precious time in the advocacy and promotion. This overall process is set such that the buying inertia of a customer is very high taking more time to convert into revenue. By the time a customer is ready to buy a technology after a pilot project, there is something new extra featured product or trend arrived in the market and hence impacting the business building. Due to many such reasons (not listed here), many ICT projects cannot scale-up successfully beyond the pilot project level.

Of course, there are few successful global stories in rural ICT domain that have mitigated these challenges by adopting hybrid value chain based business models along with use of ICTs for educating the farmers.

Challenges for the ICT beneficiary (rural customer)

In rural area, no customer buys the new product immediately till the trust is built. But, an encouraging fact is that there are few progressive drivers in the villages who dare to adopt new technologies at their own risk and expenses. They take initiative, visit the urban based ICT companies, dealers and try to understand the benefits of the technology. They start using it and then villagers follow them after few months. The mindset of the rural customer turns slowly towards adoption, provided their key concerns are addressed by the ICT providers. They expect the product or services to have a reasonable cost and to be available locally with assured performance for at least three to five years. Once initiated, they should be trained and in any case, should not feel like cheated and fooled. So, advocacy programs arranged by the ICT manufacturers in partnerships with NGOs or government organizations help a lot in trust building process to save the time of adoption.

Optimistic scenario for ICTs in general in Indian rural sector

By understanding the strategic importance of use of ICTs, every country should be optimistic in empowering the rural and agriculture sector with the possible tools. E.g. in India, Goa State has provided 50% subsidy for buying agro smart tools, the Karnataka State has started m-governance program, Smart Control panels (ICT based) and pumps are going to be distributed free of cost to 150K farmers in Andhra Pradesh by The Indian Government. Many NGOs and CSR projects are supporting ICT promotion in different states. Local manufacturers and service providers in ICT technologies are taking genuine interest in the rural business with innovative models.

The above points of discussions are outcome of 25 years of dedicated work in E- Irrigation by a couple from India, <u>Mr. Santosh & Mrs. Rajashree Ostwal</u>. They innovatively used mobile phone in 2004 as a low cost wireless module near the distantly located water pump for remote control and monitoring of irrigation activities. Later in 2011, a mobile phone was replaced by a GSM module. Their brand, <u>Nano Ganesh</u> and their entrepreneurial story (Ossian Agro Automation Pvt. Ltd.) has been a subject of discussions in many forums and conferences across the globe with different awards. There *are few inspiring <u>videos</u> on Nano Ganesh which will be a real evidence of sustainable success of ICT in rural sector.*

<u>http://www.e-agriculture.org/blog/challenges-adoption-icts-rural-sector-learning-nano-ganesh-ict-india</u>

5.3 Digital-Agriculture

Agriculture of the future will be digitally integrated at all stages of production, from understanding genetics to transport logistics. We are using our expertise in digital innovation and agriculture to improve decision making for farmers, agribusiness, policy-makers and researchers.

The challenge

Transforming agriculture for the future

The world is becoming ever more connected through digital technology. Smart devices are getting smaller, faster and cheaper. Medical and defense industries have been taking advantage of this digital innovation to address challenges in their sector. Similarly, smart digital services have the potential to help the agricultural industry meet its productivity and sustainability challenges.

While computing and sensor technologies have been used on Australian farms for the last two decades, adoption has been uneven and the full potential unrealized.

The curse of 'too much information' has proved challenging especially in the genomics space where we can sequence entire genomes in a matter of days but have years of analysis ahead to fully comprehend the data generated. This also means the latent value of the data is unrealized.

Risk and uncertainty is unfortunately increasing. Climate change, energy costs, availability of skilled labour and market volatility all add up, constraining decision-making for farmers and policy-makers alike.

With the internet comes increased access to information. Information technology enables consumers to selectively access, share and validate products along the entire supply chain, increasing demands on sustainability, compliance, traceability and product differentiation.

Most sectors of agriculture are interested in these technologies because of the benefits they can potentially provide in an increasingly complex and volatile decision-making environment, and where developments in automation can overcome constraints of labour scarcity and expense.

Digital agriculture has the potential to radically redefine the role of farmers and the management of large parts of the agricultural landscape.

Our response

Smart solutions for modern farming problems

'Digital agriculture' includes activities such as the development, testing and deployment of information and communication technologies (including informatics) for agricultural research, development and delivery.

As the national science agency, and Australia's largest agricultural research organization, we are combining our expertise in data and digital technologies with our agricultural knowledge and experience. Our digital agriculture research combines the disciplines of phenomics, software engineering, data analytics, precision agriculture, and farm systems management. Our focus is on research and development that has general applicability across industries and domains.

For example, we are adapting and applying sensor systems that can cheaply and accurately monitor the state of plants, animals and soils. The data generated from such a system would assist a farmer to precisely manage their inputs in order to maximize production in the most cost effective and sustainable way.

It is also important that we develop information systems which can ingest process, summarize and analyze data streams generated by multiple sensor systems and other data sources - for example, integrated systems to forecast crop yield at paddock, farm, district and national scales.

We are also working on novel modes of delivering data, information and knowledge to decision makers, including in real time and in situ. For example, we are adapting our computer decision support models that are used by hundreds of farmers and advisors across Australia so that they can be used on mobile devices in the field and with updates from sensor information on the spot.

https://www.csiro.au/en/Research/AF/Areas/Digital-agriculture

5.4 How Will Digital India Impact on Agriculture in India?

Posted on July 10, 2015 by Vibhor

The new initiative of Government of India is Digital India has recently launched by PM Narendra Modi. It aims at ensuring the government services are made available to citizens without any or through less paperwork.

The one thing which is the most useful for Rural India is the setting up of an **Online National Agriculture Trading** market to help farmers of India and increase the agriculture.

By 2019, the two-way platform will be created between Farmers and Buyers. This will be done through the broadband connectivity across the rural India.

Let us look at some of the important points which will impact Farmers in big way through this initiative.

- Farmers now have many available options to sell their produce.

- They will have the options to sell and buy fruits and vegetables and other produce across India through online platform.

- Currently Farmers have to sell their produce too few mandis and market committees and they charge high amount of tax from them.

- Farmers can sell their produce to mandis or to online platform.

- The direct link between seller and buyer will erase out the mediators which will increase the profit margin of farmers and it will also benefit the end product customer also.

- This online trade will be free of cost so it's a service with no cost again it will boost producer's income.

- An agency would be setup to monitor the smooth functioning in online trading; it will also look after the transportation facilities after the online purchase/sell.

According to me it's a good initiative but GOI has to face some challenges to make this plan successful. A proper training program, uninterrupted services, electricity, availability of smart phones, tablets and computers to almost every farmer can be big challenge.

https://vibhorsinhablogs.wordpress.com/2015/07/10/how-will-digital-india-impact-on-agriculture-in-india/

5.5   Farming goes digital: the 3rd Green Revolution

Farming goes digital: the 3rd Green Revolution

The growing capacity of smart machines to turn data into useful, timely knowledge is becoming a key driver of sustainable productivity growth in agriculture

Farming is often seen as very traditional, particularly in today's highly urbanized societies. In fact, farmers have always embraced change and today are using increasingly advanced technologies. A greater understanding of genetics has improved the seed breeding process and precision farming – using satellite sensors to tailor treatments for small areas of fields – has improved productivity while reducing the use of fertilizer and pesticides. Now comes the next stage. It may surprise some people, but farming is entering the digital age.

The constant quest for farmers is for larger and more predictable harvests from the same fields, while minimizing the use of expensive fertilizers and chemicals and spending as little time as possible in the field. This means an increasing reliance on sophisticated farm machinery which allows farmland to be ploughed, seeded, weeded, tended and harvested very efficiently.

The advent of GPS satellites allowed tractors and harvesters to be guided accurately, and other satellite-based sensors let farmers map soil moisture content or their crop's development in detail. Farmers have always understood their land and how to manage it, but systems like this have helped them get the best from each field down to the individual square meter.

But that's not the end of the story. As computing power has blossomed – we now all have smart phones with the power of a supercomputer of a few decades ago – so has the capacity to gather and analyze data. This has ushered in the era of Big Data, where novel ways have been found to make use of the vast amount of information available.

Smart machines – turning data into knowledge: Data has little value until it can be turned into knowledge, but the more data you have, the more knowledge you can create and apply. Just as Google cracked the problem of trawling through billions of Internet pages to find the ones we want to read, so agricultural suppliers and machinery manufacturers can do the same with data on weather and soil conditions.

Machinery suppliers now have their own IT whizz kids who have developed ways for data on weather, soil, seed and fertilizer to be used to manage farms much more efficiently at the touch of a screen.

At one time, a farmer had no choice but to walk his fields and hope to pick up pest or disease problems in time to limit the damage done. Entire fields were sprayed, sometimes just as a precaution, which was wasteful and costly. Today, a farmer can send up a drone to survey his crops and pick up problems in small areas, which can be nipped in the bud before they spread.

Sensors can also be mounted on tractors or other farm machinery and, combined with a database of weather patterns, can be used to help farmers plant the right seed at the right time to ensure a high yield. Other sensors can manage the machinery itself to make sure it operates efficiently, to communicate with other pieces of kit or even to order spare parts. Livestock farmers can benefit from the Big Data revolution as well. Already, automatic milking is becoming normal. Now, farmers can use sensors which tell them directly when their cows are ready for artificial insemination and when they are about to give birth.

The ability not just to collect vast amounts of data but now to analyze it to provide useful, timely knowledge provides another key tool for today's farmer. If agriculture cannot feed the growing population – especially a more prosperous one which consumes more meat – then there is no sustainable future for society. Farmers need all the help they can get to get the best from their land, season after season.

A digital revolution in the making: In the 1960s and '70s, the first green revolution used clever plant breeding to vastly increase the yield of rice and wheat at a time when the world struggled to feed a population half the size of todays. The second revolution is still in progress. This is the application of our rapidly-expanding knowledge of plant and animal genetics and ability to tweak genes to improve important traits.

And now, with hardly any public recognition as yet, comes the third of these green revolutions, the digital one, which allows farmers to make the most of the potential offered by plant and animal breeders. The key is the ability to get the best out of each square meter of soil, even each individual plant, rather than simply get a reasonable average across a whole field.

This digital revolution may just have started in Europe and the USA but, as costs continue to fall, we can foresee developing countries embracing the same changes before too long. With such a large yield gap to bridge, the third green revolution may be just what the third world needs to guarantee food security.

About CEMA

As the voice of the agricultural machinery industry, CEMA represents the 4,500 manufacturers of agricultural equipment in Europe which includes large multinational companies as well as numerous small and medium-sized enterprises (SMEs).

Newsletter issue: Edition May 2015

http://www.cema-agri.org/newsletterarticle/farming-goes-digital-3rd-green-revolution

5.6 Digital Agriculture Empowers Farmers

David Bergvinson Delhi   Print Edition: January 15, 2017

Prime Minister Narendra Modi launched Digital India on July 1, 2015 to create digital infrastructure for empowering rural communities, enabling digital delivery of services and promoting digital literacy. Given that 68 per cent of India's population is rural and agriculture is the main source of livelihood for 58 per cent of the population, one must consider the role of Digital Agriculture within Digital India. Digital Agriculture can be defined as ICT and data ecosystems to support the development and delivery of timely, targeted (localized) information and services to make farming profitable and sustainable (socially, economically and environmentally) while delivering safe, nutritious and affordable food for ALL. Rural connectivity will be key to providing low cost data and access to information. It would empower rural youth to realize their full potential, farmers to increase their profitability by accessing equitable markets and rural businesses to offer value added services.

Bittersweet Sugar

David Bergvinson, Director General, International Crops Research Institute for the Semi-Arid Tropics believes technology will be key to increasing agriculture productivity by delivering tailored recommendations to farmers based on crop, planting date, variety sown, and real-time, localized observed weather and projected market prices.

The key components to support the implementation of Digital Agriculture is Spatial (and Temporal) Data Infrastructure (SDI) and low-cost smart phones and tablets to support the bi-directional flow of data and information to rural consumers. SDI has been the key driver to support modern farming in the US, Australia and Europe as well as emerging economies of China and Brazil. Agriculture is a data-intense enterprise when one considers soil variability, moisture and nutrient levels, rainfall variability, and timing of key operations like planting and harvesting, and market price volatility. Advanced agriculture industries help farmers manage these production and market risks through the application of spatial/temporal data bases that are cloud enabled and integrated through Application Programming Interfaces (APIs). This creates a rich and dynamic data ecosystem that enables advanced analytics to inform farmers of the best economic options to maximize profitability and minimize risk - the two critical variables farmers in India would also like to manage.

Smart phones are the other key intervention as they are equipped with GPS to track where photos of field infestations or hail damage have taken place for technical support or insurance claims. Mobile phones also enable farmers to integrate into structured markets based on approved grades and standards that can be verified using calibrated photos and settlements made through mobile money. While India has over 960 million mobile phones, only 17 per cent of the population has a smart phone but this is changing quickly with over 204 million smart phone users projected for 2016. This percentage is much lower for rural consumers but this too is changing as the price point for smart phones manufactured in India is dropping as are phablets (phones and tablets that support rural education and extension).

Digital technology will be key to increasing agriculture productivity by delivering tailored recommendations to farmers based on crop, planting date, variety sown; real time localized observed weather and projected market prices. These recommendations will be based on advanced big data analytics related to down-scaled daily observed weather that is now 9 km x 9 km but will soon be under 1 km x 1 km and effectively field level that feed into crop growth models to estimate yields, harvest date and potential pest and disease outbreaks to optimize pest control measures. Remote sensing is another big data resource to support the development of derived weather products (radar), improved hydrology and watershed management, soil health, crop coverage and crop health estimates among other application. This is now complimented by Unmanned Aerial Vehicles (UAVs) that can capture multispectral images to assess crop health, damage and yield far more accurately than satellites.

The greatest impact Digital Agriculture will have is on democratization of market pricing and compressing transaction costs so that farmers capture a higher portion of the produce's marketable value. Agricultural value chains are complex with several actors along the chain but information asymmetry between the farmer and aggregator or intermediaries results in farmers having to sell into saturated, weak markets that are not based on standards. Powerful business models have emerged from Africa, Brazil and China that use big data and mobile phones to increase value chain efficiency for upstream access to appropriate inputs and credit. It also helps in targeted recommendations for improving productivity through market integration based on agreed grades, standards and prices. It is not uncommon for farm incomes to double in the case of grain crops and to quadruple in the case of perishable produce. India is well positioned to realize the same opportunities for its farmers by providing the basic spatial data infrastructure to enable coordination along the value chain.

With the Direct Benefit Transfers system and the unique identification number, Aadhaar, to support transfer of government subsidies to citizens, India is uniquely positioned to leverage these platforms to support the earlier interventions around soil health, Prime Minister Krishi Sinchayee Yojana, national markets and weather indexed insurance. When combined with spatial/temporal data infrastructure, subsidies can be validated (for example, application of fertilizer on a specific field under a targeted fertilizer subsidy programme) and targeted (e.g. digital soil map and crop to be cultivated and rainfall anticipated) to increase farm profitability and manage production and market risks that in turn give farmers confidence to invest in their farms to further increase productivity.

Digital Agriculture will also leverage social media platforms to build human capacity. One of the best examples originating from India is Digital Green. It uses participatory videos that have farmers explain best management practices to other farmers. This approach is ten times more cost effective than traditional extension services as farmers trust other farmers more given they can better relate to someone like them who are building a livelihood under similar circumstances.

Mobile money is the last key intervention that has unlocked tremendous opportunities for rural consumers in Africa and will do the same for India. Paper money is expensive and risky to rural consumers but mobile money is safer, especially for women, and costs less to transfer. Mobile money also allows rural consumers to bypass poor infrastructure to support savings and access credit.

While Digital Agriculture is most advanced in the US, the concepts are scale neutral and are being successfully applied to smallholder farmers around the globe. We need to move with a sense of urgency to apply these new tools to accelerate the pace of agriculture development to not only realize the vision of the Prime Minister of a Digital India but to facilitate the achievement of Sustainable Development Goals before 2030. Digital agriculture will also help achieve the objectives of the National Food Security Act in the most efficient, effective and equitable manner to ensure ALL have access to safe, nutritious and affordable food. ~

This is an extract of the strategy paper on Digital Agriculture submitted to the Indian Prime Minister's Office upon request.

http://www.businesstoday.in/magazine/features/digital-agriculture-empowers-farmers/story/242966.html

5.7 Agrow Book– Empowering the Agriculture Industry as a Whole

Agriculture plays a vital role in India's economy. Along with fisheries and forestry, agriculture is one of the largest contributors to the Gross Domestic Product (GDP). However, if we take a closer look at the overall contribution from agriculture to the economy, it portrays a different picture. In 2010, agriculture contributed to 19% of the total GDP, while employing over 51% of the population.

Aware of this huge gap in profitability, Hyderabad-based agtech startup, Agrowbook has been working towards driving positive transformation within the sector. Speaking of the impetus for starting up, CEO, Subhash Lode, said that it wasn't just a single turning point but a lifetime of difficulties experienced that moved him to seek solutions. And the field of technology seemed to the obvious place to look, as Subhash said, "We have observed almost every industry vertical is benefitted with Information technology interventions and we believe it's time for the agriculture vertical to embrace it too to improve on processes, as well as optimize and improve the farmer's balance sheet."

The strategy

The objective, quite plainly, was to improve profitability within the farming community by improving spend on the entire farm culture. It will include farm inputs, logistics, farm mechanizations, automation, improving the processes at various stages. Hyderabad-based startup, Agrowbook, is both an online forum and offline service for knowledge sharing, interaction and a competitive marketplace for farm produce. Subhash said that on the field, the startup works with farmers guiding them to make the right choices with farm inputs, improving logistics costs, transportation decisions, and procuring farm machines. "We also have the Agrowbook portal which caters to the information need of the farming community," he added.

The online portal provides information to more than 82,000 visitors, with more than 1800 registered users. Additionally, Agrowbook has more than 23,000 videos on agriculture and rural development which is accessed by 400 to 500 visitors globally, daily. "Close to 77% visitors are from India, 8.5% from USA and rest from other agrarian countries."

said Subhash. The offline station at Pedanallaballi, simultaneously, has catered more than 400 farmers on various farming needs including seeds, fertilizers, pesticides, and protection from wild animals and pests.

Upcoming projects

Agrowbook is also launching the Farmer Balance Sheet App – an easy way to help farmers maintain accounts that give them insights into the spend, and make informed decisions to drive profits. "We've found from our ground work that farmers don't always have strict management of their accounts. They keep a log of their expenses, but they may not account for the smaller expenses such as valuation for their efforts into cultivation. With the app, farmers can record transaction information, bills, other expenses, add notes concerning all kinds monetary exchange." said Subhash, adding, "With this information in hand, farmers can identify their profit and loss sources, to take better decisions and optimize their cultivation."

But Agrowbook does not provide solutions pertaining to farming methods only. On the contrary, it aims to enable a holistic development of the industry, as Subhash points out, "Our station is also equipped to cater Telemedicine services. Our free Wi-Fi at Rural stations enables the rural youth to access knowledge on internet, thus improving the digital literacy among rural population."

The telemedicine service accomplishes two objectives – one, is the resolution of preliminary health issues, thus controlling expenditure of time, money and physical exertion. The other, given the minimal human resources in healthcare available in rural areas, training locals in basic first aid and care can increase the network of care givers, amp up employment while ensuring proper treatment.

The way forward

Having witnessed the farming community's problems from such proximity, Subhash reiterates the importance of government support to farmers, while acknowledging that new age farmers expect more. Fortunately, Subhash says that governments are proactively identifying the hurdles and supporting technological disruptions in Agtech through incubators.

Agrowbook, additionally, intends to further this support by establishing 50 rural Agri-stations in Telangana, AP and Maharashtra by the end of 2017 while simultaneously exploring other agrarian belts in the world over. Agrowbook is partnering with Autodesk, the National Institute of Rural Development (NIRD) and Panchayati Raj to improve and push for more solutions.

Subhash believes the Agtech startups can change the scenarios on multiple fronts with the use of IoT and data management, creating low cost and value for money solutions for large number of farming families across India. With that in mind, Agrowbook is also planning to host an Open Design Centre, where selected agriculture and rural-based innovations can be designed, with easy access to funding and quick commercialization.

"Finding talent and pushing innovation in India are not the issue," said Subhash, "it is with capital access, which is big constraint." And Agrowbook is working towards eliminating that hurdle, for the farming community as well as the innovator, to enable complete development, of the industry and its tertiaries.

Great news for start-ups in Telangana!

Techstartup.in for Hyderabad is an initiative by National Association of Software and Services Companies (NASSCOM) in partnership with IBM and the Government of Telangana. This is a digital platform for start-ups in the tech ecosystem of Telangana and Andhra Pradesh. With the aim of stimulating local innovation, we want to include start-ups at all stages as part of our listing. You're running a start-up with a disruptive idea? You're started to make a business and social impact? Great, our editorial team will get in touch to feature you in a story. So, make sure you register now!

http://hyderabad.techstartup.in/feature/agrowbook-empowering-the-agriculture-industry-as-a-whole/

5.8 The Rise of Digital Farming
Willie Vogt 1 | Sep 08, 2016

It's not often you travel to Europe for two media events back to back, but that's what's happening this week with BASF and Bayer holding major global programs in Germany. And while the two competitors are definitely engaging the market in their own way, one common phrase has come from both events – digital farming.

For BASF, the answer is Maglis, which is an evolving package of programs that are designed to connect farmer, dealer and BASF specialist in ways to enhance crop yields and returns. Earlier this year we shared the global introduction of Maglis from Commodity Classic. This program has several modules under development with the first – a customer navigation tool – available in the U.S.

There are more modules at work – first introduced in Canada – that will be moving to the U.S. by season 2017, including a sustainability assessment tool that will help you "read" your farm in new ways. And there's a crop

Plan module as well, designed to bring together weather information, pest warnings and other tools in a data dashboard. BASF has been working on relationships with machinery companies so information you gather with equipment can be easily passed to this system (they have an agreement with John Deere, for example).

Over at Bayer, the work on digital farming continues, and already the company has initiated a range of partnerships to build a system that takes satellite images and helps farmers determine in-season issues that need to be addressed. In addition, the company is formulating ways for farmers and dealers to work together.

The Bayer system, which has yet to be publicly named, is under continued development. However, there's one message that came out of the media event that caught my attention. Bayer is looking at a future where you may not buy "crop protection products" but instead you would buy "clean fields."

That's a fascinating concept of buying an outcome rather than an input. With continued refinement of on-farm data collection, and use, these are the kinds of ways companies can work with farmers for enhanced results. The scenario painted during a review of the Bayer system would be that the dealer would build a program, including a custom application schedule, which would then be put in place. And if you spray your own fields, the Bayer program would send prescriptions, and you would share machine data back to the system as part of the program.

The price of the program would be based on a clean field result, and perhaps even a yield guarantee – these are all just early ideas in a program that shows the promise of digital farming. How that plays out remains to be seen, but it's a fascinating concept.

Call it digital farming, internet of things, big data, you name it we're entering a different age where technology will be put to work in some fascinating ways. We'll continue to explore those issues in upcoming blogs as these digital farming tools become available in the United States.

http://www.farmindustrynews.com/blog/rise-digital-farming

5.9   Big Data for the Next Green Revolution
BEDANGA BORDOLOI

A new call: Of technology-powered agriculture - Photo: M Srinath

From precision agriculture to real-time price updates, advanced data analytics can help farmers usher in a new era in farming

It is clear that the projected population growth and urbanization rates will have dramatic impacts on food security across the world by 2050. The impacts are multi-sectoral and extend well beyond food into infrastructure, healthcare, and technology.

However, technology has the potential to re-shape these trends for the benefit of society. Technology is disrupting all areas of agricultural value chain, driving countless opportunities and challenges particularly around profitably feeding the 9.6 billion people on Earth by 2050.

At the same time, the growing demand for food and shifting food security needs are driving innovation in the resource space. World is now more inter-connected, spawning massive data and exploration of these data can help to drive decision making that can transform the farm source-to-consumer value chain. Agri-businesses are subject to numerous regulations and consumer requirements across their supply chain. Of the several touch points along the agri-value chain, each holds critical information that can help businesses make the most of their resources, provide greater transparency in their processes and protect consumers.

Big Data has the potential to add value across each touch points starting from selection of right agri-inputs, monitoring the soil moisture, tracking prices of markets, controlling irrigations, finding the right selling point and getting the right price.

What data can do

Big-data businesses can analyze varieties of seeds across numerous fields, soil types, and climates. Similar to the way in which Google can identify flu outbreaks based on where web searches are originating, analyzing crops across farms helps identify diseases that could ruin a potential harvest. The challenges and opportunities of data is immense in a country like India with 638,000 villages and 130 million farmers speaking around 800 languages with 140 million hectares of cultivable land under 127 agro climatic regions capable of supporting 3,000 different crops and one million varieties.

Self-driven vehicles can already drive themselves across fields using Global Positioning System (GPS) signals accurate to less than inch of error thus helping farmers plant more accurately, but the real potential is what happens when this data from thousands of tractors on thousands of farms is collected, grouped and analyzed in real time.

Precision agriculture aids farmers in tailored and effective water management, helping in production, improving economic efficiency and minimizing waste and environmental impact. Recent progress in Big Data and advanced analytics capabilities and agri-robotics such as aerial imagery, sensors, and sophisticated local weather forecasts can truly transform the agri-scape and thus holds promise for increasing global agricultural productivity over the next few decades.

Right information

Farmers need accurate weather forecasts and accurate information on the inputs they can use. Optimizing input factors (e.g., nutrients, irrigation, and pest control) can help protect natural resources. The use of granular data (for example, data for every 100-meter square of a field) and analytical capability to integrate various sources of information (such as weather, soil, and market prices) will help in increasing crop yield and optimizing resource usage, lowering cost. Since, climate change and extreme weather events will demand proactive measures to adapt or develop resiliency, Big Data can bring in the right information to take informed decisions.

Big Data and advanced analytics are streamlining food processing value chains by finding the core determinants of process performance, and taking action to continually improve the accuracy, quality and yield of production. Big Data is already being used for optimizing production schedules based on supplier, customer, machine availability and cost constraints.

It can provide agri-business with greater visibility into supplier quality levels, and greater accuracy in predicting supplier performance over time. In India, every year 21 million tons of wheat is lost, primarily due to scare cold-storage centers and refrigerated vehicles, poor transportation facilities and unreliable electricity supply. Big Data has the potential of systematization of demand forecasting thus reducing such losses.

Connecting the dots

A trading platform for agricultural commodities that links small-scale producers to retailers and bulk purchasers via mobile phone messaging can help send up-to-date market prices via an app or SMS and connect farmers with buyers, offering collective bargaining opportunities for small and marginal farmers.

India should look at establishing a systematic mechanism to capture the data that could offer additional value-creating opportunities. In particular, rapid proliferation of mobile technologies in rural populations could let farmers in these areas to improve productivity based on decision made backed by better information grounded on Big Data. It also has the potential to change the agri-business models including revenue models, as businesses will have the opportunity to offer new products and services thus developing sustainable revenue streams.

Proliferation of data offers unprecedented opportunities to understand consumer needs and preferences of farmers, and to deliver tailored services and products for organizations that can make sense of this data.

Given all this, today is right time for agri-businesses to lead on defining what better practices on data use are available. There is need to formulate a business model wherein value can be captured from the scale of data being captured by different players in the agri-supply chain. Companies must act now to focus, simplify and standardize big data through an enterprise-wide data management strategy as Big Data poise to deliver the next revolution of farming.

The writer is Kuwait market leader for EY's Climate Change and Sustainability Services practice. The views are personal

(This article was published on January 13, 2017)

http://www.thehindubusinessline.com/opinion/big-data-can-transform-agriculture-in-india/article9479255.ece

5.10 Precision Agriculture in the Digital Era

The internet is playing a key role in the transformation of industries. What new opportunities is the agriculture industry facing within the digital era?

Today, more than 7 billion people are living on this planet. By 2050, the total number is estimated to reach 9.6 billion as people will be living longer as well. As economic development brings more wealth, people want and demand better-quality food. Such factors require higher efficiency in agricultural production, produce yields and quality.

In China, agricultural production has satisfied people's basic needs to survive. High-quality agricultural products, however, are in short supply, despite infrastructure and farmers' knowledge expected to grow.

The internet is playing a key role in the transformation of industries. In Internet + Agriculture, mobile internet is becoming more and more important. In rural areas, smart phones are much easier to use than computers. So, this is how to use digital technologies to boost the development of planting capacity and infrastructure construction. How can the agricultural development of China be speeded up? How can the quality of products and benefits for farmers be improved? Such questions have been put on the table of many internet giants and plant protection companies.

In March 2016, BASF launched its innovative "BASF Leading Grower" App to better serve farmers in China – helping them to improve their growing skills and productivity and starting a new precision agriculture model for the digital age.

Boost for China's agricultural transformation

"BASF will continue to offer services in every part of the value chain of agricultural products. Our commitment to helping farmers improve the quality of farming, produce and competitiveness will never change. We will strive to help farmers maximize their profits."

Jiang Weiqi, Manager, Marketing, Fungicide and Specialty Crop, Crop Protection, BASF

Agricultural production in China is still, generally, in a primary stage, with a number of problems to be solved.

Wheat and corn production areas in the north of the country have large land holdings, but farmers in the south are mostly individuals who manage their own small fields and buy agricultural supplies from retail stores. Take crop farming and protection for example. As retail stores are driven by profit, seldom do they offer to-the-point guidance to farmers whose demand volume is relatively low when they buy products for their crops. Faced with a great number of crop protection products, in addition to farming technical services that vary in quality, farmers need a way to choose products and services that are right for them.

Farmers with smaller-sized fields usually focus on short-term profit, so they often irrationally choose crops to grow based on the market trend of the year. They may easily plant the same crops or blindly change them. The consequence will be that they harvest but they don't profit. Farmers need to have their target crops well planned for longer term, as well as know more about the marketing channels of agro-products to really get both high yields and profits.

Technologies in agriculture, meanwhile, have been left behind for a long time and there are no efficient channels for communication and marketing. Agricultural profits, therefore, are so far below expectations that farmers leave their fields to work in cities. It is said that those born in the 1970s are reluctant to farm; those born in the 1980s refuse to farm; while those born in the 1990s don't even mention farming now.

In recent years, national policies have been issued one after another to encourage and support land transfer, home-based farms and large-scale growing. The number of large-scale farmers is increasing rapidly. Many far-sighted entrepreneurs born in the 1980s have also sensed the great opportunities in agriculture and have devoted themselves to it. Crop growing is no longer gloomy as more and more farmers are engaged in it.

According to Jiang Weiqi, Manager, Marketing, Fungicide and Specialty Crop, Crop Protection, BASF, these farmers are 35 to 45 in age, well-educated and with the best know-how in crop farming across the country. They are not just beneficiaries of land policies but also executors and leaders of modern agriculture in China. As the "cool" generation in agriculture, they are open-minded and willing to try more channels and platforms to learn new crop-farming technologies and products, and to conduct scientific planning in farming so as to improve productivity, quality and profit.

As smart phones have become necessities in people's lives, the BASF Leading Grower App will be able to provide and deliver in-time, comprehensive and precise agricultural and technological services to meet the needs of large-scale farmers. They will be able to manage planting more efficiently. Through their phones, farmers will receive weather reports, learn about agricultural technologies and pest control and be able to consult with BASF experts through long-distance guidance about agricultural problems.

"It is a systematic job to help farmers improve quality and profits," said Jiang. "BASF will continue to offer services in every part of the value chain of agricultural products. Our commitment to helping farmers improve the quality of farming, produce and competitiveness will never change. We will strive to help farmers maximize their profits."

Good tool for farmers

Pest control is the most common and stable operation in daily farming, independent from the changing climates each year. Fungicides, therefore, are most relevant to the quality of produce among all crop protection technologies as they strengthen a crop's resistance and immunity to changes in the environment.

As a leading supplier of fungicides, BASF has helped Chinese farmers by launching two or more high-performance and innovative fungicides in each of the past three years. Take grapes from Jiaxing, Zhejiang, for example. Grape farmers who use the BASF farming protection solution have reduced pesticide use by 50% in terms of dosage and frequency, saving on manpower costs but harvesting more and better fruits. These grapes are healthier in their looks and of better quality, so they sell for higher prices. In general, farmers who choose to use BASF's management solution for their grapes have a high return on invested capital, earning 27 times the outlay.

In the past, BASF promoted its products and usage tips through face-to-face meetings with farmers. The farmers attending such meetings numbered just a few dozen, while BASF's investment in manpower and capital is quite a lot. Most farmers didn't have access to such information, know the benefits, or communicate their problems in using the products.

Now, the BASF Leading Grower App not only promotes products and services more efficiently but also gathers information that farmers are most concerned about. They can get to know micro climates in their own fields, crops' growing stages, the pest control in each of them and practical cases for reference. Farmers can also learn about the latest crop farming technologies and solutions, make decisions and adjust operations according to weather conditions and growing cycles.

For example, a farmer in Huizhou, Guangdong, can select his village and crops via the BASF Leading Grower App, set the technology to monitor the weather in his fields and different stages (seedling, flowering and growing) in growing and pest control. The App can also serve as an automatic reminder. The farmer may be the only farming expert in the family but when he is thousands of miles away from home, he can still arrange for his family to use plant protection products and take care of the crops.

"The BASF Leading Grower App is easy to use, like a teacher and friend to farmers by their side," said Jiang. "Through smart phones, farmers can obtain crop protection solutions and products from us 24/7 in different locations. They are farming in scientific ways and can manage their business anytime, anywhere."

Big data in future agriculture

By collecting, integrating and evaluating the backstage data of the Leading Grower App, BASF is able to strengthen its farmer-relationship management. According to Jiang, when farm information is accumulated to a certain scale, big data will come into play. In future, information about farmers, field locations and yields retrieved from this App will help BASF provide services to directly connect farmers with sales terminals and lower the risks caused by incorrect marketing information that would hurt farmers' benefits. It will be another service BASF intends to provide to Chinese farmers.

In Hainan Island where mangoes grow, as farmers do not have relevant marketing information prices for the fruit are manipulated by resellers. Farmers sell their mangoes at one to two yuan per kilogram. After being transported by resellers and logistics carriers, such mangoes will be sold at 10-20 yuan per kilogram in tier-one cities such as Shanghai. In future, once farmers are able to deal directly with end users on the same platform, all information about supply and demand will be public and both farmers and consumers can benefit from such transactions.

As the BASF, Leading Grower App is further promoted and used, hundreds of thousands of farmers will contribute to the database that will provide detailed information on produce such as variety, place of origin, when they are planted and harvested. If farmers could directly connect with fruit stores and supermarkets, brand new marketing channels would be established. Farmers who used to grow the same crops en masse can, in future, avoid such scenarios by knowing market trends, making smart planning in scientific ways and selecting the right crops to plant.

In addition, other records of farming, pesticides and residues will be also saved in the BASF Leading Grower App database. "This valuable data is not only strong proof of the product's high quality but also basic support to track agricultural production in future. In this way, food safety can be guaranteed. We are looking forward to all of these prospects," said Jiang. "We have just started and it takes time to promote the BASF Leading Grower App. But BASF is already in the leading position of our industry."

Scan the QR code to download and log on to the "BASF Leading Grower" App. Invitation code: 888888.

https://www.basf.com/cn/en/company/new s-and-media/BASF-Information/Food-nutrition/Precision-agriculture-in-the-digital-era.html

5.11 How Big Data will revolutionize the Global Food Chain

By Clarisse Magnin

How big data will revolutionize the global food chain.

Advanced analytics opens vast untapped potential for farmers, investors, and emerging economies to reduce the cost of goods sold.

The way digital technologies are reshaping the relationship between consumers and brands has been hotly debated over the past few years, with much discussion of the reshaping of consumer decision journeys, the advent of multichannel marketing and sales, and the impact of smart phones and the mobile Internet on customer behavior. Yet an even bigger opportunity has been largely overlooked. By taking advantage of big data and advanced analytics at every link in the value chain from field to fork, food companies can harness digital's enormous potential for sustainable value creation. Digital can help them use resources in a more environmentally responsible manner, improve their sourcing decisions, and implement circular-economy solutions in the food chain.

Huge untapped potential

So far, most of the excitement about digital's potential in the consumer-packaged-goods industry has centered on marketing and sales. But for food producers, the opportunities begin higher upstream and end lower downstream. At the upstream end, the agricultural practices followed by dairy farmers, cacao and coffee producers, wheat and barley producers, cattle farmers, and so on result in enormous variations in commodity costs in an industry where raw materials represent easily 60 percent of the cost of goods sold (COGS).

Manufacturing and packaging also represent a substantial share of COGS, as well as contributing to companies' environmental and social footprints and food-safety risks. At the other end of the food chain, big data and advanced analytics can be used to optimize downstream activities such as waste management. Food waste causes economic losses, harms natural resources, and exacerbates food-security issues. About a third of food produced for human consumption is lost or wasted every year in a world where 795 million people—a ninth of the population—go hungry.

Cutting postharvest losses in half would produce enough food to feed a billion more people. Global food waste and loss cost $940 billion a year, have a carbon footprint of 4.4 Gt CO_2-equivalent (more than 8 percent of global greenhouse-gas emissions), and a blue-water footprint of about 250 cubic km (3.6 times the annual consumption of the US). In 2007, the amount of food wasted globally equated to 1.4 billion hectares—an area bigger than Canada—of agricultural production.

Using technology to improve areas such as climate forecasting, demand planning, and the management of end-of-life products could bring enormous social, economic, and environmental benefits. For example, the French start-up Phenix runs a web-based marketplace to connect supermarkets with end-of-life food stocks to NGOs and consumers who could use them. The platform enables the supermarkets to save the costs of disposal, gives consumable products a second life, and alleviates some of the social and environmental burden of waste.

5.12 Would You Like to Learn More About Our Consumer Packaged Goods Practice?

Visit our Big Data & Advanced Analytics page

The opportunities for digital innovation in the food chain are enormous and vary by context, with some well suited to emerging markets and others more appropriate to mature economies.

Efficiency opportunities for emerging economies

Emerging markets can tap the potential of digital in the food chain through innovations such as precision agriculture, supply-chain efficiencies, and agriculture-focused payment systems.

Precision agriculture is a technology-enabled approach to farming management that observes, measures, and analyzes the needs of individual fields and crops. By allowing farmers to apply tailored care and manage water more effectively, it boosts production, improves economic efficiency, and minimizes waste and environmental impact. Its development is being shaped by two technological trends: big-data and advanced-analytics capabilities on the one hand, and robotics—aerial imagery, sensors, sophisticated local weather forecasts—on the other. According to 2014 estimates, the global market for agricultural robotics is expected to grow from its current $1 billion to $14–18 billion by 2020.

New entrants and large companies alike are developing products and services for precision agriculture. The start-up CropX offers sensors to help farmers adjust irrigation to the needs of their soil, while Blue River uses computer vision and robotics to determine the needs of individual plants. At the opposite end of the scale, IBM has developed a highly precise weather-forecast technology, Deep Thunder, and an agriculture-specific cloud technology.

Recommendations can be adjusted in real time to reflect changing weather conditions. Soil sensors and aerial images help farmers manage crop growth centrally, with automated detection systems providing early warnings of deviations from expected growth rates or quality.

Automated systems showing the status, performance, and potential bottlenecks of critical equipment in real time can be used to optimize fleet management, thus increasing delivery reliability and preventing spoilage. Transport times can be cut in half by using smart meters to improve routing. Coupling transport-management systems with agricultural sensors can allow unified hauling of inbound transportation, generating average savings of 10 to 20 percent.

Agriculture-specific payment systems and financial services can help farmers make their economic models more resilient. Some growers use insurance contracts to offset weather risk, for instance. Insurers calculate a premium on the basis of the likelihood of a particular weather event, such as frost, and the impact it would have on a crop at a specific point in its growth cycle. The premium is paid out when the number of occurrences surpasses a predefined threshold.

Payments are another area where digital solutions can make food chains more efficient. In Kenya, Sokopepe provides a trading platform for agricultural commodities that links small-scale producers to retailers and bulk purchasers via mobile-phone messaging. Another Kenyan initiative, MFarm, provides up-to-date market prices via an app or SMS and connects farmers with buyers, offering a group selling tool for those farmers too small to market to a large buyer by themselves.

Solutions to systemic challenges for mature economies

Developed countries can use digital tools and methods to tackle challenges such as improving the safety of food, the sustainability of sourcing decisions, and companies' environmental footprints.

Food safety could be improved through the adoption of innovative technologies such as consumer food scanners that analyze a dish using spectroscopy and give users immediate  information on its composition. The European Commission recently launched a competition to develop a viable, affordable, and noninvasive food scanner, with a prize of €800,000 in funding for the winning team.

Two groups of people would derive particular benefit from these devices: sufferers from food-related illnesses such as obesity, allergies, and intolerance, and health-conscious individuals wishing to use food scanners as a complement to activity trackers. In view of the global epidemic in obesity and type-2 diabetes, estimates suggest that the market for personal food scanners could reach US $1 billion by 2020.

Sourcing decisions could be made more sustainable by adding yield-forecasting and risk-assessment tools to agronomic modeling methods to assess the impact of hyper local weather forecasts on a particular plant's yield and soil conditions. This would allow global food manufacturers to not only choose the best regions and countries to source from, but also to adapt their sourcing routes to weather challenges. These tools could also be used to determine the ideal mix of commodities in a country's agricultural portfolio, taking into account productivity levels by region.

Given the unpredictability and volatility of raw-materials costs, global food companies could derive huge benefits from finding ways to mitigate these risks while maintaining a responsible sourcing strategy toward growers.

Environmental-footprint management is another challenge that digitization can help to address. For instance, Cisco's Internet of Everything will provide consumers with the means to trace a food product back along its entire chain of production, from farmer's field to supermarket shelf. A scan able code on packaging will take users to a website that provides a detailed analysis of every stage and process undergone by that product's specific production batch.

The technology could be used to provide consumers with a guarantee of a product's environmental credentials. One of the challenges of advanced environmental practices is the difficulty of demonstrating the reality behind marketing claims and overcoming consumer skepticism, particularly where price premiums are concerned. A robust method for tracing sourcing through to origins could support this practice and make it more economically viable for food manufacturers.

Digital methods and tools are opening up opportunities for leading food companies to improve their management not only of the "last mile" of marketing and sales, but the entire journey from field to fork.

About the author(s)

Clarisse Magnin is a senior partner in McKinsey's Paris office and an EMEA leader in the Retail, Private Equity and Operations Practices; she also leads the consumer hub in France and is a global leader in the Sustainability and Resource Productivity Practice.

http://www.mckinsey.com/business-functions/digital-mckinsey/our-insights/how-big-data-will-revolutionize-the-global-food-chain

Chapter 6: Digital Transformation Initiative in India

6.1 "Make in India", "Skill India" and "Digital India" Positive signals of new Transformation

Press Information Bureau, Government of India, Ministry of Information & Broadcasting: 25-October-2016 15:32 IST

I&B Ministry to play the Facilitator's role for the M&E Sector – Venkaiah Naidu, I&B Minister delivers inaugural address at the 5th Edition of CII Big Picture Summit

Minister of Information and Broadcasting, Sri M. Venkaiah Naidu has said that digital and mobile tools have been leading to paradigm shifts in the M&E sector. The growth of varied platforms such as 4G, broadband, mobile technologies, digital media has enabled the M&E sector to move towards "Convergence across platforms and content". The Government of India's "Make in India", "Skill India" and "Digital India" campaigns were clearly positive signals of the new transformation including GST which is expected to be a game changer for the M&E sector. Sri Naidu stated this while delivering the keynote address at the inaugural function of the 5th Edition of CII Big Picture Summit at New Delhi today. The theme of this year's Summit is 'Embracing Disruption to Stay Competitive'.

Regarding opportunities in the skill sector for the M&E industry, Sri Naidu said that the Government is fully aware of the acute shortage of professionals across different segments. He mentioned that he would like the industry to give its recommendations on the steps to be taken to match demand and supply as well as the recommendations emerging from the discussions at the summit for the different sessions focusing on skill assessment and needs.

On the issue of growth prospects for the industry, Shri Naidu said that as part of the national policy, the Government would work with the industry to develop infrastructure to get the right talent at the appropriate sectors. The M&E sector in India had always been a very liberal media market and a number of initiatives had been taken including opening up and liberalizing FDI in the broadcast sector.

For the initiatives in the film sector, Sri Naidu said there is a huge opportunity to make India lead in the world as film shooting location and digital media hub for the world. Our films, actors, content, technology were expanding footprint to new and emerging global markets, and the aim of the Government was to make this transition smooth by creating an enabling regulatory environment. The Co-production agreements with other countries has ensured the projection and branding of India's soft power.

On the issue of the theme of the Conference "'Embracing Disruption to Stay Competitive", the Minister said that this process had substantially altered the business models across the world. The Indian M&E industry needed to outline a firm roadmap to ensure the convergence of networks, devices and content, the core elements of the digital entertainment process. Sri Naidu referred to the Government's Digital India and Smart City initiative that were going to have a major impact on increasing the penetration of Internet to Tier-II and Tier-III cities. He also referred to the potential of smart phones in facilitating a critical role for consumers' professional and personal lives. The Government's initiatives and private sector participation was necessary to ensure the optimal use of the potential of the digital ecosystem.

http://pib.nic.in/newsite/PrintRelease.aspx?relid=151945

6.2   Make in India

PROGRAM

The Make in India initiative was launched by Prime Minister in September 2014 as part of a wider set of nation-building initiatives. Devised to transform India into a global design and manufacturing hub, Make in India was a timely response to a critical situation: by 2013, the much-hyped emerging markets bubble had burst, and India's growth rate had fallen to its lowest level in a decade. The promise of the BRICS Nations (Brazil, Russia, India, China and South Africa) had faded, and

India was tagged as one of the so-called 'Fragile Five'. Global investors debated whether the world's largest democracy was a risk or an opportunity. India's 1.2 billion citizens questioned whether India was too big to succeed or too big to fail. India was on the brink of severe economic failure.

PROCESS

Make in India was launched by Prime Minister against the backdrop of this crisis, and quickly became a rallying cry for India's innumerable stakeholders and partners. It was a powerful, galvanising call to action to India's citizens and business leaders, and an invitation to potential partners and investors around the world. But, Make in India is much more than an inspiring slogan. It represents a comprehensive and unprecedented overhaul of out-dated processes and policies. Most importantly, it represents a complete change of the Government's mindset – a shift from issuing authority to business partner, in keeping with Prime Minister's tenet of 'Minimum Government, Maximum Governance'.

PLAN

To start a movement, you need a strategy that inspires, empowers and enables in equal measure. Make in India needed a different kind of campaign: instead of the typical statistics-laden newspaper advertisements, this exercise required messaging that was informative, well-packaged and most importantly, credible. It had to (a) inspire confidence in India's capabilities amongst potential partners abroad, the Indian business community and citizens at large; (b) provide a framework for a vast amount of technical information on 25 industry sectors; and (c) reach out to a vast local and global audience via social media and constantly keep them updated about opportunities, reforms, etc.

The Department of Industrial Policy & Promotion (DIPP) worked with a group of highly specialized agencies to build brand new infrastructure, including a dedicated help desk and a mobile-first website that packed a wide array of information into a simple, sleek menu. Designed primarily for mobile screens, the site's architecture ensured that exhaustive levels of detail are neatly tucked away so as not to overwhelm the user. 25 sector brochures were also developed: Contents included key facts and figures, policies and initiatives and sector-specific contact details, all of which was made available in print and on site.

PARTNERSHIPS

The Make in India initiative has been built on layers of collaborative effort. DIPP initiated this process by inviting participation from Union Ministers, Secretaries to the Government of India, state governments, industry leaders, and various knowledge partners. Next, a National Workshop on sector specific industries in December 2014 brought Secretaries to the Government of India and industry leaders together to debate and formulates an action plan for the next three years, aimed at raising the contribution of the manufacturing sector to 25% of the GDP by 2020. This plan was presented to the Prime Minister, Union Ministers, industry associations and industry leaders by the Secretaries to the Union Government and the Chief Secretary, Maharashtra on behalf of state governments.

These exercises resulted in a road map for the single largest manufacturing initiative undertaken by a nation in recent history. They also demonstrated the transformational power of public-private partnership, and have become a hallmark of the Make in India initiative. This collaborative model has also been successfully extended to include India's global partners, as evidenced by the recent in-depth interactions between India and the United States of America.

PROGRESS

In a short space of time, the obsolete and obstructive frameworks of the past have been dismantled and replaced with a transparent and user-friendly system that is helping drive investment, foster innovation, develop skills, protect Intellectual Property (IP) and build best-in-class manufacturing infrastructure. The most striking indicator of progress is the unprecedented opening up of key sectors – including Railways, Defense, Insurance and Medical Devices – to dramatically higher levels of Foreign Direct Investment.

A workshop titled "Make in India – Sectorial perspective & initiatives" was conducted on 29th December, 2014 under which an action plan for 1 year and 3 years has been prepared to boost investments in 25 sectors.

The ministry has engaged with the World Bank group to identify areas of improvement in line with World Bank's 'doing business' methodology. A 2 day workshop and several follow up meetings were held to formulate framework which could boost India's ranking which is currently 130 in terms of Ease of doing business.

An Investor Facilitation Cell (IFC) dedicated for the Make in India campaign was formed in September 2014 with an objective to assist investors in seeking regulatory approvals, hand-holding services through the pre-investment phase, execution and after-care support.

The Indian embassies and consulates have also been communicated to disseminate information on the potential for investment in the identified sectors. DIPP has set up a special management team to facilitate and fast track investment proposals from Japan, the team known as 'Japan Plus' has been operationalized with effect from October 2014. Similarly, 'Korea Plus', launched in June 2016, facilitates fast track investment proposals from South Korea and offers holistic support to Korean companies wishing to enter the Indian market.

Various sectors have been opened up for investments like Defense, Railways, Space, etc. Also, the regulatory policies have been relaxed to facilitate investments and ease of doing business.

Six industrial corridors are being developed across various regions of the country. Industrial Cities will also come up along these corridors.

Today, India's credibility is stronger than ever. There is visible momentum, energy and optimism. Make in India is opening investment doors. Multiple enterprises are adopting its mantra. The world's largest democracy is well on its way to becoming the world's most powerful economy.

http://www.makeinindia.com/sectors

6.3 Digital India: Transforming India Into a Knowledge Economy

With a clear vision, the present government is pushing ahead the Digital India initiative to transform the country into a digitally empowered society and a knowledge economy.

The journey towards a digitally – connected India began in the early 90s and 2000s with the introduction of a range of e – governance programmes. However, its impact was limited.

With a clear vision, the present government is pushing ahead the Digital India initiative to transform the country into a digitally empowered society and a knowledge economy. With the launch of this initiative, the government aims to reach out to citizens in the remotest of locations and make them a part of India's growth story. Since technology is a key driver in causing disruptive change, digital tools will empower citizens and prove to be a game-changer.

Digital India provides the much-needed thrust to the nine pillars of growth areas, namely Broadband Highways, Universal Access to Mobile Connectivity and Public Internet Access Programme, among others.

KEY PILLARS[1]

The Digital India programme is based on the following pillars:

- **Broadband Highways[2]**

Under this programme, high – speed broadband coverage highways will connect 250,000 villages, various government departments, universities, etc. In addition, National Information Infrastructure (NII) will ensure the integration of the network and cloud infrastructure within the country to provide high-speed connectivity to various government departments. These components include networks such as State Wide Area Network (SWAN), National Knowledge Network (NKN), National Optical Fiber Network (NOFN), Government User Network (GUN) and the Megh Raj Cloud.

- **Universal access to Mobile Connectivity[3]**

Today, there exist around 55,619 villages in India that have no mobile coverage. To cover remote villages in the northeast, a comprehensive development plan has been initiated that will be carried out in phases.

- **Public Internet Access Programme[4]**

The underlying principle of this initiative is to make 250,000 Common Service Centers (CSCs) operational at the gram Panchayat level for delivery of government services. In a similar move, 150,000 post offices will be converted into multi-service centers.

- **E-governance: Reforming government through technology[5]**

The idea is to use business process re-engineering to transform government processes and make them simple, automated and efficient. Under this, forms will be simplified and only minimum and necessary information will be collected. Similarly, there will be a tracking process for the status of online applications. To further simplify the process, use of online repositories for certificates, educational degrees, identity documents will be encouraged so that these documents do not have to be submitted in the physical form.

- ### Ekranti - Electronic Delivery of Services[6]

This pillar emphasizes on the use of technology for service delivery such as e-education, e-healthcare, technology for planning, final inclusion etc.

- ### Information for all[7]

This is to provide open access to government information and documents available online. This will enable a two – way communication between the citizens and the government through online platforms and social media. The biggest success story is MyGov.in, a platform for citizen engagement in governance, which was launched by the Prime Minister Narendra Modi on 26th July 2014 as a medium to exchange ideas or suggestions with the government.

- ### Electronics manufacturing[8]

Under this programme, the target is to reach net zero imports by 2020 through implementation in areas such as taxation, economies of scale, skill development, government procurement etc.

- ### IT for jobs[9]

This step will provide the required skills and training to enable youth to find jobs in the IT/ITes sector. This component also emphasizes on the setting up of BPOs to enable ICT-enabled growth.

- ### Early harvest programmes[10]

These early harvest programmes consist of a range of projects to be carried out within a short timeline. This includes an IT platform for messages, e-greetings from the government, biometric attendance and Wi-Fi in all universities etc.

VISION OF DIGITAL INDIA[11]

The Digital India vision provides the intensified impetus for further momentum and progress for e-Governance and would promote inclusive growth that covers electronic services, products, devices, manufacturing and job opportunities.

- **Governance and Services on demand**

Digital India aims to create a seamless ecosystem across multiple government departments to make services available on both online and mobile platforms. As part of the initiative, financial transactions would be made cashless and entitlements would be available on the cloud.[12]

- **Digital empowerment of citizens**

This programme will provide universal digital literacy to enable citizens to use the digital platform. The government services can be accessed in local languages to help users participate in the new governance mechanism. Since technology is the key driver in India's economic growth, it will spur growth in areas of governance and service delivery.

SUCCESSES OF DIGITAL INDIA[13]

- **E-Pathshala: Transforming Learning through Technology**

The Ministry of Human Resource Development introduced the e-Pathshala programme to promote 'learning on the go' among students, teachers and parents. Through this initiative, free access to NCERT books is available to students of classes 1 to 12. These books are available in both Hindi and English.[14]

- **eBiz platform**

The initiative, driven by the Department of Industrial Policy and Promotion (DIPP), seeks to provide comprehensive Government-to-Business (G2B) services to business entities with transparency, speed, and certainty. The aim is to reduce several levels of points of contact between business entities and government agencies, establish single-window services and reduce the burden of compliances.[15]

- ## My Gov platform

This is a platform for citizens to exchange ideas and suggestions with the government. Through this initiative, the government receives feedback, inputs and ideas from people regarding policy decisions and new initiatives like Digital India, Swachh Bharat, Make in India, among others.[16]

- ## Jeevan Praman

The Jeevan Praman programme enables pensioners to conveniently submit their life certificates online through this portal. The certificates are stored in the Life Certificate Repository and available to pensioners and Pension Disbursing agencies.[17]

- ## Digital Locker System

DigiLocker is a key initiative under Digital India. This programme is targeted at paperless governance and is a platform for issuance and verification of documents and certificates digitally. A dedicated cloud storage space is given to all those who register for the Digital Locker account. To make it an easy process, this storage is linked to their Aadhaar (UIDAI) number. Organizations that are registered with Digital Locker can push electronic copies of documents and certificates (e.g. driving license, Voter ID, School certificates) directly into the citizens' lockers. As per the official website, there are 39, 64, 008 registered users and 50,47,204 uploaded documents.[18]

Digital India has been introduced to ensure smooth implementation of e – governance in the country and transform the entire ecosystem of public services through the use of information technology. There is no better way to promote inclusive growth other than through the empowerment of citizens.

Source:

1 *http://www.digitalindia.gov.in/content/programme-pillars*

2 *http://www.digitalindia.gov.in/content/broadband-highways*

3 *http://www.digitalindia.gov.in/content/universal-access-mobile-connectivity*

4 *http://www.digitalindia.gov.in/content/public-internet-access-programme*

5 *http://www.digitalindia.gov.in/content/e-governance-%E2%80%93-reforming-government-through-technology*

6 *http://www.digitalindia.gov.in/content/ekranti-electronic-delivery-services*

7 *http://www.digitalindia.gov.in/content/information-all*

8 *http://www.digitalindia.gov.in/content/electronics-manufacturing*

9 *http://www.digitalindia.gov.in/content/it-jobs*

10 *http://www.digitalindia.gov.in/content/early-harvest-programmes*

11 *http://www.digitalindia.gov.in/content/vision-and-vision-areas*

12 *http://www.digitalindia.gov.in/content/vision-and-vision-areas*

13 *http://www.digitalindia.gov.in/content/approach-and-methodology*

14 *epathshala.nic.in/*

15 *http://meity.gov.in/content/e-biz*

16 *https://mygov.in*

17 *https://jeevanpramaan.gov.in*

18 *https://digilocker.gov.in/about.php*

19 *http://www.digitalindia.gov.in/*

http://www.makeinindia.com/article/-/v/digital-india-transforming-india-into-a-knowledge-economy

6.4   What we need is Digital Disruption
JAIDEEP MEHTA

The IoT will improve efficiencies, but it will also throw up organizational and leadership challenges in business.

New waves of technologies are transforming the industrial, business and governance landscape. Sample how the Delhi government is engaging with citizens through its e-governance app. everything from reporting on dirty streets to water meter readings is getting digitized.

Hold my hand soon; robotics will influence every walk of human life
William Breadberry / shutterstock.com

On another vector, YES Bank recently invested significant marketing monies to have a presence at a Nasscom conference, where its key audience was the IT industry and CIOs: they are building a business to enable digital and mobile commerce and seeking to drive more, and deeper, relationships with technology houses to drive growth.

Even as companies embrace digital technologies, commonly referred to as SMAC (social, mobile, analytics and cloud), leveraging them for business gains of various hues, the next generation of technologies is getting ready to roll. IDC has identified six key new technologies. Unlike SMAC, these six technologies, or innovation accelerators, are going to impact businesses' operating processes and paradigms, driving deeper transformation.

New internet, virtual reality

Internet of Things (IOT) is the label given to a connected world where inanimate objects 'talk' to each other, exchanging information without human intervention, and triggering business processes.

For instance, a trucking company in Delhi has used IoT to track its vehicles while monitoring essential indicators such as speed, fuel consumption and the general health of the vehicle, using an integrated system of sensors which feed data into a mobile-network-connected device. This kind of application can save the company anywhere between 10-15 per cent of operating costs through reduced pilferage, prevention of unauthorized stops and preventive maintenance.

By 2020, we expect more than 30 billion devices to be connected on to one single "new" internet.

Augmented and virtual reality, the next accelerator, has already invaded the gaming ecosystem. However, if you are a healthcare provider, you'll soon be using visors to virtually train key frontline medical staff. Or, if you happen to be the Army, virtual battlefields will enable safe and effective training of soldiers.

We also see applications in R&D, product development and in industries as disparate as interior design, retail and chemical manufacturing. For us consumers, expect it to completely transform the ecommerce experience soon as you buy from a virtual supermarket while wearing your visor and pay at the virtual self-service checkout. Technology vendors such as Samsung, Face book and many others are racing to develop next generation devices which enrich our experiences.

3D printing, robots

This can feel gimmicky, with hobbyists "printing" out things made of plastic materials in their garages. However, this accelerator is already being used to produce artificial body parts where organ replacements are required. A leading brand is launching a custom-fit, 3D-printed shoe which is 'manufactured' in the store. 3D-printed prototypes are replacing clay models whilst enabling far more detail and accuracy in product development labs: and did I mention time savings to the tune of 60-70 per cent?

3D printing can, and will, revolutionize supply chains, inventory management practices, product development and R&D methods and healthcare. Watch out for the rise of hyper-local, micro-factories which democratize manufacturing, changing it forever.

Next generation robots come in two flavours: real and virtual. Physical robots can now execute tasks that are extremely intricate. Swiss firm ABB recently showcased a robot folding a paper aeroplane and launching it into the air, demonstrating the next level of robotic dexterity, programmatic sophistication and versatility.

Robots will replace humans in all kinds of repetitive or dangerous tasks: from factory shop floors to uranium mines. The day is not far when hotel housekeeping and even engineering functions see robots playing a bigger role.

Security, thought systems

The final two innovation accelerators are not just important in themselves but also have a pervasive impact on the four above, and on a much wider ecosystem.

The tragedy of the digital age is the increasing incidences of cyber-crime — from individuals suffering phishing attacks and stolen passwords to large organizations losing confidential customer data. We are in a perpetual battle with cyber-criminals, rogue countries and malevolent employees seeking to hack, steal and sell.

Next-generation security will blend the physical and digital. CCTV cameras with face recognition technology built in ensure that if a bad actor enters the premises, the cameras can instantly trigger alarms and activate relevant business processes.

On another front, projects are on to make passwords redundant. Using a combination of biometrics and behaviour tracking, new age security systems will identify you with more certainty. The paradigm of security is also being extended to protect new age robots, IoT networks and virtual reality systems. Success is an imperative: failure will halt the onset of the digital age in its tracks.

No doubt, cognitive systems will be the most pervasive accelerator going forward. The fundamental notion is that machines can self-learn, improve and deliver superior outcomes over a period of time. This is possible due to breakthrough technologies manifested in machine learning systems, artificial intelligence platforms and big data systems. The possibilities in smart traffic management in cities are also phenomenal with cognitive systems which learn from historical traffic patterns and can, for example, automatically change the rhythm of traffic lights, or indeed dynamically set parking charges.

As a CEO, it is imperative that you understand implications of these emerging technologies: figuring out how they work could be left to someone else, but understanding what they can do is of critical importance to you.

Given the breakneck speed of evolution, coupled with the worsening skills shortages, it is not an easy or predictable ride. The promise of transformation can only be realized with visible, sustained leadership from the top, a culture that pardons innovation failures, the ability to stretch your business model and a discrete innovation investment fund.

The writer is managing director of IDC India and South Asia

(This article was published in the Business Line print edition dated June 9, 2016)

http://www.thehindubusinessline.com/todays-paper/tp-opinion/what-we-need-is-digital-disruption/article8706935.ece?ref=relatedNews

6.5   The Next-Generation Operating Model for The Digital World

By Albert Bollard, Elixabete Larrea, Alex Singla, and Rohit Sood

Companies need to increase revenues, lower costs, and delight customers. Doing that requires reinventing the operating model.

Companies know where they want to go. They want to be more agile, quicker to react, and more effective. They want to deliver great customer experiences, take advantage of new technologies to cut costs, improve quality and transparency, and build value.

The problem is that while most companies are trying to get better, the results tend to fall short: one-off initiatives in separate units that don't have a big enterprise-wide impact; adoption of the improvement method of the day, which almost invariably yields disappointing results; and programs that provide temporary gains but aren't sustainable.

We have found that for companies to build value and provide compelling customer experiences at lower cost, they need to commit to a next-generation operating model. This operating model is a new way of running the organization that combines digital technologies and operations capabilities in an integrated, well-sequenced way to achieve step-change improvements in revenue, customer experience, and cost.

A simple way to visualize this operating model is to think of it as having two parts, each requiring companies to adopt major changes in the way they work:

- The first part involves a shift from running uncoordinated efforts within silos to launching an integrated operational-improvement program organized around customer journeys (the set of interactions a customer has with a company when making a purchase or receiving services) as well as the internal journeys (end-to-end processes inside the company). Examples of customer journeys include a homeowner filing an insurance claim, a cable-TV subscriber signing up for a premium channel, or a shopper looking to buy a gift online. Examples of internal-process journeys include Order-to-Cash or Record-to-Report.

• The second part is a shift from using individual technologies, operations capabilities, and approaches in a piecemeal manner inside siloes to applying them to journeys in combination and in the right sequence to achieve compound impact.

Let's look at each element of the model and the necessary shifts in more detail:

Shift #1: From running uncoordinated efforts within siloes to launching an integrated operational-improvement program organized around journeys

Many organizations have multiple independent initiatives underway to improve performance, usually housed within separate organizational groups (e.g. front and back office). This can make it easier to deliver incremental gains within individual units, but the overall impact is most often underwhelming and hard to sustain. Tangible benefits to customers—in the form of faster turnaround or better service—can get lost due to hand-offs between units. These become black holes in the process, often involving multiple back-and-forth steps and long lag times. As a result, it's common to see individual functions reporting that they've achieved notable operational improvements, but customer satisfaction and overall costs remain unchanged.

Instead of working on separate initiatives inside organizational units, companies have to think holistically about how their operations can contribute to delivering a distinctive customer experience. The best way to do this is to focus on customer journeys and the internal processes that support them. These naturally cut across organizational siloes—for example, you need marketing, operations, credit, and IT to support a customer opening a bank account. Journeys—both customer-facing and end-to-end internal processes—are therefore the preferred organizing principle.

Transitioning to the next-generation operating model starts with classifying and mapping key journeys. At a bank, for example, customer-facing journeys can typically be divided into seven categories: signing up for a new account; setting up the account and getting it running; adding a new product or account; using the account; receiving and managing statements; making changes to accounts; and resolving problems. Journeys can vary by product/service line and customer segment. In our experience, targeting about 15–20 top journeys can unlock the most value in the shortest possible time.

We often find that companies fall into the trap of simply trying to improve existing processes. Instead, they should focus on entirely reimagining the customer experience, which often reveals opportunities to simplify and streamline journeys and processes that unlock massive value. Concepts from behavioral economics can inform the redesign process in ingenious ways. Examples include astute use of default settings on forms, limiting choice to keep customers from feeling overwhelmed, and paying special attention to the final touch point in a series, since that's the one that will be remembered the most.

In 2014, a major European bank announced a multiyear plan to revamp its operating model to improve customer satisfaction and reduce overall costs by up to 35 percent. The bank targeted the ten most important journeys, including the mortgage process, on boarding of new business and personal customers, and retirement planning. Eighteen months in, operating costs are lower, the number of online customers is up nearly 20 percent, and the number using its mobile app has risen more than 50 percent. (For more on reinventing customer journeys, see "Putting customer experience at the heart of next-generation operating models," forthcoming on McKinsey.com.)

Shift #2: From applying individual approaches or capabilities in a piecemeal manner to adopting multiple levers in sequence to achieve compound impact

Organizations typically use five key capabilities or approaches (we'll call them "levers" from now on) to improve operations that underlie journeys.

- *Digitization* is the process of using tools and technology to improve journeys. Digital tools have the capacity to transform customer-facing journeys in powerful ways, often by creating the potential for self-service. Digital can also reshape time-consuming transactional and manual tasks that are part of internal journeys, especially when multiple systems are involved.[1]

- *Advanced analytics* is the autonomous processing of data using sophisticated tools to discover insights and make recommendations. It provides intelligence to improve decision making and can especially enhance journeys where nonlinear thinking is required. For example, insurers with the right data and capabilities in place are massively accelerating processes in areas such as smart claims triage, fraud management, and pricing.

- *Intelligent process automation (IPA)* is an emerging set of new technologies that combines fundamental process redesign with robotic process automation and machine learning. IPA can replace human effort in processes that involve aggregating data from multiple systems or taking a piece of information from a written document and entering it as a standardized data input. There are also automation approaches that can take on higher-level tasks. Examples include smart workflows (to track the status of the end-to-end process in real time, manage handoffs between different groups, and provide statistical data on bottlenecks), machine learning (to make predictions on their own based on inputs and provide insights on recognized patterns), and cognitive agents (technologies that combine machine learning and natural-language generation to build a virtual workforce capable of executing more sophisticated tasks). To learn more about this, see "Intelligent Process Automation: The engine at the core of the next generation operating model."

• *Business process outsourcing (BPO)* uses resources outside of the main business to complete specific tasks or functions. It often uses labor arbitrage to improve cost efficiency. This approach typically works best for processes that are manual, are not primarily customer facing, and do not influence or reflect key strategic choices or value propositions. The most common example is back-office processing of documents and correspondence.

• *Lean process redesign* helps companies streamline processes, eliminate waste, and foster a culture of continuous improvement. This versatile methodology applies well to short-cycle as well as long-cycle processes, transactional as well as judgment-based processes, client-facing as well as internal processes.

Guidelines for implementing these levers

In considering which levers to use and how to apply them, it's important to think in a holistic way, keeping the entire journey in mind. Three design guidelines are crucial:

1. Organizations need to ensure that each lever is used to maximum effect. Many companies believe they're applying the capabilities to the fullest, but they're actually not getting as much out of them as they could. Some companies, for example, apply a few predictive models and think they're really pushing the envelope with analytics—but in fact; they're only capturing a small fraction of the potential value. This often breeds a false complacency, insulating the organizations from the learning that would otherwise drive them to higher performance because it is "already under way" or "has been tried". Having something already under way is a truism: everyone has something under way in these kinds of domains, but it is the companies that press to the limit that reap the rewards. Executives need to be vigilant, challenge their people, and resist the easy answer.

Speed and scale: Unlocking digital value in customer journeys

In the case of analytics, for example, maxing out the potential requires using sophisticated modeling techniques and data sources in a concerted, cross-functional effort, while also ensuring that front-line employees then execute in a top-flight way on the insights generated by the models.

2. Implementing each lever in the right sequence. There is no universal recipe on sequencing these levers because so many variables are involved, such as an organization's legacy state and the existing interconnections between customer-facing and internal processes. However, the best results come when the levers can build on each other. That means, in practice, figuring out which one depends on the successful implementation of another.

Systematic analysis is necessary to guide decision making. Some institutions have started by outlining an in-house versus outsource strategy rooted in a fundamental question: "What is core to our value proposition?" Key considerations include whether the activities involved are strategic or confer competitive advantage or whether sensitive data or regulatory constraints are present.

The next step is to use a structured set of questions to evaluate how much opportunity there is to apply each of the remaining levers and then to estimate the potential impact of each lever on costs and customer experience. This exercise results in each lever being assigned an overall score to help develop a preliminary point of view on which sequence to use in implementing the levers.

There's also a need to vet the envisioned sequences in the context of the overall enterprise. For example, even if the optimal sequence for a particular customer journey may be "IPA then lean then digital," if the company's strategic aspiration is to become "digital first," it may make more sense to digitize processes first.

This systematic approach allows executives to consider various sequencing scenarios, evaluate the implications of each, and make decisions that benefit the entire business.

3. Finally, the levers should interact with each other to provide a multiplier effect. For example, one bank only saw significant impact from its lean and digitization efforts in the mortgage application journey after both efforts were working in tandem. A lean initiative for branch offices included a new scorecard that measured customer adoption of online banking, forums for associates to problem solve how to overcome roadblocks to adoption, and scripts they could use with customers to encourage them to begin mortgage applications online. This, in turn, drove up usage of online banking solutions. Software developers were then able to incorporate feedback from branch associates, which made future digital releases easier to use for customers. This in turn drove increased adoption of digital banking, thereby reducing the number of transactions done in branches.

Some companies have developed end-to-end journey "heat maps" that provide a company-wide perspective on the potential impact and scale of opportunity of each lever on each journey These maps include estimates for each journey of how much costs can be reduced (measured in terms of both head count and financial metrics) and how much the customer experience can be improved.

Companies find heat maps a valuable way to engage the leadership team in strategic discussions about which approaches and capabilities to use and how to prioritize them.

Case example: The 'first notice of loss' journey in insurance

In insurance, a key journey is when a customer files a claim, known in the industry as first notice of loss (FNOL). FNOL is particularly challenging for insurers because they must balance multiple objectives at the same time:

providing a user-friendly experience (for example, by offering web or mobile interfaces that enable self-service), managing expectations in real time through alerts or updates, and creating an emotional connection with customers who are going through a potentially traumatic situation—all while collecting the most accurate information possible and keeping costs in line.

Many companies have relied on Lean to improve FNOL call-center performance. One leading North American insurer, however, discovered it could unlock even more value by sequencing the build out of three additional capabilities, based on the progress it had already made with Lean:

Digitization: This company improved response times by using digital technologies to access third-party data sources and connect with mobile devices. With these new tools, the insurer can now track claimant locations and automatically dispatch emergency services. Customers can also upload pictures of damages, and both file and track claims online. The insurer also allows some customers to complete the entire claims process without a single interaction with a company representative.

Advanced analytics: Digitization of the FNOL journey provided the insurer with more and better data faster, which in turn allowed its analytics initiative to be more effective. Now able to apply the latest modeling capabilities to better data, the company is using advanced analytics to improve decision making in the FNOL journey. For example, intelligent triage is used to close simple claims more quickly, and smart segmentation identifies claims likely to be total losses and those liable to require the special investigative unit (SIU) far earlier than before. Analytics are even being used to predict future staffing needs and inform scheduling and hiring, thereby allowing both complex and simple claims to be handled more efficiently.

Intelligent process automation (IPA): Once digital and analytics were in place, IPA was implemented. Automation tools were deployed to take over manual and time-consuming tasks formerly done by customer-service agents, such as looking up policy numbers or data from driving records. In addition to reducing costs, IPA sped up the process and reduced errors. IPA came last because the streamlining achieved by digitization and more effective use of analytics had eliminated some manual processes, so the IPA effort could focus only on those that remained.

By combining four levers—lean plus digital, analytics and IPA—this insurer drove a significant uplift in customer satisfaction while at the same time improving efficiency by 40 percent. (For more approaches to improving claims, see "Next-generation claims operating model: From evolution to revolution," forthcoming on McKinsey.com.)

Bringing it all together: Avoid creating new silos by thinking holistically

Senior leaders have a crucial role in making this all happen. They must first convince their peers that the next-generation operating model can break through organizational inertia and trigger step-change improvements. With broad buy-in, the CEO or senior executive should align the business on a few key journeys to tackle first. These can serve as beacons to demonstrate the model's potential. Next come evaluation of the company's capabilities to determine which levers can be implemented using internal resources and which will require bringing in resources from outside. Finally, there is the work of actually implementing the model. (For more on the last topic, see "How to build out your next-generation operating model," forthcoming on McKinsey.com.)

Transformation cannot be a siloed effort. The full impact of the next-generation operating model comes from combining operational-improvement efforts around customer-facing and internal journeys with the integrated use of approaches and capabilities.

About the author(s)

Albert Bollard is an associate partner in McKinsey's New York office; **Elixabete Larrea** is an associate partner in the Boston office; Alex Singla is a senior partner in the Chicago office, and Rohit Sood is a partner in the Toronto office.

The authors would like to thank Sanjay Kaniyar, Swapnil Prabha, and Deniz Cultu for their gracious support and expertise in creating this article.

http://www.mckinsey.com/business-functions/digital-mckinsey/our-insights/the-next-generation-operating-model-for-the-digital-world

6.6   The Case for Digital Reinvention

By Jacques Bughin, Laura LaBerge, and Anette Mellbye

Digital technology, despite its seeming ubiquity, has only begun to penetrate industries. As it continues its advance, the implications for revenues, profits, and opportunities will be dramatic.

As new markets emerge, profit pools shift, and digital technologies pervade more of everyday life, it's easy to assume that the economy's digitization is already far advanced. According to our latest research, however, the forces of digital have yet to become fully main stream. On average, industries are less than 40 percent digitized, despite the relatively deep penetration of these technologies in media, retail, and high tech.

The case for digital reinvention

As digitization penetrates more fully, it will dampen revenue and profit growth for some, particularly the bottom quartile of companies, according to our research, while the top quartile captures disproportionate gains. Bold, tightly integrated digital strategies will be the biggest differentiator between companies that win and companies that don't, and the biggest payouts will go to those that initiate digital disruptions. Fast-followers with operational excellence and superior organizational health won't be far behind.

These findings emerged from a research effort to understand the nature, extent, and top-management implications of the progress of digitization. We tailored our efforts to examine its effects along multiple dimensions: products and services, marketing and distribution channels, business processes, supply chains, and new entrants at the ecosystem level (for details, see sidebar "About the research"). We sought to understand how economic performance will change as digitization continues its advance along these different dimensions. What are the best-performing companies doing in the face of rising pressure? Which approach is more important as digitization progresses: a great strategy with average execution or an average strategy with great execution?

The research-survey findings, taken together, amount to a clear mandate to act decisively, whether through the creation of new digital businesses or by reinventing the core of today's strategic, operational, and organizational approaches.

More digitization and performance pressure—ahead

According to our research, digitization has only begun to transform many industries (Exhibit 1). Its impact on the economic performance of companies, while already significant, is far from complete.

This finding confirms what many executives may already suspect: by reducing economic friction, digitization enables competition that pressures revenue and profit growth. Current levels of digitization have already taken out, on average, up to six points of annual revenue and 4.5 points of growth in earnings before interest and taxes (EBIT). And there's more pressure ahead, our research suggests, as digital penetration deepens (Exhibit 2).

While the prospect of declining growth rates is hardly encouraging, executives should bear in mind that these are *average* declines across *all* industries. Beyond the averages, we find that performance is distributed unequally, as digital further separates the high performers from the also-rans. This finding is consistent with a separate McKinsey research stream, which also shows that economic performance is extremely unequal. Strongly performing industries, according to that research, are three times more likely than others to generate market-beating economic profit. Poorly performing companies probably won't thrive no matter which industry they compete in.

At the current level of digitization, median companies, which secure three additional points of revenue and EBIT growth, do better than average ones, presumably because the long tail of companies hit hard by digitization pulls down the mean. But our survey results suggest that as digital increases economic pressure, all companies, no matter what their position on the performance curve may be, will be affected.

Uneven returns on investment

That economic pressure will make it increasingly critical for executives to pay careful heed to where—and not just how—they compete and to monitor closely the return on their digital investments. So far, the results are uneven. Exhibit 3 shows returns distributed unequally: some players in every industry are earning outsized returns, while many others in the same industries are experiencing returns below the cost of capital.

These findings suggest that some companies are investing in the wrong places or investing too much (or too little) in the right ones—or simply that their returns on digital investments are being competed away or transferred to consumers. On the other hand, the fact that high performers exist in every industry (as we'll discuss further in a moment) indicates that some companies are getting it right—benefiting, for example, from cross-industry transfers, as when technology companies capture value in the media sector.

Where to make your digital investments

Improving the ROI of digital investments requires precise targeting along the dimensions where digitization is proceeding. Digital has widely expanded the number of available investment options, and simply spreading the same amount of resources across them is a losing proposition. In our research, we measured five separate dimensions of digitization's advance into industries: products and services, marketing and distribution channels, business processes, supply chains, and new entrants acting in ecosystems.

Facing up to digital disruption: Reinventing the core with bold business strategy

How fully each of these dimensions has advanced, and the actions companies are taking in response, differ according to the dimension in question. And there appear to be mismatches between opportunities and investments. Those mismatches reflect advancing digitization's uneven effect on revenue and profit growth, because of differences among dimensions as well as among industries. Exhibit 4 describes the rate of change in revenue and EBIT growth that appears to be occurring as industries progress toward full digitization. This picture, combining the data for all of the industries we studied, reveals that today is average level of digitization, shown by the dotted vertical line, differs for each dimension. Products and services are more digitized, supply chains less so.

To model the potential effects of full digitization on economic performance, we linked the revenue and EBIT growth of companies to a given dimension's digitization rate, leaving everything else equal. The results confirm that digitization's effects depend on where you look. Some dimensions take a bigger bite out of revenue and profit growth, while others are digitizing faster. This makes intuitive sense. As platforms transform industry ecosystems, for example, revenues grow—even as platform-based competitors put pressure on profits. As companies digitize business processes, profits increase, even though little momentum in top-line growth accompanies them. The biggest future impact on revenue and EBIT growth, as Exhibit 4 shows, is set to occur through the digitization of supply chains. In this dimension, full digitization contributes two-thirds (6.8 percentage points of 10.2 percent) of the total projected hit to annual revenue growth and more than 75 percent (9.4 out of 12 percent) to annual EBIT growth.

Despite the supply chain's potential impact on the growth of revenues and profits, survey respondents say that their companies aren't yet investing heavily in this dimension. Only 2 percent, in fact, report that supply chains are the focus of their forward-looking digital strategies (Exhibit 5), though headlining examples such as Airbnb and Uber demonstrate the power of tapping previously inaccessible sources of supply (sharing rides or rooms, respectively) and bringing them to market. Similarly, there is little investment in the ecosystems dimension, where hyper scale businesses such as Alibaba, Amazon, Google, and Tencent are pushing digitization most radically, often entering one industry and leveraging platforms to create collateral damage in others.[1]

Instead, the survey indicates that distribution channels and marketing are the primary focus of digital strategies (and thus investments) at 49 percent of companies. That focus is sensible; given the extraordinary impact digitization has already had on customer interactions and the power of digital tools to target marketing investments precisely. By now, in fact, this critical dimension has become "table stakes" for staying in the game. Standing pat is not an option.

The question, it seems, looking at exhibits 4 and 5 in combination, is whether companies are overlooking emerging opportunities, such as those in supply chains that are likely to have a major influence on future revenues and profits. That may call for resource reallocation. In general, companies that strategically shift resources create more value and deliver higher returns to shareholders. This general finding could be even truer as digitization progresses.

Structuring your digital reinvention

Our survey results also suggest companies are not sufficiently bold in the magnitude and scope of their investments (see sidebar "Structuring your digital reinvention"). Our research (Exhibit 6) suggests that the more aggressively they respond to the digitization of their industries—up to and including initiating digital disruption—the better the effect on their projected revenue and profit growth. The one exception is the ecosystem dimension: an overactive response to new hyper scale competitors actually lowers projected growth, perhaps because many incumbents lack the assets and capabilities necessary for platform strategies.

As executives assess the scope of their investments, they should ask themselves if they have taken only a few steps forward in each dimension—by digitizing their existing customer touch points, say. Others might find that they have acted more significantly by digitizing nearly all of their business processes and introducing new ones, where needed, to connect suppliers and users.

To that end, it may be useful to take a closer look at Exhibit 6, which comprises six smaller charts. The last of them totals up actions companies take in each dimension of digitization. Here we can see that the most assertive players will be able to restore more than 11 percent of the 12 percent loss in projected revenue growth, as well as 7.3 percent of the 10.4 percent reduction in profit growth. Such results will require action across all dimensions, not just one or two—a tall order for any management team, even those at today's digital leaders.

Looking at the digital winners

To understand what today's leaders are doing, we identified the companies in our survey that achieved top-quartile rankings in each of three measures: revenue growth, EBIT growth, and return on digital investment.

We found that more than twice as many leading companies closely tie their digital and corporate strategies than don't. What's more, winners tend to respond to digitization by changing their corporate strategies significantly. This makes intuitive sense: many digital disruptions require fundamental changes to business models. Further, 49 percent of leading companies are investing in digital more than their counterparts do, compared with only 5 percent of the laggards, 90 percent of which invest less than their counterparts. It's unclear which way the causation runs, of course, but it does appear that heavy digital investment is a differentiator.

Leading companies not only invested more but also did so across *all* of the dimensions we studied. In other words, winners exceed laggards in both the *magnitude* and the *scope* of their digital investments (Exhibit 7). This is a critical element of success, given the different rates at which these dimensions are digitizing and their varying effect on economic performance.

Strengths in organizational culture underpin these bolder actions. Winners were less likely to be hindered by siloed mind-sets and behavior or by a fragmented view of their customers. A strong organizational culture is important for several reasons: it enhances the ability to perceive digital threats and opportunities, bolsters the scope of actions companies can take in response to digitization, and supports the coordinated execution of those actions across functions, departments, and business units.

Win

So, we found a mismatch between today's digital investments and the dimensions in which digitization is most significantly affecting revenue and profit growth. We also confirmed that winners invest more, and more broadly and boldly, than other companies do. Then we tested two paths to growth as industries reach full digitization.

The first path emphasizes strategies that change a business's scope, including the kind of pure-play disruptions the hyper scale businesses discussed earlier generate. As Exhibit 8 shows, a great strategy can by itself retrieve all of the revenue growth lost, on average, to full digitization—at least in the aggregate industry view. This kind of superior strategy with median performance in the non-strategy dimensions of McKinsey's <u>digital-quotient</u> framework—including agile operations, organization, culture, and talent— yields total projected growth of 4.3 percent in annual revenues.

Most executives would fancy the kind of ecosystem play that Alibaba, Amazon, Google, and Ten cent have made on their respective platforms. Yet many recognize that few companies can mount disruptive strategies, at least at the ecosystem level. With that in mind, we tested a second path to revenue growth.

Companies in this profile lack a disruptive strategic posture but compensate by being in the top 25 percent for all the other elements of digital maturity.[2]This fast-follower profile allows more room for strategic error—you don't have to place your bets quite so precisely. It also increases the premium on how well you execute. The size of the win is just slightly positive at 0.4 percent in annual revenue growth: 5.3 percent from good (but not best-in-class disruptive) strategy and an additional 7.1 percent through top-quartile digital maturity. This is probably good news for incumbents, since many of them are carefully watching tech start-ups (such as those in fintech) to identify the winning plays and then imitating them at their own bigger scale. That approach, to be sure, demands cutting-edge agility to excel on all the operational and organizational aspects of digital maturity.

In the quest for coherent responses to a digitizing world, companies must assess how far digitization has progressed along multiple dimensions in their industries and the impact that this evolution is having—and will have—on economic performance. And they must act on each of these dimensions with bold, tightly integrated strategies. Only then will their investments match the context in which they compete.

About the author(s)

Jacques Bughin is a director of the McKinsey Global Institute and a senior partner in McKinsey's Brussels office; **Laura LaBerge** is a senior practice manager of Digital McKinsey and is based in the Stamford office; and **Anette Mellbye** is an associate partner in the London office. The authors wish to thank Dan Lovallo, Soyoko Umeno, and Nicolas van Zeebroeck for their contributions to this article.

http://www.mckinsey.com/business-functions/digital-mckinsey/our-insights/the-case-for-digital-reinvention

6.7 The seven decisions that matter in a digital transformation: A CEO's guide to reinvention

By Peter Dahlström, DriekDesmet, and Marc Singer

The seven decisions that matter in a digital transformation: A CEO's guide to reinvention

A successful digital transformation requires making trade-off decisions. Here's how successful CEOs guide their business's reinvention.

Being the CEO of a large company facing digital disruption can seem like being a gambler at a roulette table. You know you need to place bets to win, but you have no idea where to put your chips.

Of course, digital transformations aren't games of chance. But they do require big and bold commitments during uncertainty to reinvent the business rather than just improve it.

Many of the digital initiatives large incumbents have already tried to date have tended to operate at the margins of the business. Innovation labs or apps can be useful for learning and can even provide a boost to the company. Meanwhile, the legacy business remains in place, largely unperturbed.

Without a transformation of the core—the value proposition, people, processes, and technologies that are the lifeblood of the business—any digital initiative is likely to be a short-term fix. The legacy organization will inevitably exert a gravitational pull that drives a reversion to established practices. Reinvention of a business is, by its nature, bold. But it's one thing to be bold; it's another to be thoughtfully bold. A digital reinvention requires the

CEO to make tough decisions, which involve hard trade-offs that it is tempting to ignore, defer, or rush into. Yet knowing which decisions to prioritize and how to implement them can make the difference between a successful transformation effort and one that struggles.

These decisions occur in the four phases of a successful digital transformation program:

- Discovering the ambition for the business based on where value is migrating
- Designing a transformation program that targets profitable customer journeys
- Delivering the change through an ecosystem of partners
- De-risking the transformation process to maximize the chances of success

In each of these areas, the CEO has a lot of things to do, from modeling new behavior to driving a change in culture to executing strategy.[1] But this article focuses on some of the big decisions CEOs need to make, and how they can go about making them. Based on our experience with dozens of digital transformations, we believe these seven decisions are the most important ones.

DISCOVER—Set the ambition for the business.

Decision 1: Where the business should go

Few decisions are more momentous than choosing the business direction. While the almost existential nature of this decision can seem overwhelming, most incumbents don't have a choice, since they are already facing disruptions that can threaten their long-term viability.

Data and analysis, as well as a disciplined framework for thinking through options, provide a helpful structure for making the decision. As a starting point, we recommend a thoughtful review of the market and business based on those stalwarts of economic analysis, supply and demand.[2] It's important that any analysis be dynamic and forward-looking, based on an understanding of how digital technology could lead to changes in the future.

Almost every notable digital innovation we've seen has been based on using connectivity and data to transform the customer experience or to reshape products and services by allowing customers to interact with them in new ways. So that's a good basis for thinking through the possibilities. Incumbents can also look to approaches used by digital innovators—both within and outside their sectors—to spur fresh thinking.[3]

While analysis is crucial, it is no substitute for imagination. C. S. Lewis called imagination "the organ of meaning," and CEOs need to tap into it. One approach might be to imagine how the industry would work if it were completely digitized.[4] Often, a creative leap is needed to identify how the firm might serve customers in new ways across their entire journey. We have found 24-hour hackathons with senior leaders to be a very effective way to break through old thinking and encourage executives to adopt completely new ways of doing things.[5]

GE is an example of an incumbent that envisioned how its industry would evolve and acted in response. CEO Jeff Immelt noted that "15 percent or 20 percent of the S&P 500 valuation is consumer Internet stocks that didn't exist 15 or 20 years ago. The consumer companies got none of that ... If you look out 10 or 15 years ... that same value is going to be created in the industrial Internet".[6] Based on this insight, GE launched GE Digital, a software and analytics group that works closely with all the company's business units, and Predix, a branded digital platform that invites developers to build new applications using GE data.

DESIGN—create a plan for the digital transformation.

Decision 2: Who will lead the effort?

A program that will deliver the needed degree of transformation is not something CEOs can delegate; they must lead the charge themselves.

Some CEOs, like Daniel Gilbert, cofounder of Quicken Loans, serve as the public face of the company's digital-transformation program. Gilbert was the primary evangelist for Quickens Rocket Mortgage initiative, touting it as the "mortgage industry's iPhone moment."

CEOs, however, can't do this on their own. Like the conductor of an orchestra, the CEO provides vision and ongoing direction. But a group of other senior leaders needs to drive the effort day-to-day. Thus, a key decision for the CEO is selection of the members of the orchestra, based on the skills needed to be harmonious and effective.

One criterion for inclusion, naturally, must be skill in and knowledge of digital. That's why some CEOs turn to a chief digital officer (CDO). Appointing a CDO is the right answer for many companies, but it's only part of the solution.

This decision needs to extend putting in place the right team of people to drive the change. Since digital affects almost every aspect of the business and requires an unprecedented level of coordination across the entire organization, any leadership group has to include executives from multiple functions. While it can be important to have people, who are visionary and inspiring, the team will also need respected executives with a deep understanding of the mechanics of the business, as well as expertise in change management. In addition, the CEO should select leaders who embody and will forward the key values of a digital culture: customer-centricity, a collaborative mind-set, and a tolerance for risk.

This leadership team doesn't need to be large. In fact, it can be quite small, as long as its members, and the people working with them, have the requisite skills. At Starbucks, for example, Howard Schultz had the CIO and CDO guide a decade-long digitization effort that has driven widespread adoption of mobile payments at North American stores, tightly coupled with the company's customer-loyalty program. At a European energy company, it was a COO, CMO, and CSO (chief sales officer) who led the charge.

Decision 3: How to 'sell' the vision to key stakeholders

Any change effort requires active communication of the vision and an explanation of why it's necessary. For this reason, the CEO needs to decide not only what to say but also how—and how long—to communicate.

One approach is to think of the change program as a product and brand it. When Angela Ahrendts took over as CEO of Burberry, she launched a bold Art of the Trench campaign and an aggressive move into digital, which signaled her high level of ambition and rejuvenated the organization. In early 2014, Ralph Hamers, CEO of ING Group, announced his vision for the company, called Think Forward, Act Now. Its goal was to deliver a differentiating customer experience through faster innovation and better use of analytics. Late in 2016, Hamers updated the vision with Accelerating Think Forward, which focused on mobile banking.[9]

It's crucial to decide when to communicate and with whom. The CEO should focus first on winning over influencers both inside and outside the company, then on propagating the change to their networks. CEOs also need to adopt a campaign mentality. This means delivering crisp and clear messages, in a steady cadence, using all relevant formats and channels. It's an influencing program, so messages need to be tailored to each audience—from employees to the board to shareholders.

A bold, long-term orientation, well communicated to all key stakeholders, can be a crucial counterbalance against pressures to hit short-term financial targets once the transformation program begins.

Decision 4: Where to position the firm within the digital ecosystem

New companies are able to challenge established businesses because an ecosystem of relatively cheap and plentiful resources—from technologies to platforms to vendors—is in place. This has been a boon to disruptive attackers, but the same resources can be used by incumbents, too.

CEOs need to figure out which capabilities, skills, and technologies available in the ecosystem complement and support their business's strategic ambitions. How much to rely on these relationships and how to structure them, are also crucial decisions. Making them requires a clear sense of how to secure the company's most valuable assets, such as relationships with customers or data.

Michael Busch, the CEO of Thalia, Germany's leading bookstore, systematically evaluated the entire supply chain before launching his company's digital book offering. He created a network of alliances with other book retailers and partnered with Deutsche Telekom, which provided the technology and digital distribution backbone. He did not, however, make any agreements that separated Thalia from its customers, which it saw as its core value.

Over the past decade, BBVA Compass, a Spanish bank with a growing global presence, has aggressively remade itself into a digital organization.[10] In 2016, it launched an API marketplace, which allows fintech start-ups to build apps that interface with BBVA's back-end systems. This arrangement channels the energy and creativity of entrepreneurs while ensuring that BBVA retains a leadership position within the ecosystem.

Decision 5: How to decide during the transformation

As boxer Mike Tyson once said, echoing Joe Louis, "Everyone has a plan 'til they get punched in the mouth."[11] No matter how well a transformation effort is designed, there will be surprises and unforeseen developments. To deal with this reality, the CEO and top team need to decide on governance and escalation rules to allow for inevitable course corrections.

Frequent check-ins—at least weekly—with senior leaders should be planned to gauge whether the digitization effort is on course and institute changes if it is not. That sounds like a lot, but devoting even one hour a week to a program that transforms the company is just 1 to 2 percent of a CEO's time. The challenge is to book this time and stick to it.

To support this approach, the CEO needs a dashboard developed to track progress on key initiatives that reflect the ambitions of the transformation. A digital transformation is a long-term effort, and as a result, yardsticks that focus on the short term, like ROI, can be misleading. Nontraditional metrics that evaluate digital adoption, such as new registrations on digital channels or digital-engagement levels, are better gauges of the progress of a digital transformation.[12]

DELIVER—execute the transformation plan, allowing for ongoing adaptation and adjustment.

Decision 6: How to allocate funds rapidly and dynamically

The key lever CEOs and senior teams have to drive a digital transformation is resource allocation. This isn't just about making sure resources get to the right places, a decision CEOs already make as part of their everyday work. With a digital transformation, the CEO needs to decide what the allocation process should be and at what tempo it should operate.

Our research shows that raising a company's Digital Quotient, or DQ®, requires targeted allocation of both capital and operating expenditures.[13] The CEO and top team should act like venture capitalists by following a digital initiative's progress closely, pulling the plug for projects that lag expectations, and investing more in those that do well.

This requires speeding up budgeting processes, which at large companies tend to follow annual cycles. During a digital transformation, budgeting should shift from annual to quarterly or even monthly cycles.

Succeeding with a digital transformation often requires cutting budgets for legacy operations. In the midst of its transformation effort, a large bank realized that even after making massive investments in digital, branches still accounted for 90 percent of its operating expenses—and that 70 to 80 percent of the transactions done in branches could be executed digitally. In response, they shifted almost all future capital spending to digital, closed a number of branches, and launched a program to migrate customers who relied on branches for routine services to ATMs or web/mobile channels.

DE-RISK—Increase transformation's prospects for success.

Decision 7: What to do when

More than 70 percent of transformation programs fail.[14]While the decisions covered in this article go a long way toward improving the odds, loss of momentum can undo even the best transformation efforts. To forestall that possibility, CEOs should carefully decide how to sequence the transformation for quick wins that yield revenue payoffs and reduce costs, gains that can then be reinvested. One e-tailer, for example, unlocked $300 million in just five months by prioritizing initiatives with the fastest payback. That turned into more than $800 million within a year, thanks to momentum from the early windfall.

Effective sequencing requires clear criteria to evaluate the potential payoff of various parts of the transformation initiative. These should include a hard-nosed assessment of projected benefits, the time needed to capture them, dependencies, investments required, and impact on the overall transformation journey. Sequencing with an eye toward cumulative effect is also necessary, so the business builds towards a cohesive digital whole rather than a jumble of loosely affiliated programs, which can undermine the ultimate benefits of scale. Digital is the defining challenge for today's generation of CEOs. And the decisions they make will determine whether their businesses thrive or fade.

http://www.mckinsey.com/business-functions/digital-mckinsey/our-insights/the-seven-decisions-that-matter-in-a-digital-transformation

6.8   Digital Transformation in India
ANIL BHANSALI, 17 OCTOBER 2016

The way societies operate and interact with each other has drastically changed with the advent of the digital revolution. Over the years, the impact of technology has been profound, not just in terms of making our lives easier, but also in terms of our approach to the way we carry out tasks, solve problems and resolve issues.

There is no doubt that our leaders understand the role that technology can play in realizing the vision for India's growth – it is at the core of the Digital India programme and a key driver across all plans devised by the Indian Government over the last two years. The government recognizes the transformative power of technology and sees it as an enabler for the change that we all seek- be it in delivering better citizen services, digitizing education records, efficient and productive functioning, or using technology to provide a new social security platform.

Cloud is really at the core of the technology revolution that we see around us. Today, cloud computing is making it possible to drive intelligence and insights from the immense magnitude of data available, converting it into predictive and analytical power. This power puts data and cloud computing at the centre of the analysis and action that governments are taking to address different societal issues.

Education, agriculture and healthcare are critical for the progress of our country, and the ability of software to make an impact in these areas will ensure that we are successful in empowering our citizens. We are partnering different state governments as well as private and public institutions to come up with solutions that have the potential to fundamentally handle major challenges in these three sectors.

Keeping kids in school

India has more than 250 million students enrolled in government and private schools. While this is one of the largest school enrolment figures in the world, unfortunately, more than 70 percent of children never complete their education. With the objective of preventing dropouts, we are working with the Government of Andhra Pradesh to help identify students at risk of dropping out and design targeted intervention programmes.

This is done by applying machine learning and advanced visualization techniques that take into account multiple data points, including a student's board exam performance, post-exam enrolments, school facilities, and teachers' abilities and skills. This solution has been taken to 10,000 government schools across Andhra Pradesh and has produced 600,000 predictions. We now have a 360-degree view of students, mapped using close to 100 variables. The interface also allows officers to counsel students accordingly.

Bringing much needed information to farmers

Agriculture is the backbone of the Indian economy. The sector is the largest generator of employment in the country, and accounts for 16 percent of our GDP and over 10 percent of our exports. However, changing weather patterns have resulted in millions of farmers facing an uncertain future due to crop failure. We have partnered with ICRISAT (International Crop Research Station for Semi-Arid Tropics – a United Nations agency) to analyze volumes of data on weather forecasts, local rainfall and soil conditions. This data was analyzed to develop a "Sowing Date" application that tells farmers the right sowing date to maximize their yield.

Access to this platform for farmers was simplified by providing information to farmers via SMSes in Telugu. In addition, we also collaborated with ICRISAT for the Government of Andhra Pradesh on another solution - a Personalized Village Advisory Dashboard, developed using Power BI tools - to provide an instant overview across several environmental factors that determine a healthy crop yield. The pilot was conducted at the start of the kharif season in Devenakonda village, located in the Kurnool district of Andhra Pradesh.

Assessing the efficacy of medical treatments

In healthcare, we are collaborating with LV Prasad Eye Institute, a not-for-profit eye health institute that offers comprehensive patient care, rehabilitation services and high-impact rural eye health programmes, on a machine learning and data analytics model. Using Eye Smart, an award winning ophthalmic electronic medical record and hospital management system, and Microsoft Azure, LVPEI has registered over 400,000 new patients digitally.

This helps the institute predict the success of Lasik eye surgeries based on past medical records and surgical parameters, providing doctors with actionable insights and enabling them to develop better treatment plans and interventions. The impact of this can be tremendous. In India alone, an estimated 12 million people are blind and 54 million people are visually impaired. 72 percent of these cases are treatable. This unique solution can ensure breakthrough work not just in eye care, but also in other critical areas like diabetes, heart-related illnesses, infectious diseases, and child health as well.

Unending opportunity

These are just three instances in education, agriculture and healthcare that really opens our eyes to what is possible with the cloud. Closely tied to the power of cloud computing is the fact that the benefits of the digital transformation will be all encompassing only when its citizens are digitally empowered. It is, therefore, critical to provide low cost internet access to the masses and bring several million people on the right side of the digital divide.

This is where low-cost and effective technologies such as TV White Space can play an instrumental role. They have the potential to accelerate rural internet, and become the backbone of a Digital India, by providing much needed access to technology and extending opportunities to the underserved. We are also working with the Government of Maharashtra to develop a smart village in Harisal, in collaboration with an ecosystem of partners.

These are but a few glimpses of how technology can transform India and the world. Digital India seeks to transform India into an empowered society. We are a proud and committed partner in driving this transformative change that the country is experiencing. We believe we have the platforms, technologies and solutions to support India's digital transformation and positively impact the lives of a billion people.

https://yourstory.com/2016/10/digital-transformation-in-india/

6.9 Union Budget (2017-18): Promoting Digital Payments (Digital Economy) Towards Less-Cash Society.

Dated 1st Feb 2017

Digital Economy – Budget 2017

Digital Economy is one of 10 central themes for Budget-2017 for establishing speed, accountability and transparency in the system.

Digital Economy

- 125 lakh people have adopted the BHIM app so far. The Government will launch two new schemes to promote the usage of BHIM; these are, Referral Bonus Scheme for individuals and a Cash Back Scheme for merchants

- Steps would be taken to promote and possibly mandate petrol pumps, fertilizer depots, municipalities, Block offices, road transport offices, universities, colleges, hospitals and other institutions to have facilities for digital payments, including BHIM App.

- Aadhaar Pay, a merchant version of Aadhaar Enabled Payment System, will be launched shortly

- A Mission will be set up with a target of 2,500 crores digital transactions for 2017-18 through UPI, USSD, Aadhaar Pay, IMPS and debit cards.

- A proposal to mandate all Government receipts through digital means, beyond a prescribed limit, is under consideration.

- Banks have targeted to introduce additional ₹10 lakh new POS terminals by March 2017. They will be encouraged to introduce ₹ 20 lakh Aadhaar based POS by September 2017.

- Proposed to create a Payments Regulatory Board in the Reserve Bank of India by replacing the existing Board for Regulation and Supervision of Payment and Settlement Systems.

PROMOTING DIGITAL ECONOMY

- Under scheme of presumptive income for small and medium tax payers whose turnover is upto ₹ 2 crores, the present, 8% of their turnover which is counted as presumptive income is reduced to 6% in respect of turnover which is by non-cash means.

- No transaction above ₹ 3 lakh would be permitted in cash subject to certain exceptions

- Cash expenditure allowable as deduction, both for revenue as well as capital expenditure, to be limited to Rs 10,000. Similarly, the limit of cash donation which can be received by a charitable trust is being reduced from Rs10,000/- to Rs 2000/-.

- Miniaturised POS card reader for m-POS (other than mobile phones or tablet computers), micro ATM standards version 1.5.1, Finger Print Readers / Scanners and Iris Scanners and on their parts and components for manufacture of such devices to be exempt from BCD, Excise/CV duty and SAD.

- Increased digital transactions will enable small and micro enterprises to access formal credit. Government will encourage SIDBI to refinance credit institutions which provide unsecured loans, at reasonable interest rates, to borrowers based on their transaction history.

- The digital payment infrastructure and grievance handling mechanisms shall be strengthened. The focus would be on rural and semi urban areas through Post Offices, Fair Price Shops and Banking Correspondents.

- Steps would be taken to promote and possibly mandate petrol pumps, fertilizer depots, municipalities, Block offices, road transport offices, universities, colleges, hospitals and other institutions to have facilities for digital payments, including BHIM App.
- A proposal to mandate all Government receipts through digital means, beyond a prescribed limit, is under consideration.
- Government will consider and work with various stakeholders for early implementation of the interim recommendations of the Committee of Chief Ministers on digital transactions.

http://cashlessindia.gov.in/Union_Budget_(2017-18).html

6.10 What Do the Numbers Reveal About India's Digital Acceptance Post-Demonetization?

TARUSH BHALLA, 18 FEBRUARY 2017

Point-of-Sale transactions saw 88 percent rise, while mobile wallets transactions doubled. This is the emergence of a new normal and the real numbers of digital payments during demonetization.

(Photo credit: Shutter stock)

There is much buzz around the failures of demonetization, with the Reserve Bank of India (RBI) getting flak for not revealing the real numbers on the old tender notes that came back to the banks. But as the February bulletin from the Mint Road reveals, the much-criticized move gave way to an increase in digital payments during November and December.

Although provisional, the data, when pitched against RBI's data from October (pre-demonetization), paints an interesting story of how India took to digital payments in the wake of the unexpected cash crunch.

Following are some of the major observations from the bulletin:

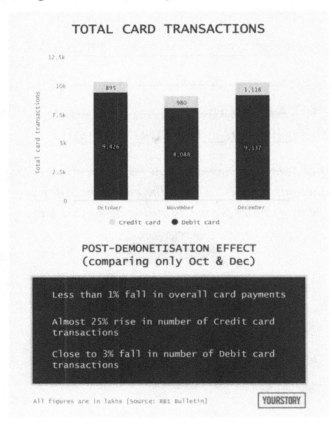

1) Decline in total card transactions

Quite contrary to popular belief, the total number of card transactions declined during the month of November, when the government ceased the tender of Rs. 500 and Rs. 1,000 notes.

While the total number of card transactions in the country in October 2016 stood at 10,321 lakh transactions, the total number of card transactions fell to 9,068 lakh transactions in November. December saw an increase from this number, to 10,255 lakh transactions in the country, **registering less than a percent decline in number** (as shown above).

But what is interesting is that the total number of credit card transactions saw a slow uptake from 895 lakh transactions in October to 980 lakh transactions in November and subsequently settled at 1,118 lakh transactions in December.

However, the transactions on debit cards said a different story, exhibiting a decline from 9,426 lakh transactions in October to 8,088 lakh transactions in November and a slow pick-up to 9,137 lakh transactions in December.

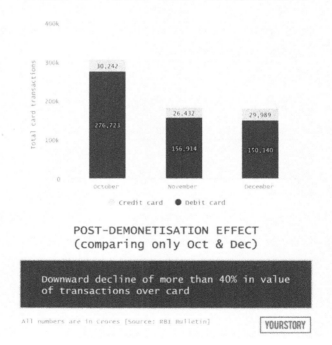

The reason

So, what could be the reason for this? **A major reason for this is the currency crunch and heavy limits on withdrawal that kept people away from the ATMs.** As proved by the data from RBI, **the total amount of debit card usage at ATMs fell from 8,020.6 lakh transactions to 5,740 lakh transactions in November and rose to 5,921 lakh transactions in December.**

The value of these withdrawals slipped from Rs. 2,54,781 crores in October to Rs. 1,25,297 crores transactions in November and surprisingly kept slipping to Rs. 1,06,266 crores in December.

Moreover, there was a sharp decline of more than 40 percent in the total value of card transactions as well, falling from Rs. 3,06,965 crores in October, to Rs. 1,80,219 crores in December.

But as we dug deeper into the report, we saw that this decline in card transactions gave way to a sudden and forceful change in the Indian mentality towards seeking alternative methods of digital payments like m-wallets, UPI (Unified Payments Interface).

2) Point-of-Sale

The **total number of card transactions over point-of-sale (PoS) saw a whopping 88-percent rise** when October's numbers were compared with that of December (the month by which the real impact of these alternative payment methods could be measured). Debit card usage at PoS grew from 1,406 lakh transactions in October to 2,348 lakhs in November and subsequently 3,215 lakh transactions in December, standing at a more than 100-percent rise since October. Even credit cards saw a 25-percent rise in transactions at PoS machines (as shown in chart below).

The value of card transactions on PoS machines shot up more than 41 percent from October (Rs. 51,883 crores) to Rs. 73,762 crores in December. The value of debit card transactions over PoS machines was the highest gainer, rising slowly from Rs. 21,941 crores in October to Rs. 31,616 crores in November and Rs. 43,874 crores in December. Overall, there was more than a 100-percent increase in uptake.

CARD TRANSACTIONS AT POINT-OF-SALE (POS)

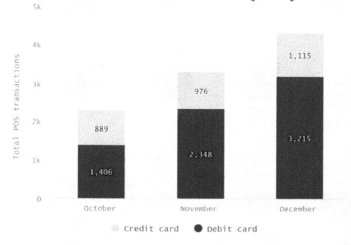

POST-DEMONETISATION EFFECT (comparing only Oct & Dec)

Close to 88% rise in PoS transactions

More than 25% rise in Credit card transactions at PoS machines

More than 100% rise in Debit card transactions at PoS machines

All figures are in lakhs [Source: RBI Bulletin]

YOURSTORY

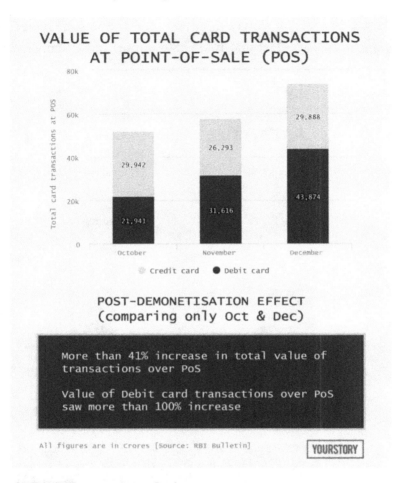

VALUE OF TOTAL CARD TRANSACTIONS AT POINT-OF-SALE (POS)

Total card transactions at POS

	October	November	December
Credit card	29,942	26,293	29,888
Debit card	21,941	31,616	43,874

Credit card   ● Debit card

POST-DEMONETISATION EFFECT (comparing only Oct & Dec)

More than 41% increase in total value of transactions over PoS

Value of Debit card transactions over PoS saw more than 100% increase

All figures are in Crores [Source: RBI Bulletin]   YOURSTORY

3) Digital payment solutions

Total usage of digital solutions shot up by more than 100 percent

But what could be the most pertinent reveal of the bulletin is the numbers on digital solutions usage, which saw more than a 105-percent rise in the number of transactions. These include mobile wallets, pre-paid cards as well as paper vouchers such as Sodexo. The average value on digital payment solutions also grew by 62 percent.

The number grew from 1,269 lakh total transactions and value of Rs. 6,022 crores in October to 1,690 lakh total transactions of Rs. 5,010 crores in November. The sharp incline, however, was seen in December, with 2,610 lakh total transactions holding a total value of Rs. 9,770 crores.

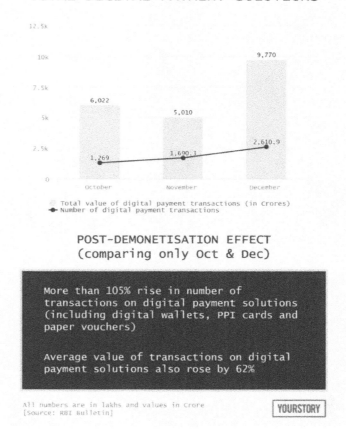

4) Mobile wallets became the new king

The RBI bulletin shows show the steep rise in usage of mobile wallets for many Indians, to deal with the cash crunch. **There was close to a 114-percent rise in the number of wallet transactions between October and December.** While the total number of wallet transactions stood at 995 lakhs, it successively grew to 1,380.9 lakhs in November and shot up to 2,131 lakh transactions in December.

Even the total value of transactions rose: it was Rs. 3385 crores in October, Rs. 3305 crores in November and subsequently doubled up to Rs. 7,448 crores in December (as shown in the chart below).

These numbers, however, still don't prove the tall claims of six million transactions daily by some wallet companies, made in the month of December.

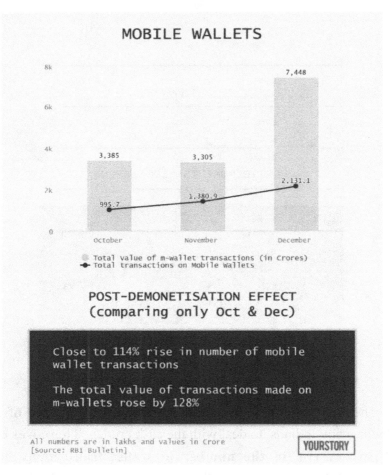

5) Mobile banking

The value of transactions for mobile banking grew 30 percent.

On the mobile banking front, the total number of transactions grew from 780.8 lakh transactions valued at Rs. 1,13,578 crores in October to 896.1 lakh transactions in December valued at Rs. 1,48,583 crores.

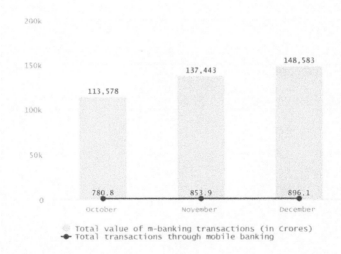

6) Physical infrastructure (PoS and ATMs)

Further, the government mandated installation of 10 lakhs new PoS machines by March. The actual number of ATMs in October were 2,19,578, which grew nominally to 2,20,166 ATMs in November 2016. But the branches saw a decline, to 2,19,866 ATMs, in December.

In December, PoS machines in the country registered a 12-percent rise from October. The total count was 15,12,068, which grew nominally to 15,89,263 in November and shot up to 17,05,423 PoS machines by the end of December.

While the RBI should provide clarity on how many bank notes came in as a result of the demonetization, its bulletin has shown that the announcement proved to be a huge success in the government's sight to increase digital acceptance in the country.

https://yourstory.com/2017/02/digital-india-post-demonetisation/

ABOUT THE AUTHOR

Award winning Key Note Speaker at International Level, Professor Ajit Kumar Roy is an acclaimed researcher and consultant. Prof. Roy obtained his M.Sc. degree in Statistics and joined Agricultural Research Service (ARS) of Indian Council of Agricultural Research (ICAR) as a Scientist (Statistics) in 1976. In recent past was engaged as National Consultant (Impact Assessment), for East &North Eastern States of India at National Agricultural Innovation Project (World Bank funded) of ICAR. Earlier he had served as a Consultant (Statistics) at Central Agricultural University, Agartala. Earlier had served at CIFA, ICAR, as Principal Scientist and was involved in applied research in the areas of ICT, Statistics, Bioinformatics Analytics, and Economics. At International level, he served as a Computer Specialist at SAARC Agricultural Information Centre (SAIC), Dhaka, Bangladesh for over 3 years.

The author with over 45 years of research and teaching experience in Statistical Analysis, Analytics, and information & Knowledge management edited twenty books and several conference proceedings. Besides, published over 100 articles in refereed journals. His recent best-sellers are 'Cashless Economy in India-Present Scenario, Potential, Prospect and Challenges Ahead'; Post Demonetization Budget-2017- Expectations, Apprehensions and Reality'; 'Facts and Figures of Demonetization in India-Reactions, Views and Comments; Big Data and Data Science Initiative in India- Upcoming Job Opportunities: Big data Job Opportunities in India (Big Data-Series-4 Book 1);'Applied Big Data Analytics'; 'Impact of Big Data Analytics on Business, Economy, Health Care and Society'; 'Data Science - A Career Option for 21st Century'; 'Self Learning of Bioinformatics Online'; 'Applied Bioinformatics, Statistics and Economics in Fisheries Research' and 'Applied Computational Biology and Statistics in Biotechnology and Bioinformatics'; Emerging Technologies of the 21st Century.

He is a Member, Organizing Committee Board for the 6th International Conference on 'Biometrics and Biostatistics' to be held during, November 13-14, 2017 Atlanta, Georgia, USA. Editorial Board Member, Jacobs Journal of Biostatistics, Jacobs Publishers, 900 Great Hills, Trail # 150 w, Austin, Texas. He now works as Visiting Professor, question setter and examiner of four Indian Universities.